INFORMATION

INFORMATION

A Reader

EDITED BY
ERIC HAYOT,
ANATOLY DETWYLER,
LEA PAO

Columbia University Press
New York

Columbia University Press
Publishers Since 1893
New York   Chichester, West Sussex
cup.columbia.edu

Copyright © 2022 Columbia University Press
All rights reserved

Library of Congress Cataloging-in-Publication Data
Names: Hayot, Eric, 1972– editor. | Detwyler, Anatoly, editor. | Pao, Lea, editor.
Title: Information : a reader / edited by Eric Hayot, Anatoly Detwyler, Lea Pao.
Other titles: Information (Hayot, Detwyler, Pao)
Description: New York : Columbia University Press, [2021] | Includes index.
Identifiers: LCCN 2020030682 (print) | LCCN 2020030683 (ebook) |
    ISBN 9780231186209 (hardcover; acid-free paper) | ISBN 9780231186216
    (trade paperback; acid-free paper) | ISBN 9780231546546 (ebook)
Subjects: LCSH: Information science—Philosophy. | Information science—
    Social aspects.
Classification: LCC Z665 .I582 2021 (print) | LCC Z665 (ebook) |
    DDC 020—dc23
LC record available at https://lccn.loc.gov/2020030682
LC ebook record available at https://lccn.loc.gov/2020030683

Columbia University Press books are printed on permanent
    and durable acid-free paper.
Printed in the United States of America

Cover design: Milenda Nan Ok Lee
Cover art: sylverarts Vectors © Shutterstock

CONTENTS

INFORMED SOCIETY   285

INFORMATION

INFORMATION: A READER

An Introduction

ERIC HAYOT

W e live, we are told, in an age of information. And though at first glance our sense of this new life with and as information seem to stem from a series of recent technological transformations—most prominently the rise of electrical and digital methods of encoding, compression, storage, and networking—information as we now understand it has been the subject of human activity since the rise of oral culture over 10,000 years ago and probably before that as well. We know from analysis of the written works of Homer, for instance, that the poets who recited his work did not do so entirely from memory, but built their individual performances from algorithmic structures that allowed them to act flexibly and creatively within a larger pattern. We know too that the patterns of drumming used for long-distance communication across West African forests employed structures of redundancy designed to compensate for the relatively small throughput of their communication technology. And we know from the earliest written discussions of the value of writing that literacy was considered to have both potentially salutary and potentially damaging social, political, and personal effects, ranging from the stunting of the individual capacity for memory to the mimicry of authoritative knowledge. Hence Socrates's worrying to Phaedrus, around 370 BCE, that writing might diminish the mind's ability to hold things clearly before it; hence the great book-burning project of Qin Shi Huang, the first ruler of a unified Chinese empire, in the third century BCE.

Beginning from this transhistorical account of the social role played by information makes the concept's relation to the humanities fairly clear.

All societies are information societies; the social is, in some strong sense, both the outcome of a series of processes for managing, organizing, and passing information on, as well as itself a process for managing future outcomes. The social is not *only* that, to be sure; but the social is always *also* that, from the beginning. And about such topics the humanistic sciences—history, philosophy, the study of culture, the arts, and of the lives of communities and of the individuals who make them up—will have a great deal to say. The light humanistic inquiry casts onto the past will refract, inevitably, onto our present information age, and onto the futures that it imagines for itself.[1]

All that sounds great. So why does "information and the humanities" feel, nonetheless, like such an unlikely and uncomfortable pairing?

Because what this confident assertion of the relevance of the topic to the method ignores is, precisely, the role information currently plays in our social lives. One need only remember the many ways in which the contemporary meanings and uses of the word-concept "information" codify—or are felt to codify, same thing—positions and values about society, culture, meaning, and history that feel, for a variety of reasons, inimical to the basic assumptions of humanist thought to understand why the arrival of information on the shores of humanistic inquiry might make many humanists feel anxious. Facebook, Twitter, WeChat, Palantir—technologies of corruption and control ranging from police use of facial recognition software to the corporate manipulation of media to the quantitative assessment of educational outcomes: information has already taken over everything else, and now it is coming for the humanities as well.

What are these ideas about information that seem somehow contrary to the very presumptions of the humanities? Let's make a list:

(1) That the information age in which we live is characterized specifically by a series of technological advances that produce a radical break with the pre-electrical/digital past, and that, what's more, that break must be resolutely understood as the result of progress. At its worst this position holds that all knowledge produced prior to the arrival of information is now obsolete.

(2) That the information society is, like information itself, politically and philosophically neutral, and that, therefore, its benefits and goods need not be understood as necessarily embedded within—and somehow connected to—the ugly histories of capitalism and imperialism alongside which the information society emerges, or to the various other modes of control and complicity that might cause one to be suspicious about such claims to neutrality.

(3) That this informational neutrality extends itself to matters of social representation, including matters of race, gender, and disability, and that therefore both the masculinity and the Whiteness of information as a concept and as

a field of social practice have nothing to do with information per se, and are mere epiphenomena of other aspects of the social.

(4) That information has nothing, also, necessarily to do with the apparatuses of state or corporate control, even if the entire discipline of statistics, or the rise of data mining, or of communication and surveillance techniques now associated with Silicon Valley corporations or spy agencies have always been developed with the command and management of the social in mind.

(5) That information produces only social benefits, in terms of speed of communication and management, or in terms of organization and storage of social and institutional knowledge, and does not—by, for instance, relying on the vast production of equivalences and the reduction of instances to patterns and trends—trample the specificity of individual people, historical contexts, or social groups, making them "manageable" and "knowable" in profoundly impoverished terms.

(6) That, in keeping with its general neutrality, "information" correctly describes the elements of a symbolic act (linguistic or otherwise) that remain fundamentally independent of their context, even if—as humanists keep trying to show everyone, with some limited success—everything has a context, and that there is therefore no such thing as information, in a strong ontological sense.

(7) That information-driven knowledge practices can and should replace the comparatively fuzzy, mealy-mouthed, ambiguous epistemologies of the traditional humanities, with their too-clever analysis of language, their imputation of impossible-to-disprove unconscious motivations, or their reliance on a variety of figures like catachresis, chiasmus, or paradox, figures that are simply figments of literary imagination, and that in fact this process is, happily, already well under way. Witness the rapid quantification of knowledge in the mixed disciplines—political science, sociology, psychology, and anthropology—over the last four decades, and the more recent uses of computational methods in fields like history ("cliometrics") or literature ("the digital humanities"), all of which will finally put paid to the humanities and their vague, language-dependent bullshit.

You get some sense of the humanist reaction to this range of propositions from the following paragraph of John Durham Peters' now-classic 1988 essay on the history of the word "information":

This essay aims to treat information in the way that it does not want to be treated: as a word which has a history full of inversions and compromises. Information is a term that does not like history. Dretske (1981), for example, opines: "In the beginning there was information. The word came later"; Beniger (1986) similarly takes information to be equiprimordial with life itself: he locates its emergence in the primordial soup of self-replicating proteins. Such views effectively take information out of history and in so doing neglect the history and grounds of their own modes of discourse. Information is, after all, a word with a history: it is a cultural invention that has come to prominence at a certain point in time, in a specific constellation of interests. Once that history is grasped, information clearly shows itself, contra Dretske, not to be a fit successor to the Word.[2]

In recent decades Peters has gone on to become one of the great theorists and critics of the techno-utopian drive behind a certain version of information thinking. And here, thirty years ago you can already see the grounds of his critique: Peters' absolute insistence on history and historicity, his justified contempt for those who do not see that their own concepts refer not to ontological qualia, but to context-bound reifications of ways of thought. And you see also some of his critique's moral-rhetorical valence, visible in a vision of historical development in which information has usurped the rightful position of language, language that directs itself not only to the more human dimensions of the social, but also to its theological or even specifically Christian ones. For how else can one understand Peters's final phrase, in which information is "not . . . a fit successor" to the word? Or his capitalization of that final Word? In this way one can see a phrase like "information and humanities" as a translation of the eternal agon between God and Mammon, the human and the inhuman, the living and the dead.

One of the many senses in which we live in an information age, then, will be the one in which our age is not only dominated by information, which might well be true for any number of ages, but in which our age is dominated by a certain rhetoric of information, and by information's conceptual dominance across a wide variety of fields—as well as the *response to that dominance*. The (idea of the) fundamental *neutrality* of the modern information concept, and indeed the (idea of the) more fundamental neutrality of the forms of knowledge from which it draws sustenance, and which it sustains in turn, threatens any theory of society or of social action that depends for its analysis on the idea that *interest* constitutes one of the major motivators of social behavior and social life. For if one turns technological progress into a philosophy of history, or insists that quantitative analysis produces laws of social management as inexorable, unalterable, and inhuman as the laws of motion, then there really is not much room in your conceptualization of human life for the humanities, for politics, or for arguments about the two. It's just a matter of assembling the datasets, disrupting the old, outdated patterns, and moving forward into a Luddite-free, predictable future.

As far as the modern rhetoric of information is concerned, one ur-text of this vision of an engineering-driven philosophy comes from Warren Weaver's introduction to *The Mathematical Theory of Communication* (1949). The book itself belongs right at the center of the contemporary information regime, the center of what we will be calling the "Shannon knot"—a critical disruption or turn in the history of the information concept that shaped, for good and ill, the information discourse of the next sixty years. Though most of the book was written by the Bell Systems engineer Claude Shannon, and is highly technical in nature, Weaver's introduction, and some of Shannon's other work, extended the force of its innovation quite widely into other social areas, launching a thousand thinkpieces, a thousand academic conferences, a thousand books, a thousand grant proposals, and indeed a thousand thousand responses to its provocative arguments about the nature of modern society. This Shannon moment establishes the framework within much of what we think about information as a global or even universal concept is debated and understood.

Weaver's introductory essay begins to do this work by conflating "information," operating in a relatively restricted sense to refer to electrical impulses traveling along a radio frequency or a telephone wire, and "communication," which is after all not just that. He writes:

> The word communication will be used here in a very broad sense to include all the procedures by which one mind may affect another. This, of course, involves not only written and oral speech, but also music, the pictorial arts, the theater, the ballet, and in fact all human behavior. In some connections it may be desirable to use a still broader definition of communication, namely, one which would include the procedures by means of which one mechanism (say automatic equipment to track an airplane and compute its probable future positions) affects another mechanism (say a guided missile chasing this airplane).[3]

What is incredible about this passage—the confident rapidity of its movement from communication to "all human behavior" and thence to all procedures whereby mechanisms affect one another—is also what has been widely derided in humanist responses to information theory (some of which appear in this volume). It would be unfair, however, to make Weaver solely responsible for its presumptions. The process whereby engineering comes in to solve the problems of philosophy has its roots in the scientific positivism of the nineteenth century. And that positivism has its roots in turn in the ongoing human quest for natural or universal laws whose incontrovertibility and general applicability will clear up the complexities of human interests and supervene the time-bound nature of social life.

Indeed, one sees quite precisely in the combination of the Weaver essay and the Shannon material both the logic a binary structure that imagines a rough separation between the philosophical elements of the problem (Weaver) and the purely technical ones (Shannon). Later in his career, having seen the information concept take off in all sorts of wild philosophical and anthropological directions, Shannon would attempt to re-restrict the discussion to a set of purely technical terms. But the philosophical cat was already out of the technological bag—in fact the cat was never in the bag, *pace* Schrödinger, since the very distinction between philosophy and technology is itself an artifact of the kind of information-logic that both produces the Shannon/Weaver volume in the first place, and then reinscribes itself as a binary in the putative division between the two sections of the book. In short, there is in fact at the very heart of the idea of information, and of the history of information, precisely the kind of distinction between the technological and the social that information culture seems to address—and of course fails to fully address, insofar as it begins, insofar as it is born, from a theory of the total separation of the technical and the social that has never in human actuality taken place.

The obnoxious reach of Weaver's sentences nonetheless perfectly captures the version of a technologizing drive that dominates *this* era, and belongs to the more general process that places the social status and epistemological legitimacy of the humanities under so much contemporary threat. On these grounds, then, the idea of information as it functions in contemporary society is for a humanist thinker legitimately both threatening and terrible. And the introduction of the concept into traditional humanistic fields, as for instance proposed by a reader like this one, a sign of the continued and unstoppable epistemological surrender.

But here we are. And there are, it seems to me, two grounds on which all humanists should be interested in information, and should become familiar both with the canon associated with the Shannon knot, and with all of the ways in which information can be used if one moves *beyond* or *around* that knot, to think of information in ways that express rather than deny the best epistemological instincts of humanistic thought.

The first is that information in both its modern and pre-modern uses directs us to fairly fundamental problems of philosophy and language. In its pre-modern use in the Western linguistic tradition—a use that extends from Plato through the eighteenth century, and is retained anachronistically in the phrase "for your information"—information refers to the in-forming of a substance, the ways in which a concept or idea gives shape to an actual instantiation of something. In this way the idea of the tree in-forms the tree, as in Plato, or the idea of God in-forms the mind of the human—and therefore the human mind is a pathway back to God—for a medieval European theologian. For this usage of the word, then, we might say that the study of information leads us into the basic distinction between form and content, and therefore toward the study both of the history of philosophical relations between form and content, but also the social organization of those relations: for instance, in literature, in the idea of genre; and in sociology, in the relation between nation-state and citizen, or realm and subject.

As for the modern use, which develops, as Peters notes, somewhere around 1800: in it information becomes what we think of it as today, namely a morse-lized, contextless piece of . . . something like meaning or data or "thing to know." That it is hard to describe or name what information is *of* is one indica-tion of the work done by the concept. This morselized, decontextualized qual-ity is what allows us to imagine that information does anything but in-form in the older sense; information is that which has no fixed form, but can be passed on from one person to another, or one medium to another, without either being significantly altered in itself, or altering that which it touches. Think of, for instance, how we use the word to describe what happens when one person asks another when the train is coming. It does not matter whether the second person sings, shouts, or whispers the answer, or indeed whether it is delivered in German, Spanish, or Chinese, or whether again it appears in a book, on a pamphlet, or is projected in ten-foot-high letters on the side of Trump Tower; in any of these cases the "information" is *the thing that stays the same across iterations*. This idea that something stays the same—that there would be something that would stay the same, and that it could be differenti-ated from all the things that differ—is fundamental to the very idea of repe-tition or repeatability, and therefore again to both the idea of language as it is both experienced and theorized from the beginning of its human use, as well as to the idea of culture or the social from that same beginning. It seems use-ful therefore, whatever one thinks about the technocratic impulse associated with information discourse, that we have *information* as a word to describe this thing, this reification of a feature of the social, which everyone needs and uses all the time. This is so even if the actual work of humanist thinking in the twentieth century—especially since poststructuralism—has been inexorably to refuse the idea of repetition, and to insist over and over again on the ways in which context, be it historical, linguistic, or mediatic, makes absolutely no two actions, be they social or linguistic, identical. Though this is of course true at some level—you never step in the same river twice—at some other level it is patently not so, since otherwise you would have to abandon the possibility of recognizing it as a different *river*.

Both the modern and pre-modern history of the European word *informa-tion*, then, open up onto fairly broadly conceivable problems in both language use and social organization. What's more, to see that information has histor-ically functioned to refer to both sets of problems suggests that the problems may well be conceptually related. And here one should not, I think, get too excited about the fact that the changes through which the information con-cept goes seem to involve a fairly radical movement between opposites—from information as the thing that shapes and gives form to information as form-less content. For it is well known that opposition is a particularly strong form of relation. Any student of Freud will understand that the transfer between opposites is as much an indication of complementarity, mutual imbrication, and desire, as it is a sign of blockage or antagonism.

I have referred so far to information as a European word, and of course it is. But analogues for the word exist in non-European languages, of course, and analogues for what we recognize as information-related ideas or processes occur all over the place. Our argument here is not that there is something called "information" and that its European history tells us what it is; it is that there is something we might refer to in English as information, and that a comparative study of information-like processes around the world and across historical time will help us understand both the general social use of some kind of ur-concept, as well as illuminate the particularities of the European experience (or experiences) of that concept in history. So for instance: a folktale about someone being deceived by appearances is, no matter when or where it takes place, a quite practical theorization and articulation of the form-content distinction—it looked like a coyote, but really it was Coyote—as it relates to information; and any ritual is, likewise, an act that expresses ideas about similarity—we walk in a circle because the sky is the shape of a circle—or, better, that produces within itself an active theory of similarity that becomes available for other uses. The scope of these questions is as broad as the history of the species.

So much for the first reason why humanists ought to be interested in, and to contend with, information—and indeed struggle to develop counter-concepts, counter-reifications that might not simply cede the word "information" to its contemporary technocratic use.

The second reason is that one can think of information as a concept that brings together three related social processes, each of which directs us to broad fields of human activity. Let's call them storing, organizing, and communicating. Let me take them in order. Storing is meant to refer to the entire world whereby the things we today call knowledge or information are preserved over time, as well as the politics that determine their preservation. Because no storing happens without a medium of storage, and therefore without the reification of either a material substrate as a means of storage—paper, clay tablets, stone, floppy disks—or a social process as a means of storage—institutionalization of storytelling, the development of school systems, rituals of all types, memorization and memorialization—the idea of storing carries us toward the entire discipline of a very broadly conceived media studies. And of course because someone, or groups of someones, have to decide what should be stored, and how, and to match storage methods to storage value, storing opens on to the questions raised in Derrida's *Archive Fever*, but also in any number of less theoretical and highly practical contexts, as for instance in the work done to develop the first libraries of the African American experience, as Laura Helton has shown, and many more things besides.[4] What should we keep? How should we keep it? These are the questions of storage, and of course the question of how exactly we know that the "what" that we store is the same as the "what" retrieved from storage opens on to deep questions of philosophy, history, politics, and identity.

Organization: at the limit of the various neurobiological processes that limit the human capacity to remember, as well as the limit of the various socio-institutional processes that aim to extend that capacity—in institutions of various types, in codes of law, and of course in the various technologies that interface with individual and social memory, including writing—one encounters the need to reduce long lists of things to shorter lists of categories. Whether these categories involve types of people, which therefore helps a society organize its rules of marriage and incest, preserving a certain social stability through the codification of moieties of all types, types of plants or animals, types of gods, types of stories, types of laws or political activity, types of sex or sexuality—all of these belong to the general field of organizing. Organizing will inevitably draw on patterns that can themselves be named and described—hierarchies, Venn diagrams, opposites, lists, Greimasian semiotic squares, orders—which could be the subject of a certain analysis. All such organizations of the real will have an uneasy relationship with the inevitable forms of difference, complexity, and misfitted-ness that historical actuality incessantly throws at us, which means that any act of organizing is, necessarily, an act of epistemological violence, though a violence that remains absolutely necessary to the possibility of continuity in the social. The tension between a descriptive organization and a proscriptive one, and the social effects of both types, which can never be distinct, also belongs to this general category of analysis.

As for communication, it will perhaps be the most obviously relevant to literary humanists, since it addresses the entire realm of meaning, and the relation between the literal and the figural, with which we are already familiar. Indeed, the aspects of the Shannon moment that have had the most purchase on literary studies stem directly from the excitement and anxiety provoked by the spread of Shannonian information theory across the disciplines in the 1950s and 1960s. Their results may be seen in the work of linguists like Roman Jakobson or literary critics like Yuri Lotman, and more broadly in the great split between what one might think of as continental semiotics, on the one hand, and Anglo-American semiotics, on the other. Some of the modern tension around this problem might be thought of as a reaction to competing names for the act of meaning-making that come up around information theory: if one thinks of meaning-making as fundamentally driven by the creator of a message, then we might speak here of transmitting, and focus on the work of transmitters and transmission, of the production of messages by individuals or machines that operate essentially as monads in the social. If on the other hand one recognizes that any act of meaning-making assumes some kind of audience, and is therefore ontologically, from the beginning, a matter of *dialogue*, then any act of so-called transmitting makes no sense unless included in a much broader process of social communication and expectation, and is far from neutral as a result.

A third and final reason: for many years now any number of humanists working outside departments of literature and history narrowly conceived, less caught up in the immediacy of a certain humanist rejection of information-life, have in fact done an immense amount of important and interesting work on the concept. These colleagues work in fields like library science, or history of science, or indeed in the social sciences. Their work constitutes an important ground for this very book. Indeed, one might think of this volume (and its companion reader) as an attempt to bridge the gap between the information-oriented work of scholars like Safiya Noble, whose PhD is in Library and Information Science, or Virginia Eubanks, a political scientist, both of whom have done so much to illuminate the social effects of the algorithmic organization of culture, and the fields of literature, rhetoric, history, and continental philosophy, which have not yet done enough work on such topics. If we do not understand storing, organizing, and communicating in richer and more transhistorical ways, if we do not see their deep connection to the most basic interests of humanist inquiry, then we will simply think less richly and less well.

What then, among all these processes, is information? It is not prior to them. It follows them. The processes, and the social needs they meet, for beings living in time, are as fundamental as any reified extension of their activity. Information, considered as a social form, is not, in such a view, a primary substance. It is rather an outgrowth of specific human practices and action. It appears in the world because it meets a specific human-social need, namely the need to have words and concepts that, among other things, help us describe the relation between content and form, or to talk about the things that we store, organize, or transmit to one another, that reify, in whatever way, things that make it easier for us to manage, to get by or get along, to accomplish our goals. This is true whether a culture has the particular word *information* or not, in the same way that it is true that a culture has a power structure or uses knowledge, whether or not it has those specific words or their near equivalents in another language. Indeed, one of the tasks going forward will be to engage in a comparative study of information-concepts, with the understanding that information itself is only one of many such concepts, and not the master-term of the entire system, with the idea of producing a list of information-near-equivalents, each of which would help adumbrate the larger social process that governs their necessity, or lack of necessity. For if one encounters a culture without the idea of information, a culture that lives purely "in the moment," that would surely add to our understanding of the range of capacities of the human animal. Any comparative, transhistorical list of information-concepts would have to be supported by an equally rich list of related or connected terms, since no one today can know what information means without understanding the difference our contemporary structure of knowledge proposes between that term and ideas like knowledge, data, or wisdom, not to mention gossip, news, or feeling, each of which relates differently to the idea of information and, in a system constructed by negative differences, constructs it (for our time). A complete description of such a system for a given social and historical moment would come close to mapping out the entire Foucauldian order of things that would define its status as a certain kind of information society.

And so, these two books.

The first, which you have before you, is a reader. It includes material mostly written in and around the mid-century technological and theoretical transformations which produce our contemporary information age, and which have brought to the fore the idea of information as a social concept. This material constitutes, in many respects, the editorial collective's opening gambit at building a canon for the broad-based humanistic study of information. It is organized into five parts.

Part one, "The Shannon Knot," lays out some of the critical texts written in, around, after, and in historical and philosophical judgment of the initial arrival of information theory into mass consciousness. Though one of the major arguments of these two books is that this set of texts and concerns cannot and should not delimit our sense of what information is or how it should be studied, the knot nonetheless had such a profound influence on both intellectual and popular conceptions of information that today one can barely think of information without it. The task of doing so begins with a reading of these texts and their embeddedness within a postwar milieu profoundly invested in military and paramilitary applications of technology, and with a recognition, as well, that to think of information studies as merely the critique of this status would be to remain fundamentally trapped within it. The 1949 moment is only one commencement of many, but it is an important one. We must understand it to move beyond it.

The second part, "Order, Number," refers specifically to the idea of organization. It showcases the analysis of organization across a number of fields, including the epistemological, the mediatic, the numerical or statistical, and the physical.

The third part is "The Work of Art." Why does this seemingly more limited and focused topic interrupt a sequence of what might otherwise be thought of as headings of general interest? It is because the work of art has for a long time constituted a kind of testing ground for theories of information (as well as for theories of language), either by virtue of being almost entirely excluded from them, by virtue of being placed to the side as a special category of cultural activity to be dealt with once the important basic problems have been solved, or by virtue of standing in as an extreme test of any total theory of information-work. In this way the work of art has a special status in the history of information, both for the ways that it has been fundamentally excluded from the idea of information, and this by both information-philes and information-phobes, and for the ways in which various adventurers have attempted, in the wake of the Shannon knot, to ravel it into that particular set of mysteries.

The work of art belongs, to be sure, to a larger ecology of cultural production, one of the major features of which involves the production of various material substrates, such as voice or writing, and conceptual forms like genres and categories, that organize it. "Media Ecologies" begins with orality and literacy, moves from the arts of memory to twentieth century technological forms of all types, and closes, finally, with a glimpse at the role information and media metaphors have played in the description and research activity of the biological sciences. There we find DNA, binding together in a metaphorical double helix biotic existence and writing: the so-called book of life.

The reader's final part, "Informed Society," turns its attention to the specifically social and political consequences of information-gathering and information-organization. It is primarily focused on the modern period, and specifically on the forms of hope associated with the idea of a participatory democracy composed of equally educated citizens, figured by the idea of the informed voter, for instance, as well as the forms of threat or anxiety posed by regimes of surveillance and control, and sometimes of self-surveillance and self-control. The reader's final words are given over to Steven Marks, who, in placing information within a history of capitalism that extends well before its putative origin in the Shannon of 1948–1949, indicates something of the historical range that would, while grasping the study of this field firmly in a historical context, allow us also to move outside and beyond it, and to learn, from that outside, new ways of thinking information's very socio-historical essence or being.

As for the Keywords volume for which this work stands as a companion, it contains its own introduction. But it needs to be said somewhere that both the range of research areas and the range of participants in that second volume aim not only to showcase some of the most interesting contemporary work in the humanistic study of information, but also to act as a rebuke to the relatively White, male, and technocratic makeup and focus of the information-canon presented in the reader. That Whiteness, maleness, and technocratism are features of the historical appearance of the information society and of information theory as fields of experience and study is not in question. In this they reflect, of course, the dominance of White men in the production of knowledge of all types in twentieth century Europe and the United States, as well as the larger positions of dominance—in both soft and hard power—that those regions held during the postwar period. But they also reflect something critical about the nature of information as it has been used and understood in the last seventy years. I refer to information's alleged semiotic and political neutrality and its context-independence. Information technically conceived shares these two

forms of social positioning with the idealized figure of Enlightenment knowledge, whose arguments or actions ought not to depend on the speaker's wealth,
status, gender, race, or social position. That the advantages of this neutrality
have been unevenly distributed—that their distribution has often served the
continued dominance of the dominant, and thus the general forces of racism,
classism, and sexism—is well known. It is in fact the nature of White privilege
(or masculine privilege) that it speaks and acts from a position of blankness, and
therefore universality, that does not extend beyond its borders, so that a White
man gives voice to "knowledge," while a woman gives voice only to "knowledge
from a woman's point of view," the colonizer to a managerial understanding of
situations, and the colonized only to a fractured conceptualization of the social
whole, limited by the fact of their being dominated in the first place. And so on.

That the privilege of neutrality has been unjustly withheld from the full
realm of the social does not mean that such neutrality does not or should not
exist, but it does suggest that the production of information theory, and indeed
the overall orientation toward a certain vision of technological society—whose
political avatar is libertarianism—has not been especially White and male by
virtue of a simple coincidence. It seems likely, rather, a matter of convenience or
collusion. What this means for the future of information studies in the humanities is clear: we will not succeed in truly understanding, or even studying,
information in an epistemologically serious manner unless we diversify both
our areas of concern and the producers of our knowledge. Only in this way
will, in the decades to come, the range of something like *Information: Keywords*
return to inflect the future editions of a book like *Information: A Reader*, with
all the happy results for our collective efforts to understand ourselves and the
world that such a promise implies.

* * *

Two last things. First: this volume preserves the citational formats of the
original works. In the attempt to keep the amount of scholarly information
manageable, we have chosen to omit reference lists for in-text parenthetical
citations. Readers who wish to further tug on a citational thread should consult the original work.

Second: it would be churlish to close without noting that this book and the
companion Keywords volume would not have been possible without a great
deal of institutional and personal support and intellectual exchange. Foremost
among these was the environment and friendship made possible by Penn State's
Center for Humanities and Information, and particularly—since it spawned
the very idea of this project—the community of scholars and thinkers that surrounded the center in its first two years of operation. This included not only the
editors named here but also Bonnie Mak, Laura Helton, John Russell, Pamela

Vanhaitsma, and the many postdoctoral and visiting fellows who made up the life of the center. Olivia Brown, Yiming Ma, and Alysa Hickey provided infrastructural support, as did Carey Eckhardt, Susan Welch, and Eric Silver. Sarah Osment helped us out of an editorial jam at a critical moment. We're also grateful to the team at Columbia University Press, and especially to Philip Leventhal, for their share in the work.

Notes

1. What is the social? A lifeworld, a container, and a shaped and shaping form for human historical interaction. I assume that there has never not been the social; the social is the life-form of the species, as it is of primates and many other mammals; a made structure composed of individual units, whose actions collectively generate a set of patterns, habits, and other forms of repetition—including the form we call "language"—some of which constitute the unconscious background, some the contested foreground, of ordinary (and historical) life.

2. John Durham Peters, "Information: Notes Toward a Critical History," *Journal of Communication Inquiry* (July 1988): 10.

3. Claude E. Shannon and Warren Weaver, *The Mathematical Theory of Communication* (Urbana: University of Illinois Press, 1963), 4. Unfortunately the press refused to give us permission to reprint a larger excerpt of Weaver's essay in this volume.

4. Laura Helton, "Making Lists, Keeping Time: Infrastructures of Black Thought, 1900–1950," in *Against a Sharp White Background: Infrastructures of African American Print*, ed. Brigitte Fielder and Jonathan Senchyne (Madison: University of Wisconsin Press, 2019), 82–108; Jacques Derrida, *Archive Fever: A Freudian Impression*, trans. Eric Prenowitz (Chicago: University of Chicago Press, 1997).

THE SHANNON KNOT

I
n July 1948 there appeared in the *Bell System Technical Journal* the
first part of an article that laid out mathematical calculations for measuring and managing the rate of flow and the degree of uncertainty in
signal processing. It began:

> The recent development of various methods of modulation such as PCM and
> PPM which exchange bandwidth for signal-to-noise ratio has intensified the
> interest in a general theory of communication.

Observe the scale of the sentence. The opening noun phrase—"the recent development of" a series of technical methods for doing certain things, communicated in technical terms (modulated PCM, PPM, bandwidth, signal-to-noise
ratio)—gives way to a verb—the development has "intensified"—that has as its
object an "interest." An interest in what? In nothing less than "general theory of
communication," a theory, that is, that will be general, covering (one assumes)
all aspects of the thing to be discussed, and, moreover, will be a general theory
of something already quite general—namely, communication.

The nontechnical reader will be forgiven for not even realizing communication was at issue, at least until the appearance of the sentence's final word. And
indeed the surprise technically minded readers might have felt, in 1948, that the
scope of the project announced in this first sentence had, for their troubles, an
explanation waiting around the corner. Communication, the article went on to
say, is conceived here as the problem of "reproducing at one point either exactly

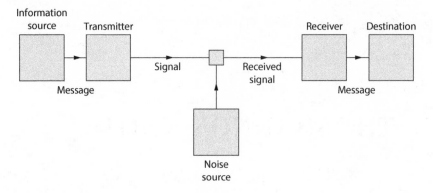

0.1 Schematic diagram of a general communication system.

or approximately a message selected at another point," a problem illustrated on the article's second page with a schematic diagram.

Leave aside for the moment whatever thoughts you might have, as a humanist, about the definition of communication here (is it really a matter of "reproducing" messages?), or whatever objections you might have to the diagram (does communication only really go in one direction, from a source to a destination?). Notice instead simply the scope and range of the opening of this article, the confident theorization of communication that follows from the technical details, and the assurance that what will be sought in these pages is a *general* theory of it. And know this: that from these beginnings—the sentence, the diagram, the articles (part 1 was followed by part 2, published in October), and their republication as a short book in 1949, *The Mathematical Theory of Communication*, with an introduction by Warren Weaver—was launched the entire field of modern information theory, with all its enormous effects, including, for starters, the effects that make words like bandwidth or signal-to-noise ratio far more familiar to ordinary readers in 2021 than they would have been to their grandparents, or great-grandparents, seventy years earlier. At their limit, the effects of information theory have gone far beyond adjustments to the common lexicon: they have shaped new academic fields, including the study of natural language processing and computational linguistics; they have generated technical advances ranging from statistical models for data compression and the development of digital transmission methods, all of which lead directly into modern computing, media systems, and data management and storage. And they are responsible, also, for the more general conceptualization of the postwar period, and our period, as an information age, as a historical era defined and organized in some fundamental way by a new relationship to this thing called *information*.

The particular alliance between technical interest—for the articles were written as their author, Claude Shannon, tried to solve certain problems in the transmission of voices over telephone wires—and social or even anthropological scope, the desire to produce nothing less than a theory of communication in general, was typical of the excitement produced by the postwar U.S. military-industrial-cultural complex. Shannon did the work that appeared under the aegis of "A Mathematical Theory of Communication" as he worked for Bell Labs on a contract funded directly by the World War II–era National Defense Research Committee. Its most immediate concerns owed a great deal to the problems of military communication and cryptography that were so critical to that period, and whose technical developments led to, among other things, the development of the modern digital computer.

But even in its infancy information theory's scope was wider than the military needs that spawned it. Shannon's work on communication drew on other work done in and around military projects at MIT in the war years, including research on problems related to artillery and anti-aircraft fire control. The fire control work was most prominently theorized by Norbert Wiener, whose *Cybernetics; or, Control and Communication in the Animal and the Machine* also appeared in the *annus mirabilis* of 1948. Wiener's book begins with a discussion of the problems of tracking planes with anti-aircraft fire, but moves on to consider the entire realm of operations that involve what Wiener called "feedback"—the process whereby an operator, such as the helmsman of a ship, or a thermostat, responds to changes in environmental conditions like the wind or the water or the temperature and adjusts its operations accordingly. These operations, Wiener argued, could be thought of not only as forms of intelligence, but also forms of social organization, operating at statistical scales both large and small (consider the way a population of living beings might adjust its reproductive patterns in response to food surpluses or shortages, to shifts in climate or in political governance.) As with Shannon's, the power of Wiener's work came from its integration of a variety of scientific tools, including mathematics and statistics, and its pan-cultural, even universal ambitions. "Information is information, and not matter or energy," Wiener wrote in the first pages of *Cybernetics*; to him is owed, therefore, one of the first articulations of information as an ontological category on the order of what were then recognized as the only two fundamental forces in the universe.

The excitement surrounding all this information talk was expanded and extended by a series of ten conferences held on cybernetics between 1946 and 1953, organized by the Josiah Macy Jr. Foundation. The Macy Conferences, as these were known, brought together academics and researchers from across the disciplines, with the goal of breaking down disciplinary barriers and of leveraging the new scientific knowledge into the humanities and the social sciences. Their participants included linguists, philosophers, sociologists, and psychologists, as well as biologists, zoologists, physicists, engineers, computer scientists, neuroscientists, and physicians, who together composed a veritable who's who of American intellectual life at the time. Together, the series of reactions to cybernetics and information theory, which spread from the Macy conferences across the entire world—touching, for instance, the work of the linguist Roman Jakobson or the anthropologist Claude Lévi-Strauss, among many, many others—constitute the core of what the editors of these two books have called the Shannon knot, the network of talks, articles, books, ideas, disagreements, innovations, successes, failures, missed opportunities, and general ferment that has made information the socially important concept it is today.

The Shannon knot thus explains many of the selections reproduced here, including the material from Shannon and Wiener, and the work of Macy participants Gregory Bateson and Donald MacKay, as well as that of Harold Garfinkel, whose advisor, the American sociologist Talcott Parsons, also presented at the Macy meetings. We have reproduced material from Shannon's original article, but not from Warren Weaver's important introduction to *The Mathematical Theory of Communication*, as we were not able to obtain copyright permission from the University of Illinois Press.

The resonance of the work done between 1948 and 1960 echoes long down the years, spreading from its initial spaces into a wider variety of fields, producing commentary, extension, and critique. Responses have to some extent differed in tone depending on field; in analytic philosophy, for instance, Fred Dretske's work, partially reproduced here, launched a long and mainly positive engagement with the texts of information theory, some of which leads directly into the contemporary development of a philosophy of information by a number of thinkers, including Luciano Floridi, Rafael Capurro, and many others. In more explicitly humanistic arenas, however, the reaction to both the work done around the knot and to the general social shifts caused by the rise of information technologies has been most frequently suspicious and negative, particularly as it responds to the various techno-utopianisms and fantasies of bureaucratic management and control that emerge from them. John Durham Peters' text is a touchstone here, while N. Katherine Hayles shows us how theorists based in literary criticism have attempted both to understand and to remediate some of the information work for positive purposes. Peter Janich's work, which comes more directly from philosophy, also pursues a fairly skeptical line when it comes to evaluating the claims made by information theory to have radically reorganized our understanding of the universe. The final excerpt in this section comes from the French philosopher and historian of technology Matthieu Triclot, and demonstrates the ways in which, some seven decades later, we might begin to think the legacy of the work done in and around 1949.

A final word, on the relation of this section to the rest of the book. This section comes first in this reader because the Shannon knot, more than anything else, has given us the concept of information—both the social concept, and the technical-scientific one—that we have today. This dominance makes it impossible, or at least unserious, to think "information" without passing through the knot. But that does not mean that such a conceptualization of information is correct, either technically or pragmatically; nor does it suggest that humanists ought to spend all their time fighting against this dominance—a move that would, ironically, simply continue to affirm it. The goal of the project is not to assert the Shannon knot's centrality but to place it in a historical context, and then to use that context to recalibrate and relocate our sense of both the humanist possibilities, and the *human* possibilities, of a more complex understanding of information as a social form: to begin the Shannon knot, as we do here, but then to move, as you will in subsequent sections, having passed through it, finally beyond it, to other, richer topographies.

Eric Hayot

CLAUDE SHANNON, FROM
A MATHEMATICAL THEORY OF
COMMUNICATION (1948)

By the time Shannon (1916–2001) wrote these words, he was already known for having developed a theory of circuit design that used Boolean algebra to simplify switching relays used in telephone systems. During the war, much of his work focused on cryptography; at Bell Labs he met with Alan Turing, then visiting from England to help with cryptographic work; Turing showed Shannon his 1936 paper on the "universal Turing machine." The work below comes out of the intersection between Shannon's interest in the logical and electronic representation of symbolic systems, and the more practical problems of telephonic communication. Much of the material in Shannon's work is highly technical; we have included enough of it here to give readers untrained in advanced mathematics a full sense of the work.

Introduction

The recent development of various methods of modulation such as PCM and PPM which exchange bandwidth for signal-to-noise ratio has intensified the interest in a general theory of communication. A basis for such a theory is contained in the important papers of Nyquist[1] and Hartley[2] on this subject. In the present paper we will extend the theory to include a number of new factors, in particular the effect of noise in the channel, and the savings possible due to the statistical structure of the original message and due to the nature of the final destination of the information.

The fundamental problem of communication is that of reproducing at one point either exactly or approximately a message selected at another point. Frequently the messages have meaning; that is they refer to or are correlated according to some system with certain physical or conceptual entities. These semantic aspects of communication are irrelevant to the engineering problem. The significant aspect is that the actual message is one selected from a set of possible messages. The system must be designed to operate for each possible selection, not just the one which will actually be chosen since this is unknown at the time of design.

If the number of messages in the set is finite then this number or any monotonic function of this number can be regarded as a measure of the information produced when one message is chosen from the set, all choices being equally likely. As was pointed out by Hartley the most natural choice is the logarithmic function. Although this definition must be generalized considerably when we consider the influence of the statistics of the message and when we have a continuous range of messages, we will in all cases use an essentially logarithmic measure.

The logarithmic measure is more convenient for various reasons:

1. It is practically more useful. Parameters of engineering importance such as time, bandwidth, number of relays, etc., tend to vary linearly with the logarithm of the number of possibilities. For example, adding one relay to a group doubles the number of possible states of the relays. It adds 1 to the base 2 logarithm of this number. Doubling the time roughly squares the number of possible messages, or doubles the logarithm, etc.

2. It is nearer to our intuitive feeling as to the proper measure. This is closely related to (1) since we intuitively measure entities by linear comparison with common standards. One feels, for example, that two punched cards should have twice the capacity of one for information storage, and two identical channels twice the capacity of one for transmitting information.

3. It is mathematically more suitable. Many of the limiting operations are simple in terms of the logarithm but would require clumsy restatement in terms of the number of possibilities.

The choice of a logarithmic base corresponds to the choice of a unit for measuring information. If the base 2 is used the resulting units may be called binary digits, or more briefly *bits*, a word suggested by J. W. Tukey. A device with two stable positions, such as a relay or a flip-flop circuit, can store one bit of information. N such devices can store N bits, since the total number of possible states is 2^N and $\log_2 2^N = N$. If the base 10 is used the units may be called decimal digits. Since

$$\log_2 M = \log_{10} M / \log_{10} 2$$
$$= 3.32 \log_{10} M,$$

a decimal digit is about $3\frac{1}{3}$ bits. A digit wheel on a desk computing machine has ten stable positions and therefore has a storage capacity of one decimal digit. In analytical work where integration and differentiation are involved the base e is sometimes useful. The resulting units of information will be called natural units. Change from the base a to base b merely requires multiplication by $\log_b a$.

By a communication system we will mean a system of the type indicated schematically in Fig. 1. It consists of essentially five parts:

1. An *information source* which produces a message or sequence of messages to be communicated to the receiving terminal. The message may be of various types: (a) A sequence of letters as in a telegraph or teletype system; (b) A single function of time $f(t)$ as in radio or telephony; (c) A function of time and other variables as in black and white television—here the message may be thought of as a function $f(x,y,t)$ of two space coordinates and time, the light intensity at point (x,y) and time t on a pickup tube plate; (d) Two or more functions of time, say $f(t)$ $g(t)$, $h(t)$—this is the case in "three-dimensional" sound transmission or if the system is intended to service several individual channels in multiplex; (e) Several functions of several variables—in color television the message consists of three functions $f(x,y,t)$, $g(x,y,t)$, $h(x,y,t)$ defined in a three-dimensional continuum—we may also think of these three functions as components of a vector field defined in the region—similarly, several black and white television sources would produce "messages" consisting of a

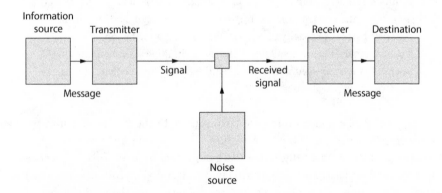

1.1 Schematic diagram of a general communication system.

number of functions of three variables; (f) Various combinations also occur, for example in television with an associated audio channel.

2. A *transmitter* which operates on the message in some way to produce a signal suitable for transmission over the channel. In telephony this operation consists merely of changing sound pressure into a proportional electrical current. In telegraphy we have an encoding operation which produces a sequence of dots, dashes and spaces on the channel corresponding to the message. In a multiplex PCM system the different speech functions must be sampled, compressed, quantized and encoded, and finally interleaved properly to construct the signal. Vocoder systems, television and frequency modulation are other examples of complex operations applied to the message to obtain the signal.

3. The *channel* is merely the medium used to transmit the signal from transmitter to receiver. It may be a pair of wires, a coaxial cable, a band of radio frequencies, a beam of light, etc.

4. The *receiver* ordinarily performs the inverse operation of that done by the transmitter, reconstructing the message from the signal.

5. The *destination* is the person (or thing) for whom the message is intended.

We wish to consider certain general problems involving communication systems. To do this it is first necessary to represent the various elements involved as mathematical entities, suitably idealized from their physical counterparts. We may roughly classify communication systems into three main categories: discrete, continuous and mixed. By a discrete system we will mean one in which both the message and the signal are a sequence of discrete symbols. A typical case is telegraphy where the message is a sequence of letters and the signal a sequence of dots, dashes and spaces. A continuous system is one in which the message and signal are both treated as continuous functions, e.g., radio or television. A mixed system is one in which both discrete and continuous variables appear, e.g., PCM transmission of speech.

We first consider the discrete case. This case has applications not only in communication theory, but also in the theory of computing machines, the design of telephone exchanges and other fields. In addition the discrete case forms a foundation for the continuous and mixed cases which will be treated in the second half of the paper. [...]

2. The Discrete Source of Information

We have seen that under very general conditions the logarithm of the number of possible signals in a discrete channel increases linearly with time. The capacity to transmit information can be specified by giving this rate of increase, the number of bits per second required to specify the particular signal used.

We now consider the information source. How is an information source to be described mathematically, and how much information in bits per second is produced in a given source? The main point at issue is the effect of statistical knowledge about the source in reducing the required capacity of the channel, by the use of proper encoding of the information. In telegraphy, for example, the messages to be transmitted consist of sequences of letters. These sequences, however, are not completely random. In general, they form sentences and have the statistical structure of, say, English. The letter E occurs more frequently than Q, the sequence TH more frequently than XP, etc. The existence of this structure allows one to make a saving in time (or channel capacity) by properly encoding the message sequences into signal sequences. This is already done to a limited extent in telegraphy by using the shortest channel symbol, a dot, for the most common English letter E; while the infrequent letters, Q, X, Z are represented by longer sequences of dots and dashes. This idea is carried still further in certain commercial codes where common words and phrases are represented by four- or five-letter code groups with a considerable saving in average time. The standardized greeting and anniversary telegrams now in use extend this to the point of encoding a sentence or two into a relatively short sequence of numbers.

We can think of a discrete source as generating the message, symbol by symbol. It will choose successive symbols according to certain probabilities depending, in general, on preceding choices as well as the particular symbols in question. A physical system, or a mathematical model of a system which produces such a sequence of symbols governed by a set of probabilities, is known as a stochastic process.[3] We may consider a discrete source, therefore, to be represented by a stochastic process. Conversely, any stochastic process which produces a discrete sequence of symbols chosen from a finite set may be considered a discrete source. This will include such cases as:

1. Natural written languages such as English, German, Chinese.

2. Continuous information sources that have been rendered discrete by some quantizing process. For example, the quantized speech from a PCM transmitter, or a quantized television signal.

3. Mathematical cases where we merely define abstractly a stochastic process which generates a sequence of symbols. The following are examples of this last type of source.

(A) Suppose we have five letters A, B, C, D, E which are chosen each with probability .2, successive choices being independent. This would lead to a sequence of which the following is a typical example.

> B D C B C E C C C A D C B D D A A E C E E A
> A B B D A E E C A C E E B A E E C B C E A D.

This was constructed with the use of a table of random numbers.[4]

(B) Using the same five letters let the probabilities be .4, .1, .2, .2, .1, respectively, with successive choices independent. A typical message from this source is then:

$$\text{A A A C D C B D C E A A D A D A C E D A}$$
$$\text{E A D C A B E D A D D C E C A A A A A D.}$$

(C) A more complicated structure is obtained if successive symbols are not chosen independently but their probabilities depend on preceding letters. In the simplest case of this type a choice depends only on the preceding letter and not on ones before that. The statistical structure can then be described by a set of transition probabilities $p_i(j)$, the probability that letter i is followed by letter j. The indices i and j range over all the possible symbols. A second equivalent way of specifying the structure is to give the "digram" probabilities $p(i,j)$, i.e., the relative frequency of the digram $i\,j$. The letter frequencies $p(i)$, (the probability of letter i), the transition probabilities $p_i(j)$ and the digram probabilities $p(i,j)$ are related by the following formulas:

$$p(i) = \sum_j p(i,j) = \sum_j p(j,i) = \sum_j p(j)p(i)$$
$$p(i,j) = p(i)p_i(j)$$
$$\sum_j p_i(j) = \sum_i p(i) = \sum_{i,j} p(i,j) = 1$$

As a specific example suppose there are three letters A, B, C with the probability tables:

$p_i(j)$		j			i	$p(i)$	$p_i(i,j)$		j		
		A	B	C	A	$\frac{9}{27}$			A	B	C
	A	0	$\frac{4}{5}$	$\frac{1}{5}$	B	$\frac{16}{27}$		A	0	$\frac{4}{15}$	$\frac{1}{15}$
i	B	$\frac{1}{2}$	$\frac{1}{2}$	0	C	$\frac{2}{27}$	i	B	$\frac{8}{27}$	$\frac{8}{27}$	0
	C	$\frac{1}{2}$	$\frac{2}{5}$	$\frac{1}{10}$				C	$\frac{1}{27}$	$\frac{2}{135}$	$\frac{1}{135}$

A typical message from this source is the following:

$$\text{A B B A B A B A B A B A B A B A B B B A B B B B B A B A B A B A B A B A B B B A}$$
$$\text{C A C A B B A B B B B A B B A B A C B B B A B A}$$

The next increase in complexity would involve trigram frequencies but no more. The choice of a letter would depend on the preceding two letters but not on the message before that point. A set of trigram frequencies $p(i, j, k)$ or equivalently a set of transition probabilities $pij(k)$ would be required. Continuing in this way one obtains successively more complicated stochastic processes. In the general n-gram case a set of n-gram probabilities $p(i_1, i_2, \ldots, i_n)$ or of transition probabilities $P_{i_1, i_2, \ldots, i_{n-1}}(i_n)$ or is required to specify the statistical structure.

(D) Stochastic processes can also be defined which produce a text consisting of a sequence of "words." Suppose there are five letters A, B, C, D, E and 16 "words" in the language with associated probabilities:

.10 A	.16 BEBE	.11 CABED	.04 DEB
.04 ADEB	.04 BED	.05 CEED	.15 DEED
.05 ADEE	.02 BEED	.08 DAB	.01 EAB
.01 BADD	.05 CA	.04 DAD	.05 EE

Suppose successive "words" are chosen independently and are separated by a space. A typical message might be:

DAB EE A BEBE DEED DEB ADEE ADEE EE DEB BEBE BEBE BEBE ADEE BED DEED DEED CEED ADEE A DEED DEED BEBE CABED BEBE BED DAB DEED ADEB.

If all the words are of finite length this process is equivalent to one of the preceding type, but the description may be simpler in terms of the word structure and probabilities. We may also generalize here and introduce transition probabilities between words, etc.

These artificial languages are useful in constructing simple problems and examples to illustrate various possibilities. We can also approximate to a natural language by means of a series of simple artificial languages. The zero-order approximation is obtained by choosing all letters with the same probability and independently. The first-order approximation is obtained by choosing successive letters independently but each letter having the same probability that it has in the natural language.[5] Thus, in the first-order approximation to English, E is chosen with probability .12 (its frequency in normal English) and W with probability .02, but there is no influence between adjacent letters and no tendency to form the preferred digrams such as TH, ED, etc. In the second-order approximation, digram structure is introduced. After a letter is chosen, the next one is chosen in accordance with the frequencies with which the various letters follow the first one. This requires a table of digram frequencies $pi(j)$. In the third-order approximation, trigram structure is introduced. Each letter is chosen with probabilities which depend on the preceding two letters.

3. The Series of Approximations to English

To give a visual idea of how this series of processes approaches a language, typical sequences in the approximations to English have been constructed and are given below. In all cases we have assumed a 27-symbol "alphabet," the 26 letters and a space.

1. Zero-order approximation (symbols independent and equiprobable).

   XFOML   RXKHRJFFJUJ   ZLPWCFWKCYJ   FFJEYVKCQSGHYD
   QPAAMKBZAACIBZLHJQD.

2. First-order approximation (symbols independent but with frequencies of English text).

   OCRO HLI RGWR NMIELWIS EU LL NBNESEBYA TH EEI
   ALHENHTTPA OOBTTVA NAHBRL.

3. Second-order approximation (digram structure as in English).

   ON IE ANTSOUTINYS ARE T INCTORE ST BE S DEAMY ACHIN D
   ILONASIVE TUCOOWE AT TEASONARE FUSO TIZIN ANDY TOBE
   SEACE CTISBE.

4. Third-order approximation (trigram structure as in English).

   IN NO IST LAT WHEY CRATICT FROURE BIRS GROCID
   PONDENOME OF DEMONSTURES OF THE REPTAGIN IS
   REGOACTIONA OF CRE.

5. First-order word approximation. Rather than continue with tetragram, . . ., *n*-gram structure it is easier and better to jump at this point to word units. Here words are chosen independently but with their appropriate frequencies.

   REPRESENTING AND SPEEDILY IS AN GOOD APT OR COME CAN DIF-
   FERENT NATURAL HERE HE THE A IN CAME THE TO OF TO EXPERT
   GRAY COME TO FURNISHES THE LINE MESSAGE HAD BE THESE.

6. Second-order word approximation. The word transition probabilities are correct but no further structure is included.

   THE HEAD AND IN FRONTAL ATTACK ON AN ENGLISH WRITER
   THAT THE CHARACTER OF THIS POINT IS THEREFORE ANOTHER
   METHOD FOR THE LETTERS THAT THE TIME OF WHO EVER TOLD
   THE PROBLEM FOR AN UNEXPECTED.

The resemblance to ordinary English text increases quite noticeably at each of the above steps. Note that these samples have reasonably good structure out to about twice the range that is taken into account in their construction. Thus in (3) the statistical process insures reasonable text for two-letter sequences, but four-letter sequences from the sample can usually be fitted into good sentences. In (6) sequences of four or more words can easily be placed in sentences without unusual or strained constructions. The particular sequence of ten words "attack on an English writer that the character of this" is not at all unreasonable. It appears then that a sufficient complex stochastic process will give a satisfactory representation of a discrete source. [. . .]

Notes

1. Nyquist, R., "Certain Factors Affecting Telegraph Speed," *Bell System Technical Journal*, April 1924, p. 324; "Certain Topics in Telegraph Transmission Theory," *A.I.E.E. Trans.*, v. 47, April 1928, p. 617.
2. Hartley, R. V. L., "Transmission of Information," *Bell System Technical Journal*, July 1928, p. 535.
3. See, for example, S. Chandrasekhar, "Stochastic Problems in Physics and Astronomy," *Reviews of Modern Physics*, v. 15, No. I, January 1943, p. 1.
4. Kendall and Smith, *Tables of Random Sampling Numbers*, Cambridge, 1939.
5. Letter, digram and trigram frequencies are given in *Secret and Urgent* by Fletcher Pratt, Blue Ribbon Books, 1939. Word frequencies are tabulated in *Relative Frequency of English Speech Sounds*, G. Dewey, Harvard University Press, 1923.

NORBERT WIENER, FROM
CYBERNETICS; OR, CONTROL
AND COMMUNICATION IN THE
ANIMAL AND THE MACHINE (1948)

Wiener (1894–1964), a child prodigy and polymath, was for a time far better known than Shannon, as his interests in philosophy and sociology meant that he did much more to connect his mathematical and engineering work to larger trends involving social life. Cybernetics, the science that Wiener developed to describe a quasi-universal theory of the mechanisms whereby systems reproduced themselves, was the outcome of these ambitions. The selections below are drawn from the beginning and the end of the book, and give some sense of its overall range. You will recognize in the opening reference to anti-aircraft fire a connection to the opening paragraph of Weaver's introduction to Shannon, cited in the introduction.

Introduction

[. . .] At the beginning of the war, the German prestige in aviation and the defensive position of England turned the attention of many scientists to the improvement of anti-aircraft artillery. Even before the war, it had become clear that the speed of the airplane had rendered obsolete all classical methods of the direction of fire, and that it was necessary to build into the control apparatus all the computations necessary. These were rendered much more difficult by the fact that, unlike all previously encountered targets, an airplane has a velocity which is a very appreciable part of the velocity of the missile used to bring it down. Accordingly, it is exceedingly important to shoot the missile, not at the target, but in such a way that missile and target may come together in space at some time in the future. We must hence find some method of predicting the future position of the plane.

The simplest method is to extrapolate the present course of the plane along a straight line. This has much to recommend it. The more a plane doubles and curves in flight, the less is its effective velocity, the less time it has to accomplish a mission, and the longer it remains in a dangerous region. Other things being equal, a plane will fly as straight a course as possible. However, by the time the first shell has burst, other things are *not* equal, and the pilot will probably zig-zag, stunt, or in some other way take evasive action.

If this action were completely at the disposal of the pilot, and the pilot were to make the sort of intelligent use of his chances that we anticipate in a good poker player, for example, he has so much opportunity to modify his expected position before the arrival of a shell that we should not reckon the chances of hitting him to be very good, except perhaps in the case of a very wasteful barrage fire. On the other hand, the pilot does not have a completely free chance to maneuver at his will. For one thing, he is in a plane going at an exceedingly high speed, and any too sudden deviation from his course will produce an acceleration that will render him unconscious and may disintegrate the plane. Then too, he can control the plane only by moving his control surfaces, and the new regimen of flow that is established takes some small time to develop. Even when it is fully developed, it merely changes the acceleration of the plane, and this change of acceleration must be converted, first into change of velocity and then into change of position, before it is finally effective. Moreover, an aviator under the strain of combat conditions is scarcely in a mood to engage in any very complicated and untrammeled voluntary behavior, and is quite likely to follow out the pattern of activity in which he has been trained. [. . .]

It will be seen that for the second time I had become engaged in the study of a mechanic-electrical system which was designed to usurp a specifically human function—in the first case, the execution of a complicated pattern of computation, and in the second, the forecasting of the future. In this second case, we should not avoid the discussion of the performance of certain human functions. In some fire-control apparatus, it is true, the original impulse to point comes in directly by radar, but in the more usual case, there is a human gun-pointer or gun-trainer or both coupled into the fire-control system, and acting as an essential part of it. It is essential to know their characteristics, in order to incorporate them mathematically into the machines they control. Moreover, their target, the plane, is also humanly controlled, and it is desirable to know its performance characteristics.

Mr. Bigelow and I came to the conclusion that an extremely important factor in voluntary activity is what the control engineers term *feedback*. [. . .] In doing this, we have made of communication engineering design a statistical science, a branch of statistical mechanics. The notion of statistical mechanics has indeed been encroaching on every branch of science for more than a century. We shall see that this dominance of statistical mechanics in modern physics has a very vital significance for the interpretation of the nature of time. In the case of communication engineering, however, the significance of the statistical element is immediately apparent. The transmission of information is impossible save as a transmission of alternatives. If only one contingency is to be transmitted, then it may be sent most efficiently and with the least trouble by sending no message at all. The telegraph and the telephone can perform their function only if the messages they transmit are continually varied in a manner not completely determined by their past, and can be designed effectively only if the variation of these messages conforms to some sort of statistical regularity.

To cover this aspect of communication engineering, we had to develop a statistical theory of the *amount of information*, in which the unit amount of information was that transmitted as a single decision between equally probable alternatives. This idea occurred at about the same time to several writers, among them the statistician R. A. Fisher, Dr. Shannon of the Bell Telephone Laboratories, and the author. Fisher's motive in studying this subject is to be found in classical statistical theory; that of Shannon in the problem of coding information; and that of the author in the problem of noise and message in electrical filters. Let it be remarked parenthetically that some of my speculations in this direction attach themselves to the earlier work of Kolmogoroff[1] in Russia, although a considerable part of my work was done before my attention was called to the work of the Russian school.

The notion of the amount of information attaches itself very naturally to a classical notion in statistical mechanics: that of *entropy*. Just as the amount of information in a system is a measure of its degree of organization, so the entropy of a system is a measure of its degree of disorganization; and the one is simply the negative of the other. This point of view leads us to a number of considerations concerning the second law of thermodynamics, and to a study of the possibility of the so-called Maxwell demons. Such questions arise independently in the study of enzymes and other catalysts, and their study is essential for the proper understanding of such fundamental phenomena of living matter as metabolism and reproduction. The third fundamental phenomenon of life, that of irritability, belongs to the domain of communication theory and falls under the group of ideas we have just been discussing.[2]

Thus, as far back as four years ago, the group of scientists about Dr. Rosenblueth and myself had already become aware [of] the essential unity of the set of problems centering about communication, control, and statistical mechanics, whether in the machine or in living tissue. On the other hand, we were seriously hampered by the lack of unity of the literature concerning these problems, and by absence of any common terminology, or even of a single name for the field. After much consideration, we have come to the conclusion that all the existing terminology has too heavy a bias to one side or another to serve the future development of the field as well as it should; and as happens so often to scientists, we have been forced to coin at least one artificial neo-Greek expression to fill the gap. We have decided to call the entire field of control and communication theory, whether in the machine or in the animal, by the name *Cybernetics*, which we form from the Greek χυβερνήτης or *steersman*. [. . .]

I have said that this new development has unbounded possibilities for good and for evil. For one thing, it makes the metaphorical dominance of the machines, as imagined by Samuel Butler, a most immediate and non-metaphorical problem. It gives the human race a new and most effective collection of mechanical slaves to perform its labor. Such mechanical labor has most of the economic properties of slave labor, although, unlike slave labor, it does not involve the direct demoralizing effects of human cruelty. However, any labor that accepts the conditions of competition with slave accepts the conditions of slave labor, and is essentially slave labor. The key word of this statement is *competition*. It may very well be a good thing for humanity to have the machine remove from it the need of menial and disagreeable tasks, or it may not. I do not know. It cannot be good for these new potentialities to be assessed in the terms of the market, of the money they save; and it is precisely the terms of the open market, the "fifth freedom," that have become the shibboleth of the sector of American opinion represented by the National Association of Manufacturers and the *Saturday Evening Post*. I say American opinion, for as an American, I know it best, but the hucksters recognize no national boundary.

Perhaps I may clarify the historical background of the present situation if I say that the first industrial revolution, the revolution of the "dark satanic mills," was the devaluation of the human arm by the competition of machinery. There is no rate of pay at which a United States pick-and-shovel laborer can live which is low enough to compete with the work of a steam shovel as an excavator. The modern industrial revolution is similarly bound to devalue the human brain, at least in its simpler and more routine decisions. Of course, just as the skilled carpenter, the skilled mechanic, the skilled dressmaker have in some degree survived the first industrial revolution, so the skilled scientist and the skilled administrator may survive the second. However, taking the second revolution as accomplished, the average human being of mediocre attainments or less has nothing to sell that it is worth anyone's money to buy.

The answer, of course, is to have a society based on human values other than buying or selling. To arrive at this society, we need a good deal of planning and a good deal of struggle, which, if the best comes to the best, may be on the plane of ideas, and otherwise—who knows? I thus felt it my duty to pass on my information and understanding of the position to those who have an active interest in the conditions and the future of labor, that is, to the labor unions. [. . .]

Information, Language, and Society

[. . .] Suppose I find myself in the woods with an intelligent savage who cannot speak my language and whose language I cannot speak. Even without any code of sign language common to the two of us, I can learn a great deal from him. All I need to do is to be alert to those moments when he shows the signs of emotion or interest. I then cast my eyes around, perhaps paying special attention to the direction of his glance, and fix in my memory what I see or hear. It will not be long before I discover the things which seem important to him, not because he has communicated them to me by language, but because I myself have observed them. In other words, a signal without an intrinsic content may acquire meaning in his mind by what he observes at the time, and may acquire meaning in my mind by what I observe at the time. The ability that he has to pick out the moments of my special, active attention is in itself a language as varied in possibilities as the range of impressions that the two of us are able to encompass. Thus social animals may have an active, intelligent, flexible means of communication long before the development of language.

Whatever means of communication the race may have, it is possible to define and to measure the amount of information available to the race and to distinguish it from the amount of information available to the individual. Certainly no information available to the individual is also available to the race unless it modifies the behavior of one individual to another, nor is even that behavior of racial significance unless it is distinguishable by other individuals from other forms of behavior. Thus the question as to whether a certain piece of information is racial or of purely private availability depends on whether it results in the individual assuming a form of activity which can be recognized as a distinct form of activity by other members of the race, in the sense that it will in turn affect their activity, and so on.

I have spoken of the race. This is really too broad a term for the scope of most communal information. Properly speaking, the community extends only so far as there extends an effectual transmission of information. It is possible to give a sort of measure to this by comparing the number of decisions entering a group from outside with the number of decisions made in the group. We can thus measure the autonomy of the group. A measure of the effective size of a group is given by the size which it must have to have achieved a certain stated degree of autonomy.

A group may have more group information or less group information than its members. A group of non-social animals, temporarily assembled, contains very little group information, even though its members may possess much information as individuals. This is because very little that one member does is noticed by the others and is acted on by them in a way that goes further in the group. On the other hand, the human organism contains vastly more information, in all probability, than does any one of its cells. There is thus no necessary relation in either direction between the amount of racial or tribal or community information and the amount of information available to the individual.

As in the case of the individual, not all the information which is available to the race at one time is accessible without special effort. There is a well-known tendency of libraries to become clogged by their own volume; of the sciences to develop such a degree of specialization that the expert is often illiterate outside his own minute specialty. [. . .]

One of the lessons of the present book is that any organism is held together in this action by the possession of means for the acquisition, use, retention, and transmission of information. In a society too large for the direct contact of its members, these means are the press, both as it concerns books and as it concerns newspapers, the radio, the telephone system, the telegraph, the posts, the theater, the movies, the schools, and the church. Besides their intrinsic importance as means of communication, each of these serves other, secondary functions. The newspaper is a vehicle for advertisement and an instrument for the monetary gain of its proprietor, as are also the movies and the radio. The school and the church are not merely refuges for the scholar and the saint: they are also the home of the Great Educator and the Bishop. The book that does not earn money for its publisher probably does not get printed and certainly does not get reprinted.

In a society like ours, avowedly based on buying and selling, in which all natural and human resources are regarded as the absolute property of the first business man enterprising enough to exploit them, these secondary aspects of the means of communication tend to encroach further and further on the primary ones. [. . .]

Thus on all sides we have a triple constriction of the means of communication: the elimination of the less profitable means in favor of the more profitable; the fact that these means are in the hands of the very limited class of wealthy men, and thus naturally express the opinions of that class; and the further fact that, as one of the chief avenues to political and personal power, they attract above all those ambitious for such power. That system which more than all others should contribute to social homeostasis is thrown directly into the hands of those most concerned in the game of power and money, which we have already seen to be one of the chief anti-homeostatic elements in the community. It is no wonder then that the larger communities, subject to this disruptive influence, contain far less communally available information than the smaller communities, to say nothing of the human elements of which all communities are built up. Like the wolf pack, although let us hope to a lesser extent, the State is stupider than most of its components.

This runs counter to a tendency much voiced among business executives, heads of great laboratories, and the like, to assume that because the community is larger than the individual it is also more intelligent. Some of this opinion is due to no more than a childish delight in the large and the lavish. Some of it is due to a sense of the possibilities of a large organization for good. Not a little of it, however, is nothing more than an eye for the main chance and a lusting after the fleshpots of Egypt.

There is another group of those who see nothing good in the anarchy of modern society, and in whom an optimistic feeling that there must be some way out has led to an overvaluation of the possible homeostatic elements in the community. Much as we may sympathize with these individuals and appreciate the emotional dilemma in which they find themselves, we cannot attribute too much value to this type of wishful thinking. [. . .]

I mention this matter because of the considerable, and I think false, hopes which some of my friends have built for the social efficacy of whatever new ways of thinking this book may contain. They are certain that our control over our material environment has far outgrown our control over our social environment and our understanding thereof. Therefore, they consider that the main task of the immediate future is to extend to the fields of anthropology, of sociology, of economics, the methods of the natural sciences, in the hope of achieving a like measure of success in the social fields. From believing this necessary, they come to believe it possible. In this, I maintain, they show an excessive optimism, and a misunderstanding of the nature of all scientific achievement.

All the great successes in precise science have been made in fields where there is a certain high degree of isolation of the phenomenon from the observer. We have seen in the case of astronomy that this may result from the enormous scale of certain phenomena with respect to man, so that man's mightiest efforts, not to speak of his mere glance, cannot make the slightest visible impression on the celestial world. In modern atomic physics, on the other hand, the science of the unspeakably minute, it is true that anything we do will have influence on many individual particles which is great *from the point of view of that particle.* [. . .] As far as these effects are concerned, the intervals of time concerned are large from the point of view of the individual particle and its motion, and our statistical theories have an admirably adequate basis. In short, we are too small to influence the stars in their courses, and too large to care about anything but the mass effects of molecules, atoms, and electrons. In both cases, we achieve a sufficiently loose coupling with the phenomena we are studying to give a massive total account of this coupling, although the coupling may not be loose enough for us to be able to ignore it altogether.

It is in the social sciences that the coupling between the observed phenomenon and the observer is hardest to minimize. On the one hand, the observer is able to exert a considerable influence on the phenomena that come to his attention. With all respect to the intelligence, skill, and honesty of purpose of my anthropologist friends, I cannot think that any community which they have investigated will ever be quite the same afterward. Many a missionary has fixed his own misunderstandings of a primitive language as law eternal in the process of reducing it to writing. There is much in the social habits of a people which is dispersed and distorted by the mere act of making inquiries about it. In another sense from that in which it is usually stated, *traduttore traditore*.

On the other hand, the social scientist has not the advantage of looking down on his subjects from the cold heights of eternity and ubiquity. It may be that there is a mass sociology of the human animalcule, observed like the populations of *Drosophila* in a bottle, but this is not a sociology in which we, who are human animalcules ourselves, are particularly interested. We are not much concerned about human rises and falls, pleasures and agonies, *sub specie aeternitatis*. Your anthropologist reports the customs associated with the life, education, career, and death of people whose life scale is much the same as his own. Your economist is most interested in predicting such business cycles as run their course in less than a generation or, at least, have repercussions which affect a man differentially at different stages of his career. Few philosophers of politics nowadays care to confine their investigations to the world of Ideas of Plato.

In other words, in the social sciences we have to deal with short statistical runs, nor can we be sure that a considerable part of what we observe is not an artifact of our own creation. An investigation of the stock market is likely to upset the stock market. We are too much in tune with the objects of our investigation to be good probes. In short, whether our investigations in the social sciences be statistical or dynamic—and they should participate in the nature of both—they can never be good to more than a very few decimal places, and, in short, can never furnish us with a quantity of verifiable, significant information which begins to compare with that which we have learned to expect in the natural sciences. We cannot afford to neglect them; neither should we build exaggerated expectations of their possibilities. There is much which we must leave, whether we like it or not, to the un-"scientific," narrative method of the professional historian.

Notes

1. Kolmogoroff, A. N., "Interpolation and Extrapolation von stationären Zufälligen Folgen," *Bull. Acad. Sci. U.S.S.R.*, Ser. Math. 5, 3–14 (1941).
2. Schrödinger, Erwin, *What Is Life?*, Cambridge University Press, Cambridge, England, 1945.

HAROLD GARFINKEL, FROM
TOWARD A SOCIOLOGICAL THEORY OF INFORMATION (1952)

Garfinkel (1917–2011), a sociologist, belongs (with Erving Goffman) to the "descriptive turn" in American sociology. Against large-scale, even structuralist approaches favored by his PhD advisor, Talcott Parsons, Garfinkel proposed "ethnomethodology," a mode of sociological work that relied on neutral descriptions of the practical ways in which social actors accomplish their goals. Garfinkel was exposed to the revolution in information theory while at Harvard, where he finished his PhD in 1952; in his last two years of study he also taught at Princeton, where he developed an extensive outline for a course on information. Those materials, from which the excerpt below is drawn, are gathered together in *Toward a Sociological Theory of Information,* edited by Anne Rawls and published by Routledge in 2009.

II. Some Desired Properties of the Thing Called "Information"

The following list was devised by going over some of the more prominent ways that sociologists as well as others have treated "information." The list is long but by no means complete. The trick is to find a definition that so constitutes the thing we are after that these properties are retained.

In whatever way we define "information" it would be desirable above all that the thing be conceived of as an existent and that it be capable of fairly precise empirical description.[1]

Further, it should at every point be "coupled" to—to use a phrase that Wiener employs—and be dependent for its existence upon physical as well as behavioral processes. We require that a system of signals and a system of information be capable of being not only coupled but *variably* coupled in the sense that while this information would depend upon signal characteristics that it not be given in one-to-one fashion with signal characteristics. We require that it be possible to perform physical operations that will affect it while at the same time logical operations like matching, counting, comparing, classifying, measuring, be possible with it.

It should be capable of being doubted, believed, tested, and recalled. One should be able to "invest" it with degrees of certainty. It should be capable of being an object of the experiences of love, hate, respect, fear, judgment, and so on.

It needs to be capable of remaining invariant under variations of signaling characteristics. It needs to be capable of spatial and temporal patterning. One should be able to refer meaningfully to its "existing in amount" at least in the sense that in more than a metaphorical sense one could talk of a person having it while another person does not. We would like it to stand in some clear and determinate relationship to the notions of signal, message, error randomness, order, memory, feed-back, communication, and communicative path, channel, and route though without sacrifice of sociological problems to engineering metaphors.

It needs to be transmissible from one physical spatial point to another. It must be transformable. It must be so defined that it makes sense to speak of its being differentially distributed within a social structure. It must be capable of being stored. It must allow of caretaker rights to it; of rights and costs of acquisition; of rights of use, control, and transfer. It must be capable of being lost, changed, bought and sold; it must be capable of being "priced."

It must make sense to talk of its clarity or ambiguity, of its uniqueness and typicality; of its private, public, personal, impersonal, anonymous or identified character. Usage must permit the category of ignorance, i.e., its presence or absence but without implying any notion of a finite total and without assigning motivational status to either information or ignorance. It must be capable of being used within the requirement of a sociologically conceived actor who is capable of autonomously altering as well as inventing or creating not only the rules of his own operation but this information as well. It needs to be capable of dissolving into randomness on the one hand, of having a probabilistic character, or at the other extreme of being so completely determined as to have the convincingness for the experiencer of apodicity.

It must be capable of acquisition through procedures other than and in addition to those of logico-empirical science. Further, the actor must be capable of acquiring it even though he fails in his make-up to approximate even closely the characteristics of the rational man.

It must somehow be found not only in the wide-awake attitudes of everyday life and be acquired through the senses, but must be found in the cloud-cuckoo worlds of dreams, fantasy, scientific theory, the theater, children's play, etc. It must deal with tables, persons, motives, centaurs, laws, and ghosts.

It must make sense to speak of information about information. It must in an important sense require for its objective status a statement about the person as a perceiver and a world that is simultaneously constituted through the notion of the perceiver, yet it must be capable of being treated independently of the perceiver.

It must be capable of treatment not only with reference to the notion of purpose, i.e., its instrumental character, but with reference to usage for its own sake and without reference to the accomplishment of a purpose, i.e., its expressional character.

On top of all this the definition must be general enough in its designation to cover this ground, but specific enough and with enough internal structure to permit its immediate use in generating questions, theorems, concepts, measurements, and so on.

As the confidence men put it, the good sucker always wants the best of it.

III. The Conditions within Which a Definition of Information Will be sought

[. . .] We have then our first specification of the thing, "information," I experience it not as liked, loved, hated, wished for, doubted, but *judged*. Or to borrow from the terminology of logic, I experience it in the mode of its affirmative meaning. To use Husserl's language, I "live in" its sense of affirmation. I do not affirm *about*; I affirm *that*. As I look at the Kriegsspiel board, I see directly the sense, the meaning, "I have completed my move without capturing a piece." When I consider the possibility that his king is not on the back row, I experience in its affirmative sense the question of where his king may be if it is not on the back row.

And now what else is required? (1) *For the case of signs:* Insofar as the experiencer actualizes something as the thing indicated by the sign, the thing indicated as it is experienced in the affirmative mode will be called the experiencer's information or "what he knows." (2) *For the case of expressions:* Insofar as the experiencer actualizes the object of an expression, that is, insofar as he effects the coincidence of the meaning and the thing meant—which can be done as was pointed out previously through a perception, a fantasized image, or an idea—the unity of meaning and thing meant as the coincidence presents a specified object will, insofar as the experiencer "lives in" the affirmative mode of the coincidence be known as his information or "what he knows."

So much for the notion of information in general. A very touchy problem remains to be handled: the problem of information storage. Temporarily I would like to propose the following view. Instead of conceiving the coincidence of meaning and thing meant as a little package that gets tied together and filed away in the recesses of memory, "put on the drum," to be drawn out again when the need arises, I would prefer (though again only to take a stand on the problem) to regard information as something not recalled but re-created out of the resources of the available order of possibilities of experience, available sensory materials, actions, etc. Thus preferred usage would be to talk of a communicant as knowledge*able* rather than talking of his knowledge. What he knows he knows only in the moment of knowing and not otherwise. I'm still peering at this notion with a stranger's eyes and so I'm in bad need of some very searching conversation. What I'm after is somehow to resolve the bothersome dilemma between information as a momentary product of experience and information as an atemporal sum of things experienced.

Inasmuch as the empirical procedure for testing recall consists of matching the "recollected" item with the original expressional input, it might be that we can abandon the notion of knowledge held in potentiality of recall as unnecessary and perhaps as even scientifically sterile, while addressing ourselves to the task of considering what conditions of the communicant's make-up and what conditions of social structure give us the probabilities of a certain kind of "re-creation" when the task of recall is set to the communicant. At any rate, I much prefer the notion of memory as a describable set of operations by which a previous meaningful experience is reproduced or re-presented to the notion of a memory as a container. However, I'm not insistent, only puzzled.

With this much to go on, let's turn now to some kinds of information.

Note

1. [Editor's Note: This does not mean that it exists as information independently of being perceived as such. But, rather that it has physical existence period—independently of being perceived—it is not a concept or a "meaning."]

DONALD MACKAY, FROM "THE PLACE OF 'MEANING' IN THE THEORY OF INFORMATION" (1955)

MacKay (1922–1987) graduated in 1943 in Physics from the University of St Andrews and was immediately drafted into work on radar for the British Admiralty. His encounter with the physical limits to shortening radar pulses eventually became central to his contributions to Information theory. MacKay spent much of his career studying the differences between computers and the human brain, contributing to the fields of neuroscience and information theory. A participant in the 1951 Macy conference, MacKay strove in subsequent years to emphasize the human dimensions of information exchange, teaching at Kings College, London, and then at the University of Keele in Staffordshire. The essay below is a shortened version of a lecture he gave at the London Symposium on Information Theory, 1955. It was published, along with a number of MacKay's other papers on similar topics, in *Information, Meaning, and Mechanism* (MIT Press, 1969).

Introduction

It is now seven years since Shannon published his papers on a 'Mathematical Theory of Communication.' In this he defined a quantity which he called 'amount-of-information,' which is essentially a logarithmic measure of the statistical unexpectedness (reciprocal of probability) of the message concerned.

Since the unexpectedness of a message need have no direct connection with its semantic content or meaning, Shannon wisely insisted that the concept of 'meaning' was outside the scope of his theory.

This innocent statement by Shannon has given rise to two unfortunate consequences.

In the first place the original sense of Shannon's warning has sometimes been forgotten and he is credited with the view that the whole theory of information (which includes his own theory of the unexpectedness of information as a vital part) has nothing to do with 'meaning.'

Secondly, and largely in consequence of this, the idea has become current that the whole subject of meaning is not satisfactory for the information theorist. 'Subjective,' 'vague,' 'dangerous,' are the adjectives with which it is often smothered.

Now there is no doubt that the idea of 'meaning' has subjective aspects, that it is vague in many people's minds, and that it still in fact provokes debate among philosophers of the subject: it is at least as 'dangerous' in these respects as the idea of 'information' itself. But it is no more so; and in this paper I venture to outline a tentative account of the place of 'meaning' in the theory of information which I hope, though dealing by definition with the human subject, may be objective, precise and (sufficiently) safe. [. . .]

Meaning

At the outset we must note that it is not only statements which may be said to have meaning. We speak also of the 'meaning' of other expressions such as questions, commands and even exclamations. In seeking to define an equivalent of the term in the language of information theory, we must be careful not to imply too narrow a definition.

I do not mean that we must find an omnibus equivalent which can be substituted directly for all uses of 'meaning' in everyday speech; but it does seem reasonable for the reader to demand, and the information-theorist to accept, the principle that, in the early stages particularly, the technical equivalent of a common term should conform as far as possible with common usage. The technician's effort to sharpen the concept should at least in principle allow the technical equivalent to be substituted for the term, without violation of basic sense or grammar, in as many contexts as possible.

Let us now picture a communication process in which you send a message (*M*) to me. For example, *M* might be "Someone is waiting for you outside." Now we may assume that by sending *M* to me you intend to produce some effect on me. If you had sent a message in gibberish or in a language unknown to me, you might have intended only to distract and puzzle me; but since the message *M* is in English, we will take it that you intend me to understand it and to appreciate its meaning. What kind of effect is this? Obviously it need not be an immediate change in my observable pattern of behaviour. What you are concerned with is my 'total state of readiness:' in objective terms, the set or matrix of conditional probabilities of different possible patterns of behavior in relevant circumstance. For example, when I leave the room you want me to behave as if I expected to find someone outside, and so forth. It is, then, the conditional-probability matrix or 'C.P.M' which you want to affect in a particular way, by my 'understanding the meaning' of your message. If the C.P.M. is already in the desired state—if for example I know already that someone is waiting for me—then your object has already been achieved. Your object, then, is not necessarily to bring about a change in the C.P.M., but to establish a certain state of (part of) the C.P.M. for activity, internal (e.g. perceptual) or external (e.g. motor activity).

What then of the meaning of your message? We must clearly distinguish between (a) the meaning intended by the sender, (b) the meaning understood by the receiver, and (c) the conventional meaning. But if we take (b), for example, can we define the received meaning as simply the change that takes place in B's behaviour? Attempts have been made to define the meaning of a message simply as the behaviour-pattern it produces in the receiver; but this I think will not do. To begin with, we would not say that a message has no meaning if the receiver already knows what it is saying. A message does not lose its *meaning* through being repeated. And then purely on linguistic grounds one could scarcely regard the behaviour resulting from receipt of a message as synonymous with its received meaning. Any number of sentences in which 'meaning' is normally used would become grammatical nonsense, if this 'definition' were substituted,

On the other hand, the received meaning is certainly closely tied up with the behavioural consequences, if we include internal as well as external activity under 'behaviour.' We may reasonably say that the consequent internal and external behaviour-pattern in principle shows or demonstrates the received meaning.

Can we then define the received meaning as the change in the C.P.M. for internal and external activity? Again our objection would apply, that a repeated message may produce no significant change. Can we identify the meaning with the state of the C.P.M. rather than the change? Again the linguistic objections are I think conclusive. The meaning of a message is not identical with the state it produces. It is *identified by* the state it produces. This represents some progress. A message read for a second time produces—or should produce—substantially the same state of the relevant C.P.M. Its meaning is the same. What technically precise phrase can we substitute then for 'meaning' here?

I suggest that the received meaning of the message be defined, not as the resulting state of the C.P.M but *as the selective function of the message on an ensemble of possible states of the C.P.M.* 'Selective function' here implies of course a relationship, not a happening.

Tentatively we take as our basic definition of 'meaning,' then, the selective function on a specified set or ensemble, or for short 'selective function.' This leaves room for as many subdivisions or the concept as there are different definable ensembles; but I have not yet come across any instances in which one cannot consistently replace 'meaning' by 'selective function' or 'selective operation,' leaving the sense unaltered, and giving often considerable illumination.

Corresponding to our distinctions between intended, received, and conventional meaning, we now have distinctions between (*a*) the selective function intended by the originator; (*b*) the selective function actually exercised; (*c*) the selective function on the ensemble of states of a conventional symbolic representational system.

In what follows we shall not always recapitulate these, but the necessary modifications to the argument to make it apply in cases (*a*), (*b*), or (*c*) will be obvious.

Some Test Cases

Let us take a few examples. To begin with, let us consider the term 'meaningless.' 'This message or word is meaningless,' on our definition, becomes 'This message or word lacks a selective function . . . it has no selective relationship to . . .' To what? Immediately our definition suggest that the statement '*X* is meaningless' is incomplete. This we should expect, for a sentence may easily be meaningful to one man and gibberish to another. Meaninglessness is a relative concept, and a precise definition of meaning would be useless unless it automatically reminded us of this.

Now it is possible for something to lack a selective function for two reasons: (*a*) one or more of its component terms may be undefined—may have no selective function—so that the total selective operation is undefined; (*b*) two or more of the component selective functions may be incompatible, so that the total selective operation cannot be completed.

Correspondingly, we find two kinds of meaningless sentence. 'The gups are plec' is meaningless to most of us for the first reason. 'The water is isosceles' is meaningless for the second. On the other hand, 'This stochastic process is stationary' is probably meaningless to most of our fellow-mortals for the first reason; and 'The radiation from a horn-fed cheese' (actual title of a paper on Microwaves!) perhaps equally meaningless for the second.

Consider next the notion of 'synonymy.' One objection to any attempt to define meaning is that 'Two concepts may have the same meaning on one definition of the term, but different meanings on another.' For example, does 'an equilateral plane figure with four right-angled corners' have the same meaning as 'a square'? Our answer is quite clear. If we translate 'meaning' by 'selective function' we see at once that identity of selective function (synonymy) is going to depend on the particular ensemble on which we propose to test the selective function. The fact that various proposed 'definitions' of meaning have given different answers from common sense may merely be evidence that they were not sufficiently fundamental. If attempts are made to define a relation in terms of only one of its terminals, we must expect apparent paradoxes to result. Thus 'an equilateral plane figure with four right-angled corners' has the same selective function as 'a square' on the ensemble of plane geometric figures. It may have quite a different selective function on the ensemble of my states of imaginative activity.

What then of a message which states something I know already or a message which is repeated? As long as we define the meaning as the selective function rather than the effect there is no paradox in the fact that the effect on second hearing may be negligible. The selective operator which formally represents the meaning of a message is usually (in mathematical jargon) 'idempotent:' the immediate repetition of the selective operation should yield an unchanged result. Admittedly the fact that it has been repeated may itself have meaning—may have a selective function of its own. This however is quite distinct from the meaning of the message itself which is unchanged.

Here we begin to renew contact with information theory. We are accustomed to saying that a mere repetition of the same message (in the absence of noise) has no selective-information-content for the receiver, because the ensemble on which it operates the second time has only one member with non-zero probability. Selective-information-content in fact measures the size of the change brought about by a given selective operation. A second hearing of our message causes no change, and so has no selective-information-content; but it has the same selective function and so on our definition the same meaning as before. If, on the other hand, it did not exercise the appropriate selective function on first hearing, we say it was misunderstood. Its selective function, and hence its received meaning, on second hearing may then be different.

It is of course a psychological fact that if the same phrase or sentence is repeated sufficiently often it temporarily loses its meaning. Here is a further test of our definition, and again it not only survives, but shows the phenomenon itself in a fresh light. Repetition robs a sentence of meaning-to-the-subject—of 'selective function on the ensemble of states of the subject's C.P.M.,' we would say. This not only makes sense, but suggests various experimental questions as to the processes by which constant repetition of symbolic stimuli leads temporarily to their 'uncoupling' from the selective system governing the subject's C.P.M.

So we might go on. The meaning (intended, received, conventional) of a command, a question, or an exclamation, for example, can likewise be defined as their selective function on a specified ensemble of responses. The detailed discussion of questions, commands, and other non-descriptive messages would have taken us too far, but the outlines of their treatment from the present standpoint will probably be clear enough. For the moment it is sufficient to note that our technical definition of meaning appears to be equally applicable in all such cases. Differences there are in plenty, but they are differences in the ensemble on which selective function is exercised, rather than differences in the basic concept of meaning in each case.

One remaining use of 'meaning' is in a rather different category. We sometimes speak of the meaning of objects or events which are not messages. An overcast sky 'means' that rain is imminent; or a mud-pie on the front doorstep 'means' that the children have been playing there.

Here the object is a sign of what it 'means,' but not a symbol. It thus does not have an intended or a conventional selective function; but the meaning which we attribute to it can still be defined as its selective function on the ensemble of states of our C.P.M. The concept of meaning once again admits of one and the same definition.

The Relevant Ensembles

At this point—if not before—an objection may well be raised. Not everything which alters the total C.P.M. for activity is a message; nor would it necessarily be described as meaningful. Thus our definition might seem to be too broad.

In one sense it certainly is. We have seen already that in any particular case we must fill it out by specifying whether the selective function is intended, actual, or conventional, and saying for what ensemble it is defined. Our purpose has been to discover, if we can, a satisfactory basic concept from which the various common senses of 'meaning' can be derived by making these various distinctions. By extracting the common factor of 'selective function' (i.e. selective relationship to an ensemble specified or implied) we have, I hope, found the first term in a 'family tree' of sub-definitions which we must expect to ramify as widely as the range of relevant ensembles.

On the other hand, a definition of meaning must not be mistaken for a sufficient criterion of meaningfulness. Our object is to provide a technical equivalent for the term 'meaning' where it is in fact used, not to legislate as to where it should be used. The latter is largely an empirical task—to discover, if we can, the range of relevant ensembles presupposed in our basic definition of meaning.

Here we may note only a few pointers.

First, what distinguishes the perception of a meaningful object or event from that of a meaningless one? Essentially, the first leads or could lead to a further inference. To say 'X means Y' is to imply that a further representation,

Y, is logically justified, given *X*. Even to say '*X* is meaningful' is to imply that some further representational activity is logically justified by *X*, whether or not the speaker is able to carry it out.

Thus the range of ensembles to which a meaningful object or event has a selective relationship by virtue of its meaning is restricted to those of representational states. In the human organism, for example, we may presume that there are certain internal states of the information flow system which constitute implicit representations of the subject's world of activity, both conceptual and physical.

To ask in detail what characterizes representational states of the information flow system would take us too far, and I discussed the question elsewhere.[1] But we may draw one more basic dividing line. A typical pattern of activity— walking out of the room expecting to find a friend outside the door—is directed to the achievement of a hierarchy of 'goals': to maintain balance, to avoid the corner of the table, to find the door handle, and so forth. If the table, for example, is moved, the corresponding 'goal-setting' alters if I become aware that it has moved. The hierarchy of goal-settings represents, in a definite sense, what I know or believe concerning my world of activity. Our suggestion is, briefly, that the internal representational activity of the human organism takes the form of the selection of goal-settings—including the conditional probabilities of their alteration. The ensembles presupposed in our definition of meaning are ensembles of goal-settings in the above sense.

What then of 'conventional meaning,' as given for example in dictionaries? What an entry in a dictionary does is to replace an unfamiliar selective operator by an equivalent whose selective function for the user is presumed to be established. The ensemble concerned is in the first instance that of established selective operators; but the term 'established' presupposes a 'standard user' whose ensemble of representational states is ultimately in question.

This discussion applies equally to natural and to artificial languages. The only difference is that whereas natural sentences may modify the C.P.M. (state of readiness) for other than symbolic responses, sentences in an artificial language affect only the C.P.M. for perception and manipulation of the symbols themselves.

Mechanical Translation

Our present line of thought has a bearing on the vexed question of mechanical translation. When as children we learn to translate from one language to another we may begin by trying to substitute one word directly for another with the help of a dictionary. As we progress, we gradually pass over to a quite different kind of procedure. We try to discover what the original author *wants to convey* in the new language. In short, we pass over from thinking solely in terms of the symbols to thinking in terms of the dispositions intended to be evoked by the symbols. This is what distinguishes insightful translation from what some would prefer to call mere transcription.

A corresponding distinction exists between two different approaches which are covered by the name of mechanical translation. The first, at present almost universal, produces a translation by a correlation of syntactic structure in the two languages. No understanding is needed, in principle, of the dispositions intended to be evoked by the material to be translated. For this reason I would suggest that even Professor Yngve's ingenious 'transition language'[2] would perhaps be better termed a 'transition code,' since its function is not to select dispositions but rather symbols.

The second approach would be to make, as all intermediate step, a representation of the *dispositions* intended to be evoked by the material to be translated. A translation could then be achieved by producing, as the output, expressions in the other language which evoked the same dispositions. I know of no practical work being carried out on these lines, and I suspect that it may have to wait for our understanding of information-processing in the human organism; but the product of such a translating device would, I think, be much closer to what we normally desire of a human translator.

The difference would be shown most easily in the kinds of fault to which each translation would be liable. A translation on the first principle should quite faithfully reflect the syntactic structure of the original, but could easily fail seriously to convey the meaning. A translation on the second principle might allow only a loose inference to the syntactic structure of the original, but should on the whole faithfully reproduce its meaning.

'Meaning' in the Formalism of Information Theory

We may now seek to connect this approach with the author's earlier representation of meaning in the formalism of information theory. The state of a representational system can be described by enumerating the states of each of its independent degrees of freedom. If there are l of these, each may be associated with one dimension of an l-dimensional 'information-space,' so that any given state is represented by a point or region of this space.

A particular message may now be pictured as selecting a particular region, which may be identified by the vector (or distribution of vectors) linking it to the origin. The meaning of the message is then represented by the orientation of this vector, relative to the vector basis. Where the meaning is imprecise, the selective operation is imprecise, and the orientation of the vector correspondingly distributed statistically.

Some further details of this representation have been discussed in Chapter 6. For the moment we note only that the orientation of the vector specifies and corresponds one-to-one with the selective function of the message. The two approaches thus unite in an illuminating way, since the term 'selective function,' although the best I can suggest at the moment, is not ideally explicit; and the orientation of a selective 'arrow' provides a useful thought-model of what is intended by the term.

Conclusions

1) It appears from our investigation that the theory of information has a natural, precise, and objectively definable place for the concept of meaning.

2) The meaning of a message may be defined as its selective function on a specified ensemble.

3) The selective-information-content of the message measures logarithmically the size of the change brought about by its selective operation on the same ensemble.

4) The relevant ensemble comprises different possible states of a representational system. In the human organism these are states of the conditional-probability matrix (C.P.M.) governing goal-setting activity. Where the human C.P.M. is in question, the relevant probabilities cannot of course be estimated objectively (nor, probably, subjectively). This does not, however, prevent the concept from being objectively defined; nor does it preclude the possibility that these probabilities are determined by an objectively definable physical state of the organism.

5) The basic concept of meaning as selective function subdivides according to the ensembles for which the function is defined. The distinctions between intended meaning, received meaning, and conventional meaning are automatically preserved.

6) It may be too much to expect that every idiomatic usage of 'meaning' will be adequately translated by 'selective function,' but the concept seems to apply equally readily in relation to questions, commands, and other non-propositional utterances, and to non-symbolic objects possessing significance.

7) Since meaning, as thus defined, has as fine gradations as the gradations of human C.P.M.'s, the ideal of an unambiguous universal language would seem to be unrealizable. The most hopeful ideal approximation would be a language the primitive individuals of which represented the independent degrees of freedom of the human C.P.M. which are common to all normal humans. It may well prove the best, if not the most practicable solution to the problems of context and the like in mechanical translation to use an ideal language based on this principle as an intermediary between the original and

final languages. Unfortunately the completion of a truly basic language on these lines waits on our understanding of the human C.P.M.

Notes

1. MacKay, D. M. "Mentality in Machines." *Proc. Arist. Soc. Suppt.*, 1952, XXVI, pp. 61–86.
2. Yngve, V. H. "The Translation of Languages by Machine." In E. C. Cherry (Ed.), *Information Theory*. London: Butterworths, 1956, pp. 195–205.

CLAUDE SHANNON, "THE BANDWAGON" (1956)

This short essay, published in 1956, shows Shannon coming to terms with the increasing popularity of the terms he had put forward seven years earlier. It responded to an article published by L. A. De Rosa, chairman of the Professional Group in Information Theory, that had asked explicitly whether the group should seek to expand its purview to such fields as management, biology, psychology, and linguistic theory.

Information theory has, in the last few years, become something of a scientific bandwagon. Starting as a technical tool for the communication engineer, it has received an extraordinary amount of publicity in the popular as well as the scientific press. In part, this has been due to connections with such fashionable fields as computing machines, cybernetics, and automation; and in part, to the novelty of its subject matter. As a consequence, it has perhaps been ballooned to an importance beyond its actual accomplishments. Our fellow scientists in many different fields, attracted by the fanfare and by the new avenues opened to scientific analysis, are using these ideas in their own problems. Applications are being made to biology, psychology, linguistics, fundamental physics, economics, the theory of organization, and many others. In short, information theory is currently partaking of a somewhat heady draught of general popularity.

Although this wave of popularity is certainly pleasant and exciting for those of us working in the field, it carries at the same time an element of danger. While we feel that information theory is indeed a valuable tool in providing fundamental insights into the nature of communication problems and will continue to grow in importance, it is certainly no panacea for the communication engineer or, a fortiori, for anyone else. Seldom do more than a few of nature's secrets give way at one time. It will be all too easy for our somewhat artificial prosperity to collapse overnight when it is realized that the use of a few exciting words like information, entropy, redundancy, do not solve all our problems.

What can be done to inject a note of moderation in this situation? In the first place, workers in other fields should realize that the basic results of the subject are aimed in a very specific direction, a direction that is not necessarily relevant to such fields as psychology, economics, and other social sciences. Indeed, the hard core of information theory is, essentially, a branch of mathematics, a strictly deductive system. A thorough understanding of the mathematical foundation and its communication application is surely a prerequisite to other applications. I personally believe that many of the concepts of information theory will prove useful in these other fields—and, indeed, some results are already quite promising—but the establishing of such applications is not a trivial matter of translating words to a new domain, but rather the slow tedious process of hypothesis and experimental verification. If, for example, the human being acts in some situations like an ideal decoder, this is an experimental and not a mathematical fact, and as such must be tested under a wide variety of experimental situations.

Secondly, we must keep our own house in first class order. The subject of information theory has certainly been sold, if not oversold. We should now turn our attention to the business of research and development at the highest scientific plane we can maintain. Research rather than exposition is the keynote, and our critical thresholds should be raised. Authors should submit only their best efforts and these only after careful criticism by themselves and their colleagues. A few first rate research papers are preferable to a large number that are poorly conceived or half-finished. The latter are no credit to their writers and a waste of time to their readers. Only by maintaining a thoroughly scientific attitude can we achieve real progress in communication theory and consolidate our present position.

GREGORY BATESON, FROM "THE CYBERNETICS OF 'SELF': A THEORY OF ALCOHOLISM" (1972)

Bateson (1904–1980), trained as an anthropologist, did fieldwork in New Guinea and Bali in the 1930s, and spent his World War II years working for the British Office of Special Services, designing propaganda to undermine the morale of enemy combatants. In the years following the war, his range of research interests expanded to include systems theory, cybernetics, linguistics, sociology, and biology. He was a major participant in the Macy conferences. This essay was published in a collection of Bateson's short works, *Steps to an Ecology of Mind* (1972). That book shows Bateson applying cybernetics to the broader field of evolutionary anthropology, arguing that societies themselves can be understood as complex, large-scale feedback systems.

The Epistemology of Cybernetics

What is new and surprising is that we now have partial answers to some of these questions. In the last twenty-five years extraordinary advances have been made in our knowledge of what sort of thing the environment is, what sort of thing an organism is, and, especially, what sort of thing a mind is. These advances have come out of cybernetics, systems theory, information theory, and related sciences.

We now know, with considerable certainty, that the ancient problem of whether the mind is immanent or transcendent can be answered in favor of immanence, and that this answer is more economical of explanatory entities than any transcendent answer: it has at least the negative support of Occam's Razor.

On the positive side, we can assert that *any* ongoing ensemble of events and objects which has the appropriate complexity of causal circuits and the appropriate energy relations will surely show mental characteristics. It will compare, that is, be responsive to *difference* (in addition to being affected by the ordinary physical "causes" such as impact or force). It will "process information" and will inevitably be self-corrective either toward homeostatic optima or toward the maximization of certain variables.

A "bit" of information is definable as a difference which makes a difference. Such a difference, as it travels and undergoes successive transformation in a circuit, is an elementary idea.

But, most relevant in the present context, we know that no part of such an internally interactive system can have unilateral control over the remainder or over any other part. The mental characteristics are inherent or immanent in the ensemble as a *whole*.

Even in very simple self-corrective systems, this holistic character is evident. In the steam engine with a "governor," the very word "governor" is a misnomer if it be taken to mean that this part of the system has unilateral control. The governor is, essentially, a sense organ or transducer which receives a transform of the *difference* between the actual running speed of the engine and some ideal or preferred speed. This sense organ transforms these differences into differences in some efferent message, for example, to fuel supply or to a brake. The behavior of the governor is determined, in other words, by the behavior of the other parts of the system, and indirectly by its own behavior at a previous time.

The holistic and mental character of the system is most clearly demonstrated by this last fact, that the behavior of the governor (and, indeed, of every part of the causal circuit) is partially determined by its own previous behavior. Message material (*i.e.*, successive transforms of difference) must pass around the total circuit, and the *time* required for the message material to return to the place from which it started is a basic characteristic of the total system. The behavior of the governor (or any other part of the circuit) is thus in some degree determined not only by its immediate past, but by what it did at a time which precedes the present by the interval necessary for the message to complete the circuit. There is thus a sort of determinative *memory* in even the simplest cybernetic circuit.

The stability of the system (*i.e.*, whether it will act self-correctively or oscillate or go into runaway) depends upon the relation between the operational product of all the transformations of difference around the circuit and upon this characteristic time. The "governor" has no control over these factors.

Even a human governor in a social system is bound by the same limitations. He is controlled by information from the system and must adapt his own actions to its time characteristics and to the effects of his own past action.

Thus, in no system which shows mental characteristics can any part have unilateral control over the whole. In other words, *the mental characteristics of the system are immanent, not in some part, but in the system as a whole.*

The significance of this conclusion appears when we ask, "Can a computer think?" or, "Is the mind in the brain?" And the answer to both questions will be negative unless the question is focused upon one of the few mental characteristics which are contained within the computer or the brain. A computer is self-corrective in regard to some of its internal variables. It may, for example, include thermometers or other sense organs which are affected by differences in its working temperature, and the response of the sense organ to these differences may affect the action of a fan which in turn corrects the temperature. We may therefore say that the system shows mental characteristics in regard to its internal temperature. But it would be incorrect to say that the main business of the computer—the transformation of input differences into output differences—is "a mental process." The computer is only an arc of a larger circuit which always includes a man and an environment from which information is received and upon which efferent messages from the computer have effect. This total system, or ensemble, may legitimately be said to show mental characteristics. It operates by trial and error and has creative character.

Similarly, we may say that "mind" is immanent in those circuits of the brain which are complete within the brain. Or that mind is immanent in circuits which are complete within the system, brain *plus* body. Or, finally, that mind is immanent in the larger system—man *plus* environment.

In principle, if we desire to explain or understand the mental aspect of any biological event, we must take into account the system—that is, the network of *closed* circuits, within which that biological event is determined. But when we seek to explain the behavior of a man or any other organism, this "system" will usually *not* have the same limits as the "self"—as this term is commonly (and variously) understood.

Consider a man felling a tree with an axe. Each stroke of the axe is modified or corrected, according to the shape of the cut face of the tree left by the previous stroke. This self-corrective (*i.e.*, mental) process is brought about by a total system, tree-eyes-brain-muscles-axe-stroke-tree; and it is this total system that has the characteristics of immanent mind.

More correctly, we should spell the matter out as: (differences in tree)—(differences in retina)—(differences in brain)—(differences in muscles)—(differences in movement of axe)—(differences in tree), etc. What is transmitted around the circuit is transforms of differences. And, as noted above, a difference which makes a difference is an *idea* or unit of information.

But this is not how the average Occidental sees the event sequence of tree felling. He says, "*I* cut down the tree" and he even believes that there is a delimited agent, the "self," which performed a delimited "purposive" action upon a delimited object.

It is all very well to say that "Billiard ball A hit billiard ball B and sent it into the pocket"; and it would perhaps be all right (if we could do it) to give a complete hard-science account of the events all around the circuit containing the man and the tree. But popular parlance includes *mind* in its utterance by invoking the personal pronoun, and then achieves a mixture of mentalism and physicalism by restricting mind within the man and reifying the tree. Finally the mind itself becomes reined by the notion that, since the "self' acted upon the axe which acted upon the tree, the "self" must also be a "thing." The parallelism of syntax between "*I* hit the billiard ball" and "The ball hit another ball" is totally misleading.

If you ask anybody about the localization and boundaries of the self, these confusions are immediately displayed. Or consider a blind man with a stick. Where does the blind man's self begin? At the tip of the stick? At the handle of the stick? Or at some point halfway up the stick? These questions are nonsense, because the stick is a pathway along which differences are transmitted under transformation, so that to draw a delimiting line *across* this pathway is to cut off a part of the systemic circuit which determines the blind man's locomotion.

Similarly, his sense organs are transducers or pathways for information, as also are his axons, etc. From a systems-theoretic point of view, it is a misleading metaphor to say that what travels in an axon is an "impulse." It would be more correct to say that what travels is a difference, or a transform of a difference. The metaphor of "impulse" suggests a hard-science line of thought which will ramify only too easily into nonsense about "psychic energy," and those who talk this kind of nonsense will disregard the information content of *quiescence.* The quiescence of an axon *differs* as much from activity as its activity does from quiescence. Therefore quiescence and activity have equal informational relevance. The message of activity can only be accepted as valid if the message of quiescence can also be trusted.

It is even incorrect to speak of the "message of activity" and the "message of quiescence." Always the fact that information is a transform of difference should be remembered, and we might better call the one message "activity–not quiescence" and the other "quiescence–not activity."

Similar considerations apply to the repentant alcoholic. He cannot simply elect "sobriety." At best he could only elect "sobriety–not drunkenness," and his universe remains polarized, carrying always both alternatives.

The total self-corrective unit which processes information, or, as I say, "thinks" and "acts" and "decides," is a *system* whose boundaries do not at all coincide with the boundaries either of the body or of what is popularly called the "self" or "consciousness"; and it is important to notice that there are *multiple* differences between the thinking system and the "self" as popularly conceived:

(1) The system is not a transcendent entity as the "self" is commonly supposed to be.

(2) The ideas are immanent in a network of causal pathways along which transforms of difference are conducted. The "ideas" of the system are in all cases at least binary in structure. They are not "impulses" but "information."

(3) This network of pathways is not bounded with consciousness but extends to include the pathways of all unconscious mentation—both autonomic and repressed, neural and hormonal.

(4) The network is not bounded by the skin but includes all external pathways along which information can travel. It also includes those effective differences which are immanent in the "objects" of such information. It includes the pathways of sound and light along which travel transforms of differences originally immanent in things and other people–and especially *in our own actions.*

It is important to note that the basic—and I believe erroneous—tenets of popular epistemology are mutually reinforcing. If, for example, the popular premise of transcendence is discarded, the immediate substitute is a premise of immanence in the body. But this alternative will be unacceptable because large parts of the thinking network are located outside the body. The so-called "Body-Mind" problem is wrongly posed in terms which force the argument toward paradox: if mind be supposed immanent in the body, then it must be transcendent. If transcendent, it must be immanent. And so on.

Similarly, if we exclude the unconscious processes from the "self" and call them "ego-alien," then these processes take on the subjective coloring of "urges" and "forces"; and this pseudodynamic quality is then extended to the conscious "self" which attempts to "resist" the "forces" of the unconscious. The "self" thereby becomes itself an organization of seeming "forces." The popular notion which would equate "self" with consciousness thus leads into the notion that ideas are "forces"; and this fallacy is in turn supported by saying that the axon carries "impulses." To find a way out of this mess is by no means easy. [. . .]

Alcoholic "Pride"

[. . .] This hierarchy of contexts within contexts is universal for the communicational (or "emic") aspect of phenomena and drives the scientist always to seek for explanation in the ever larger units. It may (perhaps) be true in physics that the explanation of the macroscopic is to be sought in the micro-scopic. The opposite is usually true in cybernetics: without context, there is no communication.

In accord with the negative character of cybernetic explanation, "informa-tion" is quantified in negative terms. An event or object such as the letter K in a given position in the text of a message *might* have been any other of the limited set of twenty-six letters in the English language. The actual letter excludes (*i.e.,* eliminates by restraint) twenty-five alternatives. In comparison with an English letter, a Chinese ideograph would have excluded several thousand alternatives. We say, therefore, that the Chinese ideograph carries more information than the letter. The quantity of information is conventionally expressed as the log to base 2 of the improbability of the actual event or object.

Probability, being a ratio between quantities which have similar dimensions, is itself of zero dimensions. That is, the central explanatory quantity, infor-mation, is of zero dimensions. Quantities of real dimensions (mass, length, time) and their derivatives (force, energy, etc.) have no place in cybernetic explanation.

The status of energy is of special interest. In general in communicational systems, we deal with sequences which resemble stimulus-and-response rather than cause-and-effect. When one billiard ball strikes another, there is an energy transfer such that the motion of the second ball is energized by the impact of the first. In communicational systems, on the other hand, the energy of the response is usually provided by the respondent. If I kick a dog, his immediately sequential behavior is energized by his metabolism, not by my kick. Similarly, when one neuron fires another, or an impulse from a micro-phone activates a circuit, the sequent event has its own energy sources.

Of course, everything that happens is still within the limits defined by the law of energy conservation. The dog's metabolism might in the end limit his response, but, in general, in the systems with which we deal, the energy supplies are large compared with the demands upon them; and, long before the supplies are exhausted, "economic" limitations are imposed by the finite number of available alternatives, *i.e.,* there is an economics of probability. This economics differs from an economics of energy or money in that probability—being a ratio—is not subject to addition or subtraction but only to multiplicative pro-cesses, such as fractionation. A telephone exchange at a time of emergency may be "jammed" when a large fraction of its alternative pathways are busy. There is, then, a low probability of any given message getting through.

In addition to the restraints due to the limited economics of alternatives, two other categories of restraint must be discussed: restraints related to "feedback" and restraints related to "redundancy."

We consider first the concept of feedback:

When the phenomena of the universe are seen as linked together by cause-and-effect and energy transfer, the resulting picture is of complexly branching and interconnecting chains of causation. In certain regions of this universe (notably organisms in environments, ecosystems, thermostats, steam engines with governors, societies, computers, and the like); these chains of causation form circuits which are *closed* in the sense that causal interconnection can be traced around the circuit and back through whatever position was (arbitrarily) chosen as the starting point of the description. In such a circuit, evidently, events at any position in the circuit may be expected to have effect at *all* positions on the circuit at later times.

Such systems are, however, always *open*: (*a*) in the sense that the circuit is energized from some external source and loses energy usually in the form of heat to the outside; and (*b*) in the sense that events within the circuit may be influenced from the outside or may influence outside events. [. . .]

JOHN DURHAM PETERS, FROM
"INFORMATION: NOTES TOWARD
A CRITICAL HISTORY" (1988)

Peters (b. 1958), a media theorist and historian, published this essay a
year after writing a long and biting review of James Beniger's *The Control Revolution* (Harvard University Press, 1986). Beniger's book, Peters
had argued, typified a kind of apotheosis of information-thinking: contextless, value-neutral, it presented a theory of control without a theory of power; it produced a theory of life and technology that excluded
all forms of culture and the humanities. In this essay Peters attempts to
restore to the idea of information some of its missing historical depth,
and to remind the reader that the concepts we use to govern our sense
of the world are developed by humans in specific historical situations,
and change, by virtue of human attention, in other ones. Only a deep
understanding of all the things information has been can keep us from
being blinded by the dazzle of what information is—or what we are told
that it is—today.

[. . .]

I

*"Concepts, like individuals, have their histories and are just as incapable
of withstanding the ravages of time as are individuals. But in and through
all this they retain a kind of homesickness for the scenes of their childhood"*
(Søren Kierkegaard 1965/1841, 47).

The term *information* enters English via Latin and is first attested in the four-teenth century. From the Latin *informare* (to instruct) and *informatio* (idea, instruction, concept, doctrine), came a cluster of senses—*information* as an *item of new knowledge*—that more or less still prevails. But in the environment fashioned by Aristotle's disciples in the late middle ages—preeminently Thomas Aquinas—*informatio* and *information* were used in a broader sense to account for the way that the universe is ordered. According to their reading of Aristotle, the universe of matter is given shape and identity by the forms or essences that imbue it. The intelligibility of material objects owes to the forms that *in-form* them shaping them from within. This doctrine which was later dubbed *hylomorphism* (from Aristotle's *hyle* or matter and *morphe*, or form) served as a master principle in much late medieval religion and science. As Jacob (1973, 20) writes. "In the sixteenth century, each mundane object, each plant and each animal can always be described as a particular combination of matter and form. Matter always consists in the same four elements. An object is thus characterized by form alone . . . [W]hen an object is created, it is the form that is created. When the object perishes, only the form disappears, not the matter . . ." *Information* was a term that took part in a vocabulary that described how matter was imbued with the intelligible order of forms. It belonged to a social world very different from our own, one still "enchanted" and governed by complex networks of similitudes, resemblances, and corre-spondences (Foucault 1970, 17–44; Hacking 1975, 39ff; Toulmin 1982, 224–5). Even when *information* was used in the sense of giving someone a report, it belonged to a world of animated essences and living forms quite divergent from our own.

Some seventeenth-century examples, all cited in the *Oxford English Dictio-nary*, illustrate this divergence and *information*'s original concern with order and structure. A character in a play by George Chapman (1961/1605, 105), answering a companion's laments about the "faithlessness of women" delivers an elaborate conceit comparing love to the sun:

> I tell thee Love is Nature's second sun;
> Causing a spring of virtue where he shines,
> And as without the sun, the world's great eye.
> All colours, all beauties, both of Art and Nature,
> Are given in vain to men, so without love,
> All beauties bred in women are vain;
> All virtues born in men lie buried,
> For love informs them as the sun doth colors . . .

Chapman provides, in passing, hylomorphic accounts of vegetation, astron-omy, color, love, virtue, and beauty, showing in each case how the material in question is made vital by something without it that *informs* it. This work of informing has nothing to do with gaining information in today's sense, but in receiving the envigorating sources of life. [. . .]

II

"If mine were the privilege of choosing, from among the Immortals, a patron saint of Communication, I should undoubtedly ask for twins—gemini, John Locke and David Hume" (Cherry 1955, 45).

In the feverish demolition of medieval institutions in the seventeenth and eighteenth centuries, the notion that *information* consisted in the activity or process of endowing some material entity with form remained largely unchanged. But the notion that the universe was ordered by forms fell into disrepute and the context of this in-forming shifted from matter to mind. Both changes inaugurated a massive inversion in the meaning of *information*.

The intellectual revolution in the early modem period can be described as three parallel assaults on the idea that the universe had any underlying "form" or set of "forms": in psychology, the removal of spirits from bodies; in politics, an attack on the holiness of the church and the necessity of the crown; and in metaphysics the denial of "intelligible essences" (Unger, 1975). In place of spirits or souls came minds, egos, or *cogitos*; in place of a divinely instituted social order came a huge but fragile Leviathan, both arbitrary and inescapable; in place of "direct perception" came "perceptions" and "impressions" in all their opacity, density, and potential deception—what Francis Bacon called "the uncertain light of the sense." [. . .]

III

[. . .] Between the middle of the eighteenth and the middle of the nineteenth centuries, there arose a new kind of empiricism no longer bound by the scale of the human body. The state became a knower; bureaucracy its senses; statistics its *information*. [. . .] But how did the term migrate from empiricism to bureaucracy?

We gain a clue from the history of *statistics*, as a term and a practice. In the eighteenth century, *statistics* (which was translated, as in the quote above, from the German term *Statistik*) was the name for the comparative (and often, competitive) study of *states*. How did it happen that the study of states became the science of making imperceptible aggregates perceptible in numerical arrays? The scale of the modern state presents its managers and citizens with a problem:

it is out of sight and out of grasp. It must be made visible. Anderson (1983) quite brilliantly argues that modern nation states are "imagined communities." He shows how novels and newspapers, whose flowering as forms of communication coincides with the rise of modern states in the eighteenth century, provided some of the means by which people could envision a vast community of fellow nationals all intimately linked at a distance. These forms give people a panoramic *tour d'horizon* of a world far too vast for mortal eyes. They are fine for giving citizens a vision of what they belong to. But rulers don't want to rule over an imaginary state: they need to make policy, control populations, tax incomes, raise armies. They need facts. And so, statistics arose as the study of something too large to be perceptible—states and their climates, their rates of birth, marriage, death, crime, their economies, and so on—and secondly, as a set of techniques for making those processes visible and interpretable. Statistics, like newspapers, novels, and encyclopedias, have the aim of representing entities too large for an empiricism based on the individual's senses. They are a tool for rendering the invisible visible, for making that which one could formerly only imagine into something factual and manageable. (That *population* is still used as a technical term for all aggregates testifies to the state origins of statistics, as does the very word.) Providing societies with such a panoramic vision is today one of the major tasks of the news media (which traffic, of course, in "information"). The use of multiple cameras so that the TV viewer can be "everywhere at once" (Katz and Dayan 1985) is a form of vision already implicit in the structure of such eighteenth-century forms of social representation as statistics, newspapers, novels, and encyclopedias.

People who, thanks to statistics, "see" something intellectually they could not see sensually, are put in a curious position. They know something that they can never experience for themselves. They have a kind of knowledge that no mortal can have. Statistics offer a kind of gnosis, a mystic transcendence of individuality, a tasting of the forbidden fruit of knowledge. But what a strange and ironically modern kind of gnosis! It is not a mystic insight into the nature of the universe, but a cross-sectional glimpse of a population's behaviors at a single moment. The actuarial table is a kind of degraded mysticism, a form of secular omniscience (checked, as always, by probabilities). This new kind of knowledge—knowledge that absolves individuals from the claims of deixis, of existing at one place and at one moment—is of course none other than information. Information is knowledge with the human body taken out of it. *Information*, which in empiricism had meant the experience of an individual, with statistics came to mean the experience of the state, insofar as the state can be said to have experience. Implicit in statistics is a kind of knower not subject to mortal limits. The nation poses starkly the problem of a collective subject of knowledge (Khoo, 1988). [. . .]

IV

[. . .] The twentieth century version of the ongoing romance with information technology in America tends less toward religion than to science and, as I will argue, military technology. The catalyst for the contemporary discourse on information is undoubtedly the diffusion of "information theory" and its terms through the American academy after World War Two. Information theory developed as an outcome of the above described "information practice" of state bureaucracy. More specifically, it came from research on telephony at Bell Labs starting in the 1920s, and on cryptography during the war. Shannon's *Mathematical Theory of Communication* (1964/1948) was many things for many people. It gave scientists a fascinating account of information in terms of the old thermodynamic favorite, *entropy*, gave AT&T technical means for "shaving" frequencies and thus economizing by getting more calls on one line, and gave American culture a vocabulary well suited to its new status as world leader in military machinery. It was explicitly a theory of "signals" and not of "significance." Warren Weaver's commentary on Shannon's theory (1964/1949), which was probably read more often than Shannon outside of electrical engineering (Ritchie 1986), insisted that the theory had nothing to do with "meaning," and only with the degrees of freedom one had in choosing signals for one's message. But as the terms diffused through American intellectual life—and they did at violent speed, as Dahling documents (1957)—these provisos were little heeded. *Information* could not help but take on a substantive sense. Indeed, the theory may have seemed so exciting because it showed how to make something already familiar through the bureaucratic institutions of everyday life into a lofty concept of science and technology. It offered an indirect way to transfigure bureaucracy, to give it a halo.

One consequence of the diffusion of information-theoretic ideas was the rewriting of the great chain of being in informational terms. On the smallest level, where the secrets of life are "coded, stored, and transmitted" we find Watson and Crick, the discoverers of the double helix, writing of DNA as a code containing "genetical information." Neural synapses are switchboards and nerves are telephone lines (reversing the metaphor: in the nineteenth century, telegraphs and telephones were "nerves"), and the messenger RNA proteins are dubbed "informosomes." Moving up to physiology, one hears of hormones and enzymes as messages. The human brain is an "information-processer." In the social world, we hear that marriages will work better when men and women "communicate more" and "share information about their feelings" with each other; that good managers must communicate effectively (i.e., share information) with employees; and internationally, that there must be a new order in the flow of information between states. Finally, a few radio receivers vigilantly await some "information" from the outermost reaches of the universe, in the quest for extraterrestrial intelligence.

The academy is another clear example of the infiltration of the discourse of information. Several specialties define themselves in terms of the production, manipulation, and interpretation of information: computer science, electrical engineering, statistics, expository writing, library science, psycholinguistics, management science, a major portion of economics, journalism, and communication research. The recent interdisciplinary confluence under the name "cognitive science" would not be possible, one senses, without *information* as intellectual connective tissue. Some have gone so far (Beniger 1986) as to suggest that all intellectual inquiry into human affairs should redescribe itself in terms of a new trinity of concepts: information, communication, and control. Such schemes are the latest appearance of the dream of unified science that runs from Descartes to Carnap; information has been a stimulant to such dreams, just as geometry, evolution, thermodynamics, statistics, and mathematical physics have been in earlier days.

What kinds of effects does this transmogrification of discursive landscape have? What kinds of things does it allow us to think and say, and what not? One indication can be found in the opening paragraph of a text that did much to make information theory available for interdisciplinary poaching: Weaver's commentary on Shannon (1964/1949). Consider Weaver's innocently enthusiastic first paragraph (1964, 1):

> The word *communication* will be used here in a very broad sense to include all the procedures by which one mind may affect another. This, of course, involves not only written and oral speech, but also music, the pictorial arts, the theater, the ballet, and in fact all human behavior. In some connections it may be desirable to use a still broader definition of communication, namely, one which would include the procedures by means of which one mechanism (say automatic equipment to track an airplane and compute its probable future positions) affects another mechanism (say a guided missile chasing this airplane).

This gem is quite typical of the whole movement to informationalize the world. Observe the rhythms of Weaver's intellectual imperialism. He starts with the favorite social situation of the empiricists: how does one "mind" affect another? His abstraction is benefitted by his modesty ("all") and his instrumental view ("procedures"). Then we travel through language, the fine arts, and somehow come out on human behavior (the ride is getting increasingly bumpy). Then Weaver "broadens" his definition by introducing Korean war military technology.

An extraordinary category, this, including music and missiles, speech and servomechanisms. What made this string of sentences, this patch of discourse, intelligible—and exciting—to so many thinkers in the 1950s and even today? What form of life allows these sentences to hang together? (If there had been a conspiracy, which there wasn't, it would be hard to imagine a neater way to colonize zones of human action such as talk, art, and dance for bureaucratic convenience than through the circulation of the doctrine that human culture is a matter of information.)

Information technology as we know it is the child of war. There is nothing inherently martial in it, but *information*'s language-games in the twentieth century have never strayed far from a mix of management, military, and machines. The two great technologies of the second world war—the computer and the Bomb—share more than a common origin in physical science. They share a common cultural space and symbolism. Information is often spoken of in nuclear terms: its half-life (as it decays like radioactive matter), it explodes if it fissions too fast, its molecular or granular quality. It shares semiotic space with subatomic physics, coming in bits, flashes, bursts, and impulses, and is often treated as mental photons: the minimal quanta of the cognitive stuff.

Both the Bomb and Information, moreover, cater to our pleasure in possible apocalypse, the exhilaration moderns (so used to the thrill of the new) feel in contemplating self-destruction. The end of the quest for novelty is death, the biggest bang of them all. Berman (1982) persuasively portrays modernity as the experience of everything solid melting into air. The Bomb is a means of accelerating the turnover in the realm of matter, information of intellect. Both help to constantly revolutionize material and intellectual means of production. Both appeal to the love of absolute novelty, to the longing for those fresh beginnings and frontiers of various sorts that America specializes in. Information stands at the frontier of knowledge, while the Bomb sits at the outer edge of human history. Both are means for making the future different from the past. One stands at the latest, and the other at the last, moment of history. [. . .]

References

Anderson, Benedict 1983. *Imagined Communities: Reflections on the Origin and Spread of Nationalism*. London: Verso.

Bacon, Francis. 1967. *The Great Instauration*. In *The English Philosophers from Bacon to Mill*, ed. E. A. Burtt. New York: Random House. First published 1620.

Beniger, James. 1986. *The Control Revolution: Economic and Technological Origins of the Information Society*. Cambridge: Harvard University Press.

Benjamin, Walter. 1968. The Work of Art in the Age of Mechanical Reproduction. In *Illuminations: Essays and Reflections*, ed. Hannah Arendt Translated by Harry Zohn. New York: Schocken. First published 1935.

Benjamin, Walter 1968. The Storyteller. In *Illuminations: Essays and Reflections*, ed. Hannah Arendt Translated by Harry Zohn. New York: Schocken. First published 1936.

Benjamin, Walter. 1968. Theses on the Philosophy of History. In *Illuminations: Essays and Reflections*, ed. Hannah Arendt Translated by Harry Zohn. New York: Schocken. Written 1940.

Berman, Marshall. 1982. *All That is Solid Melts into Air: The Experience of Modernity*. New York: Simon and Schuster.

Browne, Thomas. 1981. *Pseudodoxia Epidernica*. Edited by R. Robbins. Oxford: Clarendon Press. First published 1646.

Burchfield, R. W., ed. 1986. *A Supplement to the Oxford English Dictionary*, vol. 4. Oxford: Clarendon Press.

Carey, James W. and Quirk. John, 1970. The Mythos of the Electronic Revolution. *The American Scholar* 39(2):219–41; 39(3):395–424.

Carey, James W. 1983. Technology and Ideology: The Case of the Telegraph. In *Prospects: The Annual of American Cultural Studies*, vol. 8, ed. Jack Salzman. Cambridge: Cambridge University Press, 303–325.

Chapman, George. 1961. All Fools. In *The Plays of George Chapman: The Comedies*, vol. I, ed. Thomas Marc Parrott. New York: Russell and Russell. First published 1605.

Cherry, Colin. 1955. "Communication Theory" and Human Behavior. *Studies in Communication*. London: Martin, Seeker, and Ward, 45–67.

Cooley, Chuck. 1894. The Theory of Transportation. *Publications of the American Economic Association* 9 (May): 227–370.

Dahling, Randall Louis. 1957. *Shannon's Information Theory: The Spread of an Idea*. Unpublished master's thesis. Stanford University.

Dretske, Fred I. 1981. *Knowledge and the Flow of Information*. Cambridge: M.I.T. Press.

Fleming, Donald. 1967. Attitude: The History of a Concept. *Perspectives in American History* 1:287–365.

Foucault, Michel. 1970. *The Order of Things*. New York: Random House.

Gadamer, Hans-Georg. 1982. *Truth and Method*. Translated by John Cumming and Garrett Barden. New York: Crossroad.

Hacking, Ian. 1975. *The Emergence of Probability*. Cambridge: Cambridge University Press.

Hirsch, E. D. 1987. *Cultural Literacy: What Every American Needs to Know*. Boston: Houghton Mifflin.

Hooper, W. 1911. Statistics. *Encyclopedia Britannica*. 11th edition, vol. 25. Cambridge: Cambridge University Press. 806–11.

Hume, David. 1978. *A Treatise of Human Nature*. Edited by Peter Nidditch. Oxford: Oxford University Press. First published 1739.

Jacob. François. 1973. *The Logic of Life*. Translated by Betty Spillman. New York: Pantheon.

Kant, Immanuel. 1974. *Kritik der reinen Vernunft*. Edited by Wilhelm Weischedel. 2 vols. Frankfurt: Suhrkamp. First published 1781.

Katz, Elihu and Dayan, Daniel. 1985. Media Events: On the Experience of Not Being There. *Religion* 15 (July):305–314.

Khoo, Paul. 1988. *Representing the Nation in Politics and Fiction*. Unpublished honor's thesis, Stanford University.

Kierkegaard, Søren. 1965. *The Concept of Irony, With Constant Reference to Socrates*. Translated by Lee M. Capel. Bloomington: Indiana University Press. First published 1841.

Kipling, Rudyard. 1902. Wireless. *Scribner's Magazine* 32 (August): 129–43.

Kittler, Friedrich. 1987. Gramophone, Film, Typewriter. *October* 41 (Summer):101–118. Translated by Dorothea von Mücke.

Littlebury, Isaac. 1976. Translator's preface. *History of Herodotus*. London: reprint, New York: AMS. First published 1737.

Locke, John. 1975. *An Essay Concerning Human Understanding*. Edited by Peter Nidditch. Oxford: Oxford University Press. First published 1690.

Lovejoy, A. O. 1966. *The Great Chain of Being: A Study of the History of an Idea*. Cambridge: Harvard University Press. Lectures given in 1933.

Marx, Leo. 1964. *The Machine in the Garden: Technology and the Pastoral Ideal in America*. New York: Oxford University Press.

Milton, John. 1968. *Paradise Lost and Paradise Regained*. Edited by Christopher Ricks. New York: New American Library. First edition of *Paradise Lost* 1667: revised 1674.

Mumford, Lewis. 1970. *The Pentagon of Power*. New York: Harvest. National Geographic. 1983. 163:5 (May).

Paisley, William. 1984. Communication in the Communication Sciences. In *Progress in the Communication Sciences*. vol. 5. Edited by Milton Voigt and Brenda Dervin. Norwood, NJ: Ablex, 1–43.

Peters, John Durham. 1987. The Control of Information. *Critical Review* 1(4):5–23.

Ricoeur, Paul. 1971. The Model of the Text: Meaningful Action Considered as a Text. *Social Research* 38:529–62.

Ritchie, David. 1986. Shannon and Weaver: Unraveling the Paradox of Information. *Communication Research* 13(2):278–98.

Shannon, Claude. 1964. The Mathematical Theory of Communication. In Claude Shannon and Warren Weaver. *The Mathematical Theory of Communication*. Urbana: University of Illinois Press. First published July and October 1948 in *Bell System Technical Journal*.

Spitzer, Leo. 1948. *Essays in Historical Semantics*. New York: Vanni.

Toulmin, Stephen. 1982. *The Return to Cosmology*. Los Angeles: University of California Press.

Unger, Roberto Mangabeira. 1975. *Knowledge and Politics*. New York: Free Press.

Weaver, Warren. 1964. Recent Contributions to the Mathematical Theory of Communication. In Claude Shannon and Warren Weaver. *The Mathematical Theory of Communication*. Urbana: University of Illinois Press. First published 1949.

Weber, Max. 1946. Science as a Vocation. In *From Max Weber*, ed. Hans Gerth and C. Wright Mills. New York: Oxford University Press. Speech given in 1919.

Wiener, Norbert. 1948. *Cybernetics, or Control and Communication in the Animal and the Machine*. Cambridge: M.I.T. Press.

N. KATHERINE HAYLES, FROM "CONTESTING FOR THE BODY OF INFORMATION: THE MACY CONFERENCES ON CYBERNETICS" (1999)

Hayles (b. 1943) is a literary critic and media theorist who worked as a research chemist for the Xerox corporation before earning a PhD in English literature (in 1977). Her work focuses on the intersections between science and literariness, and particularly on the ways in which technological developments shape the history of literary production. More broadly, as you will see in the selection below (taken from *How We Became Posthuman* [Chicago, 1999]), she is an intellectual historian, showing us how the ways concepts develop and travel, shaping the ways in which we think, and do not think, about the world we live in.

When and where did information get constructed as a disembodied medium? How were researchers convinced that humans and machines are brothers under the skin? Although the Macy Conferences on Cybernetics were not the only forum grappling with these questions, they were particularly important because they acted as a crossroads for the traffic in cybernetic models and artifacts. This chapter charts the arguments that made information seem more important than materiality within this research community. Broadly speaking, the arguments were deployed along three fronts. The first was concerned with the construction of information as a theoretical entity; the second, with the construction of (human) neural structures so that they were seen as flows of information; the third, with the construction of artifacts that translated information flows into observable operations, thereby making the flows "real."

Yet at each of these fronts, there was also significant resistance to the reification of information. Alternate models were proposed; important qualifications were voiced; objections were raised to the disparity between simple artifacts and the complex problems they addressed. Reification was triumphant not because it had no opposition but because scientifically and culturally situated debates made it seem a better choice than the alternatives. Recovering the complexities of these debates helps to demystify the assumption that information is more essential than matter or energy. Followed back to moments before it became a black box, this conclusion seems less like an inevitability and more like the result of negotiations specific to the circumstances of the U.S. techno-scientific culture during and immediately following World War II.

The Macy Conferences were unusual in that participants did not present finished papers. Rather, speakers were invited to sketch out a few main ideas to initiate discussion. The discussions, rather than the presentations, were the center of interest. Designed to be intellectual free-for-alls, the conferences were radically interdisciplinary. The transcripts show that researchers from a wide variety of fields—neurophysiology, electrical engineering, philosophy, semantics, literature, and psychology, among others—struggled to understand one another and make connections between others' ideas and their own areas of expertise. In the process, a concept that may have begun as a model of a particular physical system came to have broader significance, acting simultaneously as mechanism and metaphor. [. . .]

The Meaning(lessness) of Information

The triumph of information over materiality was a major theme at the first Macy Conference. John von Neumann and Norbert Wiener led the way by making clear that the important entity in the man-machine equation was information, not energy. Although energy considerations are not entirely absent (von Neumann discussed at length the problems involved in dissipating the heat generated from vacuum tubes), the thermodynamics of heat was incidental. Central was how much information could flow through the system and how quickly it could move. Wiener, emphasizing the movement from energy to information, made the point explicitly: "The fundamental idea is the message . . . and the fundamental element of the message is the decision."[1] Decisions are important not because they produce material goods but because they produce information. Control information, and power follows. [. . .]

We are now in a position to understand the deeper implications of information as it was theorized by Wiener and Shannon. Note that the theory is formulated entirely without reference to what information means. Only the probabilities of message elements enter into the equations. Why divorce information from meaning? Shannon and Wiener wanted information to have a stable value as it moved from one context to another. If it was tied to meaning, it would potentially have to change values every time it was embedded in a new context, because context affects meaning. Suppose, for example, you are in a windowless office and call to ask about the weather. "It's raining," I say. On the other hand, if we are both standing on a street corner, being drenched by a downpour, this same response would have a very different meaning. In the first case, I am telling you something you don't know; in the second, I am being ironic (or perhaps moronic). An information concept that ties information to meaning would have to yield two different values for the two circumstances, even though the message ("It's raining") is the same.

To cut through this Gordian knot, Shannon and Wiener defined information so that it would be calculated as the same value regardless of the contexts in which it was embedded, which is to say, they divorced it from meaning. *In context*, this was an appropriate and sensible decision. *Taken out of context*, the definition allowed information to be conceptualized as if it were an entity that can flow unchanged between different material substrates, as when Moravec envisions the information contained in a brain being downloaded into a computer. Ironically, this reification of information is enacted through the same kind of decontextualizing moves that the theory uses to define information as such. The theory decontextualizes information; Moravec decontextualizes the theory. Thus, a simplification necessitated by engineering considerations becomes an ideology in which a reified concept of information is treated as if it were fully commensurate with the complexities of human thought.[2]

Shannon himself was meticulously careful about how he applied information theory, repeatedly stressing that information theory concerned only the efficient transmission of messages through communication channels, not what those messages mean. Although others were quick to impute larger linguistic and social implications to the theory, he resisted these attempts. Responding to a presentation by Alex Bavelas on group communication at the eighth Macy Conference, he cautioned that he did not see "too close a connection between the notion of information as we use it in communication engineering and what you are doing here . . . the problem here is not so much finding the best encoding of symbols . . . but, rather, the determination of the semantic question of what to send and to whom to send it."[3] For Shannon, defining information as a probability function was a strategic choice that enabled him to bracket semantics. He did not want to get involved in having to consider the receiver's mindset as part of the communication system. He felt so strongly on this point that he suggested Bavelas distinguish between information in a channel and information in a human mind by characterizing the latter through "subjective probabilities," although how these were to be defined and calculated was by no means clear.

Not everyone agreed that it was a good idea to decontextualize information. At the same time that Shannon and Wiener were forging what information would mean in a U.S. context, Donald MacKay, a British researcher, was trying to formulate an information theory that would take meaning into account. At the seventh conference, he presented his ideas to the Macy group. The difference between his view and Shannon's can be seen in the way he bridled at Shannon's suggestion about "subjective probabilities." In the rhetoric of the Macy Conferences, "objective" was associated with being scientific, whereas "subjective" was a code word implying that one had fallen into a morass of unquantifiable feelings that might be magnificent but were certainly not science. MacKay's first move was to rescue information that affected the receiver's mindset from the "subjective" label. He proposed that both Shannon and Bavelas were concerned with what he called "selective information," that is, information calculated by considering the selection of message elements from a set. But selective information alone is not enough; also required is another kind of information that he called "structural." Structural information indicates how selective information is to be understood; it is a message about how to interpret a message-that is, it is a metacommunication. [. . .]

Since structural information indicates how a message should be interpreted, semantics necessarily enters the picture. In sharp contrast to message probabilities, which have no connection with meaning, structural information was to be calculated through changes brought about in the receiver's mind. "It's raining," heard by someone in a windowless office, would yield a value for the structural information different from the value that it would yield when heard by someone looking out a window at rain. To emphasize the correlation between structural information and changes in the receiver's mind, MacKay offered an analogy: "It is as if we had discovered how to talk quantitatively about size through discovering its effects on the measuring apparatus."[4] The analogy implies that representations created by the mind have a double valence. Seen from one perspective, they contain information about the world ("It's raining"). From another perspective, they are interactive phenomena that point back to the observer, for this information is quantified by measuring changes in the "measuring instrument," that is, in the mind itself. And how does one measure these changes? An observer looks at the mind of the person who received the message, which is to say that changes are made in the observer's mind, which in turn can also be observed and measured by someone else. The progression tends toward the infinite regress characteristic of reflexivity. Arguing for a strong correlation between the *nature* of a representation and its *effect*, MacKay's model recognized the mutual constitution of form and content, message and receiver. His model was fundamentally different from the Shannon-Wiener theory because it triangulated between reflexivity, information, and meaning. In the context of the Macy Conferences, his conclusion qualified as radical: subjectivity, far from being a morass to be avoided, is precisely what enables information and meaning to be connected.

The problem was how to quantify the model. To achieve quantification, a mathematical model was needed for the changes that a message triggered in the receiver's mind. The staggering problems this presented no doubt explain why MacKay's version of information theory was not widely accepted among the electrical engineers who would be writing, reading, and teaching the textbooks on information theory in the coming decades. Although MacKay's work continued to be foundational for the British school of information theory, in the United States the Shannon-Wiener definition of information, not MacKay's, became the industry standard. [. . .]

Circling the Observer

[. . .] In March 1976, two decades after the conferences had ended, Margaret Mead and Gregory Bateson were sitting with Stewart Brand at Bateson's kitchen table in a rare joint interview. Brand asked them about the Macy Conferences. They agreed that including the observer was one of the central problems raised by the cybernetic paradigm. Reaching for a scrap of paper, Bateson sketched a diagram (which Brand included in the published interview) of the communication system as it was envisioned before cybernetics. The drawing shows a black box with input, output, and feedback loops within the box. The space labeled "Engineer" remains outside the box. A second drawing represents Bateson's later understanding of cybernetics. Here the first black box, along with the names "Wiener, Bateson, Mead," is encapsulated within a larger box. In this drawing, the observers are included *within* the system rather than looking at it from the outside. The interview turned to a discussion of the dynamics that had prevailed at the Macy Conferences. Mead commented, "Kubie was a very important person at that point." She added: "McCulloch had a grand design in his mind. He got people into that conference, who he then kept from talking." Bateson continued, "Yes, he had a design for how the shape of the conversation would run over five years—what had to be said before what else could be said." When Brand asked what that design was, Bateson answered, "Who knows?" But Mead thought it was "more or less what happened."[5]

Brand wanted to know why cybernetics had run out of steam. "What happened?" he asked repeatedly. His sense of the situation is confirmed by correspondence exchanged between the transcript editors—Heinz von Foerster, Margaret Mead, and Hans Teuber—after the tenth conference in 1953. Fremont-Smith and McCulloch wanted the transcripts published, just as the transcripts for the previous four conferences had been published. But Teuber disagreed, noting that the discussions were too rambling and unfocused; if published, he said, they would be an embarrassment. Although he was the junior member of the editorial board, he stood his ground. He wrote to Fremont-Smith, sending a copy of the letter to McCulloch, that if the others decided to publish over his objections, he wanted his name removed from the list of editors.[6] As the junior member, he had the most to lose; the others already had established reputations. McCulloch must have written a stiff note in reply, for Teuber answered defensively. He insisted that the issue was not his reputation but the quality of the transcripts. "From your note, it is obvious that I sound stuffy to you and Walter. Do tell him that I wanted to get off the list of editors, not because I am worried about reputations, but simply because I can't do enough for this transcript to get it into any sort of shape. The transactions of this last meeting simply do not add to the earlier ones—they detract. Granted, there are a few sparks, but there is not enough of the old fire. I owed it to you and Frank Fremont-Smith to speak my mind on this matter."[7] Mead worked out a compromise. The three speakers would publish their talks as formal papers, and McCulloch's summary of all the conferences would be used as an introduction. No one thought of suggesting more conferences or more transcripts. It was the end of an era.

Notes

1. "Conferences on Feedback Mechanisms and Circular Casual Systems in Biology and the Social Sciences" (March 8–9, 1946), p. 62, Frank Fremont-Smith Papers, Francis A. Countway Library of Medicine, Harvard University, Cambridge, Mass.

2. Richard Doyle discusses the reification of information in the context of molecular biology in *On Beyond Living: Rhetorical Transformations in the Life Sciences* (Stanford: Stanford University Press, 1997). See also Evelyn Fox Keller's analysis of the disembodiment of information in molecular biology in *Secrets of Life, Secrets of Death: Essays on Language, Gender, and Science* (New York: Routledge, 1992), especially chapters 5, 8, and the epilogue. Lily E. Kay critically analyzes the emergence of the idea of a genetic "code" in "Cybernetics, Information, Life: The Emergence of Scriptural Representations of Heredity," *Configurations* 5 (winter 1997): 23–92. For a discussion of how this disembodied view of information began to circulate through the culture, see Dorothy Nelkin and M. Susan Lindee, *The DNA Mystique: The Gene as a Cultural Icon* (New York: W. H. Freeman and Company, 1995).

3. Heinz von Foerster, Margaret Mead and Hans Lukas Teuber, eds. *Cybernetics: Circular Casual and Feedback Mechanisms in Biological and Social Sciences*, vols. 6–10 (Josiah Macy J. Foundation, 1952) (Eighth Conference, 1951), 8:22. The published series is hereafter cited as *Cybernetics* with the number and year of the conference and the volume number indicated.

4. Donald M. MacKay, "In Search of Basic Symbols," *Cybernetics* (Eighth Conference, 1951), 8:222. A fuller account can be found in Donald M. MacKay, *Information, Mechanism, and Meaning* (Cambridge: MIT Press, 1969).

5. Stewart Brand, "'For God's Sake, Margaret': Conversation with Gregory Bateson and Margaret Mead," *Co-Evolution Quarterly* (summer 1976), 32, 34 (Bateson's diagram is on p. 37).

6. Letter dated November 8, 1954, McCulloch Papers, B/M139, Box 2.

7. Letter dated November 22, 1954, McCulloch Papers, B/M139, Box 2.

PETER JANICH, FROM
WHAT IS INFORMATION? (2006)

Janich (1942–2016) was a German philosopher of science. Trained in the methods of the Erlangen school, and later the developer of an approach called "methodical culturalism," Janich spent his life arguing against the idea that scientific concepts describe things in nature. Instead, he wrote, they should be thought of as expressions of human investment and human social production, essentially as the results of what he called "mouth-work," as a parallel to the technological innovation of "craftwork." In the selection below we see him trying to rethink Shannon and Weaver's theory of communication by theorizing it from the ground up—from the fact, for instance, that all human communication begins, as he says, in a conversation between two people.

"Can You Hear Me Now?": Telecommunications' Semantic *Deus Ex Machina*

To attend to and solve the technical problems of the transmission of messages does not require one to abstain from developing a philosophy of language that would deal with the classical questions regarding the meaning and value of linguistic utterances. From a philosophical perspective, there is nothing to criticize about the endeavor (it has been extraordinarily technically successful). But things are otherwise when it comes to the reduction of human language to telecommunicational structures, that is, to the temporal patterns and processes of physical effects and the taking of these latter *as complete solutions to questions of meaning and value.*

Unfortunately, that's exactly what Shannon and Weaver's "Mathematical Theory of Communication/Information," and indeed the whole tradition that follows the paradigm it establishes, does. Where, as with Morris, syntax takes disciplinary precedence over semantics and pragmatics, or, with Weaver, the problems of physical transmission between a coding and decoding machine become a theory of meaning and value of communicative acts "to a significant degree," the scope of language philosophy remains suspiciously unfulfilled.

A certain ideology has thus opened a path. That path originates, undeniably, in the use of the means of formal logic for the analysis of the language of mathematics and physics. That analysis, in turn, enacts a theory (which is itself the product of a great deal of intellectual effort). And this latter imagines an *enclosed system of language*, to which the syntactic and, following it, the semantic and pragmatic analyses finally refer. This prehistory grounds the later understanding of speech in the telecommunications context, treating it as the mere selection from a pre-given quantity of signs or sign combinations and describing it statistically as a Markov process.

It doesn't take a language philosopher to see two things in an initial glance. First, actual human speech does not involve the selection of words or sentences or text from a pre-given repertoire; that kind of selection process happens, maybe, when you use a telephone book or a rhyming dictionary. Second, the reduction of language to syntax or signal-structures makes it impossible to ask two (seemingly relevant) questions: (1) how do two communicating beings mutually understand each other? and (2) how would you ever test that understanding?

It is now possible to gather together the mistakes of this entire approach. They involve, first, its basic understanding of language as *monologistic*; second, the assumption of the existence of a naive external perspective, lying outside the processes of communication, when it comes to questions of semantics and pragmatics, that is, for questions of the meaning and value of verbal utterance; and third, talking about signs and signals (not to mention the various psychological contexts and circumstances that surround language, including the influence of mental images or the desire to produce an effect on a receiver), while describing what are in truth exclusively scientific or technical processes that might best be defined as successions of causal effects.

Let me explain. (1) The understanding of language is *monological* because the smallest unit of the transmission of a message from origin to destination, the equivalent of a telecommunicative "atom," does not include any anticipation or effect of the receiver's expected (linguistic, sender-directed) *response*. As the examples of the telephone and telegraph make clear, we're not talking here about real telephonic communication in its commonly understood sense (which would include speech and counterspeech, that is, *dialogue*) but rather about technical equipment of the types used to make announcements on train station platforms. Someone says something on one side, and on the other side a voice comes out of a loudspeaker. Travelers on the platform have no apparatus with which to respond to the announcement. As for the telegraph, it consists (in the examples) of an operator who uses a keypad to enter the signals that translate a telegram into Morse code. On the other side, there is only a receiving machine, like a pen that marks dots and lines on a band of paper. No one imagines an apparatus that would send back some kind of answer.

Naturally, the theorist of communication would gladly recognize that this is so and willingly expand the system to include the components of sender, channel, and receiver, now applied to the people and places in the opposite direction. This answer is good enough, on technical grounds. But as a description of the process and concept of communication, it simply will not do. That's because it requires us to believe—and this is why I say that its understanding of language is "monological"—that the problem of understanding between origin and destination either *does not or cannot take place* or that it cannot be resolved by the communicators themselves but only by an external observer. This lucky fellow would describe the impact of misunderstanding on the message destination with all the distance appropriate to a (behaviorist) natural scientist, whose semantic and pragmatic competence would allow him to explain the relationship between that misunderstanding and whatever happened at the message origin.

On to (2): this monological model of language is a consequence of the resort to behaviorism in Morris or of the reference to semiotics in Weaver. Together these produce the classical caricature of the two behaviorists. They do not greet each other by asking "how are you?" because this would require of each individual an impossible degree of introspection, semantic competence, and pragmatic orientation; instead, they ask "how am I" because only the other of the speaker can, from a "scientific" outside, observe and resolve the question of how the speaker is doing, what he would like to say, what his utterances mean, and whether those utterances are successful.

Obviously the pre- and extratechnical principles that govern communication work otherwise, as do those governing communication via technical means like telephones or telegraphs. It's always the communicators themselves who judge and resolve the questions of meaning and value of what is communicated. No deus ex machina descending from the clouds, no Archimedean observer or scientific behaviorist from beyond the world, no God's-eye view, comes to confer meaning and value upon technically transmitted, physically determined transmission processes and effects. In every circumstance and every context, even when it comes to the evaluation of the philosophies of language and theories of information and communication, it is the case that language-using humans themselves, as speakers and hearers, produce and understand the meaning, value, and coherence of their linguistic acts and use pragmatic and semantic components to do so. That's how they regularly exchange their roles as speaker and hearer.

As for (3): in telecommunications it is strictly illegitimate to speak of "signals" or "signs" or "character sets," because we are dealing here only with the structure of physical parameters as they appear historically in space and time. Electromagnetic waves, for example, have structures, which can be produced by a loose contact in a defective plug or an erratically running motor in a refrigerator. These can be taken for signals, for instance, in the search for a problem by a repairman, who would perceive the irregular rattle of the fridge, hear crackling in a socket, or smell something burning. But only a purpose-oriented, understanding receiver of spatiotemporal changes in physical parameters can turn a clatter or a stink into a signal. The same is true on the sender's side of the telecommunicative paradigm. The goal-directed and purposeful invention, construction, and development of machines (in the context of intentional address, speech, and communication between humans) is the *necessary condition* that allows us to talk about signs, character sets, and signals. If, on the other hand, rain falls through a leaky roof onto the keyboard of a working computer, triggering some kind of "command" that, if the PC is connected to the Internet, has some actual effect in the world, we're still not dealing with signals or signs. Anyone who described things otherwise would presumably have to be willing to claim, absurdly, that a mouse "calculates" when it runs over the keypad of a calculator, thereby triggering some change in the signs on the machine's display.

These examples go so far as to prove that the essentially formalist and materialist approach of the logical empiricist tradition, like the materialism of the cyberneticists, requires a deus ex machina, a conceptual outsider, to get from the technical apparatuses and their causal effects, on one hand, to linguistic meaning, semantic recognition, or even influences on "mental images," on the other. In chapter 5, a methodical and systematic approach that repairs the errors we have seen so far will show that meaning and value do not just randomly emerge from physical patterns ("more than one could . . . naively suspect") but that, even so, human dialogue that produces meaning and value in relation to an addressee can in fact be reduced to its physical aspects, in the service of expanding human communication through technology by making it transportable across space and time.

All done? Telecommunications' Pragmatic Deficit

And so telecommunications' deus ex machina is a semantic sham: using words like "sign" or "signal" makes it seem as though coding, transmission, and decoding machines have something to do with the meaning and value of human communication. But this is not the only mistake, and not the only sleight of hand that grants the theory a philosophical and social scope that it does not actually have. In both the language philosophy privileged by Morris and the telecommunications paradigm that organizes Shannon and Weaver, the same issues that make a muddle of semantic issues appear once again when it comes to the pragmatic realm.

I showed earlier how, in Morris's representation of semiotics, syntactics emerged as the leader of the trio syntactics, semantics, pragmatics (first via a casual mention, then in a simple argument, and finally as a conceptual prerequisite for the entire system). The communications complex of the theoretical tradition inaugurated by Shannon and Weaver continues, even in our contemporary communication, information, and entertainment technologies, to deal only with "syntactic" machines. However fancily or intelligently programmed, using "fuzzy logic" or creating "neural networks," whether digital or analog, these machines feature only causal reciprocity between switches, whether these latter follow the principles of a simple on-off mechanism (digital) or a lamp dimmer (analog).

It would be difficult to exaggerate the degree to which the entire debate about information concepts, theories, and technologies relies on retroactive, analytic, top-down argumentation. The cry of the army of technicians, scientists, philosophers, and journalists that have taken on this conceptual battlefield would seem to be "All done!" What's done, what's laid out in front of us as given or assumed, includes the logical, mathematical, and scientific-technical theories that find their way into information and communication theories and technologies; human language, with its syntactic, semantic, and pragmatic structures; language philosophy and its canonical-dogmatic orientation toward syntax, which places it before semantics and pragmatics; the idea that systems theory comes before systems; that systems come before components; that the reflex mechanism of a squirrel-hunting dog comes before its description in a semiotic theory; that the machines called "sender" and "receiver" come before the desire of one human being to say something to another. In the backward world of the communications complex, all conceptual ordering is *reversed*.

Everyone in this world knows, attends to, and practices this reverse ordering, even when it contradicts her own sense of things. Naturally, a person *first* decides to say something to someone, *before* she can arrive at the question of whether the circumstances require sending her a letter, recording a message on tape, or using the telephone or telegraph. Naturally, a person *first* learns how to act in the world (including how to use nonlinguistic actions appropriate to his culture and its various codified action sequences, such as the basic tasks of daily life, including eating, getting dressed, living, taking care of others, and so on) before inventing, building, or using telecommunication machines. Naturally, a *person* first learns to speak (in communicative situations) *before* delivering a self-directed monologue that works out a mathematical proof. Naturally, there *first* have to be functioning, that is, accomplished and successful, communications, in which the participants regularly switch roles between speaker and listener, and naturally, such a scene first requires an understanding of the meaning of what is said ("functioning communication") and a recognition of its shared meaning ("successful communication"), *before* the structure and noise of a single transmission from origin to destination (an utterance directed by one person to another) can be analyzed. Naturally, there *first* has to be a plan for a complex artificial construction (like a telephone system) *before* its technical realization can take place, and naturally, the technical system has first to be built *before* it can start to function; naturally, the system (like a telephone) must first function *before* it can be used. And naturally, the possibility of this entire sequence of steps can *only in retrospect* be described from a top-down perspective.

Though the communications complex's pragmatic deficit begins, then, with a methodically ungrounded ordering of syntax, semantics, and pragmatics, it is the product of a more general misunderstanding of the fact that the entire world of objects that we are discussing here would not be *available* were it not for human action. Decisions about functioning and nonfunctioning (*Gelingen und Mißlingen*), success and failure (*Erfolg und Mißerfolg*), happen in the realm of human action.[1] Only from there can one move on to technologies or theories.

You can sum up this analysis of the semantic and pragmatic deficits of the communications complex in one (admittedly long) sentence: the dogmatic division of theoretical philosophy in the logical empiricist tradition (via the amputation of pragmatics, particularly of the latter's productive, constructive elements) and the emphasis on analytic, that is, resolution-oriented methods, led its followers to believe that only the ready-to-hand products of science and technology, and not the human endeavors and reasonings that led to them, would permit an accurate understanding the world. Which is, after all, a pretty fundamental mistake.

Note

1. These two pairs are near-synonyms and would usually both be translated into English as "success" and "failure." *Gelingen* and *Mißlingen* have more of a sense of action or process, of accomplishment or failure to accomplish or carry out some act. Janich uses the two pairs together throughout to emphasize different aspects of communicative activity; here we translate *Gelingen* and *Mißlingen* as "functioning" and "nonfunctioning" and *Erfolg* and *Mißerfolg* as "success" and "failure."—Trans.

MATTHIEU TRICLOT, FROM
THE CYBERNETIC MOMENT (2008)

Triclot (b. 1976) is a French philosopher and historian of science whose first book, from which this selection is taken, offered a lengthy and complex rethinking of the history of cybernetics. The book begins by remarking on the history of the discipline. After its tremendous early popularity in the 1950s and 1960s, by the 1980s cybernetics was largely considered passé; the energy associated with it had flowed into such fields as information theory, neuroscience, and evolutionary anthropology. Why look at a "failed" science, Triclot asks? What can such a science teach us about the way that ideas work? And how can we, in returning to the site of this "failure," gain a sense of what might have been lost—intellectually or socially—by the abandonment of a field that attempted so boldly to unite humanistic and scientific approaches to the study of human life?

How does one come to see information where one previously saw only matter or energy? What about the cybernetic moment makes possible the constitution of information as an object of science? What are the contours of information's "ecological niche," to use Hacking's metaphor? What set of conditions allowed the discourse of information to birth itself, and flourish, at the turn of the 1950s?

First, a condition of *observability*. In the technical milieu stemming from the war, it becomes possible to talk about information or information processing in the context of a wide range of machines that no one would before have placed in the same category. We can observe the activity of information processing when we code messages, filter signals, program calculators, and so on. But the simple fact of being able to observe a class of phenomena and to regroup them in a common category is not enough. The vocabulary of information has a specific function in the technical milieu; it reveals the essential unity of a wide range of important and quasi-simultaneous developments. The communicating machines, the telephone and the telegraph, from which the technical vocabulary of information originates, deal with information; the new radars deal with information; automatons that shoot, automatons that calculate, and finally the human beings who are themselves included in these apparatuses, who act with the machine, providing it with a filtered, evaluated information, adjusting its behavioral deviations according to its intended purpose, reducing margins of contingency, etc.: all these deal with information too.

This technical vector of observability is tied directly to a philosophical vector. When it comes to machines, talking about the processing of information or about communication in general is anything but neutral. It is as if a human function, one of the most specifically human functions, the one that involves speech and the relationship with others, intelligence and society, had been transferred to machines. In reality, the machines haven't, literally, taken anything from us; it makes more sense to say that a function invented for the machines has been transferred to human beings: only after we began to consider machines through the lens of information processing and exchange do we perceive human activities of communication in the same way. But this transfer reopens a wide range of problems associated with the mechanistic stance in philosophy, with the status of thought, with finality, and with the boundary between organism and machine. The cannon that tracks and fires automatically raises questions about the specific difference between living beings and machines, and announces the resorption of telos [*finalité*] by the mechanism; the computer dramatizes the status of intelligence and the latter's possible reduction to symbolic calculation, and so on. The vocabulary of information and of information processing has thus not only permitted a unification of the technical realm, but also has unified it in such a way that this synthesis is immediately linked to philosophical questions. This articulation between the technical milieu and a renewed mechanistic philosophy of intelligence and of the living guaranteed, for the concept of information, a social distribution that it would not otherwise have obtained. Could we have had the technique without the philosophy, the machines without the neo-mechanism? Certainly; outside the United States, in the Soviet Union, cybernetics was first introduced as a set of technical developments, whereas the mechanistic philosophy that accompanied it, which did not conform to the doctrine of the regime, was left by the wayside; after Stalin's death, the situation was reversed.[1] The alliance of technique and philosophy that is typical of the American cybernetics shapes the local conditions of the emergence of information discourse.

To these technical and philosophical vectors one must add an *epistemological* vector. Cybernetics conceived the notion of information as a term pertaining, ultimately, to a discipline of physics: statistical mechanics. This decision played a crucial role in the split generated by the notion of information in the 1950s. For cyberneticians, the choice of statistical mechanics relied on an explicit rejection of logic, as they made the crazy bet that mathematical logic would be reabsorbed by and in the physics of automatons. Linked to the philosophical vector, this primacy of statistical mechanics opens the possibility of an extension of the notion of information to the field of the living, and to the study of the nervous system in particular. Physics, fortified by the concept of information, was thereby able to constitute for some time a possible approach to biological phenomena, until molecular biology outperformed the pretensions of cyberneticians. Statistical mechanics is the true instrument of the imperialist pretensions of cybernetics towards life sciences or sciences of the mind.

The "ecological system" of information would not be complete without a last vector: *politics*. The information techniques are deeply imbricated in the research stemming from the Second World War and become, from the end of the 1940s on, an essential component of the Cold War. Among the cyberneticians, Norbert Wiener attempted desperately to extract information discourse from war logic, to promote communication as a social value and to explore new modes and methods of research; these efforts explain the unique form that cybernetic discourse took in the years that followed. Information sits at the crossroads of this more humanist position, on one hand, and the material and ideological layout of the Cold War on the other. The history of information reflects this liberal and often radical engagement with the world, which sought to ally the life sciences to the human ones. The result of all this is that information itself appears divided along technical, philosophical, epistemological, or political vectors. We encounter either the code or the signal, a symbolic program or a theory of automatons, the simulation of mind or the production of an artificial brain, formal logic or statistical mechanics, an information society or a Cold War . . . Such a description of the conditions that allowed information discourse to flourish, which takes its logic from a series of oppositions on the technical, philosophical, epistemological, and political levels, leads essentially to two major fields of research: first, it allows us to highlight the issues attached to the initial conceptualization of information; and second, it permits us to develop a specific type of analysis of an original science, cybernetics, that differentiates itself along a number of important lines from the traditional disciplines studied by history or philosophy of science.

To study the history of the concept of information as a function of division or bifurcation offers several advantages. On the philosophical level, thinking this way allows us to situate and to analyze what appears to be a fundamental sticking point of all conceptualizations of information. From one perspective, information can be considered as a disembodied term, opposed to matter, like some kind of spiritual ether circulating without support at the surface of the planet. But information can also refer to the singular form of a signal, as it did when Wiener identified the organism with a message. Faced with this cleavage of possibilities, which can be perceived already in a purely technical milieu, cybernetics made the epistemological and philosophical choice of the second representation.

This divide between the symbol and the signal constitutes a genuine philosophical sticking point, one rooted in opposed conceptions of the relation between form and matter, matter and signification, body and mind, and organism and machine. From this perspective, cybernetics appears as one of the techno-scientific and contemporary avatars of the much more ancient monist materialist position. What matters here is less, however, a desire to connect cybernetics to timeless philosophical problems, than the attempt to see how such fundamental philosophical antinomies can take shape, shift, extend or, on the contrary, sharpen, at a given time and space. Cybernetics inscribes its materialistic philosophy within a specific machinic universe, a specific context. Automated weapons and calculators that store programs present an opportunity to redistribute our conceptual maps, or to ask new questions about the natures of intelligence, signification or finality.

Bringing this divide to light thus enables us to interrogate, on the level of history and from a new perspective, the constitution of cognitive sciences. In a way, in order to constitute themselves, those sciences had to separate themselves from cybernetics and from its conception of information. The defeat of cybernetics probably masked this divide, making it seem as though the scientific decisions about artificial intelligence were the only possible ones, as though they were the natural solution to the problem of information. This was certainly not the case, as we might gather from the return to a reactualized connectionism, or from the ways in which the development of the artificial life program today reprises certain divisions of the 1950s. These opposing views on the intellectual treatment of information permit us to resolve the historical enigma of cybernetics: how did this science, triumphant at the end of the 1940s, almost completely disappear over the following decade, to be superseded by the programs of artificial intelligence? This defeat must be analyzed at the level of concepts as a philosophical opposition, rooted in both the contemporary state of technological discourse and development, and the political engagements of the era.

Beyond the historical and philosophical theses on the structuring of the concept of information, this work proposes an argument of a second order, involving the methods appropriate to the study of a science like cybernetics. Cybernetics is a genuinely unusual science: it did not manage to establish itself as a recognized discipline, and yet its vocabulary and its concepts have largely won the field, and have spread over the entire space of contemporary discourse; it opens onto questions that are profoundly and inalienably philosophical, and yet is deeply engaged in concrete and arduous technical developments. How can one trace the epistemology of a failure? What can this incongruous philosophical activity taking place amidst the machines finally mean? An ordinary solution that would begin by distinguishing between serious scientific developments, on the one hand, and their ideological consequences, on the other hand, does not seem (at least in this case) satisfactory. How can one comfortably divide science from ideology, or even established science from outdated science, in the case of a general theory and logic of automatons, for example? What meaning can one give to the analogy between the computer and the brain that structures such a theory? Taking the analogy as a simple ideological supplement to a pure and perfect science of calculators obliterates a whole zone of intermediary work in which the meaning of concepts gets negotiated. The science-ideology divide, taken as a primary tool of analysis, leads inevitably to the misrecognition of both the meaning and the actual effectiveness of any number of developments in cybernetics.

I have chosen to interpret the philosophical part of cybernetics essentially as a discussion of paradigms, in the sense developed by Thomas Kuhn.[2] Reflecting on the meaning of the concept of information in cybernetics is like a kind of gamble on the future, on the productivity of the research programs. Such a hypothesis prevents one from reducing cybernetics to a simple ideological discourse, or even to the in-between form of a "scientific ideology," as Canguilhem might have it.[3] Philosophical discussion among cyberneticians is not devoid of scientific value, even if such a discussion could not be reduced to a canonically formal and scientific "demonstration." Kuhn writes that the choice of a paradigm corresponds to a decision about the nature of fundamental concepts, about the type of object that is under examination, and on the major choices of methodology. Such decisions incarnate themselves often in one privileged example, to which one always returns. In cybernetics, the meaning of conceptual terms was consistently negotiated by means of two reference examples: that of the automated cannon tracking its target by means of negative feedback, and the analogy between the computer and the brain. Such negotiations can never be settled by the scientific method itself, by the reference to an objective and final reality; they are, on the contrary, operations that consist in fixing simultaneously an object and its method. We are in the same situation as Quine and Neurath's sailor, forced to repair the boat without having the possibility of reaching harbor, forced to modify the architecture of our discourse without having access to the final architecture of things.

Cybernetics is arguably a rather exceptional specimen of the work of paradigms, both because of their expansive appearance within the discipline, and because of the range of fields to which they seem to apply. Cybernetics is simply an attempt to think together three of the most important scientific developments of the last century. It is a reflection on the powers of statistical mechanics as applied to the fields of the living and of the mind. It attempts to hold together statistical mechanics, one of the greatest achievements of theoretical physics of the end of the nineteenth century and the beginning of the twentieth, as well as molecular biology and cognitive sciences—two of the most generative scientific programs of the second half of the twentieth century. The fact that molecular biology is not cognitive science, and that neither belongs to the field of statistical mechanics, may appear obvious today, but that wasn't the case at the end of the 1940s. Cybernetics embodied the dream of a vast unification of sciences under a physicalist concept of information. Such a project has an obvious relevance, not only from a scientific standpoint, but also for a reflection on the conceptual architecture of contemporary sciences, and in particular on the way they use the notion of information. Cybernetics may have produced fewer scientific results than it did philosophical ones, as Minsky notes, but it nevertheless constitutes a literally extraordinary moment of the history of sciences of the twentieth century; it cannot be reduced to an ideological parenthesis.

The study of this intermediary zone between science and philosophy turns out, also, to be very productive in regards to the question of technique. Cybernetics invites us to break free from an essentialist position. There is a zone of indetermination between technical features, their theoretical formalization and the representation of the possible uses of the machine; in this zone the real meaning of artifacts is at play. The computer, in particular, cannot be reduced to the simple application of Turing's results, as many people say. The delayed definition of calculators as information-processing machines processing information results from a complex process in which artifacts, logic models, research contracts and metaphors collide. The study of cybernetics illuminates this intermediary space of ontological determination, where the meaning of artifacts comes from an assemblage of heterogeneous constraints. From this perspective, cybernetics gives us an overview of the complex situation of the technosciences.

The study of cybernetics thus leads us to reflect on the modes of production of contemporary knowledge. We have been looking at a science engaged in technique, engaged in war, but which also thought about its own condition and sought to propose a new mode of scientific practice, one related to a non-technocratic mode of scientific engagement. It is regrettable that this aspect of its history has been buried or concealed, or demeaned via the caricature of a dehumanized technoscience. In such readings, philosophy always arrives too fast and too early in order to judge the productions of science; it does not take into account either the philosophy of the scientists, or their authentic commitment. How can one link the production of scientific concepts and the field of practice? How can one build a history of concepts that is neither a purely internal history of ideas of their diffusion, nor an externalizing sociology of laboratories or of institutions, or, even worse, a mixture of both? The solution probably consists in trying to account for the rules of concept-formation, the conditions that preside over the constitution of the objects of the discourse. Such conditions are never purely discursive, because discourse is always a matter of practice. Speaking is doing. This is the lesson of the historical epistemology program *à la française*, that of Bachelard, Canguilhem, Foucault, but also that of Hacking, which offers a specific way to articulate knowledge and practice: an epistemology that does not conceive the latter as a superstructural effect of the former, but questions simultaneously both their conditions of possibility and engagements with, and in, the real. The history of cybernetics, in all its variety and richness, furnishes us a sample of such a program.

Translated by Julien Jeusette and Eric Hayot

Notes

1. On this subject, see Slava Gerovitch, *From Newspeak to Cyberspeak* (Cambridge, MA: MIT Press), 139.
2. Thomas Kuhn, *The Structure of Scientific Revolutions*.
3. Georges Canguilhem, *Idéologie et rationalité dans l'histoire des sciences de la vie* (Paris: Vrin, 2000).

ORDER, NUMBER

L earning and cognition are grounded in pattern recognition. Whether in the form of an infant's feeding schedule, the electromagnetic radiation given off by the sun, or the arrangement of letters and spaces on this page, patterns communicate information about their systems. And they reveal all the more if disrupted: a nurse responds with alarm to a flatlining heart monitor, and an abnormally warm January in Chicago sparks awareness of climate change. Conversely, rendering a physical or social system as a pattern or set of possible patterns makes it possible to summarize its dynamics, describe past changes, and anticipate future trends. This section explores techniques and practices that have evolved alongside modern concepts of information, in the process reordering the ways in which we know and manage the various systems of the world, from the very small—particles and genes—to the very large—national populations and economies.

To begin, let us acknowledge the long shadow cast by the Shannon knot upon any consideration of information's relationship to order. Order, along with its sibling, organization (OED: to arrange into a structured whole; to systematize; to put into a state of order), both feature prominently in the early language and concepts of information science and cybernetics. When Shannon borrowed the notion of entropy from thermodynamics, he equated the measurement of information with the measurement of a system's disorder. Too much entropy, and a message is nothing more than a random, indecipherable jumble of elements (conversely, a message with zero entropy contains only uninterrupted sameness, communicating nothing new about its state to a recipient). Norbert Wiener, too, placed order at the center of his new science, describing the cybernetic principle of homeostasis as an entity's maintenance of order through the process of feedback with its environment. Along with Erwin Schrödinger, Wiener was fond of describing such a purposive entity as a living being in terms of negative entropy, meaning its drive to upkeep its state of organization against the universe's natural tendency toward deterioration and total entropy. For Wiener, this effort was the grounds of an existentialist struggle, which he characterized with typical grandiosity: "the declaration of our own nature and the attempt to build an enclave of organization in the face of nature's overwhelming tendency to disorder is an insolence against the gods and the iron necessity that they impose. Here lies tragedy, but here lies glory too."[1]

Yet information was already closely linked with organization and order well before entropy was introduced into the discussion. Indeed, information's etymology reveals the importance of order from as early as its entry into English from Latin in the fourteenth century. Charting its progress in his seminal essay, "*Information*: Notes Toward a Critical History" (see Part One), John Durham Peters shows how information connoted order at this early stage, naming the principle by which all matter in the universe was thought to be innately given shape and structure by abstract forms. Subsequently, with empiricism in the seventeenth and eighteenth centuries came the search for a new source of order. Information became a thing of the senses as the locus of order became the mind rather than an external metaphysical principle. However, it is in the third phase, starting around the middle of the eighteenth century, that information pivots toward achieving its present colloquial sense thanks to the rise of *statistics*, the systematic study of a state. Unlike the knowledge held by an individual, whose limited sensorium makes it impossible to experience more than a tiny fraction of the world, statistics could theoretically know a vast multitude of subjects or citizens of state, subsequently making it apprehensible to an individual in compressed or abbreviated form. Tools like "the actuarial table [present] a kind of degraded mysticism, a form of secular omniscience (checked, as always, by probabilities). This new kind of knowledge—knowledge that absolves individuals from the claims of deixis, of existing at one place and at one moment—is of course nothing other than information. Information is knowledge with the human body taken out of it," Peters tells us. In place of the knowing individual is bureaucracy, the apparatus for coordinating labor to aggregate and process large sets of data. In our era of "big" data analysis, one readily perceives how this bureaucratic form of information work has grown in complexity and reach, particularly with the advent of digital computing.

The selected readings in this section catalog how various aspects of this dimension of information developed in different disciplines and realms of life.

We begin with an excerpt from Michel Foucault's monumental work, *The Order of Things*, a book which remains startling thanks to its powerful demonstration of how attention to the practices and concepts of ordering can reveal a historical period's episteme, the grounds that a priori underlie its knowledge production. He argues that the logics of filiation and the identity of things underwent several significant shifts in modern Europe, beginning around the seventeenth century when earlier modes of ordering according to similarity were superseded by new, rationalist approaches to ordering that emphasized measurement and drawing of categorical distinctions. Mary Poovey's classic study of the double-entry account book in the fifteenth and sixteenth centuries, meanwhile, shows the rhetorical appeal of information in the emergence of ledger keeping. The numeric notation of economic transactions as discrete bits of information was appealing, she argues, on account of its arithmetical precision, rather than the system's (questionable) accuracy of representation. Both studies feature media of ordering, sorting, and classifying, including lists, tables, and printed books (to which could be added other contemporary forms, like architecture, cabinet of curiosities, and the bureau): instruments and forms of empiricist knowledge aimed at managing human error and uncertainty, taking knowledge production out of the hands of the individual in ways that anticipate the collaborative enterprise of statistics.

These systems of ordering were embedded within changing social institutions—laboratories, merchant houses, libraries—that dotted a changing landscape of discipline and control. The dynamic between information and power is clearer in the dispensation of organizations like the national statistics bureaus described by Ian Hacking in his classic history of probability and inferential knowledge. Information was crucial for overseas administration, too, as Thomas Richards establishes in the case of late nineteenth-century British literature and its articulation of anxieties and fantasies of colonial rule through the lens of thermodynamics and entropy.

The remaining selections are all more or less bound up in the Shannon knot, illustrating not only the breadth of information science since its inception, but more importantly, how new ideas about information's role in self-organizing social and natural systems further hastened the declining fortunes of individual, embodied ways of knowing. Though Friedrich Hayek could not draw directly on Shannon's theorem in his essay, "The Use of Knowledge in Society," his imaginative figuration of commodity prices as a mechanism of information distribution paved the way for economists' reinvention of the liberal market as a kind of societal computer. In "The Mathematics of Man," Claude Lévi-Strauss embraces the formalization of behavior in game theory to envision a new, quasi-numeric principle of social ordering and arrangement for anthropology. The contemporary impulse to mathematize in informatic terms is all the more evident in other realms of analysis, including biology. Indeed, the living, physical body came to appear to be constituted by writing and governed by algorithms, as Lily Kay illustrates in her work on the intersection between information science and new modes of modern biopower such as gene analysis and mapping.

To conclude, we submit one final way this section is poignant to our work as humanists. As the range of techniques and purview of pattern recognition expand, we now see its regular application within the humanities under signs like "macroanalysis," "distant reading," and "cultural analytics." Broader yet is the impact of the digital, whose profound—and frequently unanticipated—transformations of individual life and cultural expression have ushered in what some have called an era of the post-human. Plainly, neither the latter nor the digital humanities fall directly within this section's scope. But in collectively investigating the longstanding nexus between order and number, the following texts will prompt the reader to situate these relatively recent methods and subjects within the longer arc of humanity's mutual reconfiguration with information.

Anatoly Detwyler

Note

1. From Wiener's autobiography, *I Am a Mathematician*; the quote is taken from Steve J. Heims's forward to *The Human Use of Human Beings* (London: Free Association Books, 1989), xiii.

MICHEL FOUCAULT, FROM *THE ORDER OF THINGS: AN ARCHAEOLOGY OF THE HUMAN SCIENCES* (1966)

The French historian and philosopher, Foucault (1926–1984) focused much of his influential career on the development of the modern individual subject against a backdrop of increasingly refined forms of institutional coercion and control. *The Order of Things* offers a demonstration of "archaeology," Foucault's method for revealing an era's episteme by teasing out its particular schemes of ordering and classifying the world so as to know it. Analyzing the organizational logics and material practices that underlie an episteme—including the lists and tables, indexes and inventories, libraries and archives which help shape them—Foucault identifies three stages in Europe's modern history. At stake in this epistemic story is the formation a new object of knowledge, "man," who appears only after 1800 alongside new disciplines of economics, biology, and linguistics. Here we excerpt two parts. In the first, from the preface, Foucault contemplates a fictional taxonomy whose apparent, unsettling absurdity calls attention to the constructed-ness of our own episteme. In the second part, Foucault describes the episteme of what he calls the Classical period (ca 1650–1800), representing a shift from categorizing things by similitude toward a more informatic logic of ordering centered on difference, measurement, and ordering.

Preface

This book first arose out of a passage in Borges, out of the laughter that shattered, as I read the passage, all the familiar landmarks of my thought—*our* thought, the thought that bears the stamp of our age and our geography—breaking up all the ordered surfaces and all the planes with which we are accustomed to tame the wild profusion of existing things, and continuing long afterwards to disturb and threaten with collapse our age-old distinction between the Same and the Other. This passage quotes a 'certain Chinese encyclopaedia' in which it is written that 'animals are divided into: (a) belonging to the Emperor, (b) embalmed, (c) tame, (d) suckling pigs, (e) sirens, (f) fabulous, (g) stray dogs, (h) included in the present classification, (i) frenzied, (j) innumerable, (k) drawn with a very fine camelhair brush, (l) *et cetera*, (m) having just broken the water pitcher, (n) that from a long way off look like flies.' In the wonderment of this taxonomy, the thing we apprehend in one great leap, the thing that, by means of the fable, is demonstrated as the exotic charm of another system of thought, is the limitation of our own, the stark impossibility of thinking *that*.

But what is it impossible to think, and what kind of impossibility are we faced with here? Each of these strange categories can be assigned a precise meaning and a demonstrable content; some of them do certainly involve fantastic entities—fabulous animals or sirens—but, precisely because it puts them into categories of their own, the Chinese encyclopaedia localizes their powers of contagion; it distinguishes carefully between the very real animals (those that are frenzied or have just broken the water pitcher) and those that reside solely in the realm of imagination. The possibility of dangerous mixtures has been exorcized, heraldry and fable have been relegated to their own exalted peaks: no inconceivable amphibious maidens, no clawed wings, no disgusting, squamous epidermis, none of those polymorphous and demoniacal faces, no creatures breathing fire. The quality of monstrosity here does not affect any real body, nor does it produce modifications of any kind in the bestiary of the imagination; it does not lurk in the depths of any strange power. It would not even be present at all in this classification had it not insinuated itself into the empty space, the interstitial blanks *separating* all these entities from one another. It is not the 'fabulous' animals that are impossible, since they are designated as such, but the narrowness of the distance separating them from (and juxtaposing them to) the stray dogs, or the animals that from a long way off look like flies. What transgresses the boundaries of all imagination, of all possible thought, is simply that alphabetical series (a, b, c, d) which links each of those categories to all the others.

Moreover, it is not simply the oddity of unusual juxtapositions that we are faced with here. We are all familiar with the disconcerting effect of the proximity of extremes, or, quite simply, with the sudden vicinity of things that have no relation to each other; the mere act of enumeration that heaps them all together has a power of enchantment all its own: 'I am no longer hungry,' Eusthenes said. 'Until the morrow, safe from my saliva all the following shall be: Aspics, Acalephs, Acanthocephalates, Amoebocytes, Ammonites, Axolotls, Amblysto-mas, Aphislions, Anacondas, Ascarids, Amphisbaenas, Angleworms, Amphipods, Anaerobes, Annelids, Anthozoans. . . .' But all these worms and snakes, all these creatures redolent of decay and slime are slithering, like the syllables which designate them, in Eusthenes' saliva: that is where they all have their *common locus*, like the umbrella and the sewing-machine on the operating table; startling though their propinquity may be, it is nevertheless warranted by that *and*, by that *in*, by that *on* whose solidity provides proof of the possibility of juxtaposition. It was certainly improbable that arachnids, ammonites, and annelids should one day mingle on Eusthenes' tongue, but, after all, that welcoming and voracious mouth certainly provided them with a feasible lodging, a roof under which to coexist.

The monstrous quality that runs through Borges's enumeration consists, on the contrary, in the fact that the common ground on which such meetings are possible has itself been destroyed. What is impossible is not the propinquity of the things listed, but the very site on which their propinquity would be possible. The animals '(i) frenzied, (j) innumerable, (k) drawn with a very fine camelhair brush'—where could they ever meet, except in the immaterial sound of the voice pronouncing their enumeration, or on the page transcribing it? Where else could they be juxtaposed except in the non-place of language? Yet, though language can spread them before us, it can do so only in an unthinkable space. The central category of animals 'included in the present classification,' with its explicit reference to paradoxes we are familiar with, is indication enough that we shall never succeed in defining a stable relation of contained to container between each of these categories and that which includes them all: if all the animals divided up here can be placed without exception in one of the divisions of this list, then aren't all the other divisions to be found in that one division too? And then again, in what space would that single, inclusive division have *its* existence? Absurdity destroys the *and* of the enumeration by making impossible the *in* where the things enumerated would be divided up. Borges adds no figure to the atlas of the impossible; nowhere does he strike the spark of poetic confrontation; he simply dispenses with the least obvious, but most compelling, of necessities; he does away with the *site*, the mute ground upon which it is possible for entities to be juxtaposed. A vanishing trick that is masked or, rather, laughably indicated by our alphabetical order, which is to be taken as the clue (the only visible one) to the enumerations of a Chinese encyclopaedia. . . . What has been removed, in short, is the famous 'operating table'; and rendering to Roussel a small part of what is still his due, I use that word 'table' in two superimposed senses: the nickel-plated, rubbery table swathed in white, glittering beneath a glass sun devouring all shadow—the table where, for an instant, perhaps forever, the umbrella encounters the sewing-machine; and also a table, a *tabula*, that enables thought to operate upon the entities of our world, to put them in order, to divide them into classes, to group them according to names that designate their similarities and their differences—the table upon which, since the beginning of time, language has intersected space.

That passage from Borges kept me laughing a long time, though not without a certain uneasiness that I found hard to shake off. Perhaps because there a rose in its wake the suspicion that there is a worse kind of disorder than that of the *incongruous*, the linking together of things that are inappropriate; I mean the disorder in which fragments of a large number of possible orders glitter separately in the dimension, without law or geometry, of the *heteroclite*; and that word should be taken in its most literal, etymological sense: in such a state, things are 'laid', 'placed', 'arranged' in sites so very different from one another that it is impossible to find a place of residence for them, to define a *common locus* beneath them all. *Utopias* afford consolation: although they have no real locality there is nevertheless a fantastic, untroubled region in which they are able to unfold; they open up cities with vast avenues, superbly planted gardens, countries where life is easy, even though the road to them is chimerical. *Heterotopias* are disturbing, probably because they secretly undermine language, because they make it impossible to name this *and* that, because they shatter or tangle common names, because they destroy 'syntax' in advance, and not only the syntax with which we construct sentences but also that less apparent syntax which causes words and things (next to and also opposite one another) to 'hold together.' This is why utopias permit fables and discourse: they run with the very grain of language and are part of the fundamental dimension of the *fabula*; heterotopias (such as those to be found so often in Borges) desiccate speech, stop words in their tracks, contest the very possibility of grammar at its source; they dissolve our myths and sterilize the lyricism of our sentences.

It appears that certain aphasiacs, when shown various differently coloured skeins of wool on a table top, are consistently unable to arrange them into any coherent pattern; as though that simple rectangle were unable to serve in their case as a homogeneous and neutral space in which things could be placed so as to display at the same time the continuous order of their identities or differences as well as the semantic field of their denomination. Within this simple space in which things are normally arranged and given names, the aphasiac will create a multiplicity of tiny, fragmented regions in which nameless resemblances agglutinate things into unconnected islets; in one corner, they will place the lightest-coloured skeins, in another the red ones, somewhere else those that are softest in texture, in yet another place the longest, or those that have a tinge of purple or those that have been wound up into a ball. But no sooner have they been adumbrated than all these groupings dissolve again, for the field of identity that sustains them, however limited it may be, is still too wide not to be unstable; and so the sick mind continues to infinity, creating groups then dispersing them again, heaping up diverse similarities, destroying those that seem clearest, splitting up things that are identical, superimposing different criteria, frenziedly beginning all over again, becoming more and more disturbed, and teetering finally on the brink of anxiety.

The uneasiness that makes us laugh when we read Borges is certainly related to the profound distress of those whose language has been destroyed: loss of what is 'common' to place and name. Atopia, aphasia. Yet our text from Borges proceeds in another direction; the mythical homeland Borges assigns to that distortion of classification that prevents us from applying it, to that picture that lacks all spatial coherence, is a precise region whose name alone constitutes for the West a vast reservoir of utopias. In our dreamworld, is not China precisely this privileged site of space? In our traditional imagery, the Chinese culture is the most meticulous, the most rigidly ordered, the one most deaf to temporal events, most attached to the pure delineation of space; we think of it as a civilization of dikes and dams beneath the eternal face of the sky; we see it, spread and frozen, over the entire surface of a continent surrounded by walls. Even its writing does not reproduce the fugitive flight of the voice in horizontal lines; it erects the motionless and still-recognizable images of things themselves in vertical columns. So much so that the Chinese encyclopaedia quoted by Borges, and the taxonomy it proposes, lead to a kind of thought without space, to words and categories that lack all life and place, but are rooted in a ceremonial space, overburdened with complex figures, with tangled paths, strange places, secret passages, and unexpected communications. There would appear to be, then, at the other extremity of the earth we inhabit, a culture entirely devoted to the ordering of space, but one that does not distribute the multiplicity of existing things into any of the categories that make it possible for us to name, speak, and think.

When we establish a considered classification, when we say that a cat and a dog resemble each other less than two greyhounds do, even if both are tame or embalmed, even if both are frenzied, even if both have just broken the water pitcher, what is the ground on which we are able to establish the validity of this classification with complete certainty? On what 'table', according to what grid of identities, similitudes, analogies, have we become accustomed to sort out so many different and similar things? What is this coherence—which, as is immediately apparent, is neither determined by an *a priori* and necessary concatenation, nor imposed on us by immediately perceptible contents? For it is not a question of linking consequences, but of grouping and isolating, of analysing, of matching and pigeon-holing concrete contents; there is nothing more tentative, nothing more empirical (superficially, at least) than the process of establishing an order among things; nothing that demands a sharper eye or a surer, better-articulated language; nothing that more insistently requires that one allow oneself to be carried along by the proliferation of qualities and forms. And yet an eye not consciously prepared might well group together certain similar figures and distinguish between others on the basis of such and such a difference: in fact, there is no similitude and no distinction, even for the wholly untrained perception, that is not the result of a precise operation and of the application of a preliminary criterion. A 'system of elements'—a definition of the segments by which the resemblances and differences can be shown, the types of variation by which those segments can be affected, and, lastly, the threshold above which there is a difference and below which there is a similitude—is indispensable for the establishment of even the simplest form of order. Order is, at one and the same time, that which is given in things as their inner law, the hidden network that determines the way they confront one another, and also that which has no existence except in the grid created by a glance, an examination, a language; and it is only in the blank spaces of this grid that order manifests itself in depth as though already there, waiting in silence for the moment of its expression.

The fundamental codes of a culture—those governing its language, its schemas of perception, its exchanges, its techniques, its values, the hierarchy of its practices—establish for every man, from the very form, the very first, the empirical orders with which he will be dealing and within which he will be at home. At the other extremity of thought, there are the scientific theories or the philosophical interpretations which explain why order exists in general, what universal law it obeys, what principle can account for it, and why this particular order has been established and not some other. But between these two regions, so distant from one another, lies a domain which, even though its role is mainly an intermediary one, is nonetheless fundamental: it is more confused, more obscure, and probably less easy to analyse. It is here that a culture, imperceptibly deviating from the empirical orders prescribed for it by its primary codes, instituting an initial separation from them, causes them to lose their original transparency, relinquishes its immediate and invisible powers, frees itself sufficiently to discover that these orders are perhaps not the only possible ones or the best ones; this culture then finds itself faced with the stark fact that there exists, below the level of its spontaneous orders, things that are in themselves capable of being ordered, that belong to a certain unspoken order; the fact, in short, that order *exists*. As though emancipating itself to some extent from its linguistic, perceptual, and practical grids, the culture superimposed on them another kind of grid which neutralized them, which by this superimposition both revealed and excluded them at the same time, so that the culture, by this very process, came face to face with order in its primary state. It is on the basis of this newly perceived order that the codes of language, perception, and practice are criticized and rendered partially invalid. It is on the basis of this order, taken as a firm foundation, that general theories as to the ordering of things, and the interpretation that such an ordering involves, will be constructed. Thus, between the already 'encoded' eye and reflexive knowledge there is a middle region which liberates order itself: it is here that it appears, according to the culture and the age in question, continuous and graduated or discontinuous and piecemeal, linked to space or constituted anew at each instant by the driving force of time, related to a series of variables or defined by separate systems of coherences, composed of resemblances which are either successive or corresponding, organized around increasing differences, etc. This middle region, then, insofar as it makes manifest the modes of being of order, can be posited as the most fundamental of all: anterior to words, perceptions, and gestures, which are then taken to be more or less exact, more or less happy, expressions of it (which is why this experience of order in its pure primary state always plays a critical role); more solid, more archaic, less dubious, always more 'true' than the theories that attempt to give those expressions explicit form, exhaustive application, or philosophical foundation. Thus, in every culture, between the use of what one might call the ordering codes and reflections upon order itself, there is the pure experience of order and of its modes of being. [. . .]

Chapter 3: Representing

II Order

At the beginning of the seventeenth century, during the period that has been termed, rightly or wrongly, the Baroque, thought ceases to move in the element of resemblance. Similitude is no longer the form of knowledge but rather the occasion of error, the danger to which one exposes oneself when one does not examine the obscure region of confusions. 'It is a frequent habit,' says Descartes, in the first lines of his *Regulae*, when we discover several resemblances between two things, to attribute to both equally, even on points in which they are in reality different, that which we have recognized to be true of only one of them.'[1] The age of resemblance is drawing to a close . . . It is no longer sixteenth-century thought becoming troubled as it contemplates itself and beginning to jettison its most familiar forms; it is Classical thought excluding resemblance as the fundamental experience and primary form of knowledge, denouncing it as a confused mixture that must be analysed in terms of identity, difference, measurement, and order. Though Descartes rejects resemblance, he does so not by excluding the act of comparison from rational thought, nor even by seeking to limit it, but on the contrary by universalizing it and thereby giving it its purest form. Indeed, it is by means of comparison that we discover 'form, extent, movement and other such things'—that is to say, simple natures—in all subjects in which they may be present. And, moreover, in a deduction of the type 'all of A is B, all of B is C, therefore all of A is C', it is clear that the mind 'makes a comparison between the term sought and the term given, to wit A and C, with relation to the knowledge that both are B.' In consequence, if one makes an exception of the intuition one may have of a single thing, one can say that all knowledge 'is obtained by the comparison of two or more things with each other.'[2] But in fact, there can be no true knowledge except by intuition, that is, by a singular act of pure and attentive intelligence, and by deduction, which links the observed evidence together. How then can comparison, which is required for the acquisition of almost all knowledge and which, by definition, is neither an isolated observation nor a deduction, stand as an authority for a true thought? 'Almost all the labour accomplished by human reason consists without doubt in rendering this operation possible.'[3]

There exist two forms of comparison, and only two: the comparison of measurement and that of order. One can measure sizes or multiplicities, in other words continuous sizes or discontinuous sizes; but in both cases the use of measurement presupposes that, unlike calculation, which proceeds from elements towards a totality, one considers the whole first and then divides it up into parts. This division results in a number of units, of which some are merely conventional or 'borrowed' (in the case of continuous size) and others (in the case of multiplicities or discontinuous sizes) are the units of arithmetic. The comparison of two sizes or two multiplicities requires, in any case, that they both be analysed according to a common unit; so that comparison effected according to measurement is reducible, in every case, to the arithmetical relations of equality and inequality. Measurement enables us to analyse like things according to the calculable form of identity and difference.[4]

Order, on the other hand, is established without reference to an exterior unit: 'I can recognize, in effect, what the order is that exists between A and B without considering anything apart from those two outer terms'; one cannot know the order of things 'in their isolated nature', but by discovering that which is the simplest, then that which is the next simplest, one can progress inevitably to the most complex things of all. Whereas comparison by measurement requires a division to begin from, then the application of a common unit, here, comparison and order are one and the same thing: comparison by means of order is a simple act which enables us to pass from one term to another, then to a third, etc., by means of an 'absolutely uninterrupted'[5] movement. In this way we establish series in which the first term is a nature that we may intuit independently of any other nature; and in which the other terms are established according to increasing differences.

Such, then, are the two types of comparison: the one analyses into units in order to establish relations of equality and inequality; the other establishes elements, the simplest that can be found, and arranges differences according to the smallest possible degrees. Now, it is possible to use the measurement of sizes and multiplicities in establishing an order; arithmetical values can always be arranged according to a series; a multiplicity of units can therefore be arranged according to an order such that the difficulty, which previously lay in the knowing of measurement, comes finally to depend solely on the consideration of order.[6] And it is precisely in this that the method and its 'progress' consist: the reduction of all measurement (all determination by equality and inequality) to a serial arrangement which, beginning from the simplest, will show up all differences as degrees of complexity. After being analysed according to a given unit and the relations of equality or inequality, the like is analysed according to its evident identity and differences: *differences* that can be thought in the order of *inferences*. However, this order generalized form of comparison can be established only according to its position in the body of our acquired knowledge; the absolute character we recognize in what is simple concerns not the being of things but rather the manner in which they can be known. A thing can be absolute according to one relation yet relative according to others;[7] order can be at once necessary and natural (in relation to thought) and arbitrary (in relation to things), since, according to the way in which we consider it, the same thing may be placed at differing points in our order.

All this was of the greatest consequence to Western thought. Resemblance, which had for long been the fundamental category of knowledge—both the form and the content of what we know—became dissociated in an analysis based on terms of identity and difference; moreover, whether indirectly by the intermediary of measurement, or directly and, as it were, on the same footing, comparison became a function of order; and, lastly, comparison ceased to fulfil the function of revealing how the world is ordered, since it was now accomplished according to the order laid down by thought, progressing naturally from the simple to the complex. As a result, the entire episteme of Western culture found its fundamental arrangements modified. And, in particular, the empirical domain which sixteenth-century man saw as a complex of kinships, resemblances, and affinities, and in which language and things were endlessly interwoven—this whole vast field was to take on a new configuration. This new configuration may, I suppose, be called 'rationalism'; one might say, if one's mind is filled with ready-made concepts, that the seventeenth century marks the disappearance of the old superstitious or magical beliefs and the entry of nature, at long last, into the scientific order. But what we must grasp and attempt to reconstitute are the modifications that affected knowledge itself, at that archaic level which makes possible both knowledge itself and the mode of being of what is to be known.

These modifications may be summed up as follows. First, the substitution of analysis for the hierarchy of analogies: in the sixteenth century, the fundamental supposition was that of a total system of correspondence (earth and sky, planets and faces, microcosm and macrocosm), and each particular similitude was then lodged within this overall relation. From now on, every resemblance must be subjected to proof by comparison, that is, it will not be accepted until its identity and the series of its differences have been discovered by means of measurement with a common unit, or, more radically, by its position in an order. Furthermore, the interplay of similitudes was hitherto infinite: it was always possible to discover new ones, and the only limitation came from the fundamental ordering of things, from the finitude of a world held firmly between the macrocosm and the microcosm. A complete enumeration will now be possible: whether in the form of an exhaustive census of all the elements constituting the envisaged whole, or in the form of a categorical arrangement that will articulate the field of study in its totality, or in the form of an analysis of a certain number of points, in sufficient number, taken along the whole length of a series. Comparison, then, can attain to perfect certainty: the old system of similitudes, never complete and always open to fresh possibilities, could, it is true, through successive confirmations, achieve steadily increasing probability; but it was never certain. Complete enumeration, and the possibility of assigning at each point the necessary connection with the next, permit an absolutely certain knowledge of identities and differences: 'Enumeration alone, whatever the question to which we are applying ourselves, will permit us always to deliver a true and certain judgement upon it.'[8] The activity of the mind— and this is the fourth point—will therefore no longer consist in *drawing things together*, in setting out on a quest for everything that might reveal some sort of kinship, attraction, or secretly shared nature within them, but, on the contrary, in discriminating, that is, in establishing their identities, then the inevitability of the connections with all the successive degrees of a series. In this sense, discrimination imposes upon comparison the primary and fundamental investigation of difference: providing oneself by intuition with a distinct representation of things, and apprehending clearly the inevitable connection between one element in a series and that which immediately follows it. Lastly, a final consequence, since to know is to discriminate, history and science will become separated from one another. On the one hand there will be erudition, the perusal of written works, the interplay of their authors' opinions; this interplay may well, in some cases, possess an indicative value, not so much because of the agreement it produces as because of the disagreement: When the question at issue is a difficult one, it is more probable that there were few rather than many to discover the truth about it. Over against this history, and lacking any common unit of measurement with it, are the confident judgements we are able to make by means of intuitions and their serial connection. These and these alone are what constitute science, and even if we had 'read all the arguments of Plato and Aristotle, ... what we would have learned would not be sciences, it appears, but history.'[9] This being so, the written word ceases to be included among the signs and forms of truth; language is no longer one of the figurations of the world, or a signature stamped upon things since the beginning of time. The manifestation and sign of truth are to be found in evident and distinct perception. It is the task of words to translate that truth if they can; but they no longer have the right to be considered a mark of it. Language has withdrawn from the midst of beings themselves and has entered a period of transparency and neutrality.

This is a general phenomenon in seventeenth-century culture—a more general one than the particular fortunes of Cartesianism.

We must, in fact, distinguish between three things. On the one hand, there was the mechanism that, for what was really a fairly short period (not quite the last fifty years of the seventeenth century), offered a theoretical model to certain fields of knowledge such as medicine or physiology. There was also an attempt, rather diverse in the forms it took, to mathematicize empirical knowledge; though constant and continuous in the case of astronomy and part of physics, it was only sporadic in other fields—sometimes actually at tempted (as with Condorcet), sometimes suggested as a universal ideal and a horizon for research (as with Condillac or Destutt), and sometimes, too, rejected even as a possibility (by Buffon, for example). But neither this endeavour nor the at tempts of mechanism should be confused with the relation that all Classical knowledge, in its most general form, maintains with the *mathesis*, understood as a universal science of measurement and order. Under cover of the empty and obscurely incantatory phrases 'Cartesian influence' or 'Newtonian model', our historians of ideas are in the habit of confusing these three things and defining Classical rationalism as the tendency to make nature mechanical and calculable. Others are slightly more perceptive, and go to a great deal of trouble to discover beneath this rationalism a play of 'contrary forces': the forces of nature and life refusing to let themselves be reduced either to algebra or to dynamics, and thus preserving, in the depths of Classicism itself, the natural resources of the non-rationalizable. These two forms of analysis are equally inadequate; for the fundamental element of the Classical *episteme* is neither the success or failure of mechanism, nor the right to mathematicize or the impossibility of mathematicizing nature, but rather a link with the mathesis which, until the end of the eighteenth century, remains constant and unaltered. This link has two essential characteristics. The first is that relations between beings are indeed to be conceived in the form of order and measurement, but with this fundamental imbalance, that it is always possible to reduce problems of measurement to problems of order. So that the relation of all knowledge to the mathesis is posited as the possibility of establishing an ordered succession between things, even non-measurable ones. In this sense, *analysis* was very quickly to acquire the value of a universal method; and the Leibnizian project of establishing a mathematics of qualitative orders is situated at the very heart of Classical thought; its gravitational centre. But, on the other hand, this relation to the mathesis as a general science of order does not signify that knowledge is absorbed into mathematics, or that the latter becomes the foundation for all possible knowledge; on the contrary, in correlation with the quest for a mathesis, we perceive the appearance of a certain number of empirical fields now being formed and defined for the very first time. In none of these fields, or almost none, is it possible to find any trace of mechanism or mathematicization; and yet they all rely for their foundation upon a possible science of order. Although they were all dependent upon *analysis* in general, their particular instrument was not the *algebraic method* but the *system of signs*. So there first appeared general grammar, natural history, and the analysis of wealth, all sciences of order in the domain of words, beings, and needs; and none of these empirical studies, new in the Classical period and co-extensive with it in duration (their chronological frontiers are marked by Lancelot and Bopp, Ray and Cuvier, Petty and Ricardo, the first group writing around 1660 and the second around 1800–10), could have been founded without the relation that the entire *episteme* of Western culture maintained at that time with a universal science of order.

Notes

1. Descartes, *Oeuvres philosophiques* (Paris, 1963 edn., t. I, p. 77).
2. Descartes, *Regulae*, XIV, p. 168.
3. Ibid., XIV, p. 168.
4. Ibid., XIV, p. 182.
5. Ibid., VI, p. 102; VII, p. 109.
6. Ibid., XIV, p. 182.
7. Ibid., VI, p. 103.
8. Ibid., VII, p. 110.
9. Ibid., III, p. 86.

MARY POOVEY, FROM *A HISTORY OF THE MODERN FACT: PROBLEMS OF KNOWLEDGE IN THE SCIENCES OF WEALTH AND SOCIETY* (1998)

Poovey is a scholar of cultural history and literature. Her work on the changing rhetorical and epistemic force of numbers, abstraction, and uncertainty in Victorian Britain is essential reading for the scholar of information and data history. In *A History of the Modern Fact*, she traces the modern development of a discrete unit of knowledge—the fact—and its implications for knowledge systems ranging from philosophy to state-craft and political economy. The following excerpt focuses on the emergence of double-entry bookkeeping between the fifteenth and sixteenth centuries in Italy and Britain. She shows how innovations in inscription and layout made it possible to compress narrative descriptions of trans-actions into numeric information that was unprecedentedly abstract and mobile. The result: a system of economic representation whose credi-bility and moral authority stemmed from the appearance of precision, balance, and objectivity.

"This Exquisite Deep-Diving Science"[1]

Modern historians have offered two accounts of the origins of Western account-ing, each holding important clues about the epistemological issues carried over into the sciences of wealth and society. The first account tends to imply that various parts of modern accounting were developed simultaneously in different

Italian cities; and it attributes early accounting methods either to well-to-do householders' efforts to devise a system that would help in managing household economies or to Italian merchants' attempts to adapt household administrative techniques to extensive commercial enterprises.[2] The second account tends to focus on Luca Pacioli's codification of double-entry bookkeeping; it attributes the development of this kind of accounting to a university-trained elite and yokes the semantics of double-entry bookkeeping to rhetoric.[3] Although we will probably never have enough evidence to choose between these two accounts, it is possible to see that some of the issues addressed in household and mercantile accounting were preserved when accounting was codified by a Franciscan friar in 1494[4] . . .

The publication of the first double-entry bookkeeping manual constitutes the decisive episode in the histories that attribute accounting to the university elite. It also marks the moment when the relation between the spatial negotiations of power in the early modern household and the epistemological work of accounting can first be described as something more than metaphorical. That is, as an instrument for recording and monitoring the genealogical and financial secrets of a family or a family business, early accounting records can be said to have functioned *like* the study or the locked chest. Only when the rules of the double-entry system were codified, however, and published in what amounts to a textbook, does it become possible to speak of a *public system of accounting*.[5] This public system generated effects beyond individual accounting instances and did so even if merchants did not all immediately begin to keep their accounts in the double-entry form. Indeed, the formal features of the system of double-entry bookkeeping helped transform not only the claim that merchants were able to make about their status but the hegemony of the status system itself. The system was not simply *like* early modern studies, entry to which was no doubt regulated by rules that were explicit and informal but that must have varied with family circumstances. Instead, as a printed set of rules, which was specifically promoted as what we might call the industry standard, the double-entry bookkeeping system was an instrument designed to impose specific rules on a heterogeneous set of practices—to standardize bookkeeping. In promoting these standards, apologists for double-entry bookkeeping sought to make what had been a loose and class-specific set of rules governing the use of place into a generally adoptable and more easily enforced set of regulations governing writing.

More emphatically than earlier and more varied kinds of record keeping, then, double-entry bookkeeping transported the system of management unevenly realized in private households to the space of public writing. In so doing, it created a vehicle for producing public knowledge—that is, knowledge that was designed to function in public as a sign of something more than the information included in the books. Some merchants may have developed parts of the double-entry system and used them privately before textbooks began to appear (B. S. Yamey identifies the first traces of double-entry in the *massari* of Genoa as early as 1340),[6] but the method could not work as a *system* of knowledge production until it could be imitated. The social function of double-entry bookkeeping—its role as an apologist for mercantile honesty—thus coincided with the appearance of printed books about it . . .

Historians who have stressed the importance of Luca Pacioli's *De Computis er Scripuin*, have also helped us see the connection between this kind of accounting and the primary instrument by which knowledge was produced in the medieval university: rhetoric. As early as 1985, James Aho pointed out that Pacioli, a Franciscan friar who was schooled in Scholastic rhetoric—and who was a cohabitant with Leon Battista Alberti late in the latter's life—modeled the parts of the double-entry system on the major elements of Ciceronian rhetoric: *inventio*, *disposition*, and *elocution*.[7] The formal conventions of double-entry bookkeeping, Aho argues, were devised to defend commerce against the church's ban on usury, which the church fathers castigated as a sin against justice. The "case" the double-entry ledger was designed to make, according to Aho, was that the business, the facts of which the ledger recorded, was honest and that its profits did no more than offset the risk its owners incurred. The ledger made this case by following certain stylistic conventions: its contents were concise, orderly, and systematic, and its details were (presumably) faithful to the facts. The convention that gives double-entry its name—the double transcription of each transaction, once in the debit section of the ledger and once in the credit section—was intended to demonstrate that the firm's profit was legitimate, Aho concludes: for every credit I am due, this double-entry declares, l owe just so much . . .

In double-entry accounting, each transfer seeks, not simply to express the same information in different words but to write this information in abbreviated and increasingly rule-governed form. The limit toward which this process of abbreviation moved was the number, for numbers allowed one to write in short form details considered pertinent to the initial transaction. The priority accorded numbers because of their brevity and the ease of calculation they afforded, of course, privileged quantification over qualitative descriptions; the priority accorded numbers tended to make details that could be quantified seem more pertinent than details that could not. At the same time, number also allowed the writer to translate quantity into prices, and the priority accorded prices privileged commodities over other numbered items such as dates and index references.

Even though numbers were (and are) crucial to the double-entry system, however, we should not assume that they were important simply because numbers were accorded universal respect . . . or because the numbers that appeared in the double-entry books were assumed to refer to things that could be (and had been) counted.[8] In the late sixteenth century, in fact, and despite mathematicians' efforts to enhance its reputation, number still carried the pejorative connotations associated with necromancy;[9] and some of the numbers recorded in the double-entry books—specifically the prices—never pretended to refer to prices in the actual world of commerce. Instead of gaining prestige from numbers, double-entry bookkeeping helped confer cultural authority on numbers. It did so by means of the balance, which depended, as we have begun to see, on that wholly fictitious number—the number imported not to refer to a transaction but simply to rectify the books.

For late sixteenth-century readers, the balance conjured up both the scales of justice and the symmetry of God's world . . . In the double-entry system the image of the scales of justice was sub-ordinated to the figure of God's order, as if the scales had been brought to balance instead of indicating the weightier argument. Implicitly, this representation replaced the hierarchy of status, which was reinforced by rhetoric, with an equivalence or even an identity, for unequal contestants have been superseded by identical figures. The balances signaled by such figures were thus equated with justice not because one triumphed over the other but because what they displayed—the identity of two numbers—could be easily verified, first by simply comparing the two numbers and second by arithmetic, by checking the addition that produced the numbers entered at the bottom of each page. Even though number was not in itself the sign of virtue, *arithmetic*, which followed its own formal rules, constituted a system in relation to which one could judge right from wrong. In double-entry, then, the precision of arithmetic replaced the eloquence of speech as the instrument that produced both truth and virtue.

As I have already pointed out, the number added to create the ledger's balance had no referent in the actual world. It did not refer to any aspect of a commercial transaction, to a quantity of things, or to a price. Although this number had no referent, however, it did have a counterpart in the books themselves: the same number that the bookkeeper added to produce the balance on the ledger pages was then entered again on the balance sheet that appeared at the end of the ledger. On the balance sheet, the number was entered as either a credit or a debit, depending on what was necessary to offset the form it had taken in its first appearance . . . This balance sheet served to rectify the entries in the ledger, and, because balancing all the credits and debits also typically required adding a fictitious sum (carried over into another book, which constituted the starting point for a new year's or new cycle's accounts), it theoretically showed whether the business was currently in debt or making a profit.

Because double-entry bookkeeping's sign of virtue—the balance—depended on a sum that had no referent—the number added simply to produce the balance—the rectitude of the system as a whole was a matter of formal precision, not referential accuracy.[10] One could easily check whether entries had been correctly transcribed from book to book; one could tell at a glance if the sums on the ledger pages equaled each other and if the rectifying figure was correctly entered on the balance sheet; and one could easily check the arithmetic. But it was less easy to follow the course of an individual's transactions with the merchant, to tell exactly how a merchant stood with his creditors and debtors at any particular moment, or to tell whether the transactions initially recorded in the memorial were accurate. This precision, which was also a property of arithmetic, was an effect of the system of bookkeeping as a whole: only in relation to the other entries in the books could an individual entry be judged right or wrong; but in relation to those entries, the correctness of an entry could be judged absolutely, with no margin for error.

The formal precision of the accounting system made the figures recorded there seem accurate for two reasons. First, as I have just pointed out, the stages by which information was reworked from narrative to number did allow a reader to monitor the accuracy of the entries *in relation to other entries in the books*. Ensuring the accuracy of new entries, in fact, was aided by another convention that also equated both accuracy and virtue with writing according to rule. As Mellis explains, when an accountant transferred an entry from one book to another, he struck through the original entry so that he would not mistakenly enter it twice: thus, when he transferred information from the memorial to the journal, he crossed out the narrative entry in the memorial; and when he transferred a journal entry to the ledger, he struck through the former twice—once from left to right when he recorded it as a debit, and once from right to left when he recorded it as a credit.[11] This system of marks both ensured accuracy of transcription and transformed whatever errors were made in recording transactions into opportunities for displaying virtue, for if an entry was inadvertently recorded incorrectly, it was never erased, but merely struck through or marked with a cross and entered elsewhere correctly, with reference to the original, incorrect appearance.[12]

Thus the accuracy of *transcription*, which proclaimed the rectitude of the books, stood in for what could not be verified: the accuracy of the initial record of goods and transactions, which was recorded in the inventory and the memorial. Because so much more time and space were devoted to transcribing information from book to book than in making the initial record, the accuracy that could be verified assumed greater prominence than the writing that could not be checked. By the same token—and this is the second reason the system's formal precision made the figures recorded there seem accurate—the priority accorded to formal precision tended to *create* what it purported to describe. This complex effect of double-entry bookkeeping was a function of two related features of the system: its dependence on a series of personifications, and the way these personifications created writing positions that caused anyone who wrote in the books to subordinate personality (and status) to rules.

Even though the double-entry ledger's balance was the most obvious sign of the system's precision and virtue, to record the information from which that balance was derived as credits *and* debits, the bookkeeper had to create a set of personifications. Since commercial transactions were actually *either* expenditures *or* collections (or perhaps most typically, mixed transactions, as when jewels were purchased for a combination of credit, cash, and wheat), in order to write a transaction as *first* a credit and *then* a debit, the bookkeeper had to personify aspects of the business that did not necessarily correspond to actual sums of money, kinds of transactions, or even segments of the business.[13] Not only did they not refer to actual events or sums, but these fictitious entities were also not directly associated with or overseen by a single individual. "Stock" was one such personification; "Money" and "Profit and Loss" were others . . .

Even if "Money" and "Ballance" were fictions, however, as conventions of an accounting system used to demonstrate honesty, such personifications also tended to hold real individuals responsible for the fictions the double-entry system required. In other words, the "personal-moral metaphors" of accounting tended to realize what they purported to describe—by encouraging the company's agents to act as responsibly as the books represented them as being.[14] This helps explain why the fictions that might have undermined the book's display of honesty did not necessarily do so—because preserving the precision of the system required anyone who wrote in the books to act as if these fictions were true and, in so doing, to help make them so. It also helps explain how the formal precision of the books created the effect to accuracy. Even though the information recorded in the books was not necessarily accurate, the combination of the system's precision and the normalizing effect that privileging precision tended to produce created the impression that the books were not only precise, but accurate as well. This in turn was critical to the social role the double-entry system was designed to play, for what social good were accounting books if what they recorded could not be taken as accurate accounts of transactions that had actually occurred?

Notes

1. This phrase is Lewes Robert's description of accounting. See *Merchants Mappe of Commerce* (1638), 18.
2. See, for example, Raymond de Roover, "New Perspectives on the History of Accounting," *Accounting Review* 30 (July 1955): 408; B. S. Yamey, "The Functional Development of Double-Entry Bookkeeping," *Accountant*, November 1940, 333, 334–35; and Yamey, "Accounting and the Rise of Capitalism: Further Notes on a Theme by Sombert," *Journal of Accounting Research* 2 (1964): 117–36.
3. See James A. Aho, "Rhetoric and the Invention of Double-Entry Bookkeeping," *Rhetorica* 3, no. 3 (1985): 21–43; Grahame Thompson, "Early Double-Entry Bookkeeping

and the Rhetoric of Accounting Calculation," in *Accounting as a Social and Institutional Practice*, ed. Anthony G. Hopwood and Peter Miller (Cambridge: Cambridge University Press, 1994), 40–66; and Hoskin and Macve, "Writing, Examining, Disciplining," 67–97.

4. I find the argument that early accounting was associated with university-trained men persuasive because of Luca Pacioli's role in codifying double-entry bookkeeping. Nevertheless, I am puzzled by Hoskin and Macve's tendency to misstate their sources' emphasis. For example, they quote Alexander Murray as saying that the merchant's role in accounting history was "not that of a pioneer or even that of a patron of pioneers," but they neglect to point out that Murray is discussing the history of mathematics and that he does not debunk the "counting-house theory" but supplements it. More telling, they quote Michael Clanchy as stating that "the great majority of clerks and accountants . . . were trained at universities" without including the first part of this sentence: "It is possible that." Elsewhere Clancy states that "evidence is insufficient to establish for certain that most such clerks were university men," although he notes evidence that suggests they were. See Hoskin and Macve, "Writing, Examining, Disciplining," 73; Murray, *Reason and Society in the Middle Ages*, 194–94; and Michael Clanchy, "*Moderni* in Education and Government in England," *Speculum* 50 (1975): 685.

5. Grahame Thompson emphasizes the importance of printing in the codification and dissemination of double-entry bookkeeping. See Thompson, "Early Double-Entry Bookkeeping and the Rhetoric of Accounting Calculation," 55–62.

6. Yamey, "Functional Development of Double-Entry Bookkeeping," 335.

7. See Aho, "Rhetoric," 24–43. Aho points out that Pacioli was twenty-five when he met the sixty-six-year-old Alberti, and that he went to live with Alberti in 1479. It is interesting to speculate—although it must remain speculation—whether Pacioli and Alberti discussed the implications of removing accounting from the household, as publishing a textbook most surely did. On Pacioli's relation to Alberti, see also R. Emmett Taylor, *No Royal Road: Luca Pacioli and His Times* (Chapel Hill: University of North Carolina Press, 1942), chap. 8.

8. So critical are numbers to all forms of accounting that one modern analyst has called number the dominant metaphor of accounting. See Keith Robson, "Accounting Numbers as 'Inscription': Action at a Distance and the Development of Accounting," *Accounting, Organizations and Society* 17, no.7 (1992): 685, and Morgan, "Accounting as Reality Construction," 477–85.

9. For the negative connotations of number, see Taylor, *Mathematical Practitioners*, 4, and Swetz, *Capitalism and Arithmetic*, 248–49. Even Queen Elizabeth's patronage of the esteemed mathematician John Dee did little to dispel the association between number and black magic. On Dee, see Webster, *Great Instauration*, 119.

10. The distinction between precision and accuracy is not an old one; the two terms are cited in the *Oxford English Dictionary* as synonyms. Lorraine Daston has made this distinction in "Moral Economy," 8. David S. Landes also discusses the distinction; see Landes, *Revolution in Time: Clocks and the Making of the Modern World* (Cambridge: Harvard University Press, 1983), 78–83.

11. Aho describes this system; see "Rhetoric," 32. Mellis uses a system of cross-indexing to signify the transfer of entries: when the accountant entered a statement as a credit, the appropriate page number of the ledger was to be entered above a horizontal line in the left margin of the journal entry; when he transferred the entry to the debit page of the ledger, that page number should be entered below the horizontal line in the journal (*Briefe Instruction*, 43).

12. See Mellis, *Briefe Instruction*, 81.
13. This convention disappeared only in the nineteenth century. On its disappearance, see Aho, "Rhetoric," 36–37. It is noteworthy that this disappearance dovetailed with the professionalizing of accounting in Britain—as if the responsibility once "assumed" by these metaphors was transferred to the system of credentialing and certifying by which accountant's reliability was underwritten. On the nineteenth-century professionalizing of accounting, see Edgar Jones, *Accountancy and the British Economy, 1840–1980: The Evolution of Ernst and Whinney* (London: B. T. Batsford, 1981)
14. See Peter Miller and Ted O'Leary, "Accounting and the Construction of the Governable Person," *Accounting, Organizations and Society* 12, no. 3 (1987): 256–61, and Robson, "Accounting Numbers," 700. The concept of the "responsibilization of individuals" is related to the concept of "calculating selves." On "calculating selves" see Miller, "Accounting and Objectivity," 61–86. See also Aho, "Rhetoric," 38.

IAN HACKING, FROM *THE TAMING OF CHANCE* (1990)

Hacking (b. 1936) is a prominent philosopher of science. His germinal work on the history numeracy and statistics in Europe and America places him alongside people like Michel Foucault and Mary Poovey at the forefront of influential scholarship on the intersections between information, control, and modern governance. Building on Hacking's interests in the early mathematization of probability, *The Taming of Chance* describes how statistical knowledge and analysis came to supplant deterministic and mechanistic models of causality, rooting this development in new experiments with population management and the governance of social deviancy. The following comes from early on in the book in which Hacking surveys the eighteenth-century institutions responsible for developing techniques of population tabulation. The field of nation-based statistics that emerged from these institutions would cement the calculability of indeterminism and lead to the "avalanche of printed numbers" of the nineteenth century.

Public amateurs, secret bureaucrats

Trento, 11 September 1786 *I console myself with the thought that, in our statistically minded times, all this has probably already been printed in books which one can consult if the need arises.* Edinburgh, 1 January 1798

Many people were at first surprised at my using the words, Statistics and Statistical . . . *In the course of a very extensive tour, through the northern parts of Europe, which I happened to take in 1786, I found that in Germany they were engaged in a species of political inquiry to which they had given the name of Statistics. By statistical is meant in Germany an inquiry for the purpose of ascertaining the political strength of a country, or questions concerning matters of state; whereas the idea I annexed to the term is an inquiry into the state of a country, for the purpose of ascertaining* the quantum of happiness enjoyed by its inhabitants and the means of it future improvement.[1,2]

Every state, happy or unhappy, was statistical in its own way. The Italian cities, inventors of the modern conception of the state, made elaborate statistical inquiries and reports well before anyone else in Europe. Sweden organized its pastors to accumulate the world's best data on births and deaths. France, nation of physiocrats and probabilists, created a bureaucracy during the Napoleonic era which at the top was dedicated to innovative statistical investigations, but which in the provinces more often perpetuated pre-revolutionary structures and classifications. The English inaugurated 'political arithmetic' in 1662 when John Graunt drew demographic inferences from the century-old weekly Bills of Mortality for the City of London. England was the homeland of insurance for shipping and trade. It originated many other sorts of provisions guarding against contingencies of life or illness, yet its numerical data were a free enterprise hodge-podge of genius and bumbledom.

Visionaries, accountants and generals have planned censuses in many times and places. Those of the Italian city-states now provide historians with a rich texture of information. In the modern era, however, a census was an affair more of colonies than of homelands. The Spanish had a census of Peru in 1548, and of their North American possessions in 1576. Virginia had censuses in 1642–5 and a decade later. Regular repeated modern censuses were perhaps first held in Acadie and Canada (now the provinces of Nova Scotia and Quebec) in the 1660s. Colbert, the French minister of finance, had instructed all his regions to do this, but only New France came through systematically and on time. Ireland was completely surveyed for land, buildings, people and cattle under the directorship of William Petty, in order to facilitate the rape of that nation by the English in 1679. The sugar islands of the Caribbean reported populations and exports to their French, Spanish or English overlords. New York made a census in 1698, Connecticut in 1756, Massachusetts in 1764. The United States wrote the demand for a decennial census into the first article of their Constitution, thus continuing colonial practice, and even extending it, as westward the course of empire took its way, across the continent and in due course to the Philippines. Going east, the British took the same pains to count their subject peoples. India evolved one of the great statistical bureaucracies, and later became a major centre for theoretical as well as practical statistics.

Thus there is a story to be told about each national and colonial development, and each has its own flavour. For example the first Canadian enumerations were possible and exact because the people were few and frozen-in during midwinter when the census was taken. There was also a more pressing concern than in any of the regions of mainland France, for whereas the population of British North America was burgeoning, the number of fecund French families in Canada was small due to the lack of young women. To take a quite different concern, the 1776 Articles of Confederation of the United States called for a census to apportion war costs, and the subsequent Constitution ordered a census every ten years to assure equal representation of families (as a sop to the southern plantations, blacks were to be enumerated as 3/5 of a person). Six and seven decades later, those who interpreted the Constitution strictly insisted that a census could ask no question not immediately connected with representation.

No one will doubt that each region, once it takes counting seriously, becomes statistical in its own way. Stronger theses wait in the wings. For example, the nineteenth century statistics of each state testify to its problems, sores and gnawing cankers. France was obsessed with degeneracy, its interpretation of the declining birth rate.[3] The great crisis in the United States Census occurred after 1840, when it was made to appear that the North was full of mad blacks, while in the South blacks were sane and healthy—strong proof of what was good for them.[4] . . .

A survey of even one set of national statistics would be either superficial or vast. In either case it would provide excessive preparation for a reading of nineteenth-century counting. But for fear that we become fixated upon the avalanche of printed numbers that occurred after 1820 or so, I shall start with one regional example from an earlier period. I ended the last chapter by quoting Kane, writing in 1784. He wrote of the yearly registers of deaths, births and marriages which go in 'conformity to the laws of nature.' I began the present chapter quoting Goethe, who in 1786 spoke of 'our statistically minded times.' I shall use the German-speaking world, especially Prussia, as my example of those times. Graunt and the English began the public use of statistics. Peoples of the Italian peninsula and elsewhere had promulgated the modern notion of the state. But it was German thinkers and statesmen who brought to full consciousness the idea that the nation-state is essentially characterized by its statistics, and therefore demands a statistical office in order to define itself and its power.

Leibniz, my favourite witness to the emergence of probability in the seventeenth century, was the philosophical godfather of Prussian official statistics. His essential premises were: that a Prussian state should be brought into existence, that the true measure of the power of a state is its population, and that the state should have a central statistical office in order to know its power. Hence a new Prussian state must begin by founding a bureau of statistics.

He formulated this idea of a central statistical office about 1685, a few years after William Petty had made the same recommendation for England.[5] Leibniz saw a central office as serving the different branches of administration: military, civil, mining, forestry and police. It would maintain a central register of deaths, baptisms and marriages. With that one could estimate the population, and hence measure the power of a state. A complete enumeration was not yet deemed to be practicable. The population of a country, as opposed to a walled city or a colony, was in those days not a measurable quantity. Only institutions could make it one.

Leibniz had a lively interest in statistical questions of all sorts, and pursued an active correspondence on issues of disease, death and population. He proposed a 56-category evaluation of a state, which would include the number of people by sex, social status, the number of able-bodied men who might bear weapons, the number of marriageable women, the population density and age distribution, child mortality, life expectancy, distribution of diseases and causes of death.[6] Like so many of Leibniz's schemes, such a tabulation was futurology that has long since become routine fact. . . . Prussian enumerations began only with the reign of Friedrich Wilhelm I, 1713–1740, famed for administrative skills and controlled militarism. His agents had first to figure out how to count, for available numbers were far less reliable than Leibniz's rhetoric had made it appear.

Reorganization was undertaken piecemeal, starting with a machinery for registering births, deaths and marriages in the four (royal) residence cities of Brandenburg-Prussia. In 1719 an abortive enumeration of the entire state was attempted. Various systems of reporting were experimented with, and an initial summary of results was issued on 3 March 1723. By 1730 people were officially sorted into the following nine categories; landlords, goodwives, male and female children; then household members classified as journeymen, farmhands, servants, youths and maids. The rubrics endured but the subclassifications exploded. Workmen became classified according to 24 occupations, and special categories were created for the chief industry: cloth makers, fabric makers, hat makers, stocking makers etc. Quantities of worked wool were fitted into the tables. Buildings were meticulously sorted (roofed with tile or straw, new or repaired, barns or decaying), and cattle, land and roads were described. For what purpose? Often, of course, for taxation; hence the way buildings were classed. Leibniz's phrase was regularly used: determine the power of the state. What might the numbers reveal to enemies? A decree of 2 January 1733 forbade publication of the population list. It became a state secret.

If there is a contrast in point of official statistics between the eighteenth and nineteenth centuries, it is that the former feared to reveal while the latter loved to publish. An anecdote will illustrate. The energetic editor, geographer and traveller A. F. Busching published, along with much other material, two journals bulging with information about the German states and their neighbours. One, a 'magazine for new history and geography,' ran steadily during 1762–93, and the other, a 'weekly news,' between 1773 and 1787.[7] When Busching asked Frederick the Great for help in coordinating and publishing information already collected in the royal ministries, the king replied that he would not hinder Busching, who could publish anything he knew. But neither the king nor his agents would lift a finger to help him find anything out.[8]

A long string of private individuals like Busching collected and published myriad numbers. It was above all they to whom Goethe referred when, in his 1786 travelogue, he spoke of 'our statistically minded times.' Travel books less well remembered than that of Goethe would count anything. Take Johann Bernoulli's adventures in Brandenburg, Prussia, Pomerania, Russia and Poland, about the time of Goethe's more famous trip. You might expect a Bernoulli to be discerning with numbers, but not at all. When he went into a room with old master paintings, he would not describe the pictures; he whipped out his yardstick and measured their dimensions. He told the reader more about the (quite unexceptional) sizes of these paintings, than about what they depict or who made them.[9] The contents of every local statistical news-sheet were reported as he passed through. He was shocked to find that no one in Warsaw knew how many people lived in town, but was relieved to be able to insert a footnote, while the work was in press: the March 1780 issue of Busching's weekly cleared the matter up.[10]

The most systematic private statistical enterprise of mid-eighteenth-century Germany was J.P. Süssmilch's *Divine Order*. This was an intensely detailed study of births, deaths and sex ratios which revealed Providence at work.[11] He painstakingly studied parish registers and other unused data, following the model of the Englishman, Graunt: 'All that was needed' to start this kind of inquiry 'was a Columbus who should go further than others in his survey of old and well-known reports. That Columbus was Graunt'[12] . . .

Süssmilch was one of a long and open-ended line of actors on the stage of what Michel Foucault called a biopolitics 'that gave rise to comprehensive measures, statistical assessments, and interventions aimed at the entire social body or at groups as a whole.'[13] . . . German biopolitics began in earnest after the Seven Years' War in 1757–63, and here the issue was underpopulation. Perhaps a third of the people had died, and many regions were left almost empty. They required colonization in order to restore ravished farmland. Many features of Prussian statistics originate with this objective concern, augmented by the zealous administration-for-its-own-sake of Frederick the Great . . .

Aside from the tables of births, marriages and deaths, official statistics were private, for the eye of the king and his administrators. There were of course all kinds of documentation in commercial affairs, although even these tended to follow the patterns of counting people.[14] They ran parallel to the diligent productions of enthusiastic amateurs, of whom Süssmilch and Busching provide two different kinds of example. The third force in German statistical activity was the 'university statistics' from which our subject is said to take its name . . . Words on which our word 'statistics' could draw are hardly original with these professors, and probably have a better Italian pedigree than a German one. But it was undoubtedly a Gottingen scholar who fixed the very word 'Statistik.' Gottfried Achenwall thought of what he called statistics as the collection of 'remarkable facts about the state.'[15] The successor to his chair valiantly defined statistics in the words, 'History is ongoing statistics, statistics is stationary history.' The Göttingen statisticians had a strong positivist bent:

> Strictly speaking, one wants only facts from the statistician; he is not responsible for explaining causes and effects. However, he must often seize upon effects in order to show that his fact is statistically important—and moreover his work will be entirely dry, if he does not give it some life and interest by introducing, at suitable points, a mixture of history, cause and effect.[16]

The work of these men was seldom quantitative. They were opposed to number-crunching of the sort represented by Süssmilch. They thereby stand for an antinumerical and anti-averaging tradition that emerges from time to time in our history. They produced giant pull-out tables, but here one found descriptions of climates (for example) more often than measures of cloudiness. Despite this, I find a very substantial continuum between the historical-political-economic-geographic-topographical-meteorological-military surveys of the university statisticians, and, for example, the contents of Busching's two journals. Busching was thoroughly numerical—statistical in our sense of the word—but on the title pages or in the titles of many of his books he called himself an historian-geographer—a statistician in the Achenwallian sense of the word.

German culture demands definitions of concept and object. It requires an answer to the question: is X an (objective) science? Is statistics, then, a science? If so, what science is it, and what are its concepts, what its objects? 'Until now, there have been 62 different definitions of statistics. Mine will make it 63', wrote Gustav Rumelin in 1863.[17] He was director of the Württemberg statistical office, a political scientist and staunch Malthusian. I don't know which 62 he had in mind—I think that by 1863 I can do twice as well as he can, in the German literature alone. But already there had been the correct move taught by professors of philosophy: distinguish! There are two sciences. One is descriptive and non-numerical, namely the work of the university statisticians. Then there is the heir to English political arithmetic, commenced seriously in Germany by Süssmilch, C. G. A. Knies's 1850 *Statistik als selbständige Wissenschaft* furthered this conclusion, recommending that although we owe the word 'statistics' to Achenwall, we should transfer it, and use it to name the numerical studies of the political arithmeticians.[18] We ought then to say that Achenwall did something other than *Statistik*; let us call it (said Knies) *Staatskunde*.

So what? All this seems like word-play. Harald Westergaard ironically recounted this 'saga' of the word 'statistics', concluding that 'but for the curious change of names which has taken place, and which has often puzzled students of statistics, little interest would have attached to it.'[19] Westergaard implied that we would never even notice Achenwall were it not for his having institutionalized the word 'statistics' which we now use to name something numerical and non-Achenwallian.

Perhaps that opinion underestimates the university statisticians. For example, Austria established a statistical office, on the Prussian model, only in 1829. This was a systematic bureaucracy for the compilation of numerical data. Who would it employ? The staff was taken straight from the universities, where old-style university statistics continued to be taught. The subject was part of the curriculum at the six Austrian universities—Innsbruck, Padua, Pest, Prague, Venice and Vienna. It was also standard at numerous colleges and lycées. Rightly or wrongly, the Austrian administrators did not see teachers and students as doing something essentially different from what a statistical bureau should do.

The Austrian example is an objective item from bureaucratic history. At a more impressionistic level it looks as if the Prussian statistical bureaucracy was remarkably continuous with the old university statisticians. It was numerical, yes, but also descriptive. There was a great deal of resistance to theoretical French notions of 'statistical law.' The Prussian tabulations resembled those of Achenwall and Schlozer, although with numbers instead of words. Bureaucratic efficiency was combined with mathematical naiveté. The Prussian bureau was heir to university statisticians, just as it was heir to the administrative expertise of the ministries of Frederick the Great, and heir to the army of amateurs of numbers.

It was however the amateurs of numbers that most struck literary travellers such as Goethe and Bernoulli. The travel books constantly referred to local periodicals more ephemeral than Busching's, crammed with numerical tid-bits, collected with an indiscriminate enthusiasm not equalled in Britain or France. Travellers with an eye to policy and public affairs could also learn. None toured more diligently in the continent of Europe than gentlemen from the British Isles. Arthur Young's travels in Europe, and his subsequent role in agricultural reform, are well known. But such travellers did not import only agricultural technique . . . they acquired an enthusiasm for statistics.

Notes

1. Goethe at the start of his *Italian Journey*. Sir John Sinclair at the completion of his Statistical Account of Scotland. Goethe and Sinclair were travelling at almost exactly the same time.

2. J. W. Goethe, Italian Journey (1786–1788), trans. W. H. Auden and E. Mayer (New York, 1962): 21. J. Sinclair, *A Statistical Account of Scotland* (Edinburgh, 1791–99): 20, liii.

3. For a study of the consequences of this obsession, see Robert A. Nye, *Crime, Madness and Politics in Modern France: The Medical Concept of National Decline* (Princeton, 1984).

4. *Cf.* Gerald N. Grob, *Edward Jarvis and the Medical World of Nineteenth-Century America* (Knoxville, 1978).

5. W. Perry, *The Petty Papers*, ed. the Marquis of Lansdowne (London, 1927): 1, 171.

6. O. Klopp (ed.), *Die Werke von Leibniz* (11 vols., Hanover, 1864–8): 5, 303–15.

7. *Magazin für die neue Historie and Geographie* (23 vols., 1762–93), *Wochentlich Nachrichten* (1773–87). For a thorough discussion of the 'amateurs' and their weeklies or monthlies, see W. Schöne, *Zeitungswesen und Statistik: Eine Untersuchung über den Einfluss der periodischen Presse auf die Entstehung und Entwicklung der Staatswissenschaftlichen Literatur, speziell der Statistik* (Jena, 1924).

8. C. G. A. Knies, *Die Statistik als selbständige Wissenschaft: zur Lösing des Wirrfals in der Theorie und Praxis dieser Wissenschaft* (Kassel, 1850): 3.

9. Johann Bernoulli, *Reisen durch Brandenburg, Pommern, Preussen, Curland, Russland und Pohlen* (4 vols., Leipzig, 1779–80): 2, 197.

10. Ibid., 4, 86.

11. J. P. Süssmilch, *Die gottliche Ordnung in der Veränderung des menschlichen Geschlechts, aus der Geburt, dem Tode und der Fortpflanzung desselben erwiesen* (Berlin, 1741).

12. Ibid., 18.

13. Michel Foucault, *The History of Sexuality*, (New York, 1980): 138.

14. For a bibliography, see W. Sachse, *Bibliographie zur preussischen Gewerbestatistik 1750–1850* (Göttingen, 1981).

15. For a thorough history of this entire period, up to 1835, see Vincenz John, *Geschichte der Statistik: Ein Quellenmässiges Handbuch für den akademischen Gebrauch wie für den Selbstunterricht* (Stuttgart, 1884), 1.

16. A.L. Schlozer, *Staats-Gelehrtheit nach ihren Haupt-Theilen, im Auszug und Zusammenhang. Part 2. Allgemeine Statistik.* 1, *Theorie der Statistik: Nebst Ideen über das Studium der Politik überhaupt* (Gottingen, 1804): 47.

17. G. Rumelin, 'Statistik', *Tübinger Zeitschrift für Staatswissenschaft* 4 (1863): 645.

18. *Cf.* note 9.

19. H. Westergaard, *Contributions to the History of Statistics* (London, 1932): 14.

THOMAS RICHARDS, FROM *THE IMPERIAL ARCHIVE: KNOWLEDGE AND THE FANTASY OF EMPIRE* (1994)

During his career as a scholar of literature and culture, Richards wrote *The Imperial Archive,* a creatively revisionist account of the history of the British Empire through cybernetic terms of communication and control. Drawing connections between Victorian-era novels such as Rudyard Kipling's *Kim* and *Tono-Bungay* by Orson Wells and contemporary formations of geography, biology, and thermodynamics, *The Imperial Archive* argues that the massive and messy mechanism of colonial administration ultimately grounds its fantasy of mastering far-flung places in the seemingly limitless enterprise of collecting and ordering of information. Richards's emphasis on the nineteenth century as a period of incredible fecundity in the production and consumption of facts, numeric data, and information puts his work in dialog with other scholars in this volume, including C.A. Bayly and James Beniger. This excerpt is from the book's introduction.

A n empire is partly a fiction. No nation can close its hand around the world, the reach of any nation's empire always exceeds its final grasp. An empire is by definition and default a nation in overreach, one nation that has gone too far, a nation that has taken over too many countries too far away from home to control them effectively. All the great historical empires, ancient and modern, have had to come to terms with the problems of control at a distance. Empires may have armies and navies, but they also have messengers, or systems for conveying messages. The distance involved in conquest makes travel hard and knowledge of far-flung places difficult, as most of the old stories told about empires testify. In the Odyssey, Penelope has no idea what Ulysses has been up to until he returns to tell his story: After the Battle of Marathon the messenger dies. Prospero goes off to an island and has to use magic to know what is going on around him. The ocean swallows up the argosies in *The Merchant of Venice*. Robinson Crusoe gets stuck on an island. The list goes on and on, at least until the middle of the nineteenth century, when—thanks to a new set of ideas about the nature of long-distance control, ideas largely scientific in origin, borrowed from the new disciplines of geography, biology and thermodynamics—people in Britain began to think differently about what it meant to hold on to an empire. The narratives of the late nineteenth century are full of fantasies about an empire united not by force but by information. [. . .]

I have found that historians have tended to confer a lot more unity on the British Empire than is justified. Most people during the nineteenth century were aware that their empire was something of a collective improvisation. In the heyday of the Empire, the Foreign Office was small and overworked. A lot was going on, so much that the Foreign Office, which had been set up to deal with intra-European affairs, simply was not able to keep up with it all. No one office ever administered the British Empire; lacking any standing imperial bureaucracy, it was overseen by a sort of extended civil service recruited from Britain's dominant classes. The work of the Foreign Office was often done by any educated person, however unqualified, working in whatever department, stationed wherever, who felt he had to do it simply because he happened to be British. These people were painfully aware of the gaps in their knowledge and did their best to fill them in. The filler they liked best was information. From all over the globe the British collected information, for any exact civil control, of the kind possible in England, was out of the question. The Empire was too far away, and the bureaucrats of the Empire had to be content to shuffle papers.

This paper shuffling, however, proved to have great influence. It required keeping track, and keeping track of keeping track. It required some kind of archive for it all. Unquestionably the British Empire was more productive of knowledge than any previous empire in history. The administrative core of the Empire was built around knowledge-producing institutions like the British Museum, the Royal Geographical Society, the India Survey, and the universities (many of the figures of imperial myth, from T. E. Lawrence to Indiana Jones, started out in some institution of higher learning). The ideology of mid-Victorian positivism had also led most people into believing that the best and most certain kind of knowledge was the fact. The fact was many things to many people, but generally it was thought of as raw knowledge, knowledge awaiting ordering. The various civil bureaucracies sharing the administration of Empire were desperate for these manageable pieces of knowledge. They were light and movable. They pared the Empire down to file-cabinet size. The British may not have created the longest-lived empire in history, but it was certainly one of the most data-intensive. The civil servants of the Empire pulled together so much information and wrote so many books about their experiences that today we have only begun to scratch the surface of their archive. In a very real sense theirs was a paper empire: an empire built on a series of flimsy pretexts that were always becoming texts.

The truth, of course, is that it was much easier to unify an archive composed of texts than to unify an empire made of territory, and that is what they did—or at least tried to do, for most of the time they were unable to unify the knowledge they were collecting. It fell apart: ran off in many different directions like the hedgehogs in Alice's game of croquet, so much so that, in the chapters that follow, I question whether the data they collected can even be called 'knowledge.' Most Victorian epistemologies presupposed a superintending unity of knowledge. A comprehensive knowledge of the world was for most of the century the explicit goal of all forms of learning. People began the nineteenth century believing that all the knowledge in the world fell into a great standing order, a category of categories, but, after dozens of Casaubons had failed to make sense of thousands of facts squeezed into library catalogues, biological taxonomies, and philological treatises, they ended it by believing that the order of things was easier said than done. By 1900, not even the librarians at the British Museum seriously believed they would be able to chip away at this backlog of knowledge. The great monument to Victorian knowledge, the Oxford English Dictionary, wasn't completed until the late 1920's, by which time the first volumes in the series were already fifty years out of date. The intention had been to deal with old words. The practical experience of trying to order all the incoming knowledge from the Empire had forced them to reconsider whether knowledge could ever in fact be unified. These people had found themselves in the midst of the first knowledge explosion. If today we call this the 'information explosion,' it was because by the century's end many people had stopped using the word 'knowledge,' which always had something about it of a prospective unity emerging, and started using the word 'information,' with its contemporary overtones of scattered disjunct fragments of fact. [. . .]

This archive was neither a library nor a museum, though imperial fiction is full of little British libraries and museums scattered all over the globe. Rather the imperial archive was a fantasy of knowledge collected and united in the service of state and Empire. Though a literary fantasy, it was shared widely and actually had an impact on policymaking. Its impact can be quickly summed up by the way in which the word 'classification' changed its meaning in the late nineteenth century. At mid-century it meant ordering information in taxonomies; by century's end 'classified' had come to mean knowledge placed under the special jurisdiction of the state. In the fantasy of the imperial archive, the state actually succeeds in superintending all knowledge, particularly the great reams of knowledge coming in from all parts of the Empire. The myth of imperial archive brought together in fantasy what was breaking apart in fact, and it did so by conjoining two different conceptions of knowledge that may at first seem contradictory. These are the ideas of a knowledge at once *positive* and *comprehensive*. The familiar Victorian project of positive knowledge divided the world into little pieces of fact. A fact was a piece of knowledge asserted as certain, and positive knowledge was considered by both Mill and Comte to be the sum of objectively verifiable facts. The problem here of course was that facts almost never added up to anything. They were snippets of knowledge, tiny particularized units responsible for our current idea of information. It took a leap of faith to believe that facts would someday add up to any palpable sum of knowledge, and that faith often took the form of an allied belief in comprehensive knowledge. Comprehensive knowledge was the sense that knowledge was singular and not plural, complete and not partial, global and not local, that all knowledges would ultimately turn out to be concordant in one great system of knowledge. This system-building impulse was the imperial archive's great inheritance from a philosophical tradition that posited a universal and essential form of knowledge, the tradition of Leibnitz and Kant and von Humboldt, but it also took much the same ideas from a source nearer to hand, English Romanticism. Indeed it turned out that Romanticism contributed a great deal to imagining the Empire as a concordant whole. The impulse toward the universal in Shelley, the project of a complete knowledge of the world in Coleridge, the ability of Blake's visions to span the globe, the sense of a fully surveyed landscape in Wordsworth: these differing but exhaustive projects were carried forward in the literature of the Empire examined here. Though a domestic school of poetry, English Romanticism was imperial in the scope of its often-failed ambitions. In the Victorian period, Romanticism persists not only as a source of imaginary for the Empire (the Romantic poets discovered and refined the imaginary of orientalism, providing staples for travel writers and novelists alike), but as the basic animating project of the imperial archive, namely, the organization of all knowledges into a coherent imperial whole. The Victorian contribution was simply to reformulate this project as explicitly imperial and redeploy the stock imagery of Romanticism to serve the end and aims of Empire. The legacy of Romanticism was the residual conviction most Victorians shared that all knowledge, despite its modular character, should and would be united. Knowledge was expanding rapidly, but so were the means to contain it. The peculiarly Victorian confidence that knowledge could be controlled and controlling, that knowledge could be exploding and yet be harnessed as the ultimate form of power, issued from this felt merger of the Victorian project of positive knowledge with the Romantic project of comprehensive knowledge. The merger of these two projects made possible the fantasy of an imperial archive in which the control of Empire hinges on a British monopoly over knowledge.

This supplanting of power by the force of knowledge is one of the hallmarks of the twentieth century. Much of what I talk about in *The Imperial Archive* is in effect a working back from our own world, a world in which armies fund universities, corporations run laboratories, banks sponsor the arts. Power now draws its breath from knowledge, and knowledge exhales in an iron lung. Today we routinely assume that no power can possibly exist without its underlay of documents, memoranda, licenses, and files. Obvious as it may now seem, this assumption was new in the nineteenth century, when a great variety of novelists saw it being worked out in front of their eyes. If this book is mostly a work of literary criticism, it is because literature got to the subject first. Fifty years before Norbert Wiener coined the word 'cybernetics,' British writers were examining in detail the role information played in legitimating the British Empire. Two of my chapters end with discussion of Thomas Pynchon's *Gravity's Rainbow* (1973), and I have often returned to this American work of fiction because it is set in the London of 1944 and gives a picture of the chilling presence of power among the mandarins of knowledge. Pynchon's novel is poised between two empires. In it the British decant what they have learned into an intelligence network run by Americans, and the Americans learn their lesson well. The British Empire had colonies. Today's American Empire thinks not about occupying land but about watching it, and calls its colonies satellites.

This is a book, then, about the British Empire not as it was but as it was imagined to have been. This emphasis on the fantasy of empire accounts for the primary position a series of literacy readings occupies in this book. It also accounts for the fact that not all of the texts discussed deal with the Empire directly. Rather than trying to survey the entire literature of the British Empire, I have searched for the most distinctive features of the British imperial imagination. Slavery, conquest, violence, deportation, ethnocide: these are features of most empires, and though they are the focus of the work of a great imperial novelist, Joseph Conrad, they tend to play a markedly marginal role in most imperial fiction. Imperial fiction is far more frequently the site of fantasy rather than realism. Many of the typical features of this imperial fantasy have already been located and enumerated. Our understanding of the fantasies of empire, of the processes by which fantasy repels and replaces history, has been much enhanced by many recent studies probing the specific discourses and genres of empire (Edward Said on orientalism and Patrick Brantlinger on imperial gothic are exemplary here). This book seeks to add the relation between information and imperialism to this list. The fantasy of the imperial archive was a distinctive product of the late nineteenth century, as compelling in its way as the discourse of orientalism or the genre of imperial gothic. The obsession with gathering and ordering information has so far passed unremarked in imperial fiction. This book works to restore a large and missing dimension to our understanding of the imperial imagination as it applied itself to perceiving the colonial world in the nineteenth and twentieth centuries. Though I have confined myself to a few representative examples, the underlying concern with the problems of knowledge and information can be found everywhere in imperial fiction. Understanding the fantasy of knowledge elevated to global power takes us a long way toward understanding the lure, and finally the persistence, of the much larger fantasy of empire itself.

FRIEDRICH HAYEK, FROM "THE USE OF KNOWLEDGE IN SOCIETY" (1945)

Famous proponent of free market neoliberalism, the economist and philosopher Friedrich August von Hayek (1899–1992) brought the entity of information into the purview of economic scholarship beginning in the 1940s. In a debate about the efficiency of socialist economic planning, Hayek framed the social allocation of resources as an epistemic problem, asking whether a central planning agency or the free market had the knowledge to best accomplish the task. Hayek dismisses central planning because it cannot account for all the constantly changing conditions of production and distribution. Instead, he lauds the figure of the market as a knowing entity, envisioning it as a kind of processor of social information that, through the mechanism of price, continuously calculates and communicates current economic conditions to individuals in the market. This idealized vision would go on to rebrand economics as a form of information studies, eventually garnering Hayek a Nobel Prize in Economics in 1974.

[. . .]

Today it is almost heresy to suggest that scientific knowledge is not the sum of all knowledge. But a little reflection will show that there is beyond question a body of very important but unorganized knowledge which cannot possibly be called scientific in the sense of knowledge of general rules: the knowledge of the particular circumstances of time and place. It is with respect to this that practically every individual has some advantage over all others in that he possesses unique information of which beneficial use might be made, but of which use can be made only if the decisions depending on it are left to him or are made with his active cooperation. We need to remember only how much we have to learn in any occupation after we have completed our theoretical training, how big a part of our working life we spend learning particular jobs, and how valuable an asset in all walks of life is knowledge of people, of local conditions, and special circumstances. To know of and put to use a machine not fully employed, or somebody's skill which could be better utilized, or to be aware of a surplus stock which can be drawn upon during an interruption of supplies, is socially quite as useful as the knowledge of better alternative techniques. And the shipper who earns his living from using otherwise empty or half-filled journeys of tramp-steamers, or the estate agent whose whole knowledge is almost exclusively one of temporary opportunities, or the *arbitrageur* who gains from local differences of commodity prices, are all performing eminently useful functions based on special knowledge of circumstances of the fleeting moment not known to others . . .

IV

If it is fashionable today to minimize the importance of the knowledge of the particular circumstances of time and place, this is closely connected with the smaller importance which is now attached to change as such . . . One reason why economists are increasingly apt to forget about the constant small changes which make up the whole economic picture is probably their growing preoccupation with statistical aggregates, which show a very much greater stability than the movements of the detail. The comparative stability of the aggregates cannot, however, be accounted for—as the statisticians seem occasionally to be inclined to do—by the "law of large numbers" or the mutual compensation of random changes. The number of elements with which we have to deal is not large enough for such accidental forces to produce stability. The continuous flow of goods and services is maintained by constant deliberate adjustments, by new dispositions made every day in the light of circumstances not known the day before, by *B* stepping in at once when *A* fails to deliver. Even the large and highly mechanized plant keeps going largely because of an environment upon which it can draw for all sorts of unexpected needs; tiles for its roof, stationery for its forms, and all the thousand and one kinds of equipment in which it cannot be self-contained and which the plans for the operation of the plant require to be readily available in the market.

This is, perhaps, also the point where I should briefly mention the fact that the sort of knowledge with which I have been concerned is knowledge of the kind which by its nature cannot enter into statistics and therefore cannot be conveyed to any central authority in statistical form. The statistics which such a central authority would have to use would have to be arrived at precisely by abstracting from minor differences between the things, by lumping together, as resources of one kind, items which differ as regards location, quality, and other particulars, in a way which may be very significant for the specific decision. It follows from this that central planning based on statistical information by its nature cannot take direct account of these circumstances of time and place, and that the central planner will have to find some way or other in which the decisions depending on them can be left to the "man on the spot."

V

If we can agree that the economic problem of society is mainly one of rapid adaptation to changes in the particular circumstances of time and place, it would seem to follow that the ultimate decisions must be left to the people who are familiar with these circumstances, who know directly of the relevant changes and of the resources immediately available to meet them. We cannot expect that this problem will be solved by first communicating all this knowledge to a central board which, after integrating *all* knowledge, issues its orders. We must solve it by some form of decentralization. But this answers only part of our problem. We need decentralization because only thus can we ensure that the knowledge of the particular circumstances of time and place will be promptly used. But the "man on the spot" cannot decide solely on the basis of his limited but intimate knowledge of the facts of his immediate surroundings. There still remains the problem of communicating to him such further information as he needs to fit his decisions into the whole pattern of changes of the larger economic system.

How much knowledge does he need to do so successfully? Which of the events which happen beyond the horizon of his immediate knowledge are of relevance to his immediate decision, and how much of them need he know?

There is hardly anything that happens anywhere in the world that *might* not have an effect on the decision he ought to make. But he need not know of these events as such, nor of *all* their effects. It does not matter for him *why* at the particular moment more screws of one size than of another are wanted, *why* paper bags are more readily available than canvas bags, or *why* skilled labor, or particular machine tools, have for the moment become more difficult to acquire. All that is significant for him is *how much more or less* difficult to procure they have become compared with other things with which he is also concerned, or how much more or less urgently wanted are the alternative things he produces or uses. It is always a question of the relative importance of the particular things with which he is concerned, and the causes which alter their relative importance are of no interest to him beyond the effect on those concrete things of his own environment.

It is in this connection that what I have called the economic calculus proper helps us, at least by analogy, to see how this problem can be solved, and in fact is being solved, by the price system. Even the single controlling mind, in possession of all the data for some small, self-contained economic system, would not—every time some small adjustment in the allocation of resources had to be made—go explicitly through all the relations between ends and means which might possibly be affected. It is indeed the great contribution of the pure logic of choice that it has demonstrated conclusively that even such a single mind could solve this kind of problem only by constructing and constantly using rates of equivalence (or "values," or "marginal rates of substitution"), *i.e.*, by attaching to each kind of scarce resource a numerical index which cannot be derived from any property possessed by that particular thing, but which reflects, or in which is condensed, its significance in view of the whole means-end structure. In any small change he will have to consider only these quantitative indices (or "values") in which all the relevant information is concentrated; and by adjusting the quantities one by one, he can appropriately rearrange his dispositions without having to solve the whole puzzle *ab initio*, or without needing at any stage to survey it at once in all its ramifications.

Fundamentally, in a system where the knowledge of the relevant facts is dispersed among many people, prices can act to coordinate the separate actions of different people in the same way as subjective values help the individual to coordinate the parts of his plan. It is worth contemplating for a moment a very simple and commonplace instance of the action of the price system to see what precisely it accomplishes. Assume that somewhere in the world a new opportunity for the use of some raw material, say tin, has arisen, or that one of the sources of supply of tin has been eliminated. It does not matter for our purpose—and it is very significant that it does not matter—which of these two causes has made tin more scarce. All that the users of tin need to know is that some of the tin they used to consume is now more profitably employed elsewhere, and that in consequence they must economize tin. There is no need for the great majority of them even to know where the more urgent need has arisen, or in favor of what other needs they ought to husband the supply. If only some of them know directly of the new demand, and switch resources over to it, and if the people who are aware of the new gap thus created in turn fill it from still other sources, the effect will rapidly spread throughout the whole economic system and influence not only all the uses of tin, but also those of its substitutes and the substitutes of these substitutes, the supply of all the things made of tin, and their substitutes, and so on; and all this without the great majority of those instrumental in bringing about these substitutions knowing anything at all about the original cause of these changes. The whole acts as one market, not because any of its members survey the whole field, but because their limited individual fields of vision sufficiently overlap so that through many intermediaries the relevant information is communicated to all. The mere fact that there is one price for any commodity—or rather that local prices are connected in a manner determined by the cost of transport, etc.—brings about the solution which (it is just conceptually possible) might have been arrived at by one single mind possessing all the information which is in fact dispersed among all the people involved in the process.

VI

We must look at the price system as such a mechanism for communicating information if we want to understand its real function—a function which, of course, it fulfills less perfectly as prices grow more rigid. (Even when quoted prices have become quite rigid, however, the forces which would operate through changes in price still operate to a considerable extent through changes in the other terms of the contract.) The most significant fact about this system is the economy of knowledge with which it operates, or how little the individual participants need to know in order to be able to take the right action. In abbreviated form, by a kind of symbol, only the most essential information is passed on, and passed on only to those concerned. It is more than a metaphor to describe the price system as a kind of machinery for registering change, or a system of telecommunications which enables individual producers to watch merely the movement of a few pointers, as an engineer might watch the hands of a few dials, in order to adjust their activities to changes of which they may never know more than is reflected in the price movement.

Of course, these adjustments are probably never "perfect" in the sense in which the economist conceives of them in his equilibrium analysis. But I fear that our theoretical habits of approaching the problem with the assumption of more or less perfect knowledge on the part of almost everyone has made us somewhat blind to the true function of the price mechanism and led us to apply rather misleading standards in judging its efficiency. The marvel is that in a case like that of a scarcity of one raw material, without an order being issued, without more than perhaps a handful of people knowing the cause, tens of thousands of people whose identity could not be ascertained by months of investigation, are made to use the material or its products more sparingly; i.e., they move in the right direction. This is enough of a marvel even if, in a constantly changing world, not all will hit it off so perfectly that their profit rates will always be maintained at the same constant or "normal" level.

I have deliberately used the word "marvel" to shock the reader out of the complacency with which we often take the working of this mechanism for granted. I am convinced that if it were the result of deliberate human design, and if the people guided by the price changes understood that their decisions have significance far beyond their immediate aim, this mechanism would have been acclaimed as one of the greatest triumphs of the human mind . . .

CLAUDE LÉVI-STRAUSS, FROM "THE MATHEMATICS OF MAN" (1954)

Lévi-Strauss (1908–2009) was a public intellectual whose prolific scholarship reshaped the field of modern anthropology into the study of sociocultural patterns. Lévi-Strauss envisioned kinship as a system of differences among family members, analyzable as a series of binary relations that could reveal the deeper structures or code underlying all social relations and institutions. This push to make anthropology more scientific—paralleled in mid-century developments in linguistics and psychoanalysis—reveals intellectual debts to cybernetics and particularly to the Shannon's measurement of communication using terms of difference and order. Lévi-Strauss wrote "The Mathematics of Man" as the introduction to a special issue of the International Social Science Bulletin (published by UNESCO) devoted to the topic of mathematics and the social sciences. The article documents the ways in which Shannon's knot tied together different disciplines, not only by promoting data extrapolation and quantitative analysis within the social sciences, but also through Lévi-Strauss's idea of "qualitative mathematics," the inscription of social dynamics as equations, as objective as the formulas of fields like macroeconomics and demography.

When we consider the history of science, it looks as if man realized, at a very early stage, what his programme of research was to be and then, once having decided on it, took hundreds of years to acquire the means of carrying it out. In the earliest days of scientific thought, the Greek philosophers stated the problems of physics in terms of the atom, and now, two thousand five hundred years later—in a way that they probably never guessed—we are just beginning to fill in the framework which they outlined so long ago. The same might be said of the application of mathematics to the problems of mankind, for the speculations of the earliest geometers and arithmeticians were concerned with man far more than with the physical world. Pythagoras was deeply interested in the anthropological significance of numbers and figures, and Plato was much taken up with similar considerations.

In the last ten years or so these ideas, which were of such interest to the ancient world, have once more become matters of immediate practical concern; for it should be noted immediately that the developments to which this number of the International Social Science Bulletin hopes to make a modest contribution are by no means confined to the social sciences. They are also to be seen in the so-called sciences of man (if a distinction can in fact be made between the two groups). I would go even further, and say that the most sensational developments were perhaps first seen in the sciences of man—possibly because, at first sight, those sciences seem the most remote from any idea of exactitude and measurement, but also, in all probability, because the essentially qualitative object of their study made it impossible for them to 'tag along' behind traditional mathematics, as the social sciences have done for so long, and forced them to turn, from the outset, to certain novel and daring forms of mathematical thought.

The stages of this evolution can best be traced, and the fundamental changes it implies best appreciated, in the field of linguistics. From the standpoint with which we are concerned here, linguistics is in a very special position. It is classified as one of the sciences of man, but it is concerned with a social phenomenon, for language not only implies life in a society but is indeed the very foundation of that life. What sort of society could there be without language? It is the most perfect and most complex of those communication systems in which all social life consists and with which all the social sciences, each in its special field, are concerned.

Consequently, we may say that any revolution in linguistics is pertinent alike to the social sciences and to the sciences of man. Between 1870 and 1920, two basic ideas were introduced in this sphere—first under the influence of the Russian, Beaudoin de Courtenay, and later under that of the Swiss, Saussure. The first was that language is made up of separate elements, or phonemes; the second, that it is possible, by linguistic analysis, to work out systems or, in other words, combinations governed by some law of cohesion, in which, as a result, changes occurring in one part necessarily entail others, that can therefore be foreseen. The story of how these principles led to the establishment of structural linguistics—through the thinking of the Russian, Trubetskoy,[1] and the work of his followers in many lands, Jakobson, Benveniste, Sapir, Bloomfield, Hjelmslev, Sommerfelt and a number of others—is a familiar one. Structural linguistics is based on the principle that the phonemes, the microscopic elements of language, are distinct and separate (an idea probably first defined by the medieval Indian grammarians), so that, in the first place, they can be identified and, in the second, the laws by which they are associated can be determined. Those laws are quite as strict as the laws of correlation found in the natural sciences.

The laboratory research conducted independently by communication engineers was to lead, around about 1940, to very similar conclusions. In the manufacture of equipment for the artificial production of speech sounds—such as the famous *Voder*, the forerunner of a whole series of more highly developed devices—and in the theoretical elaboration of the intellectual methods governing the work of communication specialists,[2] certain main principles of interpretation can be seen in action, which are exactly the same as those at which linguistic theory had arrived—i.e. that communication among people is based on the combination of ordered elements; that, in each language, the possibilities of combination are governed by a group of compatibilities and incompatibilities; and lastly, that the freedom of choice in language, as defined within the limits of these rules, is subject, in time, to certain probabilities. Thus, by a memorable conjunction of circumstances, Saussure's famous distinction between language and speech coincides with the two great aspects of contemporary thought on physics, language being a matter of mechanical and structural interpretation, while speech, despite its apparent unpredictability, freedom and spontaneity (or perhaps because of them), provides a field for the calculus of probability. For the first time in the history of the sciences of man, it becomes possible, as in the natural sciences, to set up laboratory experiments and to check hypotheses by empirical means.

Saussure had also suggested a comparison between language and certain games of strategy, such as chess. This assimilation of language to a sort of combinative process, to which we have already alluded, was to make it possible to apply directly to linguistics the theory of games, as formulated in 1944 by J. von Neumann and O. Morgenstern.[3] As the title of the book itself indicates, the theory of games was enunciated by its authors as a contribution to the science of economics. This unexpected association between a so-called science of man and another branch of study which is generally considered to be a social science clearly brings out the fundamental factor of communication, on which all human relations are based. As the exchange of messages, in which linguistic communication consists, and the exchange of goods and services, which belongs to the realm of economics, now both admit of the same formal treatment, they begin to appear as phenomena of the same type.

Finally, as the state of a speech system is at all times governed by the immediately preceding states, language can also be connected up with the theory of servo-mechanisms, deeply influenced by biological considerations, which has become famous under the name of cybernetics.[4] Thus, in the space of a few years, specialists in such apparently distinct fields as biology, linguistics, economics, sociology, psychology, communication engineering and mathematics have suddenly found themselves working side by side and in possession of a remarkable conceptual apparatus in which they are gradually discovering that they have a common language.

It must, incidentally, be emphasized that the course of development which has been briefly outlined above is still continuing. After the contacts made between linguists and engineers in the realm of phonology, i.e. in matters still concerned with the infrastructure of language, a new and different development is at present leading the former towards a more exact formalization of the problems of grammar and vocabulary, while the technical problems of 'translating machines' are compelling the latter to think along similar lines. Some years ago the English statistician, Yule, expounded a mathematical method for the critical study of texts.[5] Today, indeed, certain religious circles, although traditionally wary of any attempt to reduce man and his reactions to purely mechanical terms, are cheerfully employing mathematical methods as an aid to the critical study of the Bible. A recent international conference of philologists, held in England during the summer of 1954, showed the growing importance of mathematical considerations in philology, literary criticism and stylistics. And there are certain premonitory signs that the history of art and aesthetics (which incidentally has often, for some centuries past, toyed with the idea) are not altogether unlikely to embark on the same path.

* * *

When social scientists venture into mathematics, they can therefore find encouragement and cheer in the assurance that they are not alone in the risks they run. In point of fact, they are being carried forward on a great surge of development, set in motion by forces which have nothing to do with them. For, as Mr. Festinger remarks at the end of his article in this issue of the Bulletin, the confidence now shown by so many social scientists in mathematical methods is due not so much to the results that they themselves have secured by those methods as to the enormous assistance that mathematics has provided in other fields, and particularly in physics.

Even so, there are certain possible misunderstandings to be avoided, and it is advisable to make clear in exactly what respects the tendency to draw together, which we have been witnessing for some years past, is novel.

Social scientists were certainly aware, well before the last ten years, that a science is not really a science until it can formulate a precise chain of propositions, and that mathematics is the best means of expression for achieving this result. Psychology, economics and demography have been using mathematical reasoning for a very long time. And, though it is true that, as regards the first of these branches of study, the use of mathematics has been confined to applied and experimental psychology (and, even there, has always been subject to criticism), in the two others the effort after mathematical accuracy and the use of mathematical methods may be said to be contemporary with the founding of the science and to have progressed concurrently with it. One might therefore be tempted to conclude that the only novel thing is the extension of processes which have long been in use elsewhere to new branches of study such as sociology, social psychology and anthropology; but this would show a complete misunderstanding of the revolution which is in progress.

Though, for at least fifty years (and more, in the case of economics and demography), the social sciences have had recourse to mathematics, it has always been for quantitative purposes. They were interested in measuring magnitudes which, in their respective fields, lent themselves to such treatment—size of population, economic resources, total 'wage hill', etc. When, as in psychology, the phenomena observed did not immediately appear to present quantitative features, an indirect approach was adopted and efforts were made, by means of a quantitative scale devised for the particular purposes in view, to discover distinctive variations whose qualitative aspects alone could be directly grasped—for example, the methods of expressing the various outward aspects of intelligence in numerical terms in an IQ scale. The whole effort at mathematical expression was thus brought down to two types of operations—firstly, to extract the quantitative aspects of observations and, secondly, to measure those aspects as accurately as possible.

These two purposes are entirely justified when there are indeed quantitative features in the facts observed and when what we hope to learn can be gleaned from those quantitative features. There is no doubt that the main justification for demography and economics is that they can make use of such methods. We wish to have quantitative information about the changes in the size of the population, the increase or decrease of its resources, etc., and there is no reason to suppose that, in the future, the above-mentioned sciences will not continue such studies very satisfactorily.

Even in this restricted field, however, difficulties are encountered. In order to abstract the purely quantitative content of population phenomena, demographers are obliged to oversimplify them. The population of which they speak has only a remote connexion with the real population; it consists of sexless individuals to whom the capacity for reproduction is undiscriminatingly ascribed, for to take couples into consideration would complicate the problem unduly from the outset. The demographer's societies are thus artificially homogeneous groups, and the most fundamental characteristics of their structure are ignored—so that, whenever it is possible to make an overall study of a society (as in ethnographical studies, owing to the fact that the groups usually considered are small), the real behaviour of the population bears very little resemblance to the abstract models of the demographers. These models are useful only for large-scale studies.

Economists have similar difficulties. In order to treat their subject quantitatively, they too must simplify, discount and distort their data. Even this is not always easy: in the economic studies included in this issue, the reader will find references to an exogenous factor which may, at any moment, upset the whole nature and order of magnitude of the forecasts. This exogenous factor is, indeed, everything that the economist has had to omit or discount in his treatment of the facts observed in order that he may deal with them as quantities. Moreover—and this is another aspect of the problem—the extrapolations of the economists can be founded only on long series of observations; and, as an economist himself points out in this issue (see the article by Mr. Tintner), the series at the economist's disposal are always, in some degree, matters of history. We are thus on the horns of a dilemma; we can either extend the series (but then their components become steadily less comparable), or we can restrict them in order to preserve their homogeneity (but then the margin of uncertainty in the forecasts increases correspondingly). Any gain in significance means an equivalent loss in accuracy of measurement, and vice versa.

This brings us up against a fundamental difficulty of measurement in the social sciences and the sciences of man. There are, no doubt, many things in our fields of study which can be directly or indirectly measured; but it is by no means certain that they are the most important things. Experimental psychology has run up against this major obstacle for years; it has measured, so to speak, for all it is worth; but whereas in the physical sciences experience proved that the progress of measurement was in direct relation to that of knowledge, in psychology it was found that the things which could be measured most satisfactorily were the least important, and that the quantification of psychological phenomena was not by any means in step with the discovery of their signification. This resulted in an acute crisis for so-called 'scientific' psychology; and, as we have just seen, the same discrepancy has been found, though probably to a lesser degree, in the other branches of study which have long been seeking to achieve 'mathematical' scientific exactitude.

* * *

Must we conclude that there is such a fundamental, irreducible difference between the natural sciences on the one hand and the social sciences and sciences of man on the other that all hope of applying to these latter the rigorous methods which have wrought so much for the former must be abandoned? Such an attitude, like that of F. A. von Hayek,[6] seems to me to reveal real obscurantism, taking this term in its etymological sense, which means obscuring a problem instead of clarifying it. The criticism to which the experimental psychologists of the beginning of this century, and the traditional economists and demographers, are open is certainly not that they have paid too much attention to mathematics, but rather that they have not paid enough; that they have simply borrowed quantitative methods which, even in mathematics itself, are regarded as traditional and largely outmoded, and have not realized that a new school of mathematics is coming into being and is indeed expanding enormously at the present time—a school of what might almost be called qualitative mathematics, paradoxical as the term may seem, because a rigorous treatment no longer necessarily means recourse to measurement. This new mathematics (which incidentally simply gives backing to, and expands on, earlier speculative thought) teaches us that the domain of necessity is not necessarily the same as that of quantity.

This distinction became clear to the present writer in circumstances which it may perhaps be permissible to recall in this context. When, about 1944, he gradually became convinced that the rules of marriage and descent were not fundamentally different, as rules of communication, from those prevailing in linguistics, and that it should therefore be possible to give a rigorous treatment of them, the established mathematicians whom he first approached treated him with scorn. Marriage, they told him, could not be assimilated either to addition or to multiplication (still less to subtraction or division), and it was therefore impossible to express it in mathematical terms. This went on until the day when one of the young leaders of the new school, having considered the problem, explained that, in order to develop a theory of the rules of marriage, the mathematician had absolutely no need to reduce marriage to quantitative terms; in fact, he did not even need to know what marriage was. All he asked was, firstly, that it should be possible to reduce the marriages observed in any particular society to a finite number of categories and, secondly, that there should be definite relationships between the various categories (e.g. that there should always be the same relationship between the 'category' of a brother's marriage and the 'category' of a sister's, or between the 'category' of the parents' marriage and 'category' of the children's). From then on, all the rules of marriage in a given society can be expressed as equations and these equations can be treated by tested and reliable methods of reasoning, while the intrinsic nature of the phenomenon studied—marriage—has nothing to do with the problem and can indeed by completely unknown.[7]

Brief and simple as this example is, it is a good illustration of the direction now likely to be followed in collaboration between mathematics and the sciences of man. In the past, the great difficulty has arisen from the qualitative nature of our studies. If they were to be treated quantitatively, it was either necessary to do a certain amount of juggling with them or to simplify to an excessive degree. Today, however, there are many branches of mathematics—set theory, group theory, topology, etc.—which are concerned with establishing exact relationships between classes of individuals distinguished from one another by discontinuous values, and this very discontinuity is one of the essential characteristics of qualitative sets in relation to one another and was the feature, in which their alleged 'incommensurability', 'inexpressibility', etc., consisted.

This mathematics of man—to be discovered along lines that neither mathematicians nor sociologists have as yet been able to determine exactly, and which is, no doubt, still to be elaborated to a very large extent—will, in any event, be very different from the mathematics which the social sciences once sought to use in order to express their observations in precise terms. It is resolutely determined to break away from the hopelessness of the 'great numbers'—the raft to which the social sciences, lost in an ocean of figures, have been helplessly clinging; its ultimate object is no longer to plot progressive and continuous movements in monotonous graphs. The field with which it is concerned is not that of the infinitesimal variations revealed by the analysis of vast accumulations of data. The picture it gives is, rather, that resulting from the study of small numbers and of the great changes brought about by the transition from one number to another. If the example is permissible, I would say that we are less concerned with the theoretical consequences of a 10 per cent increase in the population in a country having 50 million inhabitants than with the changes in structure occurring when a 'two-person household' becomes a 'three-person household'. Study of the possibilities and limitations connected with the number of members of very small groups (which, from this point of view, remain 'very small' even if the members themselves are groups of millions of individuals each) no doubt carries on a very old tradition, for the earliest Greek philosophers, the sages of China and India, and the thinkers of the peoples who lived in Africa and America in colonial times and before Columbus were all much concerned with the significance and peculiar properties of numbers. The Indo-European civilization, for Instance, had a predilection for the figure 'three', while the African and Amerindian peoples tended to think in 'fours'; and the choice made had definite logical and mathematical implications.

At all events, this return to small numbers was bound to have unforeseen consequences in the field of modern thought.

It is not, of course, for us to assess the scope of the revolution in economics caused by the work of von Neumann and Morgenstern, to which we have already alluded on several occasions. But the sociologist and the historian of thought are certainly entitled to attempt to understand the general changes in mental attitudes brought about by the introduction of new views—and not only among economists. Until recent years, the work of economists was based exclusively on statistics and function analysis. They considered large numbers and long series of variations in time and space, plotted curves from them, and endeavoured to determine correlations. Such investigations were, and quite rightly still are, very well regarded, as they make it possible to foresee or forestall certain undesirable correlations, or to perpetuate, and foster others which are considered to be desirable. To a certain extent—though people are not always agreed on how much—these speculations are useful; but they involve so much abstraction and such enormous groups of variables that, in the first place, there can never be any certainty that the suggested interpretation is the only one possible, or even the best (or indeed, in most cases, that it will produce any result); and in the second place, even on the most favourable assumption, when experience confirms the forecast in all respects, we never know quite what happens, because none of us ever encounters in real life those creations of reason with which economists habitually consort and which go by the names of marginal utility, profit-earning capacity, productivity and profit, etc.

On the other hand, when we look at the *Theory of Games*, what do we find? Firstly, no doubt, a more complicated and delicate mathematical apparatus than that found in economics or even econometric treatises. But at the same time, paradoxically enough, the things talked about are much simpler. They are no longer abstractions, but people and groups of people—generally small groups of two, three or four players, such as those made up for chess, bridge, or poker. Secondly, these players are engaged in operations which all correspond to experiences of actual life: they fight or form alliances, conspire with or against one another, co-operate or exploit each other. This, therefore, is a form of economics which aims at a very high standard of mathematical accuracy and, at the same time, resolutely concentrates on actual beings, encountered in real life, with an immediate historical and psychological significance.

When all is said and done, the specialists must decide what this new economics is worth. All I shall do is to point out that it derives from both the great schools of thought between which economics has hither to been divided—pure, or would-be pure, economics, which is inclined to treat *homo oeconomicus* as a perfectly rational individual, and sociological and historical economics as originated by Karl Marx, which aims, primarily, at providing the dialectical apparatus for a struggle. Both these schools are represented in von Neumann's theory. For the first time, therefore, so-called bourgeois and capitalistic economics and Marxist economics have a common language at their disposal. This does not mean, of course; that they are likely to come to an agreement; but at least they have common ground for discussion, and it is the mathematical approach which has made this surprising development possible.

A second example is furnished by social psychology, and more particularly by the work of Louis Guttman,[8] first presented in the monumental *American Soldier*, and again, very recently, in the collective work *Mathematical Thinking in the Social Sciences*.[9] When, at the beginning of the last world war, the American military authorities decided to call in social scientists on a very large scale in order to introduce a little order and clarity into the psychological and sociological problems of recruitment and selection, the investigators, at the very outset, came up against the difficulty of how to assign numerical values to the apparently heterogeneous answers to the questionnaires, so that they might be compared.

While Lazarsfeld was pursuing his investigations in an endeavour to provide an objective basis for the concept of character, founded on the notion of probability mechanisms,[10] Guttman struck out on quite a different line with probably more revolutionary implications. He noted that a numerical scale could be worked out immediately in certain special cases where the questions were expressed and classified in ascending order of magnitude. In a questionnaire on stature, for instance, if I ask for an answer to the following questions: Are you over 4 ft. 11 in. tall? over 5 ft. 3 in.? over 5 ft. 7 in.? and so on, any individual who answers 'yes' to the third question must automatically answer 'yes' to the preceding questions (but not necessarily to the questions coming after). Experience shows that the numerical scales so obtained show certain remarkable features of harmony and regularity, which are immediately apparent; they thus intuitively reflect the clarity of logical and psychological structure in the corresponding questionnaires. Guttman has however succeeded in, so to speak, reversing this relationship between the social sciences and mathematics. He has shown that, even for questionnaires designed on other lines, where the psychological and logical structure is not known in advance, it is always possible to rearrange the replies so as to rediscover the ideal balance. On the other hand, the manipulations by which this has been effected make it possible to break down the original questionnaire into its logical and psychological components, so that what appears to be a purely formal approach to the results of a questionnaire in fact enables us to subject it to critical scrutiny, i.e. becomes an instrument of discovery in the social sciences themselves.

In his latest publications[11] Guttman, reverting to certain traditional problems of social psychology and, in particular, to the fundamental themes in the thinking of his great forerunners, Spearman and Thurstone, throws an entirely new light on the psychological problems dealt with in the classical tradition by factor analysis; he opens up new possibilities for the methods of selection by tests, and for the theoretical interpretation of the function and value of such tests. At the same time, and certainly not deliberately, he provides historians, sociologists and anthropologists, for the first time, with a mathematical method that can be applied to the problem of the development and classification of human cultures, and that is admirably calculated to solve the difficulties and remove the contradictions which have proved a hopeless obstacle to this type of investigation ever since the days of Condorcet and Comte.

* * *

These two examples, drawn respectively from economics and from social psychology, will—I hope—give a better idea of the scope and novelty of the upheavals which are now taking place in the social sciences and the sciences of man, under the impact of the latest trends in modern mathematical thought. The articles that follow will illustrate what has been suggested above. In order to gain an accurate idea of the situation, it will, however, be essential to supplement what they have to tell us by reading the great works mentioned in this introduction, and a few others[12] the most important of which are listed in the bibliographies given in the articles in this issue of the *Bulletin*. It is also necessary, unfortunately, to allow for two difficulties.

The enormous majority of social scientists have, even now, had a classical or empirical training. Very few of them have a mathematical background and, even if they have, it is often very elementary and very conservative. The new openings offered to the social sciences by certain aspects of contemporary mathematical thinking will therefore call for a considerable effort of adaptation on the part of the social scientists. A good example of what can be done in this direction was recently set by the Social Science Research Council of the United States of America, which, during the summer of 1953, organized a mathematics seminar for social scientists at Dartmouth College in New Hampshire. Six mathematicians gave an eight-week course for 42 persons on the principles of the set theory, the group theory and the calculus of probabilities.

It is to be hoped that experiments of this sort will be made more often and more generally, but we must not be blind to the fact that they are only improvisations and makeshifts. They will probably help established social scientists not to lose their footing completely in the present upheavals; but we must also think of the rising generation, which will furnish the teachers and research workers of tomorrow. At the present time, the syllabuses of higher education make no provision for their training in mathematics. If the social sciences are really to become sciences and, to put the matter in a nutshell, are still to exist twenty years hence, reforms are urgently necessary. We can be sure, even now, that future young social scientists will need a sound, modern training in mathematics, without which they will be swept from the scientific scene. From this point of view, UNESCO has a very important duty to perform. The need for a revision of syllabuses is felt in all countries; but the teachers and administrators, most of whom have had a traditional training, are intellectually ill-equipped to plan and carry out such a revision. International action by the very few specialists throughout the world who are now able to think both mathematically and sociologically, in terms of the new situation, therefore seems particularly desirable. UNESCO would render the social sciences an incalculable service if it concentrated on working out a sort of theoretical model course in social science (which could subsequently be adapted to suit local circumstances), that would strike a proper balance between the traditional contribution of those sciences and the revolutionary new offerings of mathematical research and culture.

It would, however, be wrong to suppose that the whole problem consists simply in reorganizing instruction, so as to enable social scientists to take advantage of the latest advances in mathematical thought. It is not simply, nor indeed mainly, a question taking over methods and results from mathematics wholesale. The special needs of the social sciences, and the distinctive features of the subjects of their study, necessitate a special effort of adaptation and invention on the part of mathematicians. One-way collaboration is not enough. On the one hand, mathematics will help the advance of the social sciences but, on the other, the special requirements of those sciences will open up new possibilities for mathematics. Viewed in this light, a new form of mathematics therefore has to be developed. This cross-fertilization has, for the past two years, been the main object of the Seminar on the Use of Mathematics in the Human and Social Sciences organized at UNESCO House in 1953 and 1954 under the auspices of the International Social Science Council, in which mathematicians, physicists and biologists (on the natural science side) and economists, psychologists, sociologists, historians, linguists, anthropologists and psycho-analysts (on the human and social science side) have taken part. It is still too early to assess the results of this daring experiment; but whatever shortcomings it may have had—which are only to be expected in this period of trial and error—all involved in it are unanimous in stating that they gained much from the seminar. For man suffers quite as much, in his inner life, from 'intellectual watertight compartments' as he does, in his community life, from the distrust and hostility between different groups. By working for the co-ordination of methods of thought, which cannot forever remain entirely unrelated in the various spheres of knowledge, we are helping in the quest for an inner harmony which may be, on a different level from that with which UNESCO is concerned but no less truly, the real condition for wisdom and peace.

Notes

1. Trubetskoy, *Grundzuge der Phonologie*, 1939.
2. First systematically expounded by Claude Shannon, the engineer and mathematician, in *Mathematics Theory of Communication*, 1949.
3. J. von Neumann and O. Morgenstern, *Theory of Games and Economic Behaviour*, 1944.
4. N. Wiener, *Cybernetics, or Control and Communication in the Animal and the Machine*, 1948.
5. G. Uday Yule, *Statistical Study of Literary Vocabulary*, 1945.
6. F. A. von Hayek, *Scientism and the Study of Society*, 1952.
7. C. Lévi-Strauss, *Les structures élémentaires de la parenté*, 1949.
8. *American Soldier*. Edited by S. A. Stouffer, 4 vols., 1949–50.
9. Edited by P.F. Lazarsfeld, 1954.
10. P. F. Lazarsfeld. A Conceptual Introduction to Latent Structure Analysis, *Mathematical Thinking in to Social Sciences*, 1954, Chapter 7.
11. Louis Guttman, *A New Approach to Factor Analysis: The Radex*, op. cit., 1954, chapter 6.
12. Especially *Studies in the Scope and Method of the American Soldiers*, edited by R. K. Merton and P. F. Lazarsfeld.

LILY KAY, FROM *WHO WROTE THE BOOK OF LIFE? A HISTORY OF THE GENETIC CODE* (2000)

A biochemist-cum-historian of science, Lily E. Kay (1947–2000) wrote extensively about twentieth-century developments in life sciences, foregrounding in particular the social, cultural, and discursive dimensions that make up scientific knowledge production. *Who Wrote the Book of Life?* details the fateful adoption of information science and cybernetics into molecular biology, emblematized since World War II by the popularization of the metaphor equating DNA to a form of writing or code. The present excerpt delves into the career of Henry Quastler and his early attempts to bring Shannon's theory into the realm of genetics to analyze chromosome replication. That Quastler's comparison between the amounts of molecular information in the human body and in libraries has lost its capacity to startle us today is a testament to the degree to which once disparate fields have become integrated—rhetorically, conceptually, and operationally.

Quastler's Quest: From Biological Specificity to Information

Histories of molecular biology have generally privileged "winners' " accounts, while "losers" have gotten short shrift and, in the process of the canonization of others, stripped of recognition. Yet works written outside canonical history afford equally instructive lessons. Quastler's efforts are illuminating examples of a well-reasoned epistemic quest and curious disciplinary failure. They also provide an opportunity for situating his project within the new scientific space traced by the intersection of cybernetics, information theory, and molecular life sciences. That new space was generally characterized by the grassroot forays into cybernetics of life scientists, among them Haldane, Kalmus, Penrose, Spiegelman, Lederberg, Delbrück, Sinsheimer, Yčas, Chargaft, and Burnet, certainly conveyed an attraction; their work did not constitute formal institutional or disciplinary ventures (as would have been indicated by symposia, proceedings, and funding).

Quastler embarked on building a new subdiscipline—an information-based biology—in a technically proper form. His output, in the form of articles, reports, symposia, and edited volumes, was prolific. He achieved a measure of acclaim in the 1950s as a pioneer in a highly technical intellectually challenging branch of biology. *Science Citation Index* (1955–63) contains nearly four hundred references to his work. Many people were impressed with his biomathematical prowess and valued his theoretical framework, but his work was plagued by problems: outdated data, unwarranted assumptions, some dubious numerology, and, importantly, an inability to generate an experimental agenda. These weaknesses, coupled with Quastler's early death, led to the eventual eclipse of his quantitative studies. Yet his discursive framework survived and flourished, as did the cybernetic imagery he propagated. Its semiotic impact endured long after project fell into obscurity.

Like many European refugee scientists, Henry Quastler (1908–63) arrived in New York in 1939 from Vienna with impressive credentials and uncertain prospects. He had received a medical degree from the University of Vienna in 1932, with a focus on histology and radiology, buttressed by training in physics, chemistry, and mathematics. With his chances for a medical career in Austria rapidly dwindling after 1933, Quastler moved to Tirana, Albania, where his five-year stay led to some unusual advances. Charming, cultured, and skilled, he allegedly won the confidence of Albania's King Zog (Ahmed Bey Zogu) and became court physician. As chief of radiology at the Tirana General Hospital he managed to carry out clinical research in radiology, as well as experimental studies on malaria, the latter earning him a position in 1939 with the local bureau of Rockefeller's International Health Board. That year, with Mussolini pressing on Albania's border, the unpopular Zog fled to Greece, while Henry Quastler, rescued by Rockefeller Foundation officer Marston Bates, sailed to America. Bates had argued that Quastler possessed "a first class scientific mind—apparently a rather rare phenomenon" that would be a pity to waste. Within a year Quastler was employed as assistant radiologist at New Rochelle Hospital in New York. In 1942 he relocated to Urbana, Illinois, where he became chief radiologist of the prestigious Carle Hospital Clinic, an offshoot of the Mayo Clinic.[1]

With a penchant for research and a score of publications to his credit, Quastler soon associated himself with the University of Illinois. He made friends exceptionally easily, especially through the "Viennese mafia," as Heinz von Foerster put it. He participated informally in research, gaming a half-time appointment in radiobiology in 1947, while pursuing full-time medical practice. The University of Illinois was then modernizing and expanding its research programs, building up computing and cybernetics, molecular biology, and high-energy physics. Part of the Argonne National Laboratory Midwestern consortium, the university was then operating Betatron, a powerful electron accelerator, as a centerpiece of its high-energy physics and biomedical research. Quastler's studies of the effects of X rays on organisms and the role of the Betatron in cancer therapy fit squarely within that postwar agenda. After giving up his medical practice in 1949, he was appointed assistant professor of physiology at the new Control Systems Laboratory. The study of the therapeutic effects of radiation became his venue for "healing the world's wounds" inflicted by the atom bomb. While maintaining an active experimental program (and secret war work) in radiobiology, Quastler's scientific imagination, social skills, and relentless energies turned to applications of information theory to biology. Warren Weaver was "very well impressed by Q.," by his command of physics and by his close familiarity with the work in England.[2]

Several years in advance of a DNA-based molecular biology that featured the genome as a "text" and protein synthesis as translation of "instructions," Quastler had used these concepts to establish measures for genetic information based on knowledge of protein structure, specificity, and function. Surrounded in the late 1940s by friends such as Warren McCulloch and Heinz von Foerster (a leader of cybernetics) and captivated by the Wiener-Shannon theory, the Macy conferences, and von Neumann's lectures, Quastler joined the champions of the cybernetic vision of life. Teaming up with physicists and chemists, he combined his knowledge of cytology and genetics with his newly upgraded mathematical skills to erect an applied framework for quantifying the information flow in biological control systems. His close collaboration with Sydney M. Dancoff (1913–51) was especially significant, initiating them both into the terra incognita of cybernetics. A leading theoretical physicist of his generation, Dancoff, as participant with Quastler in the Betatron group, was branching away from quantum electrodynamics and nuclear physics to pursue his interest in biological growth, biological complexity, and reproduction as a problem of stability.[3] Their collaboration led to the first technical application of the Wiener-Shannon theory in genetics.

Quastler and Dancoff's paper, "The Information Content and Error Rate of Living Things," written in 1949, benefited from critical consultations with Salvador Luria, Sol Spiegelman, Barbara McClintock, Tracy Sonneborn, and Aaron Novick and required major revisions that delayed its publication by four years. These exchanges engaged life scientists in new ways of seeing and speaking about organisms. In a bold departure from the biological canon that natural selection serves to preserve the accuracy of replication by disposing of errors, Quastler and Dancoff proposed a cybernetic system: a chromosomal error control. Viewing replication as a high-error (mutability) process, they hypothesized a checking device—a purely statistical process—within the elements that received the messages from the chromosomes. Brushing off Luria's objections, Quastler wrote Dancoff on the fourth of July, "I believe we do like the American Constitution and stick to the system of independent checks and balances. Our next problem ought to be: how can an organism go about evolving an independent check?"[4] Nature and society, he mused, were governed by similar control mechanisms.

They envisioned the complexity of living systems in terms of high information content, and the chromosomal thread as being

A linear coded tape of instructions. The entire thread constitutes a "message." This message can be broken down into sub-units which may be called "paragraphs," "words," etc. The smallest message unit is perhaps some flip-flop which can make a yes-no decision is evident in the grown organism, we can call this smallest message unit a gene (Note that genetic alleles are two in number for each character—not three, or some other number [sic]).[5]

And if a gene was to a chromosome as a vacuum tube was to a radio, or a neuron to the nervous system, then the property of such an element would be simply that of a switch, or a relay, or an amplifier, they reasoned. As such, the statistically distributed binary decisions in the self-correcting chromosomal system seemed truly amenable to a Wiener-Shannon analysis.[6]

With that analysis, the final paper derived an information content based on hypothetical "instruction to build an organism" and proceeded to use that formula to estimate the information content of a human being in terms of atoms: 2×10^{28} bits, and of molecules: 5×10^{25} bits. The information content of a single printed page is about 10^4 bits; thus the description of a human in terms of molecules would take up to 5×10^{21} pages—many orders of magnitude greater than the content of the largest library, the authors concluded. The approximated the information content of a germ cell as 10^{11} and that of a "gene catalog" as 10^5. They then used these figures to ascertain that the generally accepted theoretical range of error rate per generation (10^{-4} and 10^{12}) agreed with the estimated theoretical range derived from Dancoff's proposed checking mechanism. Their calculations remind one that numerical similitudes and mathematical correspondences have a long history of epistemic seduction. Succumbing to what biochemist Joseph Fruton has aptly characterized as the "hypnotic power of numerology" seems to be reenacted in new forms with every scientific generation.[7]

After the blow of Dancoff's death, Quastler mobilized other colleagues for his new venture through personal appeal and local gatherings. Inspired by British and French information theorists such as Denis Gabor, Ross Ashby, Colin Cherry, Benoit Mandelbrot, and Leon Brillouin, Quastler entered into collaboration with some of them, hoping to bring a similar kind of leadership to biology. The symposium on "Information Theory in Biology," which Quastler organized in 1952 under the auspices of the Control Systems Laboratory with funding from the Office of Naval Research (ONR), was intended to be a first step in extending the "new movement" of information to the life sciences, even if it featured primarily local researchers. The often-cited symposium proceedings represented the earliest authentic effort to rewrite biology as an information science.[8]

The symposium focused on four areas: definition and measurement of information; structural analysis; functional analysis; and biosystems. Of the papers in the first area only Quastler's centered on the salient feature of information theory in biology: the mathematical interchangeability of information with specificity. His paper, "The Measure of Specificity," devised a framework and case study that supplied a persuasive argument of linking information theory to biology through the central concept of specificity. Acknowledging the stricture that "information" in the Wiener-Shannon sense did not convey meaning, he nevertheless expected to construct powerful representations in the new biosemiotic space. Information, he reasoned, related to activities of living systems—designing, deciding, messaging, differentiating, ordering, restricting, selecting, specializing, specifying, and systematizing. It could be used in operations aimed at decreasing quantities such as disorder, entropy, generality, noise, randomness, and uncertainty, and increasing the degree of design, orderliness, regularity, differentiation, and specificity. Since specificity was the governing principle in life science, Quastler reasoned that, when properly qualified, an information content would supply the exact measure of biological specificity. Establishing an estimate of "enzyme specificity" based on binary choices of "right" and "wrong" substrates he showed that the expression resembled Shannon's entropy equation. His point was that the amount of specificity could be determined without reference to causal mechanisms of the nature of "reactive gadgetry." Thus Shannon's principle that the "quantity of information in a message could be defined independently of its meaning" also obtained in biology, according to Quastler.[9]

Of course, structure mattered; it imposed definite limits on the functional range of molecules. But according to information theory, when properly applied, *any* organized structure displaying biospecificity in a form of feedback or communication—enzyme, hormone, antibody, gene—was an information carrier. Proteins epitomized biological specificity. Thus Howard University physicist Herman R. Branson expected that an information theoretical analysis of protein structure would lead to discoveries of new biological properties. Proteins possessed especially attractive properties from the standpoint of information theory, he argued:

> They are constructed much as a message, since they consist of some definite arrangement of about 20 different amino acid residues. Thus, the protein molecule could be looked upon as the message and amino acid residues as the alphabet. We do not know if the letters of this alphabet (the amino acids) are arranged in words within the message or not, that is we know nothing of the redundancy characteristics of the protein molecule.[10]

But assuming that the message was one of the many possible arrangements of the letters and spaces (i.e., neglecting intersymbol influence), one could then use the equivalence of information and negative entropy to calculate the information content in proteins, based on the content of their amino acid residues. Branson produced such calculations for nearly thirty proteins (e.g., insulin, 3.55 bits/residue; salmine, 1.43 bits/residue) and even observed regularities in the distribution of information, which he thought might represent fundamental attributes of biological systems. Specifically, he intuited that these patterns held insights into the antigenic components of proteins and into the origin and evolution of life.

In remarkable resemblance to the reasoning and symbolic representations of genetic codes only a couple of years later, Branson and his colleagues from the Control Systems Laboratory embarked on a search for intersymbol influences in protein structure, in quest of regularities in the amino acid pattern. Applying Shannon's theory, where intersymbol influences in the English language had been measured, they chose twenty paragraphs from diverse sources (want ads, textbooks, newspapers, and magazines) that matched the proteins in their sample in symbol length, treating letters as amino acids and paragraphs as proteins. (Gamow, Rich, and Yčas preferred the more dignified Milton's *Paradise Lost* as their analytic sample.) That method failed to reveal a type of intersymbol influence known to exist in language. (In hindsight their result makes sense, since the assembly of proteins is determined by nucleic acid codons, with no logical restriction on their position.) The authors concluded with the inconclusiveness of negative results but conceded to the possibility of real differences between the laws of language-construction and those governing the construction of proteins.[11]

Information based on specificity of protein structure, Quastler argued, was a necessary but insufficient condition for biological function. Structural specificity constituted an upper bound to functional specificity, with only a fraction of structural specificity finding functional expression. Focusing on antibody and gene action as forms of highly specific communication, he invited to the symposium immunochemist Felix Haurowitz from Indiana University and immunogeneticist M. R. Irwin from University of Wisconsin, with the intent of estimating the specificities associated with the function of genes and antigens. Quastler also invited Joshua Lederberg, but Lederberg remembers being "pretty quizzical" about the symposium's aims and ONR's sponsorship. Lederberg worried that recorded discussions might spill over to topics subject to security classification. The virulence of McCarthyism and the sting of the loyalty oath in the academy deterred him from such potential security entanglements.[12]

Neither Haurowitz nor Irwin possessed mathematical skills for performing information theoretical analyses. Haurowitz merely described the specificities of immunity and antibody formation based on the protein template model, and Irwin lectured on genetic specificities in human, avian, and cattle blood groups. It was Quastler who fed these qualitative accounts into his information mill to spew data on measures of functional specificities of genes and antibodies. His mathematical manipulations seemed to yield an astonishing result: functional specificity could be measured in multiples of 9 bits. Succumbing to the hypnotic power of numerology, Quastler tentatively proposed then "biological specificity is quantized in units of approximately 9 bits," suggesting a selective mechanism at work. The degree of selectivity, he hypothesized, "could be achieved by nine binary decisions under optimum conditions of maximum efficiency and error-free operation."[13]

Moving on to communication studies of "bio-systems," several participants examined the hormonal control of blood-sugar level, as a scheme where the "address of the target organ" and the "instruction" it received were encoded into the hormone at the place of production and decoded at the place of action. Another participant, Kenyon Tweedell, analyzing the development of zygotes and identical twinning, praised information theory for providing a compromise to the age-old debate of preformation versus epigenesis: specificity corresponded to preformation, epigenesis to nonspecificity. He wrote, "The information content is a set of instructions coded into the fertilized egg as dictated by genetic constitution; if a section of the instructions happens to lie in the zone which will give rise to the part to which this section refers, the part will behave as if preformed."[14] This argument preceded Francois Jacob's analysis of the "genetic program" and Delbrück's informational reinterpretation of Aristotle's theory of generation by more than a decade.

Only Henry Linschitz, a physical chemist from Syracuse University, kept a skeptical posture, offering a perceptive critique of the application of information theory to biology. Physical entropy did not provide a proper measure for the *functional* information contained within an organism, he countered. Examining the relation between structural entropy and functional organization, he questioned the applicability of information derived from entropy considerations in inert systems to living ones. Further, he believed that various problems complicated such applications, all of which related to the difficulty of defining the entropy of a system composed of *functionally interdependent* units. In a cell containing numerous protein molecules, entropy might be closely related to functional information content only if all the cell's constituents were chemically linked, so that the organized entity was truly molecular. If, on the other hand, cellular interactions occurred simply by proximity, by virtue of the existence of a common enclosing membrane, then physical entropy did not measure the essential organization of the functioning complex.[15]

One might calculate, as Linschitz did, the *physical entropy* of the cell, or its *structural organization*—the amount of negative physical entropy the cell needs to make itself—but these calculations said nothing about the way this entropy was channeled to produce a functioning cell. Functional organization was the result of nonstructural coupling between functioning units constituting the organism, he argued. (Recall that Schrödinger rejected even the equivalence of information and negentropy as a measure of structural organization.) Scientists must have also objected to the misapplication of a thermodynamics of closed systems to nonequilibrium (animate) processes.

Quastler was not deterred by these weaknesses. Shuttling back and forth along the provocative similitude linking the Wiener-Shannon measure of information with the Boltzmann-based entropy equation (a mathematical homology which did not necessarily prove the existence of an underlying common physical mechanism), he kept transporting new conceptual models and analytical tools into biology. Based on rough-and-ready estimates and piling assumption on top of hypothesis, Quastler built a semiotic house of cards: symbolic representations, quantitative relations, and numerological patterns. His pioneering investigations were not necessarily wrong, but they were devoid of predictive capability, means of theory-testing, and experimental agenda. Nevertheless they contributed to the construction of a new epistemic space, in which "biological control systems" could be represented axiomatically, independent of the knowledge of their materiality and components. By explaining precisely how cryptanalytic and mathematical principles of information theory could be applied to living systems, Quastler and his collaborators seemed to actualize the potentialities in Wiener's cybernetic vision, Shannon's communication scheme, and von Neumann's self-reproducing machines. Von Foerster's invitation to present these ideas at the Ninth Macy Conference on Cybernetics (1953) attested to Quastler's growing authority in the field.[16]

Quastler, by now, was receiving considerable scientific recognition. "If a man is 46 and famous, of fame newly confirmed on a trip in the big world, shouldn't he be showered with gifts?" Quastler asked his wife, Gertrud (a successful artist), on his birthday in 1954. "In the few months that he spent at Argonne before he came to Brookhaven he influenced more people than I would have thought possible in a few years or even in a life time," noted his colleague at Quastler's memorial service. (Quastler committed suicide the day after Gertrud's death.)[17]

Quastler refined his ideas on information theory in biology (and psychology) while pursuing his primary research on radiation biology and planning a major career move. After a brief interlude at the Argonne National Laboratory, which sponsored a large research program on clinical applications of radioisotopes and high-energy radiation, in 1955 Quastler joined the biology department of the Brookhaven National Laboratory in Upton, New York. All three national laboratories, Argonne, Oak Ridge, and Brookhaven, had their roots in the Manhattan Project and were greatly expanding in the postwar decade to form a principal research based for the AEC. These centers offered luxurious research facilities for those who could embrace the ethos of secrecy in science.[18]

The national laboratories were central to the tripartite agenda of the AEC, declared commissioner Henry D. Smythe in 1949:

> The first is to make more and better weapons. The second is to develop possible peacetime uses of atomic energy, and the third is to develop such scientific strength in the country as is needed in the long run to support the other two. . . . There are good reasons why the National Laboratories are needed and why their functions cannot be discharged by already existing research or development organizations. One of these, of course, is secrecy. . . . Another reason is . . . the advantage of gathering together a large group of men from the various divisions of science to work in close cooperation.[19]

As the only national laboratory in 1955 with a large research reactor and proton synchrotron in the billion-electron-volt range, Brookhaven offered the most expansive setting for research in radiation sciences. It also had the advantage of being formally founded in 1946 after the war, meaning it could bypass policies that constrained other national laboratories. Of the three laboratories, Brookhaven came closest to realizing the original model of a regional, cooperative research center.[20] In the 1950s, the Brookhaven symposia, sponsored by the university's biology department, centered on topics such as "Mutation" (1955), "Genetics in Plant Breeding" (1956), and "Structure and Function of Genetic Elements" (1959). These became prestigious gatherings in molecular biology.[21]

Quastler flourished at Brookhaven. While pursuing his two projects—radiation biology and information biology—his circle of collaborators and students grew steadily. In 1956 he helped organize a sequel symposium on information theory and biology, which was far more extensive than the one in 1952. Sponsored by Oak Ridge National Laboratory, Tennessee (which employed scores of life scientists in its health physics and biology divisions), the symposium focused on storage and transfer of biological information, information measures, information and ionizing radiation, aging and radiation damage, and information networks. McCulloch was invited to participate but declined, expressing his reservations about the project. He felt that information theory might not yet be suitable for probing biological complexities, and, in any case, its application hinged on cracking the genetic code. He wrote:

> I doubt whether information theory is yet properly attuned to the complexities of biological problems. To apply the theory in its present state except in a most rudimentary fashion we need to crack the code in genetics as surely as we do in the Central Nervous System. I presumed nature has somewhat optimized the code for the kind of noise it encounters, but even when we know something of the noise we cannot yet devise the optimum code enough to put a significant lower bound on the information capacity of a biological channel. . . . I have talked with Dr. Wiesner and several other members of the department and they are inclined to agree with me.

Indeed, the most illuminating aspects of the symposium—from the standpoint of the history of molecular biology—were the introduction, the papers on the generic code, and the conclusion.[22] The introduction included an elaborate primer (with exercises) on information theory originally prepared by Quastler as a technical report for the Office of Ordnance Research and, according to von Foerster, one of the best ever written on the subject. Designed to supply biologists and psychologists with the tools for recasting their problems in informational terms, this primer gave considerable attention to principles of coding as an aspect of representing information. Building on earlier studies of "protein coding" and obviously responding to the growing enchantment with the DNA "code," the primer explained symbols, alphabet, and "words" as units of representation and examined the status of different types of codes in information theory. It also probed the problem of organization in terms of systems analysis and game theory. Several exercises demonstrated how to apply these techniques to biological problems.[23] As part of the introduction, Oak Ridge biophysicist Hubert P. Yockey drew on the latest knowledge in molecular genetics, including the Watson-Crick DNA model, to devise an information-theoretical model of protein synthesis in the cell. His main argument, based on Dancoff's principle, hinged on the role of noise in the genome. He underscored the principal contribution of information theory in biology, emphasizing its ability to quantify the two key concepts of organization and specificity.[24]

George Gamow and microbiologist Martynas Yčas, engaged in an intense collaboration to decipher what by then was increasingly referred to as "the genetic code," presented a cryptographic approach synthesis. Assuming a "transfer of information from nucleic acids to proteins" and performing a cryptanalysis of the possible distribution of amino acids in two proteins, they showed that these sequences were subject to fewer strictures than language-based cryptograms; thus they expected protein decoding to be far more challenging than ordinary codes.[25] Yčas examined various "protein texts" (partial protein sequences), analyzed the frequency of occurrence of amino acids, and via the Wiener-Shannon relation, applied these findings to the problem of information storage and transfer in RNA and protein, all of it with, as he readily admitted, inconclusive results.[26]

In fact, a cloud of inconclusiveness seemed to hang over the entire 1956 symposium. The promotions of information theory in biology notwithstanding, the organizers conveyed an overanxious tone of those seeking recognition. Perhaps due to their quasi-academic status, or quizzical insecurity about their hypotheses, or just a sense of frustration, the concluding roundtable, led by Quastler, lacked the upbeat tone of earlier discussions.

> Information theory is very strong on the negative side, i.e., in demonstrating what cannot be done; on the positive side its application to the study of living things has not produced many results so far; it has not yet led to the discovery of new facts, nor has its application to known facts been tested in critical experiments. To date, a definitive and valid judgment of the value of information theory in biology is not possible.[27]

As participants put it, information theory furnished a sort of thread that enabled them to sense a continuum in the order of the universe, a means of relating existence to the nonexistence of life, a quest of regularities in irregular phenomena. It also encouraged analysis in terms of system sciences: the whole rather than its parts, the general instead of the particular, patterns rather than specific mechanisms. Information theory in biology was here to stay, they believed, but perhaps at a price of a compromise, as a discursive rather than mathematical tool. Given "the irreducibly relative nature of information measures" and the difficulties with quantitative applications, it might be "preferable to use information theory only in a semi-quantitative fashion," namely metaphorically.[28] By 1961 Yčas would reinforce this assessment. "Workers have been aware of information theory and have made qualitative use of some of its concepts," he conceded, then continued, "no explicit, and especially no quantitative use of information theory has, however, been made in practice."[29]

Nearly a decade after the emergence of the Wiener-Shannon theory and von Neumann's models of self-reproducing automata, with their promise of bringing operational techniques to "genetic communications," the technical status of information theory and cybernetics in molecular biology was dubious. By the late 1950s Shannon's skepticism regarding the applicability of information theory beyond the engineering domain seemed abundantly clear. As Cherry repeatedly stressed: information is not a commodity. He noted, "Signals do not convey information as railway trucks carry coal. Rather we should say: signals have an information content by virtue of their *potential for making selections.*" Von Foerster too voiced similar objections, arguing that it was the military context of command and control that created that confusing epistemology.[30] Yet despite the acknowledged technical impotence of information theory in molecular biology, its discursive potency intensified by compromising its technical structures. In the theory's proper form, and indeed in Quastler's mathematical analyses, all organized entities—carbohydrates, proteins, nucleic acids—contained information. Molecular geneticists (and biochemists in the late 1950s) singled out nucleic acids as the unique carriers of informational attributes. Information—as meaning and commodity—came to signify the privileged status of DNA as metaphor of a metaphor, a signification without a referent. This, however, did not diminish its scientific and cultural potency. The discourse of information linked biology to other postwar discourses of automated communication systems as a way of conceptualizing and managing nature and society. And it provided discursive, epistemic, and, occasionally, technical frameworks for the scriptural representations of genetic codes in the 1950s.

Notes

1. Coggeshall to Bates, 21 June 1939, Box 1.6, RG11, Series 704I, RAC. Letters between Bates and Sawyer 15 July and 1 August 1939, RG Personnel File. Staff Appointments Papers, R.S. 2/5/15, UIA. "Records of Training and Professional Experience" forms for Henry Quastler, 1947–55. Curtis, pp. vii-viii. The unsuccessful searches to find the Quastler Papers through the relevant institutions and family suggest that his papers are lost. I have been able to reconstruct his trajectory through several interviews: personal interview with Henry Linschitz, 16 July 1993; and with Heinz von Foerster, 26 June 1994; telephone communications with Quastler's niece, Joan Zimmerman, 2 June 1994, and with his sister, Mrs. Johanna Zimmerman, 6 and 14 June 1994; and J. Hastings, E. P. Krankeit, and Maurice Goldhaber, 15 and 17 November 1994.

2. Curtis, R. S. 2/5/15, UIA. Hewlett and Duncan, pp. 228–30. Von Foerster interview, 26 June 1994. On hiring in molecular biology at the University of Illinois, see Kay, *The Molecular Vision of Life*, p. 249. Warren Weaver Diary, 11 February 1949, Box 68, RG12.1, RAC.

3. Dancoff-Quastler Correspondence, AIP; Memorials for Sydney Dancoff, August 1951, fld.3; Dancoff's notes and incomplete manuscripts. Much of that correspondence revolves around their joint paper and the conceptual issues it raised. For a description of that collection, see also Robert C. Olby, AIP.

4. Dancoff and Quastler, pp. 263–73. Dancoff-Quastler Correspondence, fld. 1–2, passim, AIP. Quote in Quastler to Dancoff, fld. 1, 4 July 1950, AIP.

5. Dancoff-Quastler Correspondence, fld. 1; Dancoff to Quastler, 31 July 1950, AIP. In the final version of the paper Quastler offered the corrective that there were at least two generic alleles.

6. Dancoff to Quastler, 17 August 1950, p. 6, AIP.

7. Dancoff and Quastler. Fruton, "Early Theories."

8. Quastler, *Information Theory in Biology*, pp. 1–4.

9. Quastler, "The Measure of Specificity." In actuality enzyme-substrate reactions

display analog behavior, which through proper axiomatization may be theoretically "digitalized."

10. Branson, quote on pp. 84–85.

11. Augenstine, Branson, and Carver, "A Search for Intersymbol Influences in Protein Structure," pp, 105–18.

12. Lederberg to Quastler, 3 May 1951; and Lederberg to Kay, 7 July 1993. I am grateful to Joshua Lederberg for making this material available to me.

13. Haurowitz; Irwin; Quastler, "The Specificity of Elementary Biological Functions," quote on p. 188.

14. Bragdon, Nalbandov, and Osborne; and Tweedell, quote on p. 215.

15. Linschitz; and Linschitz, interview, 16 July 1993.

16. Quastler, "Feedback Mechanisms"; and von Foerster, interview, 26 June 1994.

17. Birthday file (1954), Box 3, Gertrud Quastler Papers, LC; and "In Memorium," (anonymous), 1963, Box 2, Gertrud Quastler Papers, LC.

18. Curtis. On the national laboratories, see Hewlett and Duncan, pp. 223–27; and Hewlett and Hall, pp. 252–70.

19. "Remarks by Commissioner Henry D. Smyth," 25 October 1949, pp. 4–5, Box 28.2, Series 303u, Detlev Bronk Papers, RAC.

20. Hewlett and Duncan, pp. 4, 224–25, 242–51; and Hewlett and Holl, pp. 253–54; Ramsey; and Rowe.

21. All the symposia proceedings since 1948 were published by Brookhaven National Laboratory.

22. Yockey, *Symposium on Information Theory in Biology*; McCulloch to Yockey, 25 April 1956, B M 139, McCulloch Papers, APS.

23. Quastler, "A Primer on Information Theory." According to von Foerster that primer was one of the best-written treatments of information theory; von Foerster, interview, 26 June 1994. On his contributions to information theory in psychology, see Quastler, *Information Theory in Psychology*.

24. Yockey, "Some Introductory Ideas."

25. Gamow and Yčas, "The Cryptographic Approach."

26. Yčas, "The Protein Text."

27. Quastler, "The Status of Information Theory in Biology," quote on p. 399.

28. Ibid., p. 402.

29. Yčas, "Biological Coding and Information Theory," quote on p. 256. I am grateful to Martynas Yčas for making these materials available to me.

30. Cherry, p. 169; see Chap. 1, this volume.

THE WORK OF ART

About 2,500 years ago, a work of art would change the life of Greek poet Stesichorus. It began with the story of Helen of Troy, a popular tale among poets of that time. Helen was admired for her extraordinary beauty, and scorned for causing the Trojan War, which started after Paris abducted her from her husband Menelaus and brought her to Troy. The accounts of the story vary: while some believed she was in fact abducted, others depicted her as having left her husband and gone to Troy willingly. Stesichorus, like his contemporary the Greek poet Sappho, enjoyed retelling the myth of Helen, and he, too, blamed Helen for the war. Until one fateful day, when Stesichorus woke up from a dream and discovered he had lost his sight; a result, the poet believed, of a poem he wrote describing Helen as a heartless adulteress who betrayed her husband.

Stesichorus, now wanting to take back the blasphemous mischaracterization responsible for his blindness, wrote a second poem, "The Palinode," in which he recanted the telling of the myth and suggested, instead, that Helen never went to Troy with Paris:

That story is not true,
And you did not go on the well-benched ships
and you did not reach the citadel of Troy[1]

Upon writing "The Palinode" and correcting his first version of the myth, Stesichorus, it is said, regained his sight allowing him to recover from his short and—in his view self-inflicted—blindness. The poems' drastic effects on the poet's life, even if only imagined through an eloquent anecdote, remind us of the force of a well-told story, the complexity of truth, the pain of erring and learning, and the capacity of poetry to communicate and challenge existing discourses and beliefs. What's remarkable about "The Palinode" as an act of human speech, is that the lines can only repudiate the myth at the same time as they repeat what they want to refute. By saying "that story is not true," "The Palinode" must repeat and retell the story. It must, in other words, present a truth that includes the false version in itself, only—and here Stesichorus introduces a twist—to transcend them both and suggests that Helen was neither guilty nor innocent, but that she simply was not there, because she never went to Troy. In this web of complexity lie the power and necessity of art: to allow us to recognize fact and fiction, myth and reality, but also to see how truth emerges from a complex set of relationships between truth, fictionality, arrangement, and chaos.

"The Palinode" presents an incredible example of art's investment in the processes of storage (remembering, restating, and revising the myth), transmission (choosing to compose a "counter-poem"; our knowledge of the poem through Plato), and communication (thinking about how and why to write the palinode to the achieve the best effects). These processes are the work of art—that is, they are the ways in which art facilitates communication both between the artist and the world—but also with other texts, traditions, and objects. In 1949, when Shannon and Weaver invent information as a measure of communication, they famously include the arts as information-processing activities. Like other forms of communication, they write, art follows procedures "by which one mind may affect another"[2] and so could be included in theories of information concerning such procedures. From a perspective of information, Stesichorus's "Palinode" is a daring project in testing the limits of art and the consequences of its communication—for the poet himself, who angered the Goddess and lost his sight, later for Plato, who used it in his own dialogue, and for us, learning about the myth of Helen . . . and the history of information.

Between Stesichorus and modern information theory lie more than two millennia in which humans have used art to define, test, challenge, and reinvent the boundaries of language and communication. This section of the reader, "The Work of Art," focuses on a particular moment in this history: the understanding of art vis-à-vis the newly invented mathematical concept of information. We chose this moment to illustrate the more immediate effects of information theory on arts and literature, while at the same time presenting this collection of texts—and so the concept of information—not just as an isolated historical moment, but within a larger and more complex history of questions surrounding the production, judgement, and enjoyment of art.

Shannon's formalization of communication as information-process offered a path to formulate the relationship between "art" and "information" in more practical ways. Following the popularization of information theory, philosophers and artists alike began to explore and enhance the concept of information as it applies to artistic expression, linguistic structures, and poetic composition. Beginning in the late 1950s, German philosopher Max Bense and French engineer Abraham Moles, for example, worked together to establish "Information Aesthetics" as a method to measure the information of a work of art. For Bense and Moles, art—like Shannon's information—was about organization and arrangement, and thus the "aesthetic value" of, say, a poem could with these new methods be measured and described just like any other system of signs. Their Information Aesthetics movement inspired a number of artists to produce computer and computational art, electronic literature, and media poetry—art that directly engages with information and information technology to challenge existing norms and adapt new technologies and method. Such engagement, as conceptual artist Jack Burnham wrote in 1970, would allow artists not only to use information technologies as artistic tools, but to envision how they ultimately would alter human creativity and "redefine the entire area of esthetic awareness."[3]

In the following decades, Yuri Lotman, Umberto Eco, William Paulson, and Haroldo de Campos turned to structural approaches to signs, channels, code, and meaning to rethink how language and literary or poetic texts function as communication systems. For Lotman, a text's basic function is to convey meaning between a sender and a receiver. But it also involves more complex processes of generating meaning and new information, since in order to understand a text one must bridge the difference between what one already knows and what one doesn't, between the "semantic potential" of a text, its cultural and social context, and one's own capacity to decode those meanings both within the text and outside it. Umberto Eco, in *The Open Work*, approaches these communicative processes from the angle of art as an unfinished and incomplete kind of work. Some works of art, Eco suggests, are not meant to be complete, but lend themselves to multiple and equally valid interpretations. Complicating a more straight-forward notion of the ideal passage of a message (arriving at a receiver just as the sender had intended it), the "open" work is characterized by resisting to impose definitive messages upon a text. William Paulson, in *The Noise of Culture*, proposes to define literature in terms of "noise" as a communication process not aiming at sending clear and transparent messages, but at purposefully disturbing, blocking, and preventing the transmission of information.

Questions of how literature and poetry communicate, manage, and negotiate meaning between the world, its cultural structures and traditions, and the reader were, similarly, for Haroldo de Campos, critical to understanding the value of art and the human against the backdrop of rise of technological civilizations and technocracy. De Campos found in concrete poetry—a genre of poetry using letters, words, and typography to create a visual poem—the perfect form to emphasize the materiality of language and its informational value over, for example, the verbal and romantic complexity of a sonnet. He saw the incorporation of technology and information theory into aesthetics and artistic expression as a way to make the work of art more accessible and less alienating—a way, ultimately, for humans to gain control over their technologies.

Not all embraced information and its epistemological promises. For Walter Benjamin, the new age and its turn towards information as the "new form of communication"[4] replaces the tradition of storytelling, a development that would lead to value immediacy, verifiability, and commodification over advice, experience, and sharedness. The first excerpt from Martin Heidegger's *The Origin of the Work of Art* stands apart from this collection of texts directly engaging with information theory and its vocabulary. If information theory offered new approaches to understanding the work of art, its manifestations as social and cultural products and objects, and its abilities to give form to human expression, it is because this is the kind of work art asks us, those moved, enraged, entertained, or surprised by it, to engage in. Heidegger's essay serves as a connecting point between the age-old questions of art, beauty, and truth, questions of representation, form, content, and a particular post-Shannonian approach to understanding art—extending, in this way, their immediacy beyond their historical moment.

Lea Pao

Notes

1. Stesichorus, Ibycus, Simonides. *Greek Lyric, Volume III: Stesichorus, Ibycus, Simonides, and Others*, ed. and trans. David A. Campbell (Loeb Classical Library 476) (Cambridge, MA: Harvard University Press, 1991), 93
2. Claude E. Shannon, and Warren Weaver, *The Mathematical Theory of Communication* (Urbana and Chicago: University of Illinois Press, 1963), 3.
3. See Jack Burnham, "Notes on art and information processing," published in the catalogue for the exhibition "Software. Information technology: its new meaning for art" at the Jewish Museum in New York and the Smithsonian Institution in 1970 and 1971, 11.
4. Walter Benjamin, "The Storyteller. Reflections on the Works of Nikolai Leskov," in *Illuminations*, trans. Harry Zohn (New York: Schocken, 1969), 88

MARTIN HEIDEGGER, FROM "THE ORIGIN OF THE WORK OF ART" (1950)

Heidegger (1889–1979) was a German philosopher, whose ideas had profound influence on twentieth century philosophy and hermeneutics. His main interest was the study of being (ontology), time and temporality, language, technology, and truth; his best-known works include *Being and Time* (1927), "What is Metaphysics?" (1929), "On the Essence of Truth" (1930), "The Question Concerning Technology" (1954), and "What Is Called Thinking?" (1954). Heidegger opposed the positivism and technological determinism of the 1920s and 1930s schools of logical empiricism—in "Concerning Technology," art stands in direct opposition to technological instrumentalism. In "The Origin of the Work of Art" (1950), excerpted below, Heidegger explores the meaning and nature of art. Art, within his theoretical framework of truth and being, is not intended as a means of representation, but a possibility for opening up and revealing "the truth of beings."

[...] That which gives things their constancy and pith but is also at the same time the source of their particular mode of sensuous pressure—colored, resonant, hard, massive—it the matter in things. In this analysis of the thing as matter (*hule*), form (*morphe*) is already composited. What is constant in a thing, its consistency, lies in the fact that matter stands together with a form. The thing is formed matter. This interpretation appeals to the immediate view with which the thing solicits us by its looks (*eidos*). In this synthesis of matter and form a thing-concept has finally been found which applies equally to things of nature and to use-objects.

This concept puts us in a position to answer the question concerning the thingly element in the work of art. The thingly element is manifestly the matter of which it consists. Matter is the substrate and field for the artist's formative action. But we could have advanced this obvious and well-known definition of the thingly element at the very outset. Why do we make a detour through other current thing-concepts? Because we also mistrust this concept of the thing, which represents it as formed matter.

But is not precisely this pair of concepts, matter-form, usually employed in the domain in which we are supposed to be moving? To be sure. The distinction of matter and form is *the conceptual schema which is used, in the greatest variety of ways, quite generally for all art theory and aesthetics*. This incontestable fact, however, proves neither that the distinction of matter and form is adequately founded, nor that it belongs originally to the domain of art and the art work. Moreover, the range of application of this pair of concepts has long extended far beyond the field of aesthetics. Form and content are the most hackneyed concepts under which anything and everything may be subsumed. And if form is correlated with the rational and matter with the irrational; if the rational is taken to be the logical and irrational the alogical; if in addition to the subject-object relation is coupled with the conceptual pair form-matter; then the representation has at its command a conceptual machinery that nothing is capable of withstanding.

If, however, it is thus with the distinction between matter and form, how then shall we make use of it to lay hold of the particular domain of mere things by contrast with all other entities? But perhaps this characterization in terms of matter and form would recover its defining power if only we reversed the process of expanding and emptying these concepts. Certainly, but this presupposes that we know in what sphere of beings they realize their true defining power. That this is the domain of mere things is so far only an assumption. Reference to the copious use made of this conceptual framework in aesthetics might sooner lead to the idea that matter and form are specifications stemming from the nature of the art work and were in the first place transferred from it back to the thing. Where does the matter-form structure have its origin—in the thingly character of the thing or in the workly character of the art work?

The self-contained block of granite is something material in a definite if unshapely form. Form means here the distribution and arrangement of the material parts in spatial locations, resulting in a particular shape, namely that of a block. But a jug, an ax, a shoe are also matter occurring in a form. Form as shape is not the consequence here of a prior distribution of the matter. The form, on the contrary, determines the arrangement of the matter. Even more, it prescribes in each case the kind and selection of the matter—impermeable for a jug, sufficiently hard for an ax, firm yet flexible for shoes. Such usefulness is never assigned or added on afterward to a being of the type of a jug, ax, or pair of shoes. But neither is it something that floats somewhere above it as an end.

Usefulness is the basic feature from which this entity regards us, that is, flashes at us and thereby is present and thus is this entity. Both the formative act and the choice of material—a choice given with the act—and therewith the dominance of the conjunction of matter and form, are all grounded in such usefulness. A being that falls under usefulness is always the product of a process of making. It is made as a piece of equipment for something. As determinations of beings, accordingly, matter and form have their proper place in the essential nature of equipment. This name designates what is produced expressly for an employment and use. Matter and form are in no case original determinations of the thingness of the mere thing.

A piece of equipment, a pair of shoes for instance, when finished, is also self-contained like the mere thing, but it does not have the character of having taken shape by itself like the granite boulder. On the other hand, equipment displays an affinity with the art work insofar as it is something produced by the human hand. However, by its self-sufficient presence the work of art is similar rather to the mere thing which has taken shape by itself and is self-contained. Nevertheless we do not count such works among mere things. As a rule it is the use-objects around us that are the nearest and authentic things. Thus the piece of equipment is half thing, because characterized by thingliness, and yet it is something more; at the same time it is half art work and yet something less, because lacking the self-sufficiency of the art work. Equipment has a peculiar position intermediate between thing and work, assuming that such a calculated ordering of them is permissible.

The matter-form structure, however, by which the being of a piece of equipment is first determined, readily presents itself as the immediately intelligible constitution of every entity, because here man himself as maker participates in the way in which the piece of equipment comes into being. Because equipment takes an intermediate place between mere thing and work, the suggestion is that nonequipmental beings—things and works and ultimately everything that is—are to be comprehended with the help of the being of equipment (the matter-form structure).

The inclination to treat the matter-form structure as *the* constitution of every entity receives a yet additional impulse from the fact that on the basis of a religious faith, namely, the biblical faith, the totality of all beings is represented in advance as something created, which here means made. The philosophy of this faith can of course assure us that all of God's creative work is to be thought of as different from the action of a craftsman. Nevertheless, if at the same time or even beforehand, in accordance with a presumed predetermination of Thomistic philosophy for interpreting the Bible, the *ens creatum* is conceived as a unity of *materia* and *forma*, then faith is expounded by way of a philosophy whose truth lies in an unconcealedness of beings which differs in kind from the world believed in by faith.

The idea of creation, grounded in faith, can lose its guiding power of knowledge of beings as a whole. But the theological interpretation of all beings, the view of the world in terms of matter and form borrowed from an alien philosophy, having once been instituted, can still remain a force. This happens in the transition from the Middle Ages to modern times. The metaphysics of the modern period rests on the form-matter structure devised in the medieval period, which itself merely recalls in its words the buried natures of *eidos* and *hule*. Thus the interpretation of "thing" by means of matter and form, whether it remains medieval or becomes Kantian-transcendental, has become current and self-evident. But for that reason, no less than the other interpretations mentioned of the thingness of the thing, it is an encroachment upon the thing-being of the thing. [. . .]

If all art is in essence poetry, then the arts of architecture, painting, sculpture, and music must be traced back to poesy. That is pure arbitrariness. It certainly is, as long as we mean that those arts are varieties of the art of language, if it is permissible to characterize poesy by that easily misinterpretable title. But poesy is only one mode of the lighting projection of truth, i.e., of poetic composition in this wider sense. Nevertheless, the linguistic work, the poem in the narrower sense, has a privileged position in the domain of arts.

To see this, only the right concept of language is needed. In the current view, language is held to be a kind of communication. It serves for verbal exchange and agreement, and in general for communicating. But language is not only and not primarily and audible and written expression of what is to be communicated. It not only puts forth in words and statements what is overtly or covertly intended to be communicated; language alone brings what is, as something that is, into the Open for the first time. Where there is no language, as in the being of stone, plant, and animal, there is also no openness of what is, and consequently no openness either of that which is not and of the empty.

Language, by naming beings for the first time, first brings beings to word and to appearance. Only this naming nominates beings *to* their being *from out* of their being. Such saying is a projecting of the clearing, in which announcement is made of what it is that beings come into the Open *as*. Projecting is the release of a throw by which unconcealedness submits and infuses itself into what is as such. This projective announcement forth-with becomes a renunciation of all the dim confusion in which what is veils and withdraws itself.

Projective saying is poetry: the saying of world and earth, the saying of the arena of their conflict and thus of the place of all nearness and remoteness of the gods. Poetry is the saying of the unconcealedness of what is. Actual language at any given moment is the happening of this saying, in which a people's world historically arises for it and the earth is preserved as that which remains closed. Projective saying is saying which, in preparing the sayable, simultaneously brings the unsayable as such into a world. In such saying, the concepts of an historical people's nature, i.e., of its belonging to world history, are formed for that folk, before it.

Poetry is thought of here in so broad a sense and at the same time in such intimate unity of being with language and word, that we must leave open whether art, in all its modes from architecture to poesy, exhausts the nature of poetry. [...]

Epilogue

The foregoing reflections are concerned with the riddle of art, the riddle that art itself is. They are far from claiming to solve the riddle. The task is to see the riddle.

Almost from the time when specialized thinking about art and the artist began, this thought was called aesthetic. Aesthetics takes the work of art as an object, the object of *aisthesis*, of sensuous apprehension in the wide sense. Today we call this apprehension experience. The way in which man experiences art is supposed to give information about its nature. Experience is the source that is standard not only for art appreciation and enjoyment, but also for artistic creation. Everything is an experience. Yet perhaps experience is the element in which art dies. The dying occurs so slowly that it takes a few centuries.

To be sure, people speak of immortal works of art and of art as an eternal value. Speaking this way means using that language which does not trouble with precision in all essential matters, for fear that in the end to be precise would call for—thinking. And is there any greater fear today than that of thinking? Does this talk about immortal works and the eternal value of art have any content or substance? Or are these merely the half-baked clichés of an age when great art, together with its nature, has departed from among men?

In the most comprehensive reflection on the nature of art that the West possesses—comprehensive because it stems from metaphysics—namely Hegel's *Vorlesungen über die Ästhetik*, the following propositions occur:

Art no longer counts for us as the highest manner in which truth obtains existence for itself.

One may well hope that art will continue to advance and perfect itself, but its form has ceased to be the highest need of the spirit.

In all these relationships art is and remains for us, on the side of its highest vocation, something past.[1]

The judgement that Hegel passes in these statements cannot be evaded by pointing out that since Hegel's lectures in aesthetics were given for the last time during the winter of 1828–29 at the University of Berlin, we have seen the rise of many new art works and new art movements. Hegel never meant to deny this possibility. But the question remains: is art still an essential and necessary way in which that truth happens which is decisive for our historical existence, or is art no longer of this character? If, however, it is such no longer, then there remains the question why this is so. The truth of Hegel's judgment has not yet been decided; for behind this verdict there stands Western thought since the Greeks, which thought corresponds to a truth of beings that has already happened. Decision upon the judgment will be made, when it is made, from and about this truth of what is. Until then the judgment remains in force. But for that very reason the question is necessary whether the truth that the judgment declares is final and conclusive and what follows if it is.

Such questions, which solicit us more or less definitely, can be asked only after we have first taken into consideration the nature of art. We attempt to take a few steps by posing the question of the origin of the art work. The problem is to bring to view the work-character of the work. What the word "origin" here means is thought by way of the nature of truth.

The truth of which we have spoken does not coincide with that which is generally recognized under the name and assigned to cognition and science as a quality in order to distinguish from it the beautiful and the good, which function as names for the values of nontheoretical activities.

Truth is the unconcealedness of that which is as something that is. Truth is the truth of Being. Beauty does not occur alongside and apart from this truth. When truth sets itself into the work, it appears. Appearance—as this being of truth in the work and as work—is beauty. Thus the beautiful belongs to the advent of truth, truth's taking of its place. It does not exist merely relative to pleasure and purely as its object. The beautiful does lie in form, but only because the *forma* once took its light from Being as the isness of what is. Being at that time made its advent as *eidos*. The *idea* fits itself into the *morphe*. The *sunolon*, the unitary whole of *morphe* and *hule*, namely the *ergon*, is in the manner of *energeia*. This mode of presence becomes the *actualitas* of the *ens actu*. The *actualitas* becomes reality. Reality becomes objectivity. Objectivity becomes experience. In the way in which, for the world determined by the

West, that which is, is as the real, there is concealed a peculiar confluence of beauty with truth. The history of the nature of Western art corresponds to the change of the nature of truth. This is no more intelligible in terms of beauty taken for itself than it is in terms of experience, supposing that the metaphysical concept of art reaches to art's nature.

Note

1. In the original pagination of the *Vorlesungen*, which is repeated in the Jubiläum edition edited by H. Glockner (Stuttgart, 1953), these passages occur at X, 1, 134; 135; 16. —TR.

WALTER BENJAMIN, FROM "THE STORYTELLER: REFLECTIONS ON THE WORKS OF NIKOLAI LESKOV" (1936)

Benjamin (1892–1940) was a German philosopher and critical theorist. His work on literary criticism and aesthetic theory, human experience, and technological modernity, was among the most influential work in twentieth century philosophy and thought. He belonged to the Frankfurt School, a school of Critical Theory prominent in the interwar period (1918–1939). His writings were often experiments in thought and thinking; his writing style characterized by difficult, enigmatic, fragmentary, and circular prose, belonging thus to his dialectic philosophy. His most notable essays include "The Task of the Translator" (1923), "The Work of Art in the Age of Mechanical Reproduction" (1936), and "On the Concept of History" (1940). The excerpt below comes from "The Storyteller" (1936), an essay on the art and practice of storytelling, on the difference between wisdom and information, and on changing landscape of cultural and technological practices.

I

Familiar though his name may be to us, the storyteller in his living immediacy is by no means a present force. He has already become something remote from us and something that is getting even more distant. To present someone like Leskov as a storyteller does not mean bringing him closer to us but, rather, increasing our distance from him. Viewed from a certain distance, the great, simple outlines which define the storyteller stand out in him, or rather, they become visible in him, just as in a rock a human head or an animal's body may appear to an observer at the proper distance and angle of vision. This distance and this angle of vision are prescribed for us by an experience which we may have almost every day. It teaches us that the art of storytelling is coming to an end. Less and less frequently do we encounter people with the ability to tell a tale properly. More and more often there is embarrassment all around when the wish to hear a story is expressed. It is as if something that seemed inalienable to us, the securest among our possessions, were taken from us; the ability to exchange experiences.

One reason for this phenomenon is obvious: experience has fallen in value. And it looks as if it is continuing to fall into bottomlessness. Every glance at a newspaper demonstrates that it has reached a new low, that our picture, not only of the external world but of the moral world as well, overnight has undergone changes which were never thought possible. With the [First] World War a process began to become apparent which has not halted since then. Was it not noticeable at the end of the war that men returned from the battlefield grown silent—not richer, but poorer in communicable experience? What ten years later was poured out in the flood of war books was anything but experience that goes from mouth to mouth. And there was nothing remarkable about that. For never has experience been contradicted more thoroughly than strategic experience by tactical warfare, economic experience by inflation, bodily experience by mechanical warfare, moral experience by those in power. A generation that had gone to school on a horse-drawn streetcar now stood under the open sky in a countryside in which nothing remained unchanged but the clouds, and beneath these clouds, in a field of force of destructive torrents and explosions, was the tiny, fragile human body.

II

Experience which is passed on from mouth to mouth is the source from which all storytellers have drawn. And among those who have written down the tales, it is the great ones whose written version differs least from the speech of the many nameless storytellers. Incidentally, among the last named there are two groups which, to be sure, overlap in many ways. And the figure of the storyteller gets its full corporeality only for the one who can picture them both. "When someone goes on a trip, he has something to tell about," goes the German saying, and people imagine the storyteller as someone who has come from afar. But they enjoy no less listening to the man who has stayed at home, making an honest living, and who knows the local tales and traditions. If one wants to picture these two groups through their archaic representatives, one is embodied in the resident tiller of the soil, and the other in the trading seaman. Indeed, each sphere of life has, as it were, produced its own tribe of storytellers. Each of these tribes preserves some of its characteristics centuries later. Thus, among nineteenth-century German storytellers, writers like Hebel and Gotthelf stem from the first tribe, writers like Sealsfield and Gerstäcker from the second. With these tribes, however, as stated above, it is only a matter of basic types. The actual extension of the realm of storytelling in its full historical breadth is inconceivable without the most intimate interpenetration of these two archaic types. Such an interpenetration was achieved particularly by the Middle Ages in their trade structure. The resident master craftsman and the traveling journeymen worked together in the same rooms; and every master had been a traveling journeyman before he settled down in his home town or somewhere else. If peasants and seamen were past masters of storytelling, the artisan class was its university. In it was combined the lore of faraway places, such as a much-traveled man brings home, with the lore of the past, as it best reveals itself to natives of a place. [. . .]

V

The earliest symptom of a process whose end is the decline of storytelling is the rise of the novel at the beginning of modern times. What distinguishes the novel from the story (and from the epic in the narrower sense) is its essential dependence on the book. The dissemination of the novel became possible only with the invention of printing. What can be handed on orally, the wealth of the epic, is of a different kind from what constitutes the stock in trade of the novel. What differentiates the novel from all other forms of prose literature—the fairy tale, the legend, even the novella—is that it neither comes from oral tradition nor goes into it. This distinguishes it from storytelling in particular. The storyteller takes what he tells from experience—his own or that reported by others. And he in turn makes it the experience of those who are listening to his tale. The novelist has isolated himself. The birthplace of the novel is the solitary individual, who is no longer able to express himself by giving examples of his most important concerns, is himself uncounseled, and cannot counsel others. To write a novel means to carry the incommensurable to extremes in the representation of human life. In the midst of life's fullness, and through the representation of this fullness, the novel gives evidence of the profound perplexity of the living. Even the first great book of the genre, *Don Quixote*, teaches how the spiritual greatness, the boldness, the helpfulness of one of the noblest of men, Don Quixote, are completely devoid of counsel and do not contain the slightest scintilla of wisdom. If now and then, in the course of the centuries, efforts have been made—most effectively, perhaps, in *Wilhelm Meisters Wanderjahre*—to implant instruction in the novel, these attempts have always amounted to a modification of the novel form. The *Bildungsroman*, on the other hand, does not deviate in any way from the basic structure of the novel. By integrating the social process with the development of a person, it bestows the most frangible justification on the order determining it. The legitimacy it provides stands in direct opposition to reality. Particularly in the *Bildungsroman*, it is this inadequacy that is actualized.

VI

One must imagine the transformation of epic forms occurring in rhythms comparable to those of the change that has come over the earth's surface in the course of thousands of centuries. Hardly any other forms of human communication have taken shape more slowly, been lost more slowly. It took the novel, whose beginnings go back to antiquity, hundreds of years before it encountered in the evolving middle class those elements which were favorable to its flowering. With the appearance of these elements, storytelling began quite slowly to recede into the archaic; in many ways, it is true, it took hold of the new material, but it was not really determined by it. On the other hand, we recognize that with the full control of the middle class, which has the press as one of its most important instruments in fully developed capitalism, there emerges a form of communication which, no matter how far back its origin may lie, never before influenced the epic form in a decisive way. But now it does exert such an influence. And it turns out that it confronts storytelling as no less of a stranger than did the novel, but in a more menacing way, and that it also brings about a crisis in the novel. This new form of communication is information.

Villemessant, the founder of *Le Figaro*, characterized the nature of information in a famous formulation. "To my readers," he used to say, "an attic fire in the Latin Quarter is more important than a revolution in Madrid." This makes strikingly clear that it is no longer intelligence coming from afar, but the information which supplies a handle for what is nearest that gets the readiest hearing. The intelligence that came from afar—whether the spatial kind from foreign countries or the temporal kind of tradition—possessed an authority which gave it validity, even when it was not subject to verification. Information, however, lays claim to prompt verifiability. The prime requirement is that it appear "understandable in itself." Often it is no more exact than the intelligence of earlier centuries was. But while the latter was inclined to borrow from the miraculous, it is indispensable for information to sound plausible. Because of this it proves incompatible with the spirit of storytelling. If the art of storytelling has become rare, the dissemination of information has had a decisive share in this state of affairs.

Every morning brings us the news of the globe, and yet we are poor in noteworthy stories. This is because no event any longer comes to us without already being shot through with explanation. In other words, by now almost nothing that happens benefits storytelling; almost everything benefits information. Actually, it is half the art of storytelling to keep a story free from explanation as one reproduces it. Leskov is a master at this (compare pieces like "The Deception" and "The White Eagle"). The most extraordinary things, marvelous things, are related with the greatest accuracy, but the psychological connection of the events is not forced on the reader. It is left up to him to interpret things the way he understands them, and thus the narrative achieves an amplitude that information lacks.

VII

Leskov was grounded in the classics. The first storyteller of the Greeks was Herodotus. In the fourteenth chapter of the third book of his *Histories* there is a story from which much can be learned. It deals with Psammenitus,

When the Egyptian king Psammenitus had been beaten and captured by the Persian king Cambyses, Cambyses was bent on humbling his prisoner. He gave orders to place Psammenitus on the road along which the Persian triumphal procession was to pass. And he further arranged that the prisoner should see his daughter pass by as a maid going to the well with her pitcher. While all the Egyptians were lamenting and bewailing this spectacle, Psammenitus stood alone, mute and motionless, his eyes fixed on the ground; and when presently he saw his son, who was being taken along in the procession to be executed, he likewise remained unmoved. But when afterwards he recognized one of his servants, an old, impoverished man, in the ranks of the prisoners, he beat his fists against his head and gave all the signs of deepest mourning.

From this story it may be seen what the nature of true storytelling is. The value of information does not survive the moment in which it was new. It lives only at that moment; it has to surrender to it completely and explain itself to it without losing any time. A story is different. It does not expend itself. It preserves and concentrates its strength and is capable of releasing it even after a long time. Thus Montaigne referred to this Egyptian king and asked himself why he mourned only when he caught sight of his servant. Montaigne answers: "Since he was already overfull of grief, it took only the smallest increase for it to burst through its dams." Thus Montaigne. But one could also say: The king is not moved by the fate of those of royal blood, for it is his own fate. Or: We are moved by much on the stage that does not move us in real life; to the king, this servant is only an actor. Or: Great grief is pent up and breaks forth only with relaxation. Seeing this servant was the relaxation. Herodotus offers no explanations. His report is the driest. That is why this story from ancient Egypt is still capable after thousands of years of arousing astonishment and thoughtfulness. It resembles the seeds of grain which have lain for centuries in the chambers of the pyramids shut up air-tight and have retained their germinative power to this day. [. . .]

IX

The storytelling that thrives for a long time in the milieu of work—the rural, the maritime, and the urban—is itself an artisan form of communication, as it were. It does not aim to convey the pure essence of the thing, like information or a report. It sinks the thing into the life of the storyteller, in order to bring it out of him again. Thus traces of the storyteller cling to the story the way the handprints of the porter cling to the clay vessel. Storytellers tend to begin their story with a presentation of the circumstances in which they themselves have learned what is to follow, unless they simply pass it off as their own experience. Leskov begins his "Deception" with the description of a train trip on which he supposedly heard from a fellow passenger the events which he then goes on to relate; or he thinks of Dostoevsky's funeral, where he sets his acquaintance with the heroine of his story "À Propos of the Kreutzer Sonata"; or he evokes a gathering of a reading circle in which we are told the events that he reproduces for us in his "Interesting Men." Thus his tracks are frequently evident in his narratives, if not as those of the one who experienced it, then as those of the one who reports it.

This craftsmanship, storytelling, was actually regarded as a craft by Leskov himself. "Writing," he says in one of his letters, "is to me no liberal art, but a craft." It cannot come as a surprise that he felt bonds with craftsmanship, but faced industrial technology as a stranger. Tolstoy, who must have understood this, occasionally touches this nerve of Leskov's storytelling talent when he calls him the first man "who pointed out the inadequacy of economic progress. . . . It is strange that Dostoevsky is so widely read. . . . But I simply cannot comprehend why Leskov is not read. He is a truthful writer." In his artful and high-spirited story "The Steel Flea," which is midway between legend and farce, Leskov glorifies native craftsmanship through the silversmiths of Tula. Their masterpiece, the steel flea, is seen by Peter the Great and convinces him that the Russians need not be ashamed before the English.

The intellectual picture of the atmosphere of craftsmanship from which the storyteller comes has perhaps never been sketched in such a significant way as by Paul Valéry. "He speaks of the perfect things in nature, flawless pearls, full-bodied, matured wines, truly developed creatures, and calls them 'the precious product of a long chain of causes similar to one another.'"

The accumulation of such causes has its temporal limit only at perfection. "This patient process of Nature," Valéry continues, "was once imitated by men. Miniatures, ivory carvings, elaborated to the point of greatest perfection, stones that are perfect in polish and engraving, lacquer work or paintings in which a series of thin, transparent layers are placed one on rap of the other—all these products of sustained, sacrificing effort are vanishing, and the time is past in which time did not matter. Modern man no longer works at what cannot be abbreviated."

In point of fact, he has succeeded in abbreviating even storytelling. We have witnessed the evolution of the "short story," which has removed itself from oral tradition and no longer permits that slow piling one on top of the other of thin, transparent layers which constitutes the most appropriate picture of the way in which the perfect narrative is revealed through the layers of a variety of retellings. [. . .]

YURI M. LOTMAN, "THE FUTURE FOR STRUCTURAL POETICS" (1979)

Lotman (1922–1993) was a Russian semiotician, literary theorist, and cultural historian. He taught at the University of Tartu, Estonia, and, in 1964, founded the Tartu-Moscow Semiotic School, a structuralist and post-structuralist group of thinkers developing the idea of culture as semiotic system. Their work combined structural linguistics, semiotics, and cybernetics to build a model of cultural analysis, in which works of art could be objectively analyzed as complex systems of signs. In 1984, Lotman coined the term "semiosphere," describing the space and environment in which signs operate before they gain specific linguistic, cultural, or historical meaning. Among his most important texts are *The Structure of the Artistic Text* (1977) and *Universe of the Mind: A Semiotic Theory of Culture* (1990). The text below is a short theoretical letter Lotman published in the journal *Poetics* in 1979 devoted to structural poetics. The issue included, alongside Lotman, essays by Tzvetan Todorov, Roman Jakobson, and Siegfried J. Schmidt.

Dear Colleague,

I thought it would be most convenient to reply to your questions for *Poetics* not in the academic format of an article which would bind me to a systematic and comprehensive exposition but in the form of a relaxed letter in which I can assume the right to share my latest thinking on the key current questions in poetics, even if these thoughts are as yet unripe and ill-formed.

The most crucial aspect to emerge from my own thinking and the ideas put forward by my colleagues in the development of a semiotic and structural poetics seems to me to be a radical change in the concept of the text, or more precisely, a change in the idea of the function of the text in the overall cultural context.

One of the cornerstones of the concept of the text in any of its varieties is the conviction that a text is the result of embodying a linguistic structure in some material substance. Hence whatever has concordance in the structure outside the text itself turns out to be relevant. It is this structure that is both the bearer of the meaning and the active principle. The text then is left with the passive role of manifesting the embodied structure. This notion stems, on the one hand, from Saussure's opposition of *langue* and *parole* and, on the other, from the theory of communicative systems. From this latter point of view, a text is a technical transmitting link whose function is to convey the meaning adequately in its pre-textual essence from addresser to addressee. This is precisely the basis on which, ultimately, Melčuk's "Meaning-Text" model and Žolkovskij and Ščeglov's attempts at a "generative poetics" rest. Thus we are dealing with a fundamental and well established idea. And yet it still arouses objections. Using this kind of approach the scholar looks not *at* the text, but *through* the text. The text proves to be a kind of 'packaging' which serves only to transport the structure. So we end up with the revival of the traditional opposition of form and content. Except that by 'content' we here have to understand a structure (of language, meaning or other "ideational content") which, while it exists in some ideal state, is realised in the form of the text.

This shift in orientation is particularly striking in relation to the period when Russian Formalism was proclaiming "the self-valued word" and the deautomatization of the text as a law of art if we consider texts which are artistic in nature. Notions about a work of art being a text which is different in principle from texts in primary semiotic languages and its being distinguished from them by being oriented to expression are exceptionally fruitful when they release the student's intuition. However, this thesis is suspect theoretically. In the first place, an opposition between artistic and non-artistic texts in principle is dubious on good grounds. As we see it, it is not a matter of viewing the artistic text as a special case of an ordinary language text, but the reverse: any ordinary language text manifests certain features of a work of art. One might formulate a rule: no language (in the semiotic sense), taken immanently and in isolation, is artistic, whereas any text (with the exception of metatexts and texts in artificial languages) manifests to some degree features of a work of art. One consequence of this is to deny an automatic connection between language and text.

The concept of the text as an incarnation of extra-textual 'meaning' brings us back to the traditional aesthetic position against which the Formatists were in revolt. All aestheticians who are to any extent part of the Hegelian tradition view a text as having meaning only insofar as it represents certain 'higher' essences outside itself. Whether we speak of a text as representing some social collision (Eugene Onegin as a representative of the Russian aristocracy of the beginning of the nineteenth century), or see in the expression of the cultural-psychological substratum of a period ("Žukovskij's poetry as representative of the Age of Sentimentalism"), or finally, as the manifestation of the spontaneous evolution of the spirit ("Byron's works as a moment in the development of the idea of personality")—in all cases it is not actually the text itself that interests us. It is merely a mediator between the idea in the mind of the sender of the message and the idea in the mind of its receiver. The concept of "meaning-text" brings us back to that very same psychological attitude to research and to the same kinds of methods.

And yet the very fact that this methodology is based on such a long-standing and culturally significant tradition and the fact that many distinctive results have been achieved through its application should restrain us from criticizing it too lightly, let alone dismissing it out of hand. Clearly, some aspect of the truth is revealed from positions of this kind and if we can now perceive the inadequacy of this kind of method, that too is its due.

The Formalist idea of the autonomy of the text was an attempt to switch aesthetic thought from a Hegelian to a Kantian line. However, when the Prague School began to link the neo-Kantianism of the Russian Formalists with Saussurean linguistics, a definite yielding of positions took place. The text changed from something autonomous into a manifestation of language. For even a text's orientation to expression came to be understood as an enjoyment in the text due to structure, the removal of language from the sphere of unconscious mechanisms to that of the consciously perceived. The most powerful aspects of Saussurean theory and of Formalism turned out to be far from totally compatible. This could not be said to have remained unnoticed. In particular, we may glimpse here one of the impulses for the subsequent development of the ideas of the Prague Circle, an example of which has been the whole of Roman Jakobsen's brilliant work in the field of linguo-poetics.

The predictable result of the thinking in this direction was the notion that a text (excluding, again, artificial texts) is a manifestation not of one but at least two languages. Consequently, no single text can be adequately described in terms of one sole language. In this case we may speak both of total coding through a double code, in which event one or other organisation is perceived from different readers' viewpoints and of a combination of overall codedness by some dominant code with local coding at second, third, *etc.* degrees. When this happens the play with meaning that arises in the text, the slipping between the various kinds of structural regularities, endows the text with *greater* semantic potential than ones which use any single language. The natural conclusion which followed from this was that the text did not embody meanings, but generated them. It is not a passive container, a mere receptacle for content inserted into it from outside, but a generator. But the essence of the process of generation is not only in the expansion of structures, but also, to a far greater degree, in their interaction. Their interaction in the closed world of the text becomes an active factor of culture as a working semiotic system. A text is always richer than a language and cannot be automatically computed from it. (Hence it is precisely texts that a culture is bound to commit to memory, not just languages). A text is a semiotic space within which languages interact, interfere with each other and organise themselves hierarchically.

In emphasizing this function of the text, we by no means consider it to be its sole function. In the general system of a culture texts fulfil at least two basic functions: the adequate transmission of meanings and the generation of new meanings. The first function is fulfilled best when the codes of speaker and hearer coincide most fully, hence when the text is maximally monovalent. The ideal extreme mechanism for this operation will be an artificial language and a text in the artificial language. The tendency towards standardization which brings artificial languages into being and the urge they manifest to simplify their own description which creates metalingual constructions are not exterior to linguistic activity. No culture can function without metatexts and texts in artificial languages. Since it is this aspect of the text which is most easily modelled through the use of procedures we already have at our disposal, we have tended to notice it more readily. It has become an object to be studied and has come to be identified with the text as such, thereby obscuring other aspects.

The second function finds the mechanism that suits it best in the structure of an artistic text. One could say that the whole multiplicity of texts available in different cultures arrange themselves in a field formed by two extreme poles: the artificial meta-text at one extreme, and the poetic text at the other. The closeness of some particular kind of texts to one or other extreme defines their semiotic structure. It would be a mistake to presume that the second of these two extremes can be described merely by imposing on it the model of the first. An approach of this kind means our artificially abstracting just one layer of the communication in terms of which such phenomena as the poetic text, the individuality of the text (including the individuality of the human personality as a particular kind of text), the untranslatability of the text, the conscious efforts on the part of the creator of the text to make understanding it more difficult, and so on, all become inexplicable paradoxes of culture. However, the sheer number of such paradoxes is too great for us to ignore them with a clear conscience.

The fact is that culture as an integral mechanism is served by two functionally distinct types of texts. Some, the least interesting semiotically are really just technical intermediaries in the transmission of specific constant information along the chain of communication. The principles of the "meaning-text" methods are applicable to these texts. However, it should not be forgotten that we are dealing here with the artificial text formations, or with a deliberately impoverished functioning of the text and that the complex aspects of its working are knowingly ignored in connection with the role it has acquired in the communication. But one only has to extend this principle to an artistic text to see clearly that, even with non-artistic one, it is only partially applicable. The other type of text performs not as a transmitter of meaning, but as a creator of meaning. From single cases—the transmission of an oral message along several series of parallel channels leading to a complex interweaving of verbal and iconic-gestural signs, the involvement of peripheral semiotic means, etc.—to the most complex cases of coding in the artistic text we are confronted by immanent multilingual formations, the dynamic correlation of whose elements generates new meanings. Heraclitus of Ephesus claimed that "The soul has its own Logos which grows according to its needs." The mechanism for such growth is the text.

We may compare the dynamics of the thinking of the researcher in this case with the reasoning of the chemist who, in studying sea water, would first see in it a particular case of water in general and, having separated off the formula H_2O would then refuse to investigate the residue of its composition as "outside the system." But at a second stage he would discover the presence of many other ingredients in sea water, and by setting out their chemical formulae, would put the mixture of different substances down as a fact. The third stage would be when sea water acquired for him the character of an integral chemical mechanism with its own structure and internal self-regulation combining a unity or dynamic and static principles, a mechanism manifesting qualities and potentialities which would not be characteristic of any of its separate component parts. This is the situation that the text researcher finds himself in at the present time.

It follows from what we have said so far that further text analysis may be carried on in two directions. In the first the text performs as a meaning generator. In this respect it may be compared with the mechanisms of creative thought in the human mind. The text appears as a unity consisting of at least two sub-texts, in principle organized quite differently, and a mechanism on the metalevel which unites them and guarantees their mutual transmission. In this respect, the minimal model for the text is the trope: the putting together of two sub-texts differently coded in such a way as to exclude the possibility of a mutually monovalent correspondence and yet establishing on equivalence in meaning which is realizable only within the framework of some secondary coding, generates a *new* meaning which is not present in either of the separate sub-texts. The latest research work on the asymmetry in the functioning of the right and left hemispheres of the brain and the unity of the untranslatability and the constant establishing of equivalences between texts which tend to right—or left—hemisphere consciousness,[1] allows us to postulate a parallelism between the workings of a trope (as, in fact, of any text) on the one hand, and the individual mechanism of the mind on the other.

In natural semiotic situations the generation of languages from texts is no less common than the generation of texts from languages. This may be connected with the fact that it is texts that are in many cases absorbed into the cultural memory.

Meaning-forming processes take place both due to the interaction between semiotically heterogeneous and mutually untranslatable layers of the text and as a result of complex conflicts of meaning between the text and a context that is alien to it. To the extent that an artistic text cannot be semiotically homogeneous it is in principle not homogeneous with its context. The complex multiplicity of factors and multistructuredness of any cultural (especially artistic) context makes it inevitable that any text, except when it is included in a semiotically homogeneous context, must, in a certain semiotic framework be included in a context from the point of view of which it will appear strange and alien. The combination of the internal heterogeneity of the text and the heterogeneity of the context leads to a semantic 'flicker' effect—the oscillation of meanings between several extreme constants.

The functional difference between metatexts (and, for that matter, texts in artificial languages), on the one hand, and artistic texts, on the other, is confirmed by the following consideration: a semiotic communication system begins to operate as soon as a text is introduced into it. However, in this case two operations which are in principle different can be distinguished. Where it is a question of the adequate transmission of some specific information, the operation of the system consists in the simple act of transmission. Here the optimal case will be the one where the text fully corresponds firstly to both the speaker's and the listener's codes (presuming that they are adequate), and that it includes no signifying elements which are not provided for by those code, (i.e. the text is monolayered and monovalent). These conditions are not perfectly met by artificial texts. On the other hand, texts in natural languages (just like other messages which are really produced in the communication systems of some culture) only meet these conditions to some degree.

The operation of a text proceeds in conditions which are in principle quite different when it is performing as a generator of new messages. Here the text is required to provide polyvalence in decoding process and incomplete decodability in terms of the available codes, i.e. a certain-degree of incomprehensibility. While texts of the former type behave passively, the role of the latter type is to be active.

We can imagine some device which would in principle possess all the mechanisms of thought. And yet for its potential to be realized and for the system to start working, a text would have to be introduced into it. This situation is not just hypothetical. We know that a child who has never received any texts in any form from outside shows no capacity for consciousness despite the fact that his physiological thinking apparatus is in complete working order. The machine exists, but it has not been set in motion. Ultimately, every learning process amounts to our introducing texts into our consciousness.

Observation of the process of interaction of the semiotic world of adults and children (at those stages of development when there is the greatest qualitative difference between their types of consciousness) and of the influence of developed cultures on ones that are still at earlier stages confirms that the greater the gap and, hence, the more difficult the texts of the 'upper' culture are to decode as they are introduced into the 'lower' culture, the more powerful is their speeding up effect.[2] The new text is not decoded adequately for its meaning in the source context. An unavoidable shift in its meaning takes place. Eventually the results of the historico-cultural transformations which this text undergoes in the 'upper' and 'lower' cultural context alter it to such an extent that in many cases only a special analysis can discover their common source. This suggests that the cultural-semiotic meaning of the introduction of texts from one culture into another is not in their levelling up or down but in the sleeping mechanisms of one of them being set in motion. The incomprehensibility and undecodability of a poetic-type text (or, more precisely, the difficulty of decoding it) is a form of energy; one which sets in motion the semiotic mechanism of culture.

The penetration into the depths of the text which is so characteristic of the present state of the science (whereby isomorphism is established between texts of the most different levels—from a culture as a whole to the juxtaposition of two contrasting elementary sense units) may be compared with the tendency of contemporary physics to move deeper and deeper into the elementary particles: where we had previously seen only the mechanical sum of the elements we understood, now a complex world opens up which is hard to get used to—the source of the energy of thought.

The exteriorization of the internal mechanisms of the text on the syntagmatic axis is at the basis of rhetoric. While linguistic syntagmatics link homogeneous elements in a chain, rhetoric links heterogeneous elements. Hence linguistic syntagmatics mainly add up, while rhetoric integrates, turning a sequence of texts into a Text, repeating on the macrolevel the regularities of intratextual structure.

Taking this reasoning further, one might say that what turns a culture into a Text is internal polyglottism.

Dear colleague, please accept my very warmest good wishes and excuse this long "theoretical" letter.

Ju. Lotman
Tartu, 2.1.79
(Translated by L. M. O'Toole)

Notes

1. In fact any text is a complex combination of right—and left—hemispherical semiotic structures. However, the dominance of one or other system allows us conventionally to assign them to the workings of one or other hemisphere.
2. We use the notions 'upper and 'lower' cultures entirely conventionally. The fruitful and stimulating effect of child consciousness on adult consciousness and of archaic cultures on so-called "developed" cultures which may be observed in any number of cultural situations testifies to the fact that it is precisely the difference which is 'at work,' while the notions of 'advanced' and 'backward' are both culturally and historically conventional.

ABRAHAM MOLES, FROM
INFORMATION THEORY AND ESTHETIC PERCEPTION (1958)

Moles (1920–1992) was a French electrical engineer and communication theorist who worked on the relationship between acoustics, aesthetics, sociology, and information theory. He also held PhDs in physics and psychology, and taught at universities in France, the United States, Mexico, and Germany. In the late 1950s, Moles joined Max Bense at the University of Stuttgart, which would become the intellectual and artistic center for the Information Aesthetics movement. Moles was a transdisciplinary thinker, combining Shannon and Weaver's information theory with aesthetics. Unlike Bense, whose "generative aesthetics" focused on the aesthetic value a work of art contains or produces, Moles was interested in models of perception and the ways in which humans receive and interpret signs. His book, *Information Theory and Esthetic Perception* (1973), first published in French, develops the idea that pleasure, beauty, and aesthetic feeling are the result of informational processes, which can be mathematically analyzed and understood.

The Philosophic Value of Information Theory

Dass jeder sieht die Welt in seinem Sinn
Und jeder sieht recht, soviel
ist Sinn darin.

Goethe

1. Materiality of Communication

The viewpoint characteristic of this work is that communication is material. In order to be appreciated exactly, this viewpoint must be returned to the historical circumstances which gave rise to it. What differentiates man from animals is essentially his capacity to communicate widely with his likes, and it is not an overstatement to say that what characterizes modern man is the use of artificial communication channels. Admittedly writing and optical or acoustical telegraphy, which are among the most rudimentary artificial channels, date from a relatively remote period of civilization. But the conscious realization of the materiality of communication is extremely recent. Not so long ago, the ideas transmitted by interpersonal messages were so obviously essential that they overshadowed the material aspect: The ideas "transmitted" caused the transmission to be forgotten.

For Plato, Bacon, and Spinoza, the materiality of writing was only an accessory contingency from which, properly, thought should be emancipated; the myth of the frozen words in the third book of *Pantagruel* was only a pleasant tale without philosophical value. Alone among the ancient civilizations, the Chinese and the Hebraic, by a semimystical route, approached the materiality of writing as an intrinsic value. The Chinese long considered it a sacrilege to destroy any writing whatever, no matter how uninteresting, and the Hebrews founded a finespun interweaving of logical and theological doctrine on respect for "The Book" (*Torah*).

The invention of printing led the materiality of writing to be discovered; a continually growing *economic* value has taken the place of the value of *respect*, which has been pulled to pieces. The increasing *quantity* of signs, however depreciated by their very multiplicity, made evident the concreteness of the signs' existence, independent of the ideational value they represented.

In the invention of other channels for communication through space and time, for example, telephone, radio, sound recording, picture and motion recording, *Homo faber* preceded *Homo sapiens* even more. It was necessary for these channels to be invented for people to perceive that an aliquot part of materiality, namely, the *symbol*, transcends the piece of paper or the telephone cables; to conceive, in short, the existence of a materiality of communication no matter what the mode of communication. The importance of the "ideality" of communication in the conceptual presentation was modified when it was joined by its materiality.

While in the school of Erasmus it required a mental effort which could have passed for hair-splitting to examine materiality, in the century of newspapers, radios, records, and films, materiality is pragmatically imposed:

In the modern world there is a whole class of individuals who *handle* the material support of ideas: not only printers, booksellers, messengers, and

before artificial communication channels:	ideality	materiality
after artificial communication channels:	ideality	materiality

telephone operators, but also *communication engineers.* The communication engineer sees the vector *signal,* carrying ideas he does not know or care to know, pass in the telephone wires, circuits, and amplifiers. He must deal with the problems of "crowding" wavelengths, of the delays in use of lines, or still more concretely, with the rates to be charged for each word telegraphed as a function of the distance. The quantitative aspect of information foists itself upon him.

The mass circulation press first discovered the esthetic consequences of the materiality of ideas in a new art whose very conception was foreign to traditional techniques. In the art of assembling communicated messages, the synthetic art called *page composition* or layout (for example, of a daily paper), the artist looks for an esthetic value in assembling fragments of communications that he *does not make* himself. The clear dissociation between editing and composing and the irrelevance of what is composed make evident its materiality.

Discoveries in other modes of communication confirm that this was not a fortuitous circumstance, but a general property of the materiality of communication. Everything considered, this materiality is just the classic choice the artist makes between composition and fabrication: composer and musician, painter and color fabricator, architect and contractor.

Generally, the artist does not fabricate the material with which he works. Modern techniques have *revealed* and *promoted* to their true places as artists a series of "composers": the page compositor, formerly an obscure collaborator in the printing workshop; the cutter-editor who is often the real scenarist of the movie; the sound engineer of radio and recorded music. Modern techniques have emphasized the *independence* of the roles of the maker of the material (the author followed by the typographer, the musician, the maker of colors, the scene designer followed by the photographer) and the synthesizer (the page compositor, the orchestra conductor, the painter, the stager or producer).

A new esthetics created on the basis of this remark must first essay a systematic study of the materiality of communication, in contrast with the study of ideas, which was the spirit of classical esthetics, especially in certain domains, for example, literature. Consonant with information theory, this new esthetics ought to point out that every communication process has a common element, a *metrical* one: information per se, independent of the shape of the message, of the channel it uses, and of the reactions it provokes.

The viewpoint adopted here and the objective of this work fall into place naturally in the modern state of communication and derived arts: Historically, they are at the point of understanding the generalized theory; more particularly (esthetics in the narrow sense), they try to study the messages from the external world most easily *isolated: works of art*. [. . .]

3. The Fundamental Results

The fundamental point of departure of this study, following naturally from the materiality of communication is that *information* is a *measurable quantity* which characterizes the process of communication. To communicate, near or far, is to transmit something. What is transmitted is *complexity*. Information differs essentially from meaning: Information is only a measure of complexity. To transmit a message is to make more complex the space-time surrounding the point of reception; it is to produce a microreplica of the complexity created at the origin of transmission.

Meaning rests on a set of conventions which are a priori common to the receptor and transmitter. Thus it is not *transmitted*; potentially it preexists the message. Only complexity is transmitted from the transmitter to the receptor; it is precisely what is not present at the receptor; it is what is *unpredictable*. The measure of information no more depends on the number of symbols transmitted than on the effects of these symbols; rather, it measures the *originality* of the grouping of the symbols, as opposed to the *banality* of the foreseeable.

Originality is thus among the fundamental values of the theory. In the perception of forms, *originality* opposes *intelligibility*, because only *forms* are intelligible and they reduce unpredictability, hence originality. The cleavage between the values of originality and intelligibility makes intelligibility the operational synonym of banality in the message. The etymological meaning of the word intelligence, *interligere*, justifies the assertion that what is most intelligible is what has the most bonds (liaisons), and is thus what is most often encountered in the networks of thought. The most intelligible is at the same time the most banal; the position of the mind between intelligibility and creativity is only a transposition of its position between banality and originality. The concept of originality appears necessary to the human mind as one of its *central concepts*, the existence of which structuralism postulates and Belin Milleron has pointed out. It is understandable that development of this concept should give rise to a great scientific theory.

The study of form as the union of predictable perceptual elements, either in the length of the present, or discursively in a scanning process, has led us, by connecting form with some kind of *trace* of the present in duration (instantaneous memory, immediate memory, or memorization), to consider the perception of form as the epiphenomenon of a *direct perception of auto-correlation*; the study has led us to give autocorrelation an importance which psychology has not emphasized until now. A message is a complex *form*, and its rate of information measures the complexity of the form. Information theory furnishes us a ranking of forms. The message transfers complexity from one point of the world to another.

Certain *forms*, which reduce originality by making the message assimilable, are permanent. They may be *normalized* and *repertoried*; they are *symbols*. Many symbols exist potentially in the psychophysical elements of the message; those which exist actually depend on the modes of grouping which the conventions conserved in the individual's memory find in the message. Other forms are only statistical, approximate, and inform us no more than does a *wager* about the future of the perception on the basis of its present and past state. These statistical forms are expressed by structural rules which replace the preceding symbolization.

Among these forms, one of the most important is *periodicity*, less an absolute property in the mathematical sense than a measurable quantity. Periodicity measures the regularity of the spatial or temporal development of the perception, whether or not there is a conscious *scanning* of the message. Our perception is dominated by two sorts of physical time: one rather well defined; the other more fluid, more variable, the extension of the immediately perceptible duration; the latter is the temporal "field of consciousness." With regard to the periodicity of physical phenomena, the "length of the present" separates perception of the degree of rhythmical regularity, periodicity, as a *quality of the perceived substance*, temporal or spatial, from direct perception of *rhythm* or of a foreseeability of future events.

The periodicity of an audible sound is a necessary concept in acoustics. But periodicity in the physical sense is *not known as such* by perception; rather, it is conceived as a directly apprehensible quality of the *sonic substance* (*Klangstoff*) which fills time, similar to the color of a visual impression. In the domain of sound, this analysis makes pitch an important special feature of timbre (*Klangfarbe*) when the latter has a stable dominant for longer than the length of the present. Periodicity is perceived only if it affects durations which are themselves apprehensible: Rhythms, melodies, measures, etc., considered as cyclical phenomena, have been practically neglected until now by physical science.

From the properties of symbols and rules of form in the dialectic of information, it follows that the *successive subordinations* of these symbols and rules represent important knowledge about the structure of the message. Each further restricts the repertoire of primitive elements by increasing its redundancy. Any theory of messages, in particular of artistic messages, must determine these subordinate structures, their laws, and their repertoires. This will be the goal of a "message physics," a component of experimental esthetics.

Sonic messages and musical messages in particular provide the clearest example of this message physics. The musical message must be approached in its immediate materiality, not through the artificial operating scheme of the score, which interests essentially only the performer. Phenomenological study of the message, which ought to be descriptive, reveals the existence of the successively subordinated structures, which in fact characterize the most general message. The structures are built from the psychophysical elements of hearing. Assembled according to "harmonic laws" which include operationally the concepts of harmonics and timbre, these elements compose symbols, present within the quantum of duration, whose temporal evolution constitutes the *sonic object*, an experimentally separable entity. Within the extent of the immediate memory, the groupings of sonic objects constitute sonic cells, perceived as *forms* which enter into the macrostructures. The latter irregularly alternate banality and originality.

The analysis of message structures offered by information theory suggests the possibility of creating models of sensory perception by using computing machines functioning statistically, programmed as a function of these structures.

The musical message is typical of the real artistic message. Often *repeated* to us, yet without losing its value, this message leads us to examine how the subordination of symbols is effected in several artistic messages. The musical signal shows that in reality there are two distinct and simultaneous structurings of the psychophysical messages furnished by the message, and hence two partial messages:

(1) The translatable semantic message, with universal symbolization, prepares acts and obeys an internal *metalogic* (whatever this logic may be). Information theory was originally intended for this message because the semantic part constituted an object of thought to transmit for the purpose of determining reactions in the receptor. (See Cohen, 1962.)

(2) The *esthetic* message has symbols unknown to us and rules often little known; it is untranslatable and unique.

Each of these two messages conveys its own complexity; each obeys autonomous structural laws. They are both present in different kinds of messages, in proportions depending on the roles that the messages must play. A telegraphic message is mostly semantic information. A spoken message appears in general to include equivalent proportions of these two *aspects* of information. As for the musical message, while its semantic part (musical notation) is very structured, and hence conveys a small amount of information, its esthetic part is extremely rich in information which, as a general rule, *overwhelms* the individual receptor.

Reception of the esthetic message is conditioned by the existence of a limiting information rate, both semantic and esthetic. This limit is a function of the past and memorized *culture* of the receptor, as well as of his *attention potential*. In order for a message to be intelligible to us, the complexity that it conveys must, on the average, not be *too rich*. However, artistic messages are practically always too rich. Consequently, the receiving subject is obliged to *exhaust* these messages by successive re-presentations.

If not completely determined by this condition on intelligibility, the structure of the artistic messages is nevertheless conditioned by it and must create a counterpoint between the two types of information. The two types assert themselves on the receptor alternately and irregularly in successive packages of information; the message evolves progressively toward banality in the course of time or of the scanning of the message. For example, a very rich musical message makes great use of repetition, which progressively diminishes the rate of information.

The receptor's apperceptual limit, which introduces the condition on intelligibility, plays an essential role in the complex and interacting structurings of multiple messages. Multiple messages, in a sort of concerto, are those which use different sensory information channels (sound movies, ballet, etc.) or exploit these channels in different ways (recitative, opera, illustrated books, etc.).

The materiality of communication implies that communication must obey the fundamental physical laws governing all objects. Among the first of these is the *approximation* caused by the quantification due to perceptual thresholds, and the *destruction* caused by noise, which creates uncertainty in the message.

Noise constitutes the ground against which we perceive messages from the surrounding universe. These messages must stand out sufficiently from the background to intrude upon our perception. The perpetual and disordered agitation of this background implies two *uncertainty principles* in perception:

(1) The first connects our extreme threshold of sensitivity to our a priori knowledge of the qualitative nature of this perception, namely its frequency: Uncertainty about the perceptible signal X uncertainty about its frequency = constant. Thus, we can perceive a very weak sound only by making it emerge from the background noise *and* on the condition that we have an a priori idea of its pitch or timbre.

(2) The second connects the perceptible signal to the minimum interval required to perceive it: Uncertainty about the signal X uncertainty about its duration = constant.

These universal rules play a role in the perceptual framework analogous to the uncertainty principles of Heisenberg in the framework of the material-object world of physicochemistry. [. . .]

6. Philosophical Value of Information Theory

The object of this book was essentially to *present* information theory, first rigorously, then in with some immediate *developments*, and to apply it to some of the simplest and most concrete aspects of esthetic perception, taken as a special case of ordinary perception.

In a general way, we have adopted the Hegelian method in this book. We tried to find dialectical oppositions by characterizing the two poles sufficiently to make the contrast between them stand out, then by presenting a rapid and incomplete synthesis; we tried to find in this synthesis one of the terms of new opposition and to bring forth its opposite pole. By this mechanism, overtaking and passing beyond the initial dipole, we tried ceaselessly to enlarge the initial viewpoint.

In conjunction with the fundamental dialectic order-disorder inherited from thermodynamics, information theory suggests a number of similar *dialectical dipoles* deriving from the first:

Order	Disorder
Predictable	Unpredictable
Banal	Original
Redundant	Informative
Intelligible	Novel
Simple	Complex

Each of these dialectics focuses attention on a new field of application remaining to be explored. Such a development is the task indicated for the philosopher.

As we appropriated it from communication physicists, information theory was essentially atomistic and exploratory: It decomposed messages from the environment into simple elements which it assumed, in some way not clearly stated, to be taken one by one; it followed the example of the mechanical systems which inspired it. In this form, the theory was suitable only to mechanistic psychophysics, the fecundity of which must nevertheless be emphasized. In this book we tried, in developing the concept of form, to make the theory integrative and *Gestaltist*.

The theory claims the role of a great scientific theory. Its synthetic power allows us to apprehend many disparate facts. In its development, it rediscovers some banal facts as landmarks; others, unexpected (for example, the uncertainty principles), justify it as a method of presentation.

Philosophy consumes scientific concepts in order to draw universal concepts from them; for this reason it is interested in any synthesizing theory. Although information theory, like any just beginning, remains clearly systematic, putting more emphasis on internal coherence than on agreement with other theories, the very large number of experiments and results that it can bring together in a logical perspective classes it beyond arbitrary systems.

In fact, the theory appears as a huge *Gedanken* experiment, attempting to re-create the strangeness of communication by making evident its material aspect. It was specifically this point of view which led us to the concept of sonic objects (Chap. IV).

Communication theory still raises more problems than it resolves. While it attempts to synthesize, it is also a program. Ultimately, its *heuristic* value justifies it from the philosophical viewpoint. Whatever the criticisms which can be addressed to it, and even were its essential values rejected (for example, the materiality of communication, the value of originality, the opposition between the intelligible and the original), the fact remains that like the great theories which preceded it, information theory furnishes an unlimited field for research. For this reason, it seems, necessarily, to impose its point of view in a definitive way, making acceptable the picture of the universe given by the individual's perception with all its uncertainties; it concretely returns man to the material world. In this picture, man becomes the very condition of knowledge of the world, instead of becoming asymptotically eliminated as in the science of the nineteenth century—the science which saw in an immense thermodynamics, conceived by an omniscient being, the ultimate description of the universe.

HAROLDO DE CAMPOS, FROM "THE INFORMATIONAL TEMPERATURE OF THE TEXT" (1960)

De Campos (1929–2003) was a Brazilian poet, translator, and professor of literature at Pontifícia Universidade Católica in São Paulo. He is most widely known for founding the Noigrandes poetic group in 1952, a project he engaged in with his brother Augusto de Campos and Décio Pignatari (who, among other things, translated McLuhan into Portuguese). The Noigrandes poets wrote and published concrete poetry; their manifesto "Pilot Plan for Concrete Poetry" (1958) sees in the form of concrete poetry and its material and linguistic features the ideal poetic medium in a technological age. De Campos wrote a number of theoretical, literary, and poetical essays, and translated a number of literary works from several languages (Ezra Pound, Stéphane Mallarmé, James Joyce, Dante, and others) making him a key figure of Brazilian *modernismo*. In the excerpt below, from "The Informational Temperature of the Text," de Campos uses the term "informational temperature" as a measure of "aesthetic information," rooted in both Claude Shannon's and Max Bense's work.

Concrete poetry has been accused of impoverishing language. This rebuke has often been made in almost apocalyptic terms, with some accusers speaking of "willful castration" and others going so far as to threaten the launchers of concrete poetry with a "season in Dante's Hell."

Any artistic discipline implies a voluntary restraint. In poetry, this can be seen in the terza rima of Dante or, even more pronouncedly, in the rigorous melopoeic texture of Arnaut Daniel's sestinas. In both examples, the form chosen drastically limits the poets' linguistic options. But without delving further into such generic considerations, we will attempt to develop our discussion in the objective field of modern aesthetic analysis. Information theory provides us with precise tools, free of visceral emotional appeals. In this way we can attempt to identify straightforwardly the linguistic and aesthetic characteristics which gave rise to the aforementioned censure and proceed to locate them and the poetic object which they distinguish in a wider process of formal evolution, as well as in the cultural context from which they derive their necessity and their justification.

Max Bense, in laying out his *theory of text*,[1] introduced, for aesthetic and literary purposes, B. Mandelbrot's theorem on *the informational temperature of a text*.[2] If we take 1 as the highest limit of a text's informational temperature, that temperature, in a given text, will be higher the nearer it is to 1. In such cases, for Mandelbrot "the available words are 'well employed,' even rare words being utilized with appreciable frequencies. Low temperature, on the other hand, means that words are 'badly employed,' rare words being *extremely* rare" (30). Of the first case, Mandelbrot, basing himself on Zipf,[3] gives James Joyce, whose vocabulary is "quite varied," as the example; of the second, *the language of children*.

It is necessary, however, in order to transpose these concepts into aesthetic terms, to remember Bense's admonition: Mandelbrot "limited himself to linguistic investigations," that is, his theorem is linked to "documentary or semantic information," to "factual information," and not, therefore, to "aesthetic information" (which is "inseparable from its actual accomplishment"). However, the "statistical-linguistic dimension" he reveals can furnish us an aesthetic indicator, precisely because of what "it says with respect to the text's productive process."

First conclusion: aesthetically, the concept of informational temperature is not necessarily linked to a criterion for evaluating *good* and *bad* use of words in a text, as it appears in Mandelbrot's linguistic formulation. Rather, Mandelbrot's theorem agrees with an idea of "richness of vocabulary," since he defines the "macroscopic description of the statistics of a text" as "a measure of the potential richness of its vocabulary" (28). However, richness of vocabulary and its stylistic opposite, "simplicity of vocabulary," are not, by themselves, sure indicators of the aesthetic value of a text (see appendix at the end of this essay, section 1).

Mandelbrot himself makes this felt, permitting us to suggest a fundamental aesthetic corollary at this point, when he criticizes Zipf for having considered the Joycean example as "the best model at his disposal, because of the length and variety of his works," and for having accepted the informational temperature of Joyce's texts as being the "best estimate" of the "maximum potential number of different words" for all authors, "when, in reality, that value is due to the exceptionally great potential variety of Joyce's text" (30).

Concerning "aesthetic information," it is doubtlessly true that the degree of "informational temperature" is an element in its accomplishment, an integrating factor in the artistic process that leads to it. The relative intensity or weakness of temperature, separate from any aprioristic norm of merit or demerit, can be correctly approached only when it is considered as a function of the specific creative process to which it contributes. Therefore, it will be factors of an aesthetic order, and not necessarily those of an exclusively linguistic-statistical order, which will involve the need for a higher or lower proportion, a maximum or minimum, in the informational temperature of a given artistic text, such as a poem or a piece of prose. There is, distinct from the linguistic sense, a self-sustaining concept of the "informational temperature of an aesthetic text," decidedly linked to the evolution of forms on the creative plane. [...]

Moving to "aesthetic information" and to the "artistic process" which makes it possible, it can be said that the notion of a "high informational temperature of the text" is linked to something like a craftsman's manipulation of poetry and prose. In such a procedure, the creative artist exhausts the possibilities of diversification and nuance in his or her linguistic arsenal, holding redundancy to a minimum, and elevating to the maximum the number of syntactic-semantic options. Joyce in English literature and Guimarães Rosa in Brazilian literature exemplify that artistic process, which seems of itself, in each work—or more exactly in the unified work *in progress*—to tend toward the closing of a whole cycle in the craft of verbal invention, putting it at the same time into crisis. The linguistic artifacts of both authors (Joyce's more than Rosa's) acquire a unique quality of highly personal workmanship through the elaborate handling of words and perfectionist refinement of linguistic textures. This is merely a stylistic observation and is in no way an attempt to play down the exceptional importance of these authors in the redimensioning of their respective literatures. Both were instrumental in staking out the limits of a stage of craftsmanship, well captured by Harry Levin: "The novel to end all novels."[4] This statement, which critically summarizes the position of Joyce's work, can also well characterize the correlative if less extreme position that Guimarães Rosa has come to assume in Brazilian literature.

Concrete poetry is included in a different historical and cultural dimension. Its point of departure is the "crisis of verse" generated at the end of the last [nineteenth] century by Mallarmé's "Un coup de dès" ["A Throw of the Dice]. It responds to a notion of literature not as *craftsmanship* but, so to speak, as an *industrial* process. Its product is a prototype, not the typical handiwork of individual artistry. It tends toward a minimal, simplified language, increasingly objectified and, for that reason, easily and quickly communicated. This presumes that the semantic reactions of the audience have been correctly conditioned toward structure instead of "swarms of inarticulate feelings." Its program is "the least common denominator" of language, or (paraphrasing Ogden) of an "artistically selected vocabulary minimum" (see appendix, section 3). In this way it coincides with the sense of a progressively technical civilization within which it is postulated.[5] That is why it rejects the airs and graces of craftsmanship—in spite of the seriousness with which it considers the artisan's contribution to the stockpile of extant forms—from the *art of verse* to the elaborate diversification of vocabulary in prose.[6] It has recourse in its turn to factors of proximity and likeness on the graphic-gestaltic plane, to elements of recurrence and redundancy on the semantic and rhythmic plane, to a visual-ideogrammic syntax (when not merely "combinatory") for controlling the flux of signs and rationalizing the sensible materials of a composition. This is how it limits *entropy* (the tendency to dispersion, to disorder, to the maximum informational potential of a system), fixing the informational temperature at the minimum necessary to obtain the aesthetic achievement of each poem undertaken (see appendix, section 4). [. . .]

Appendix IV

It is necessary to clarify (Bense mentions it only once) that Mandelbrot used Shannon and Weaver's concepts of *information* and *entropy* in developing his theorem of "the informational temperature" of the text: "Let us clarify, therefore, that when we speak of *information* it will always be in Shannon's sense of the word, which is precise because extremely limited" (12). In Shannon's theory of information, which is "normative, prescribing how to encode a message, given certain desires and constraints typical of a telegraphic situation," information is "a measure of one's freedom of choice when one selects a message."[7] In that theory, always related to an *information source, entropy* is a "measure of information": "The quantity which uniquely meets the natural requirements that one sets up for 'information' turns out to be exactly that which is known in thermodynamics as entropy" (12). That is to say, the expression *entropy* is related to "the amount of freedom of choice we have in constructing messages" (13), just as "in the physical sciences, the entropy associated with a situation is a measure of the degree of randomness, or of 'shuffledness' if you will, in the situation" (12). Entropy always grows, physical systems tend to become increasingly disorganized. Thus, Weaver adds that for a communication source one can say, just as he would also say it of a thermodynamic ensemble: "This situation is highly organized, it is not characterized by a large degree of randomness or of choice—that is to say, the information (or the entropy) is low" (13). It is in that sense, of *maximum de l'information*, that Mandelbrot uses the term "entropy." We can therefore conclude that a "high informational temperature" means a high degree of chance, and of *entropy*. On the other hand, Wiener[8] sees the informative content of a system as a measure of its degree of organization, and *entropy* as a measure of disorganization, one being the opposite of the other. Thus *informative content* is "essentially a *negative entropy*," while processes leading to a loss of information are strictly analogous to those in which entropy is increased. In his "Informational Aesthetics,"[9] Bense uses "information" and "entropy" to some extent in Wiener's sense of the terms. The first is defined as a measure for the "degree of order," characterizing "aesthetic cosmo-processes," where there is an "exceptional, selected distribution of elements," and the second measures the "degree of disorder," characteristic of "physical cosmo-processes." With relation to that aesthetic application, based on cybernetic nomenclature, it seems valid to say that if the limitation of the "informational maximum" in the production of a text (concrete poem) lowers the "informational temperature" in Shannon's sense (freedom of choice, chance, in relation to the lexical potential of language), it also diminishes *entropy* and consequently, in Wiener's sense of the term, increases the *organization*, the *negative entropy*, the *informative content* of the system. It is true that Bense in other essays resorts to Shannon's concept of *information*, which, as has been seen, is formulated from a different point of view from that of cybernetics. As, for example, when he studies the principle of *repetition* in the work of Gertrude Stein. There, Bense defines repetition with the term "redundancy" as "reduction in the total of aesthetic information in the process of its achievement," by means of which "the primitive originality also wanes," making it "thus possible to develop this aesthetic information as a principle of style."[10] The following text will serve as a sample of the process:

> Money is what words are.
> Words are what money is.
> Is money what words are.
> Are words what money is.

In this case, it is evident that rather than speaking of "a reduction in aesthetic information," it would be better to speak of a reduction in "informational temperature," à la Mandelbrot via Shannon, linked to the linguistic (semantic) idea of "richness of vocabulary." As Bense himself indicated in another text: "We cannot refrain from observing that concrete painting offers, in reality, little semantic information, but nevertheless relatively high values of aesthetic information."[11] This passage seems to support our proposition that there is a concept of "aesthetic informational temperature" (high or low) different from "linguistic or semantic informational temperature" (high or low). This concept can be readily applied to Stein's "exhibit," one of her best, and one which is quite close in its structural articulation to the "combinatory technique" of Eugen Gomringer's "constellations."[12]

worte sind schatten	words are shadows
schatten werden worte	shadows become words
worte sind spiele	words are games
spiele werden worte	games become words
sind schatten worte	are shadows words
werden worte spiele	do words become games
sind spiele worte	are games words
werden worte schatten	do words become shadows
sind worte schatten	are words shadows
werden spiele worte	do games become words
sind worte spiele	are words games
werden schatten worte	do shadows become words

The same concept may also be applied as a general rule to *concrete poetry*. If aesthetic information is "information about structure," "informative content" being the structure itself, the richer the former, the richer will the latter be in the sense of innovation, of inventiveness. Therefore, concrete art by reducing the work "to the aesthetically essential, to the thematics of signs," manifests in a particularly clear way the distinctive feature of aesthetic information. The selection of a structure, the choice among "x number of" structural possibilities of that one which best renders the particular problem of the poem, will be in the concrete work the Mallarméan moment of creation. This moment organizes and defines, in the sense of an irreversible decision, the raw materials of sensibility, that "torsion du concerté sur l'instant" [twisting of the concerted upon the instantaneous], in the words of the French composer Michel Fano. The dialectical poles of this decisive moment are reason and chance, intelligence and intuition, rigor and liberty. It implies, not an "abolition" but a *control*, an integration of chance in the compositional process. "The most lucid intellectual work for the clearest intuition."[13] It is there that the problem of originality is posited. It will no longer be described in terms of a thematics of content but as a *thematics of structure*. (Something altogether different, it must be once again emphasized, is that concrete poets in no way renounce the content of words. The semantic charges of the words selected are as important a working material as their sound or their graphic shape and converge with them toward the articulation of the desired structure.) It will no longer be pertinent, therefore, to speak of a "richness of vocabulary" but of a *richness of structure* which will coincide, in *concrete poetry*, without programmatical contradiction, with the most rigorous simplification and lexical transparency. In that sense, a last observation of Max Bense's seems to us to be meaningful, and we transfer it *mutatis mutandis* to concrete poetry: "In presenting instruments of perception, eternal objects of that perception[14] such as colors themselves, the measure of information and the measure of redundancy converge into a singular conjunction: Both contribute to perception, to presentification. In concrete painting *information* and *redundancy* manifest themselves as mutually integrative, complementary evidence of a single aesthetic fact." [15]

Translated by John Tolman, edited by A. S. Bessa

Notes

1. Max Bense, "Klassification in der Literaturtheorie," *Augenblick* 2 (1958).
2. B. Mandelbrot, "Linguistique statistique macroscopique," *Logique, langage et théorie de l'information*, vol. 3 of *Études d'épistemologie génétique* (Paris: Presses Universitaires de France, 1957), 1–78. Subsequent parenthetical page numbers in the text refer to this source.
3. George K. Zipf, *Human Behavior and the Principle of Least Effort* (Cambridge: Addison, 1949).
4. Harry Levin, *James Joyce* (New York: New Directions, 1960).
5. This sense is well emphasized by Max Bense, in "Klassification in der Literaturtheorie" and elsewhere.
6. "Verse," Mário Pedrose wrote, "with its unfolding movement, its cuttings and junctures, has a cultivated nature, unmistakably erudite and discursive." Mário Pedrosa, "Poeta e pintor concretista," *Jornal do Brasil* (Rio de Janeiro), 6 February 1957.
7. Claude E. Shannon and Warren Weaver, *The Mathematical Theory of Communication* (Urbana: University of Illinois Press, 1964), 9. Subsequent references appear parenthetically in the text.
8. Norbert Wiener, *Cybernetics* (New York: Wiley, 1948).
9. Max Bense, *Aesthetica II* (Baden-Baden: Agis, 1958).
10. Max Bense, "Das Existenz-Problem der Kunst," *Augenblick* 1 (1958).
11. Max Bense, *Ästhetik und Zivilisation* (Baden-Baden: Agis, 1958).
12. Jerome Rothenberg, *The Book of Hours and Constellations: Poems of Eugen Gomringer* (New York: Something Else Press, 1968).
13. Décio Pignatari, "New Poetry: Concrete," in Haroldo de Campos et al., *Teoria da poesia concreta* (São Paulo: Duas Cidades, 1975).
14. Bense here refers to the "eternal objects" of Whitehead, such as "colors or color and form relationships."
15. Max Bense, "Konkrete Malerei," in *Aesthetica III* (Baden-Baden: Agis, 1958), 88.

UMBERTO ECO, FROM
THE OPEN WORK (1962)

Eco (1932–2016) was an Italian writer, literary critic, and semiotician. He is widely known both for his novels (*The Name of the Rose*, 1983; *Foucault's Pendulum*; 1989; *Baudolino*, 2001; *Numero Zero*, 2015) and his work on media culture and semiotics. Eco's approach to semiotics is characterized by its attention to cultural phenomenon studies as communication, and its focus on the reader or interpreter of signs. Using the sender-channel-receiver model of communication, Eco gives particular importance to code in the process of signification. In order for two human beings to communicate, they need to share a common code, for otherwise they would not be able to understand the signs transmitted through language (verbal, visual, and non-verbal). His most important books on semiotics include *A Theory of Semiotics* (1976), *Semiotics and the Philosophy of Language* (1984), and *The Limits of Interpretation* (1990). In the excerpt below, from *The Open Work*, Eco proposes that literary works should be treated as "open," their multiple potential meanings are not restricted to the text itself, but constructed by readers.

The Transmission of Information

[. . .]

Thus, the larger the amount of information, the more difficult its communication; the clearer the message, the smaller the amount of information.

For this reason Shannon and Weaver, in their book on information theory, consider information as directly proportional to entropy.[1] The role played by Shannon—one of the founders of the theory—in the research on this particular question has been particularly acknowledged by other scholars in the field.[2] On the other hand, they all seem to insist on the distinction between information (here taken in its strictest statistical sense as the measure of a possibility) and the actual validity of a message (here taken as meaning). Warren Weaver makes this particularly clear in an essay aiming at a wider diffusion of the mathematics of information: "The word *information*, in this theory, is used in a special sense that must not be confused with its ordinary usage. In particular, *information* must not be confused with meaning . . . To be sure, this word information in communication theory relates not so much to what you do say, as to what you could say. That is, information is a measure of one's freedom of choice when one selects a message . . . Note that it is misleading (although often convenient) to say that one or the other message conveys unit information. The concept of information applies not to the individual messages (as the concept of meaning would), but rather to the situation as a whole . . . [A mathematical theory of communication] deals with a concept of information which characterizes the whole statistical nature of the information source, and is not concerned with the individual messages . . . The concept of information developed in this theory at first seems disappointing and bizarre—disappointing because it has nothing to do with meaning, and bizarre because it deals not with a single message but rather with the statistical character of a whole ensemble of messages, bizarre also because in these statistical terms the two words *information* and *uncertainty* find themselves to be partners."[3]

Thus, this long digression concerning information theory finally leads back to the issue at the heart of our study. But before going back to it, we should again wonder whether in fact certain concepts borrowed from information theory as tools of investigation can legitimately be applied to questions of aesthetics—if only because it is now clear that "information" has a far wider meaning in *statistics* than in *communication*. Statistically speaking, I have information when I am made to confront all the probabilities at once, before the establishment of any order. From the point of view of communication, I have information when (1) I have been able to establish an order (that is, a code) as a system of probability within an original disorder; and when (2) within this new system, I introduce—through the elaboration of a message that violates the rules of the code—elements of disorder in dialectical tension with the order that supports them (the message challenges the code).

As we proceed with our study of poetic language and examine the use of a disorder aiming at communication, we will have to remember that this particular disorder can no longer be identified with the statistical concept of entropy except in a roundabout way: the disorder that aims at communication is a disorder only in relation to a previous order.

Poetic Discourse and Information

[. . .]

Let us now turn to contemporary art and the ways in which it deliberately and systematically tries to increase its range of meanings.

According to the laws of redundancy, the probability that the article "the" will be followed by a noun or an adjective is extremely high. Similarly, after the phrase "in the event" the probability that "that" will be the next word is fairly high, whereas the probability that "elephant" will be the next word is very low. At least, this is true for the type of English we commonly use. Weaver gives numerous examples of this kind and concludes by saying that, in everyday language, a sentence such as "Constantinople fishing nasty pink" is quite improbable.[4] And yet such a sentence could be a perfect example of automatic writing as it was practiced by the Surrealists.

Let us now look at a poem by Giuseppe Ungaretti, entitled "L'Isola" ("The Island").

> A una proda eve sera era perenne
> di anziane selve assorte, scese
> e s'inoltrò
> e lo richiamò rumore di penne
> ch'erasi sciolto dallo stridulo
> batticuore dell'acqua tórrida . . .

> On a shore where evening was for ever
> Of woods enrapt and ancient, he descended,
> And advanced
> And the sound of wings recalled him,
> Sound unfettered from the shrill
> Heartbeat of the torrid water . . . [5]

There is no need to point out the various ways in which these few lines violate all linguistic probability, or to launch into a protracted critical analysis of the poem to show how, despite its lack of any conventional kind of meaning, it still conveys an immense amount of information about the island. At every new reading, this amount of information increases, endlessly expanding the message of the poem and opening up new and different perspectives, in perfect accordance with the intention of the poet who, while writing, was well aware of all the associations that an uncommon juxtaposition of words would provoke in the mind of the reader.

In other words, and to avoid overusing the technical terminology of information theory, what we most value in a message is not "information" but its aesthetic equivalent: its "poetic meaning," its "quotient of imagination," the "full resonance of the poetic word"—all those levels of signification that we distinguish from common meaning. From this point on if I use the term "information" to indicate the wealth of aesthetic meaning contained in a given message, it will be only to highlight those analogies that I deem most interesting.[6]

To avoid any possible ambiguity, I shall again emphasize that the equation "information = opposite of meaning" has absolutely no axiological function, nor could it be used as a parameter of judgment. If it could, the nursery rhyme "Hey diddle diddle / The cat and the fiddle" would have greater aesthetic value than a poem by Petrarch, just as any Surrealist *cadavre exquis* (as well as any nasty pink from Constantinople) would have greater worth than a poem by Ungaretti. The concept of information is useful here only to clarify one of the directions of aesthetic discourse, which is then affected by other organizing factors. That is, all deviation from the most banal linguistic order entails a new kind of organization, *which can be considered as disorder in relation to the previous organization, and as order in relation to the parameters of the new discourse.* But whereas classical art violated the conventional order of language *within well-defined limits,* contemporary art constantly challenges the initial order by means of an extremely "improbable" form of organization. In other words, whereas classical art introduced original elements within a linguistic system whose basic laws it substantially respected, contemporary art often manifests its originality by imposing *a new linguistic system* with its own inner laws. In fact, one might say that rather than imposing a new system, contemporary art constantly oscillates between the rejection of the traditional linguistic system and its preservation—for if contemporary art imposed a totally new linguistic system, then its discourse would cease to be communicable. The dialectic between *form* and the *possibility* of multiple meanings, which constitutes the very essence of the "open work," takes place in this oscillation, The contemporary poet proposes a system which is no longer that of the language in which he expresses himself, yet that system is not a nonexistent language;[7] he introduces forms of organized disorder into a system to increase its capacity to convey information. [. . .]

Postscript

All these points need further clarification. It would indeed be possible to show that the mathematical concept of information cannot be applied to the poetic message, or to any other message, because information (qua entropy and coexistence of *all* possibilities) is a characteristic of the *source* of messages: the moment this initial equiprobability is filtered, there is selection and therefore order, and therefore meaning.

The objection is perfectly corrected if we consider information theory only as complex of mathematical rules used to measure the transmission of bits from a source to a receiver. But the moment the transmission concerns information among human beings, information theory become a *theory of communication*, and we need to establish whether concepts borrowed from a technique used to quantify information (that is, a technique concerned with the physical exchange of signals considered independently from the meanings they convey) can be applied to human communication.

A source of information is always a focus of high entropy and absolute availability. The transmission of a message implies the selection of some information and its organization into a signifying complex. At this point, if the receiver of the information is a machine (programmed to translate the signals it receives into messages that can be rigorously referred back to a particular code, according to which every signal signifies one and only one thing), either the message has a univocal meaning or it is automatically identified with noise.

Things are, of course, quite different in a transmission of messages between people, where every given signal, far from referring univocally to a precise code, is charged with connotations that make it resound like an echo chamber. In this case, a simple referential code according to which every given signifier corresponds to a particular signified is no longer sufficient. Far from it, for, as we have already seen, the author of a message with aesthetic aspirations will intentionally structure it in as ambiguous a fashion as possible precisely in order to violate that system of laws and determinations which makes up the code. We then confront a message that deliberately violates or, at least, questions the very system, the very order—*order as system of probability*—to which it refers. In other words, the ambiguity of the aesthetic message is the result of the deliberate "dis-ordering" of the code, that is, of the order that, via selection and association, had been imposed on the entropic dis-order characteristic of all sources of information. Consequently, the receiver of such a message, unlike its mechanical counterpart that has been programmed to transform a sequence of signals into messages, can no longer be considered as the final stage of a process of communication. Rather, he should be seen as the first step of a new chain of communication, since the message he has received is in itself another *source of possible information*, albeit a source of information that is yet to be filtered, interpreted, out of an initial disorder—not absolute disorder but nonetheless *disorder in relation to the order that has preceded it*. As a new source of information, the aesthetic message possesses all the characteristics proper to the *source* of a normal informative chain.

Of course, all this quite expands the general notion of information; but the important thing here is less the analogy between two different situations than the fact that they share the same procedural structure. A message, at the outset, is a disorder whose latent meanings must be filtered before they can be organized into a new message—that is, before they can become not a work to be interpreted but an interpreted work (for example, *Hamlet* is a source of possible interpretations whereas Ernest Jones's reading of *Hamlet*, or T. S. Eliot's for that matter, is an interpreted message that has condensed a disordered quantity of information into an arrangement of selected meanings).

Obviously, neither this filtered information nor the informative capacity of the source-message can be precisely quantified. And this is where and why information theory becomes a theory of communication: it preserves a basic categorial scheme but it loses its algorithmic system. In other words, information theory provides us with only one scheme of possible relations (order-disorder, information-signification, binary disjunction, and so on) that can be inserted into a larger context, and is valid, in its specific ambit, only as the quantitative measurement of the number of signals that can be clearly transmitted along one channel. Once the signals are received by a human being, information theory has nothing else to add and gives way to either semiology or semantics, since the question henceforth becomes one of signification—the kind of signification that is the subject of semantics and that is quite different from the banal signification that is the subject of information. On the other hand, it is precisely the existence of open works (that is to say, of the openness proper to works of art, the existence of messages which manifest themselves as sources of possible interpretations) that requires an extension of the notion of information.

It would be fairly simple to show that information theory was not conceived to explain the nature of the poetic message and that, therefore, it is not applicable to processes involving both the denotative and connotative aspects of language—so simple that everybody would immediately agree with the proposition. On the other hand, it is precisely because information theory *cannot* and *should not* be applied to aesthetic phenomena that numerous scholars have tried to apply it to the field of aesthetics; likewise, it is precisely because information theory is not applicable to processes of signification that some have tried to use it to explain linguistic phenomena. Indeed, it is precisely because in their original usage the concepts pertaining to information theory have nothing to do with a work of art that, in this essay, I have tried to determine to what extent they can be applied to it. Of course, if they had been applicable to begin with, there would be no point in trying to find out whether they could be applied or not. On the other hand, the only reason I want to find out is that I think that, in the end, a work of art can be analyzed like any other form of communication. In other words, I believe that, ultimately, the mechanism that underlies a work of art (and this is what needs to be verified) *must* reveal the same behavior that characterizes the mechanisms of communication, including those types of behavior that involve the mere transmission, along one channel, of signals devoid of all connotative meaning, which can be received by a machine as instructions for a sequence of operations based on a preordained code capable of establishing a univocal correspondence between a given signal and a given mechanical or electronic behavior.

On the other hand, the objection would be insuperable if the following points were not now clear:

1. The application to aesthetics of concepts borrowed from information theory has not generated the idea of the open, polyvalent, ambiguous work of art. Rather, it is the ambiguity and polyvalence of every work of art that has induced some scholars to consider informational categories as particularly apt to explain the phenomenon.

2. The application of informational categories to phenomena of communication has by now been endorsed by a number of scholars, from Jakobson, who applied the idea of *integrated parallelism* to linguistic phenomena, to Piaget and his followers, who have applied the concepts of information theory to perception, all the way to Lévi-Strauss, Lacan, the Russian semiologists, Max Bense, advocates of the Brazilian new criticism, and so on. Such a fertile interdisciplinary and international consensus cannot be seen as a mere fad or a daring extrapolation. What we are confronting here is a categorial apparatus that may provide the key to several doors.

3. On the other hand, even if we were confronting mere analogical procedures or uncontrolled extrapolations, we would have to admit that knowledge often progresses thanks to an imagination that explores hypotheses and dares to take uncertain shortcuts. Too much rigor and an excess of honest caution can often deter one from venturing along paths that could well be dangerous but that could also lead to a plateau whence an entire new landscape would open up, with roads and highways that might have escaped a first, cursory topographic inspection.

4. The categorial apparatus of information theory appears methodologically fruitful only when inserted in the context of a *general semiotics* (although researchers are only now beginning to realize this). Before rejecting informational notions, one must verify them in the light of a semiotic rereading.

Such a semiotic endeavor could not, of course, be encompassed in this essay. The objections I have tried to answer in this postscript were for the most part raised by Emilio Garroni, author of one of the few exhaustive and scientifically sound critiques of *Opera aperta*.[8] And I do not pretend to have satisfactorily answered all his objections here. These comments are intended, in fact, to supply this essay, which still maintains its original structure despite numerous revisions, with a few answers to possible future objections. They are also designed to show how some of these answers were already implicit in the original argument, even though I did not make them explicit until stimulated by Garroni's observations. It is thanks to these observations that I have been motivated to explore this issue further.

Notes

1. R. Shannon and W. Weaver, *The Mathematical Theory of Communication* (Urbana: Illinois University Press, 1949).
2. See Goldman, *Information Theory*, pp. 330–331; and Guilbaud, *La Cybernétique*, p. 65.
3. Shannon and Weaver, *The Mathematical Theory of Communication*, pp. 99–100, 104, 106.
4. Ibid., pp. 101–102.
5. Giuseppe Ungaretti, "L'Isola," in *Life of a Man*, tr. Allen Mandelbaum (New York: New Directions, 1958), pp. 54–55.
6. The Russian Formalists had been dealing with the same question, though not in terms of information, when they came up with the theory of "estrangement," or "defamiliarization" *(priem ostrannenija)*. Extraordinarily enough, Shklovsky's article "Iskusstvo kak priëm" [Art as device]—which he wrote in 1917—already anticipated all the possible aesthetic applications of an information theory that did not yet exist. "Estrangement," for him, was a deviation from the norm, a way of confronting the reader with a device that would frustrate his systems of expectations and thereby draw his attention to a new, different poetic element. In this essay, Shklovsky is mostly concerned with illustrations of some of Tolstoy's stylistic techniques, in which the author describes familiar objects as if he had never seen them before. A similar concern with deviations, and violations, of the narrative norm is also present in Shklovsky's analysis of *Tristram Shandy*.
7. As did the Dadaists, and also Hugo Ball, who, in 1916, at the "Cabaret Voltaire" in Zurich, used to recite poetry in a strange, fantastic jargon. Similarly, certain contemporary musicians like to abandon themselves entirely to the whims of chance. All these, however, are marginal examples whose main experimental value is that they help set certain limits.
8. This essay was originally written in 1960 for the fourth issue of *Incontri musicali*. The postscript was written six years later. Garroni's critique was entitled La *crisi semantica delle arti* (Rome: Officina Edizioni, 1964), of which ch. 3 dealt with *Opera aperta*.

WILLIAM R. PAULSON, FROM
THE NOISE OF CULTURE: LITERARY TEXTS IN A WORLD OF INFORMATION (1988)

Paulson (b. 1955) is Professor of Romance Languages and Literatures at the University of Michigan. His work focuses on literary and cultural theory at the intersection of history, society, and technology. He has published three books, *Enlightenment, Romanticism, and the Blind in France* (1987), *Literary Culture in a World Transformed: a Future for the Humanities* (2001), and *The Noise of Culture: Literary Texts in a World of Information* (1988), from which the excerpt below is taken. In *The Noise of Culture*, Paulson expands Shannonian information theory to include literature as a system of information. But while in information theory a signal contains meaningful information and noise describes random fluctuations or interferences, for Paulson noise, too, can contain meaningful information. Because works of art and literature—like Eco's "open" work—are not completely isolated or self-contained, their information consists not just of clear signals, but mainly of noise, the parts of communication that produce ambiguity, complexity, misunderstanding, and unfamiliarity.

[. . .] For our purposes, Moles's concept of aesthetic information has the interest of identifying the poetic function with a specific kind of transmission channel and thus with the inevitability of noise. A language used as a pure instrument of efficient communication should be as free from noise as possible; thus if literature is to deviate from the utilitarian task of communication, it must be an imperfect process of communication, an act of communication in which what is received is not exactly what was sent. Rather than attempting to reduce noise to a minimum, literary communication *assumes* its noise as a constitutive factor of itself. This quite naturally raises doubts as to whether it is an act of communication at all, since it deliberately sacrifices the aim of communicative efficiency. These doubts do not arise from the attempt to understand literature in terms of information theory, but are a canonical feature of romantic-formalist definitions of literature. For Lev Jakubinskij, the language of poetry acquires an autonomous value when the practical, communicative purpose of language moves to the background.[1] The members of Groupe μ go further: "The final consequence of this distortion of language is that the poetic word is disqualified as an act of communication. In fact, it communicates nothing, or rather, it communicates nothing but itself. We can also say that it communicates with itself, and this intracommunication is nothing other than the very principle of form. By inserting at each level of discourse, and between levels, the constraint of multiple correspondences, the poet closes discourse on itself. It is precisely this closure that we call the opus."[2]

Paul de Man's longstanding insistence on the rhetorical dimension of language, its autonomous potential to create effects that have no counterpart in reference and cannot be resolved by grammatical reading, asserts a similar opposition between literariness and communicativity: "This gives the language considerable freedom from referential restraint, but it makes it epistemologically highly suspect and volatile. . . . Whenever this autonomous potential of language can be revealed by analysis, we are dealing with literariness and, in fact, with literature as the place where this negative knowledge about the reliability of linguistic utterance is made available."[3] De Man's view of literariness, though clearly situated in the romantic-formalist tradition, has a radicality not found in much contemporary literary theory, a radicality due in large part to his rejection of the romantic notion that literature and nonliterature can be opposed to one another and dearly separated, and also to his suspicion of the view that the work is a harmonious totality. If literary theory begins, for de Man, with the decision to treat literary language linguistically, it must subsequently encounter the impossibility of completing this task; it discovers that the literariness of language produces a residue that cannot be analyzed by grammatical means, by the procedures of linguistics extended beyond the sentence to all of discourse. "The resistance to theory is a resistance to the rhetorical or tropological dimension of language."[4] The most subtle resistance to theory thus resides in the most sophisticated of the literary theories that are committed to the resolution of textual uncertainties through grammatical or hermeneutic models. These theories aim, in effect, at an eventual reduction of the noise in the literary channel by ever more sophisticated understanding of codes and formation rules. As useful as this task may be, its considerable successes tend to mask what is most irreducibly literary about certain linguistic messages: the fact that what is received cannot coincide with what is sent, that there is, in other words, noise in the channel.

The foregoing considerations that the notion of self-organization from noise may have something to tell us about how literary texts, in spite of everything, manage to signify, how poetry can be valued as an intense, exquisite communication rather than dismissed as poor communication. All theorists of literature are aware of the seeming paradox in defining poetic function by means of its departure from the norms of communicative prose: something occurs in the poetic use of language that escapes completely the notion of "prose complicated by devices," so that the poet produces new kinds of effects not found in mere "rhetorical prose." Lotman called it the conversion of multiple ways of saying the same thing (h_1) into ways of saying multiple new things (h_2). Like Atlan's formalism of self-organization from noise, Lotman's description of this conversion takes into account the position of the observer. Lotman's h_1 existed from the author's standpoint, before transmission, and amounted to the possibility of encoding the same thing in more than one way in a given channel; his h_2 was on the side of the reader and represented an increase in information resulting from the particular form of message chosen. What is aesthetic variety from the author's perspective becomes semantic information from the reader's.

In another section of his book Lotman writes explicitly of "noise" and literary or artistic information. Here his conclusions echo almost exactly Atlan's notion of the production of information from noise: "Art—and here it manifests its structural kinship to life—is capable of transforming noise into information. It complicates its own structure owing to its correlation with its environment (in all other systems the clash with the environment can only lead to the fade-out of information)."[5] It must be noted that Lotman does not define noise in a literary context as residing within poetic language itself, as I have been suggesting in the last few pages. Rather, he refers to instances of external interference with the work of art: the missing arms of the Venus de Milo, the fading of paintings, a foreign word on a manuscript. In the relatively narrow context of Lotman's implied definition of noise, the work of art is nevertheless precisely the system in which noise can be converted into information. This fact stems, for Lotman, from the organizational nature of works of art, in other words, from a particular type of play between redundant order and informative surprise. The poetic text begins as an attempt to go beyond the usual system of a language— in which the word is a conventional sign—to a specifically artistic system, in which sounds, rhythms, and positional relations between elements will signify in new ways. The poetic text, in other words, demands of its reader that she create new codes, that she semanticize elements normally unsemanticized.[6] Aspects of language that in nonartistic communication would be extraneous to the message become elements that enter into secondary or tertiary signifying systems. Such new systems, in order to be systems, must be made of regularities and must therefore imply a degree of predictability, of redundancy. A system of versification provides an example of this: it puts in place a new system, new ways in which linguistic elements can signify, and at the same time it increases the foreseeability of certain textual features.

This would suggest that artistic texts are always more predictable than nonartistic ones, and yet the opposite seems truer to experience. Artistic texts do not become predictable, because their systems are continually disrupted by new unpredictabilities—out of which, in their turn, new systems of regularity are posited by the reader. Whereas in nonartistic communication there can be *extrasystemic* facts, aspects which are simply ignored or discarded because they are not dealt with by the code being used to interpret the message, in an artistic text there are only *polysystemic* facts, since whatever is extrasystemic at a given level, and thus destructive of regularity or predictability at that level, must be taken on as a possible index for another level, of another textural system. The multiplication of codes, or rather the creation of new and specific codes for a given genre, a given text, is the essence of the artistic text. Here is how Lotman sums up this process: "Any 'individual' fact, any thing that is 'a near miss' in an artistic text comes into being when the basic structure is complicated by additional structures. It arises as the intersection of at least two systems and takes on a special meaning within the context of each one. The greater the number of regular features intersecting at a given structural point, the greater the number of meanings this element will acquire, the more individual and extra systemic it will seem. What is extrasystemic in life is represented as polysystemic in art."[7] For the reader, one might say that where the seemingly individual fact was, there the intersection of systems shall be. What appears to be a perturbation in a given system turns out to be the intersection of a new system with the first. This is the case with many events that we call random, but what matters is that in an artistic text the random is not the gratuitous. *The principle of constructing a pattern out of what interrupts patterns is inherent in artistic communication, because this kind of communication arises by deviating from the regularities of nonartistic communication, and this deviation must be the source of whatever advantage or specificity artistic communication possesses.* In the language of the Groupe μ (and of Jean Cohen), the poetic function implies departures from norms and then the production of new kinds of relations and meaning from these departures.

The artistic text's capacity, then, to enter into correlation with external noise as into correlation with yet another system, depends simply on the properties that it already must possess to be an artistic text. If "irregularities" within the text can and must be interpreted as part of multiple systems of coherence and signification, the same can be said for "noise" arising outside the text: the already multiple layers of textual coherence are augmented by another level, this one located in the system (text + environment). "A statue tossed in the grass can create a new artistic effect if a *relation* arises between the grass and the marble." Moreover, this type of relation depends on the observer: the beholder of the fallen statue may not be able to make the needed correlations, so that "the question of whether 'noise' is transformed into artistic communication always presupposes a description of the type of culture which we take as the observer."[8] Lotman restricts the term *noise* to external disturbances of the artistic text, but his argument for what amounts to a theory of textual "complexity from noise" depends on the existence of a similar productive mechanism for dealing with internal unpredictables. The encounter of text and external noise can be productive because of the way that texts already articulate their internal noise. External noise can contribute to complexity because it does not differ fundamentally from internal noise. If the beholder can make a superior artistic work out the toppled statue, this is precisely because he was already capable of making an artistic work out of the sculpted figure when it was still standing—in spite of the irregularities in its marble, the singular position of its right arm, the fact that it was different from any statue or model he had seen before. Lotman's theorization of the role of external noise presupposes that something like noise already plays an internal role in the artistic text.

All this, however, should remind us that we are far from having settled the question of what, in literary works, may be considered noise. The concept of noise, as it arrives from the mathematical theory of information, is not entirely satisfactory for use in talking about language and literature. This puts us in the position of both needing to have the concept and needing not to have it. The difficulty arises from two definitions of noise, essentially compatible or complementary in mathematical information theory and not so elsewhere. On the one hand, noise is defined as whatever enters a message in transmission and alters it, so that whenever messages do not arrive as sent, we can speak of noise in the channel. This definition allows for a fairly reasonable extension to the ambiguities of natural and, especially, poetic language. On the other hand, noise is defined as aleatory, randomly distributed, having no rapport with the message it confuses. The two sides of the definition are compatible, even identical, in Shannon's theory: between an input and an output there is a statistical correlation, expressed as a number, X, between O and I, which corresponds to the transmission of information that has been accomplished; what is not correlated, $I-X$, is precisely what is aleatory. But in language, whereas we may accept that ambiguity is present, even ubiquitous, we find it harder to accept that this ambiguity residing in language could be without correlation to the message in which it appears. In fact, in language we have no sure way of distinguishing between message and noise, since the notion of noise as something contained in the text requires the postulation of a message existing prior to its being conveyed in language, and it is impossible in general to guarantee the existence of such a message.[9] And so we are left with a model of language, and especially poetic language, as a noisy transmission channel, but we have no way of separating exactly the noise from what is transmitted. Does this mean that any and all speculation concerning self-organization from noise and literary interpretation comes down like a house of cards? Only if such speculation depends on the ability to distinguish, *unambiguously*, between message and noise; only, in other words, if we require that our interpretive or theoretical observation of the message-noise-transmission system be itself accomplished via a channel free from noise, something like the metachannel in Moles's diagram. We can accept from the outset, however, that a noiseless metachannel does not exist. The schema of "complexity from noise" awaits us, inside and outside the text, in the reduction of the humblest rhetorical deviation as in the interpretation of the most irreducible undecidable. [. . .]

Notes

1. Quoted by Tzvetan Todorov, *Critique de la critique: Un roman d'apprentisage* (Paris, 1984), 18.
2. Group μ, *A General Rhetoric*, 12.
3. de Man, "The Resistance to Theory," 10.
4. de Man, "The Resistance to Theory," 17.
5. Lotman, *The Structure of the Artistic Text*, 75.
6. Lotman, *The Structure of the Artistic Text*, 55, 59.
7. Lotman, *The Structure of the Artistic Text*, 72.
8. Lotman, *The Structure of the Artistic Text*, 75.
9. Here is how de Man describes the inextricable relation between message and indetermination in literature: "Literature is not a transparent message in which it can be taken for granted that the distinction between the message and the means of communication is dearly established. . . . the grammatical decoding of a text leaves a residue of indetermination that has to be, but cannot be, resolved by grammatical means, however extensively conceived" (*"The Resistance to Theory,"* 15).

MEDIA ECOLOGIES

If information has a natural habitat, it is its media. Information depends on mediation: its ability to travel and to be communicated requires tools, avenues, or channels to get from point A to point B, from sender to receiver. Information can travel or flow, it can be a signal, a bit, a message, a sign, or a fact, and we can receive, obtain, derive, decode, or calculate it. All of these descriptions of information's behavior and our behavior towards information represent a small part in the complex network of mediating practices. Thinking about the difference between the information in a human cell, a black hole, or a poem requires us to define a relationship that links information and the medium that transmits it. A medium is, in the broadest sense, the means by which something is communicated or shared, and that something is, in the post-Shannon world, information.

The relationship between information and media requires to make conceptual and functional assumptions about their nature. If information is *information* regardless of whether it occurs in a unit of an organism, a region of spacetime, or a line of verse, then one must make a series of decisions about how information works and how it can remain the "same" across such vastly different environments. Information could be anything, any (measurable or decipherable or discoverable) content, independent from how or why it is transmitted. "Information," James Gleick writes, "is fungible: smoke signals and semaphores, telegraph and television, all channels carrying bits."[1] On a bigger scale, one can even make a more radical observation: "every particle in the universe," Charles Seife writes, "every electron, every atom, every particle not yet discovered, is packed with information."[2] Information is what everyone, everything, has in common; in a post-Weimar world, it becomes a "scientific entity on a par with matter and energy."[3]

Such an ontological grounding of information as a substance that "is out there," allows one to look at how, then, information can become "subject to clear, empirical, physical, and, in some cases, mathematical manipulations."[4] The possibility of these manipulations means that information—an entity, a thing in itself—exists as an object of a series of mediating practices, which, in turn, suggests that "media" can be anything from a subatomic particle to the collected works of Shakespeare printed in codex format.

For some kind of information, this independence from a particular medium is true. If someone asks how old you are, you could write your age on a piece of paper, draw lines in the sand, sing, whisper, or yell it, and you could say it in German or Chinese or English. The information will indeed be the same, regardless of how you convey it. But we also know that for other kinds of information, the means of communication matters a great deal. A tourist visiting the Louvre would be disappointed if the curators replaced the *Mona Lisa* with a different portrait but insisted that it were still the same. A music aficionado, too, would contest that the experience of their favorite piece of music remains the same regardless of whether it is recorded on tape, vinyl, or a digital format. In the first example, the choice between different media to convey information does not alter its content, whereas in the second case medium and information are inextricably linked.

"Information also has a human history," Geoffrey Nunberg writes, its history includes these media structures, systems, and technologies. In the twentieth century, Shannon's new theory of information as meaning- and, to some extent, medium-indifferent, tested the critique of media typified in the postwar field that is the Frankfurt School—Walter Benjamin, Jürgen Habermas, Max Horkheimer, and Theodor Adorno—and later in the description of media studies. "The medium, it turns out," Gleick writes about Shannonian information, "is not the message. Words, sounds, pictures or gibberish—it's still just bits."[5] "Information," unconstrained by the cultural, social, and political dimensions of its media, threatens to replace human experience[6] or advances the "mass deception" of the culture industry: "the flood of precise information and brand-new amusement make people smarter and more stupid at once."[7] The rise of the Shannonian information concept in the twentieth century and theories of media, its technologies, uses, and social demands cannot be uncoupled from each other.

The selection of texts in this section considers information's various "media ecologies," that is, the interaction between information, in all its various definitions, and media. Such ecologies aim not to resolve the conceptual fuzziness of information, as both medium-independent and medium-contingent, but include the possibility that information is, as Wolfgang Hofkirchner writes, a "superconcept," a concept that rather than settling for a definitive definition can illuminate its relation to a number of similar or overlapping concepts (data, sign, signal, message, fact, or meaning, for example).[8] From a perspective of media, information as such a "superconcept" means we can look at where similar concepts relate to practices that today we associate with information, where terminological differences can uncover conceptual affinities, or where arbitrariness or ambiguity could be a feature, not a bug.

"Media Ecologies" thus aims to draw attention to the conceptual versatility of information as it has shaped human culture and its activities. Storing, retrieving, organizing, and transmitting information are cultural practices as much as they are technological processes. Defining what information is and what it does, conjures both the concept (or superconcept) of information itself, as well as the tools, functions, and methods that imbue the media ecologies around it. Understanding information from the perspective of media, from the cave wall to the iPad, and media technologies from cuneiform to the algorithm allows us a glimpse into both the history of information's diverse functions and the impact of information-concepts on the ecologies surrounding and delineating it—and vice versa.

Frances Yates and Mary Carruthers both examine the history of memory and storage practices (in the Renaissance and the Middle Ages) and the intricate and complex mnemonic systems used to organize, store, and transmit information. Michael Hobart and Zachary Schiffman, in *Information Ages: Literacy, Numeracy, and the Computer Revolution*, argue that the history of computing, information technology, and information storage extends beyond our so-called Information Age to include the "information ages" of literacy and numeracy over 5000 years ago. While Hobart and Schiffman focus a more material history of information practices, Walter Ong turns to the transition from orality to literacy, analyzing how verbal expression and oral modes of communication require, for example, a variety of memory practices to preserve and share knowledge in the absence of writing. For Sigmund Freud, too, the question of how memory works is central to the analysis of the human mind. The mystic writing-pad, a mechanical device to write and erase notes, perfectly illustrates, according to Freud, how our psyche manages perception, permanence, conscious, and subconscious memories. Vannevar Bush, a colleague and contemporary of Shannon and Weaver, shares Freud's interest in memory devices; his focus was however, the invention of speculative and future devices like the Vocoder or the Memex.

Marshall McLuhan and Friedrich Kittler's work on media and our technological world has paved the way for modern media studies and understandings of what media are, and of what they are not. McLuhan, in *Understanding Media*, shifts the attention from the content of media to media themselves, arguing that what has changed and shape society, our consciousness, and our ability to communicate are media rather than their specific content. While McLuhan saw media as "the extensions of man" and therefore largely within human control, Friedrich Kittler emphasizes the impact technology has on human thought and action and how media and technology determine rather than extend our situation. Vilém Flusser's media philosophy, which he called communicology, connects media, its objects, and technologies to a variety of other fields, including information theory, phenomenology, semiotics, and photography. In his essays, Flusser explores how information's modes of transmission have changed from being written and inscribed to being electromagnetically and digitally communicated, and whether such a transformation represents the end of an era or an evolution. Lisa Gitelman's work on the history of new media turns to the past of writing, looking more closely at objects and materials of inscription and writing, and how they have impacted our "scriptural economy." The epistemological reward of paying attention to information's media ecologies, to the interactions among different information and information-related concepts and their environments, we hope, is to imagine and engage with a multitude of tasks, ideas, and histories of information present, past, and future.

Lea Pao

Notes

1. James Gleick, "The Lives They Lived: Claude Shannon, b. 1916, Bit Player," *New York Times*, December 30, 2001.
2. Charles Seife, *Decoding the Universe. How the New Science of Information is Explaining Everything in the Cosmos, from our Brains to Black Holes* (New York: Penguin, 2006), 3.
3. Bruce Clarke, "Information," in *Critical Terms for Media Studies*, ed. W. J. T. Mitchell and Mark B. N. Hansen (Chicago: University of Chicago Press, 2010).
4. Harold Garfinkel, *Toward a Sociological Theory of Information* (London: Paradigm, 2008), 102.
5. Gleick, "The Lives They Lived."
6. Walter Benjamin, "The Storyteller," in *Illumintions: Essays and Reflections*, trans. Harry Zohn (New York: Schocken, 1969).
7. Theodor Adorno and Max Horkheimer, *Dialectic of Englightenment*. Trans. Edmund Jephcott. (Stanford, CA: Stanford University Press, 2002).
8. Wolfgang Hofkirchner, "How to Achieve a Unified Theory of Information," *TripleC* 7, no. 2 (2009): 357–368.

FRANCES YATES, FROM
THE ART OF MEMORY (1966)

Yates (1899–1981) was an English historian, whose work focuses on the intellectual tradition and inheritance of the European Renaissance. She taught for many years at the Warburg Institute of the University of London and became widely known for her scholarly attention to magic, occult philosophy, and hermeticism within Renaissance thought and culture. Often challenged for her revolutionary ways of integrating speculative thinking, literature, theater, art, and hermetic philosophy into the writing of history, Yates stands out as a historian who transformed Renaissance histography. In her books *Giordano Bruno and the Hermetic Tradition* (1964) and *The Rosicrucian Enlightenment* (1972), Yates examines the influence of magic, esoteric, and occult practices on thinkers in early modern Europe, revealing the significance of these traditions for the formation of modern science and Renaissance humanism. Her best-known book, *The Art of Memory* (1966), from which the excerpt below is drawn, is a comprehensive study of memory and mnemonic systems from Ancient Greek and Latin sources to the scientific method emerging in the seventeenth century. Her description of the "memory palace" or "method of loci" as spatial practices to store and retain information offers an insightful perspective on both memory arts and the long history of information practices.

Mediaeval Memory and the Formation of Imagery

[. . .] The age of scholasticism was one in which knowledge increased. It was also an age of Memory, and in the ages of Memory new imagery has to be created for remembering new knowledge. Though the great themes of Christian doctrine and moral teaching remained, of course, basically the same, they became more complicated. In particular the virtue-vice scheme grew much fuller and was more strictly defined and organised. The moral man who wished to choose the path of virtue, whilst also remembering and avoiding vice, had more to imprint on memory than in earlier simpler times.

The friars revived oratory in the form of preaching, and preaching was indeed the main object for which the Dominican Order, the Order of Preachers, was founded. Surely it would have been for remembering sermons, the mediaeval transformation of oratory, that the mediaeval transformation of the artificial memory would have been chiefly used.

The effort of Dominican learning in the reform of preaching is parallel to the great philosophical and theological effort of the Dominican schoolmen. The *Summae* of Albertus and Thomas provide the abstract philosophical and theological definitions, and in ethics the clear abstract statements, such as the divisions of the virtues and vices into their parts. But the preacher needed another type of *Summae* to help him, *Summae* of examples and similitudes[1] through which he could easily find corporeal forms in which to clothe the spiritual intentions which he wished to impress on the souls and memories of his hearers.

The main effort of this preaching was directed towards inculcating the articles of the Faith, together with a severe ethic in which virtue and vice are sharply outlined and polarised and enormous emphasis is laid on the rewards and punishments which await the one and the other in the hereafter.[2] Such was the nature of the "things" which the orator-preacher would need to memorise.

The earliest known quotation of Thomas's memory rules is found in a summa of similitudes for the use of preachers. This is the *Summa de exempleis ac similitudinibus rerum* by Giovanni di San Gimignano, of the Order of Preachers, which was written early in the fourteenth century.[3] Though he does not mention Thomas by name, it is an abbreviated version of the Thomist memory rules which San Gimignano quotes.

There are four things which help a man to remember well.
The first is that he should dispose those things which he wishes to remember in a certain order.
The second is that he should adhere to them with affection.
The third is that he should reduce them to unusual similitudes.
The fourth is that he should repeat them with frequent meditation.[4]

We have to make clear to ourselves a distinction. In a sense, the whole of San Gimignano's book with its painstaking provision of similitudes for every "thing" which the preacher might have to treat is based on the memory principle. To make people remember things, preach them to them in "unusual" similitudes for these will stick better in memory than the spiritual intentions will do, unless clothed in such similitudes. Yet the similitude spoken in the sermon is not strictly speaking the similitude used in artificial memory. For the memory image is invisible, and remains hidden within the memory of its user, where, however, it can become the hidden generator of externalised imagery.

The next in date to quote the Thomist memory rules is Bartolomeo da San Concordio (i 262–1347) who entered the Dominican Order at an early age and spent most of his life at the convent in Pisa. [...] The following are Bartolomeo's rules which I translate, though leaving the sources in the original Italian:

(On order).

Aristotile in libro memoria. Those tilings are better remembered which have order in themselves. Upon which Thomas comments: Those things are more easily remembered which are well ordered, and those which are badly ordered we do not easily remember. Therefore those things which a man wishes to retain, let him study to set them in order.

Tommaso nella seconda della seconda. It is necessary that those things which a man wishes to retain in memory he should consider how to set out in order, so that from the memory of one thing he comes to another.

(On similitudes).

Tommaso nella seconda della seconda. Of those things which a man wishes to remember, he should take convenient similitudes, not too common ones, for we wonder more at uncommon things and by them the mind is more strongly moved.

Tommaso quivi medesimo (i.e. *loc. cit.*). The finding out of images is useful and necessary for memory; for pure and spiritual intentions slip out of memory unless they are as it were linked to corporeal similitudes.

Tullio nel terzo della nuova Rettorica. Of those things which we wish to remember, we should place in certain places images and similitudes. And Tullius adds that the places are like tablets, or paper, and the images like letters, and placing the images is like writing, and speaking is like reading.[5]

Obviously, Bartolomeo is fully aware that Thomas's recommendation of order in memory is based on Aristotle, and that his recommendation of the use of similitudes and images is based on *Ad Herennium*, referred to as Tullius in the third book of the New Rhetoric.[6]

What are we, as devout readers of Bartolomeo's ethical work intended to do? It has been arranged in order with divisions and sub-divisions after the scholastic manner. Ought we not to act prudently by memorising in their order through the artificial memory the "things" with which it deals, the spiritual intentions of seeking virtues and avoiding vices which it arouses? Should we not exercise our imaginations by forming corporeal similitudes of, for example, Justice and its sub-divisions, or of Prudence and her parts? And also of the "things" to be avoided, such as Injustice, Inconstancy, and the other vices examined? The task will not be an easy one, for we live in new times when the old virtue-vice system has been complicated by the discovery of new teachings of the ancients. Yet surely it is our duty to remember these teachings by the ancient art of memory. Perhaps we shall also more easily remember the many quotations from ancients and Fathers by memorising these as written on or near the corporeal similitudes which we are forming in memory. [. . .]

The attempt made in this chapter to evoke mediaeval memory can be, as I said at the beginning, but partial and inconclusive, consisting of hints for further exploration by others of an immense subject rather than in any sense a final treatment. My theme has been the art of memory in relation to the formation of imagery. This inner art which encouraged the use of the imagination as a duty must surely have been a major factor in the evocation of images. Can memory be one possible explanation of the mediaeval love of the grotesque, the idiosyncratic? Are the strange figures to be seen on the pages of manuscripts and in all forms of mediaeval art not so much the revelation of a tortured psychology as evidence that the Middle Ages, when men had to remember, followed classical rules for making memorable images? Is the proliferation of new imagery in the thirteenth and fourteenth centuries related to the renewed emphasis on memory by the scholastics? I have tried to suggest that this is almost certainly the case. That the historian of the art of memory cannot avoid Giotto, Dante, and Petrarch is surely evidence of the extreme importance of this subject.

From the point of view of this book, which is mainly concerned with the later history of the art, it is fundamental to emphasise that the art of memory came out of the Middle Ages. Its profoundest roots were in a most venerable past. From those deep and mysterious origins it flowed on into later centuries, bearing the stamp of religious fervour strangely combined with mnemotechnical detail which was set upon it in the Middle Ages.

The Memory Treatises

For the period with which the last two chapters have been concerned the actual material on the artificial memory is scanty. For the period on which we are now entering, the fifteenth and sixteenth centuries, the contrary is the case. [. . .]

In 1482, the first of the printed memory treatises appears, inaugurating what was to be a popular genre throughout the sixteenth and early seventeenth centuries. Practically all memory treatises, whether manuscript or printed, follow the "Ad Herennian" plan, rules for places, rules for images, and so on. The problem is to decide how the rules are being interpreted.

In treatises which are in the main line of descent from the scholastic tradition, the interpretations of artificial memory studied in the last chapter survive. Such treatises also describe mnemotechnic techniques of a classical character which are more mechanical than the use of the "corporeal similitudes" and which, almost certainly, also go back to earlier mediaeval roots. Besides the types of memory treatises in the main line of descent from the scholastic tradition, there are other types, possibly having a different provenance. Finally, the memory tradition in this period undergoes changes, due to the influence of humanism and the development of Renaissance types of memory. [. . .]

The student of artificial memory who used such books as these could learn the "straight mnemotechnic" from them in the descriptions of how to memorise "real" places in buildings. But he would learn it in the context of survivals of the mediaeval tradition, of places in Paradise and Hell, of the "corporeal similitudes" of Thomist memory. But whilst echoes of the past survive in the treatises, they belong to their own later times. The interweaving of Petrarch's name into the Dominican memory tradition is suggestive of increasing humanist influence. And whilst new influences are making themselves felt, there is at the same time a deterioration going on in the memory tradition. The memory rules become more and more detailed; alphabetical lists and visual alphabets encourage trivial elaborations. Memory, one often feels in reading the treatises, has degenerated into a kind of cross-word puzzle to beguile the long hours in the cloister; much of their advice can have had no practical utility; letters and images are turning into childish games. Yet this kind of elaboration may have been very congenial to Renaissance taste with its love of mystery. If we did not know the mnemonic explanation of Romberch's Grammar, she might seem like some inscrutable emblem.

The art of memory in these later forms would still be acting as the hidden forger of imagery. What scope for the imagination would be offered in memorising Boethius's *Consolation of Philosophy*,[7] as advised in a fifteenth-century manuscript! Would the Lady Philosophy have come to life during this attempt, and begun to wander, like some animated Prudence, through the palaces of memory? Perhaps an artificial memory gone out of control into wild imaginative indulgence might be one of the stimuli behind such a work as the *Hypnerotomachia Polyphili*, written by a Dominican before 1500,[8] in which we meet, not only with Petrarchan triumphs and curious archaeology, but also with Hell, divided into places to suit the sins and their punishments, with explanatory inscriptions on them. This suggestion of artificial memory as a part of Prudence makes one wonder whether the mysterious inscriptions so characteristic of this work may owe something to the influence of visual alphabets and memory images, whether, that is to say, the dream archaeology of a humanist mingles with dream memory systems to form the strange fantasia.

Amongst the most characteristic types of Renaissance cultivation of imagery are the emblem and the *impresa*. These phenomena have never been looked at from the point of view of memory to which they clearly belong. The *impresa*, in particular, is the attempt to remember a spiritual intention through a similitude; the words of Thomas Aquinas define it exactly.

The memory treatises are rather tiresome reading, as Cornelius Agrippa suggests in his chapter on the vanity of the art of memory.[9] This art, he says, was invented by Simonides and perfected by Metrodorus of Scepsis of whom Quintilian says that he was a vain and boastful man. Agrippa then rattles off a fist of modern memory treatises which he describes as "an unworthy catalogue by obscure men" and anyone whose fate it has been to wade through large numbers of such works may endorse his words. These treatises cannot recapture the workings of the vast memories of the past, for the conditions of their world, in which the printed book has arrived, have destroyed the conditions which made such memories possible. The schematic layouts of manuscripts, designed for memorisation, the articulation of a summa into its ordered parts, all these are disappearing with the printed book which need not be memorised since copies are plentiful.

In Victor Hugo's *Notre Dame de Paris*, a scholar, deep in meditation in his study high up in the cathedral, gazes at the first printed book which has come to disturb his collection of manuscripts. Then, opening the window, he gazes at the vast cathedral, silhouetted against the starry sky, crouching like an enormous sphinx in the middle of the town. "Ceci tuera cela," he says. The printed book will destroy the building. The parable which Hugo develops out of the comparison of the building, crowded with images, with the arrival in his library of a printed book might be applied to the effect on the invisible cathedrals of memory of the past of the spread of printing. The printed book will make such huge built up memories, crowded with images, unnecessary. It will do away with habits of immemorial antiquity whereby a "thing" is immediately invested with an image and stored in the places of memory. [. . .]

Mediaeval scholasticism had taken up the art of memory, and so did the main philosophical movement of the Renaissance, the Neoplatonic movement. Through Renaissance Neoplatonism, with its Hermetic core, the art of memory was once more transformed, this time into a Hermetic or occult art, and in this form it continued to take a central place in a central European tradition. [. . .]

Notes

1. Many such collections for the use of preachers were compiled; see J. T. Welter, *L'exemplum dam la littirature religieuse et didactique du Moyen Age*, Paris-Toulouse, 1927.
2. See G. R. Owst, *Preaching in Mediaeval England*, Cambridge, 1926.
3. See A. Dondaine, 'La vie et les ceuvres de Jean de San Gimignano,' *Archivum Fratrum Praedicatorum*, II (1939), p. 164. The work must be later than 1298 and is probably earlier than 1314. It was enormously popular (see *ibid.*, pp. 160 ff.).
4. Giovanni di San Gimignano, *Summa de exemplis ac sitnilitudinibus rerum*, Lib. VI, cap. xlii.
5. Bartolomeo da San Concordio, *Ammaestramenti degli antichi*, IX, viii (ed. *cit.*, pp. 85–6).
6. J. I. 47 and Pal. 54, both in the Bibliotheca Nazionale at Florence. Cf. Rossi, *Clavis universalis*, pp. 16–17, 271–5.
7. The Vienna codex 5393, quoted Volkmann, p. 130.
8. It has been established that the author of this work, Francesco Colonna, was a Dominican; see M. T. Case 11a and G. Pozzi, *Francesco Colonna, Biografia e Opere*, Padua, 1959, 1, pp. 10 ff.
9. *De vanitate scientianon*, cap. X.

MARY J. CARRUTHERS, FROM "*ARS OBLIVIONALIS, ARS INVENIENDI:* THE CHERUB FIGURE AND THE ARTS OF MEMORY" (2009)

Carruthers (b. 1941) is Erich Maria Remarque Professor Emeritus of Literature at New York University and a fellow at Oxford University. She has written a number of articles and books on the art and craft of memory, rhetoric, meditative practices, and aesthetic experience in the Middle Ages. Her pioneering book, *The Book of Memory* (1990; 2nd ed. 2008), is a classic study of medieval models, designs, training, and uses of memory across European cultures. The below excerpt is drawn from an article published in 2009, in which she traces the use of the diagram called the Cherub as an analytical tool of remembering and storing information. Her remarkable attention to abbreviation, compression, selection, organization, and visualization highlights them as crucial functions of memory processes and their rhetorical expressions—and the importance not only of the information we retain, but the information we lose and forget.

It may seem odd to begin an essay on the arts of memory by talking about forgetting, indeed, about an *art* for doing so. Surely, one would suppose, the purpose of an art of memory is exactly to forestall forgetting, to ensure that one had every single experience and bit of knowledge accumulated in a lifetime at one's immediate call, that one can in fact make of one's mind a universal encyclopedia of all that has ever been said or thought, rather as matters put on the Internet today are said to be incapable of erasure. [. . .] Themistocles, the great Athenian admiral, supposedly asked to be taught an art of forgetting because his memory was already so crowded that it needed refreshing. The emphasis in the ancient accounts is on Themistocles' remarkably complete and immediate *recollection*; the admiral's playful wish to learn forgetting, in other words, directly attests to the copiousness and security of his mnemonic inventory.[1] Forgetting has always been a necessary part of the craft of remembering. Failing to recognize this elementary condition indicates a basic misunderstanding about the purpose and function of mnemonic craft and about the nature of the mental techniques involved, including most famously the making of elaborate mental images placed in multichambered constructions. From antiquity, the arts of memory in Europe were conceived of as investigative tools for recollective reconstruction and selection, serving what we now call creative thinking. The need for structured memory storage was understood as a support for making new thought and composition, not for simply preserving all the past. I will soon return to this point, but I state it clearly now as well: the rote reiteration of a memory store is not what was intended when medieval writers spoke of *ars memorativa*. In both dialectic and rhetoric, memory craft was practiced as a tool of invention, rationally discovering and selectively recombining things one had previously learned for a particular purpose. In that sense, recollecting must always also involve some forgetting.

During his elegant, eloquent encomium on the extraordinary depth and power of his memory, St. Augustine writes:

> I arrive in the fields and vast mansions of memory, where are treasured innumerable images brought in there from objects of every conceivable kind perceived by the senses. There too are hidden away the modified images we produce when by our thinking we magnify or diminish or in any way alter the information our senses have reported. There too is everything else that has been consigned and stored away and not yet engulfed and buried in oblivion. . . . The huge repository of the memory, with its secret and unimaginable caverns, welcomes and keeps all these things, to be recalled and brought out for use when needed; and as all of them have their particular ways into it, so all are put back again in their proper places. . . . This I do within myself in the immense court of my memory, for there sky and earth and sea are readily available to me, together with everything I have ever been able to perceive in them, apart from what I have forgotten.[2]

"Apart from what I have forgotten." . . . In the cheerful admission of that phrase lies an essential divide between a modern and a medieval understanding of the cognitive function of memory. To have forgotten things is seen by us now as a failure of knowledge, however ordinary a failure it may be, and therefore a reason to distrust the power of memory altogether. Yet to have forgotten some things was understood in Augustine's culture as a necessary condition for remembering others.

It is helpful to distinguish two sorts of forgetting, resulting from different causes. There is the kind that happens because one failed to record something in the first place, the sort of thing Augustine is talking about here. This should not even be called forgetting because, as Aristotle makes clear in his treatise *On Memory and Recollection*, one cannot properly be said to remember anything until one has a mental image of it impressed in memory, which one can then later recall.[3] The other kind is deliberate and selective forgetting, the sort of forgetting that itself results from an activity of memory. One can demonstrate this from the so-called *artes oblivionales* found in a few late humanist treatises on memory art.[4] The oblivion discussed has to do with how to refresh one's search networks, not with worries about the accuracy or partialness of one's memories. As Lina Bolzoni has commented, "The techniques for forgetting handed down by the treatises are testimony to the persistence and power of the images," for they address tasks of sorting out and reducing the number of memory cues rather than suppressing or otherwise editing content one has previously learned.[5] As the story is told, Themistocles was motivated by this same need, to simplify his memory store and refresh his recollection by reducing its "crowdedness." In memory technique, crowding—either by cramming so many memories into stored places that one can no longer "see" them clearly or (even better) by deliberately covering one set of memories with others so as to rearrange their links and pathways—is always presented as the best way of forgetting something. The underlying assumption is that human memories, once constructed, cannot ever really be obliterated. They are best forgotten by being repositioned and relocated in other networks of associations.[6]

In the passage above, Augustine is certainly speaking of a consciously trained memory, one whose denizens, like prey (for he often speaks of memories as being like animals to be tracked to their lairs, whose prints or vestiges are to be followed through their familiar pathways in the forest),[7] can be rationally sought out via their particular routes when needed for use, then returned to their proper places when finished with. But this edifice, this vast treasury, is chosen and constructed. It is a work of art, using the materials of nature as all arts do, but consciously crafted for some human use and purpose. [. . .] Not only does forgetting have its honored place in an examination of *memoria*—after all, Augustine devotes a whole section of his discussion to the paradox that he can remember that he has forgotten something—but forgetting, of a sort, is essential to constructing an art of memory in the first place.

But how can this be? Here, I must return to what is meant by rote memory. Memorizing by rote or mechanically is a human capacity that certainly has its uses, even life-saving ones, as when machine operators are trained to act so habitually that the steps in a safety procedure come to them without thinking. Those valuable uses, however, are often mistakenly conflated with accuracy of reproduction, as though rote memory and accurate memory were necessarily linked. This is an easy error to make. I have done so several times myself, but I have concluded that it is a seriously misleading error.[8]

By the phenomenon of rote memory we mean iteration, the ability to repeat things without fail in the same order over and over. The virtue of rote—in a life-threatening situation, for example—lies precisely in its mindlessness. Because there is only one way to do it, something can be done with great reliability, like a tool that can perform only one task. But this is because it can be done only in one way. In other words, what is most distinctive about rote is not its accuracy but its iterability. We might say it can be accessed only along one line, and, once the procedure is started, it will unfold in the same direction in the same steps until it stops, over and over. To use an analogy from computer programming, rote memory provides a read-only memory, vital, to be sure, for a great many tasks, but neither editable nor inventive. One also requires a random-access memory; this task is particularly addressed by the structures and itineraries of *ars memorativa*.

In his lectures on Aristotle's discussion of memory and recollection, dated 1254–57, Albertus Magnus distinguishes recollective investigation from rote solely in terms of mnemonic access.[9] Recollection is a rational procedure, involving associated conceptual sequences, with a variety of starting points from which one can find (invent) what one is attempting to retrieve from memory. There are three basic categories of such starting points: from exact likeness; from opposition; or from some similarity—in Aristotle's term, "neighborliness" (*súneggus*).[10] So in any recollection procedure, one can start off from at least three different access gates instead of just one. "This," Albertus says, "is how recollecting differs from rote learning [*iterato addiscere*], since recollection can be set in motion by any" of several means, whether by the logic of the subject matter or by our own habitual associations. Rote, though, is not an investigative procedure (and is therefore not properly recollection) because it has no such navigational systems. Someone who knows only by rote, Albertus points out, has no resources if his memory fails. He simply "will not recall or recollect" what he wants.[11]

Thus, the distinction between rote recitation and recollective reconstruction hinges on the issue of mnemonic access. Discussing rote memories, Hugh of St. Victor says that people who have memorized by rote have only one point of access to what they know. Essentially, they are like people trying to find something in a book without any supporting structures: no chapters, no page numbers, no headings, no punctuation, and certainly no index. One is doomed to start at the beginning and search through the book linearly and sequentially until one finds what one wants.[12] And if, on another occasion, one wanted to find it again, one would have to go through the same laborious process—unless, of course, one had marked it in some way for quicker retrieval. What the structuring procedures learned in *ars memorativa* support is the mind's own ability, when augmented in such a way, to retrieve quickly and securely by looking for something using a good mental map. Of the Homeric rhapsodists of the ancient world—those men who were said to be able to recite all of Homer with great precision from start to finish—Xenophon commented, invoking a common ancient example of this principle, "your rhapsodists are consummate as reciters, but they are very silly fellows themselves."[13] It is not the accuracy of their recitation that is criticized but their general idiocy, their foolishness in being unable to put their knowledge to productive use. They recite only Homer and only by rote. By contrast, the structures of mnemonic art were intended to provide multiple access routes to the contents of memory, supporting the mind's unaided computational abilities with a random-access scheme. [. . .]

The ancient art of memory was conceived to serve recollection, not retention per se. This is evident from where it is discussed both in manuals of rhetoric and in the scholastic commentaries on Aristotle's brief treatise *On Memory and Reminiscence*, appended to his work *On the Soul*. Commenting on this work, both Albertus Magnus and Thomas Aquinas discuss *ars memorativa* as a tool of recollection, for memory access and retrieval of matters previously stored. In the words of Albertus, "recollection is nothing other than the investigation by memory of what has been forgotten."[14] Recollection is a rational activity, it is investigation, and it seeks to retrieve "what has been forgotten." An art of recollection is not an art to *overcome* forgetting or one that denies forgetfulness, as one might deny the existence of or obliterate an enemy. Recollection begins with what is forgotten and seeks to reconstitute the ways to recover it. This description assumes that a memory, once laid down, is always in the brain, and so can be uncovered by reconstructing its tracks (*vestigia*). [. . .]

The earliest account of memory techniques we now possess is found in a fragmentary Stoic text called *Dissoi logoi* (literally "Double Arguments," a Greek version of the curriculum exercise of arguing positive and negative sides of a question, or *argumentum in utramque partem*), in which a student is advised to make rebuslike associations to remember names and unfamiliar or difficult words.[15] Thus, to remember the name Chrysippus, one may link the syllables to an image—perhaps a golden horse (*chrysos* and *hippos*). The exercise embodied by *Dissoi logoi* was practiced and taught as a device of composition. It is significant, I think, that the other Greek text in which an art of memory is mentioned is Aristotle's *Topikōn*, where the method of analysis and composition based upon topoi of argument is likened specifically to the topoi of an art of memory, in that arguments are situated in orderly memory places (*topoi*), whence they can be called forth by recollection as needed. To investigate exactly what Aristotle meant by such "topics," and how what he may have meant differed from what Cicero meant when he in turn wrote on the "topics," and then Boethius in his turn, is not my task here. But it is clear in both these Greek texts that the work of mnemonic *techne* was associated even this early with tasks of *invention*, "finding" hard words or rational arguments.[16] It is also clearly associated with school subjects, especially (perhaps) the arts of the *trivium*, but by no means confined to these, for *memoria* was regarded as a discipline essential to them all.[17] [. . .]

Monasticism was fundamentally text-based. Augustine called memory "a kind of stomach of the mind,"[18] and in monastic writing, chewing and digestion are favored tropes for reading. Yet the conventions of monastic meditation also included vivid imagining, of buildings and other artifacts described in the Bible, for the purpose of composing additional meditation. These were sometimes called *picturae*, as in the elaborately imagined verbal *pictura* (as he calls it) of the tabernacle in Book 2 of the treatise *On the Tripartite Tabernacle* by Adam of Dryburgh, composed sometime about 1180.[19] [. . .] In meditational writing, the process of imagining these structures is commonly referred to with the verbs *pingo* and *depingo*, as well as *fingo* and its derivatives. There are many examples from the fifth century through the twelfth, and even later. Richart de Fournival (act. 1240–60), a canon of Amiens, said that all vivid text had *peinture* ("picture") as well as *parole* ("speech"), these two being the roads to the portals of memory.[20] The exact source of this recurrent medieval emphasis on mental picture-making while reading and meditating is not at all clear. Something is surely owed to the cultivation in Late Antique rhetoric of *ekphrasis* and of stylistic *enargeia* more generally as being cognitively and persuasively valuable, an emphasis that is strong as well in the rhetorical teaching of Aristotle, Quintilian, and Cicero. But the importance of imagining buildings and their furniture as a meditation device specifically those various avatars of the Temple that one finds in the Bible (Noah's Ark, the Exodus Tabernacle, Solomon's Temple, the visionary Temple Mount in Ezekiel, St. John's Heavenly City)—is directly owed to traditions of meditation and contemplative composition that were adapted into earliest Christianity from classical Judaism.[21] [. . .]

Notes

1. The story is recounted by Cicero, *De oratore* 2.299–300, and cf. 2.351. Cf. also Quintilian, *Institutio oratoria* 11.2.50, who praises Themistocles' unheard-of feat in acquiring fluent Persian within a year.
2. Augustine, *Confessiones* 10.8.12-14: "Transibo ergo et istam naturae meae, gradibus ascendens ad eum, qui fecit me, et uenio in campos et lata praetoria memoriae, ubi sunt thesauri innumerabilium imaginum de cuiuscemodi rebus sensis inuectarum. Ibi reconditum est, quidquid etiam cogitamus, uel augendo uel minuendo uel utcumque uariando ea quae sensus attigerit, et si quid aliud commendatum et repositum est, quod

nondum absorbuit et sepeliuit obliuio. . . . Haec omnia recipit recolenda, cum opus est, et retractanda grandis memoriae recessus et nescio qui secreti atque ineffabiles sinus eius: quae omnia suis quaeque foribus intrant ad eam et reponuntur in ea. . . . Intus haec ago, in aula ingenti memoriae meae. Ibi enim mihi caelum et terra et mare praesto sunt cum omnibus, quae in eis sentire potui, praeter illa, quae oblitus sum." Translated by M. Boulding (Hyde Park, NY, 1997), from the Latin text of L. Verhejien, *CCSL* 27, revised in 1990 (Turnhout, 1996), which is quoted above.

3. Aristotle, *De memoria et reminiscentia* 1.450a–b, discussing why people vary in their abilities to remember; see also his comments at 453a. I have used the Loeb Classical Library edition, translated by W. S. Hett from the 1898 text of W. Biehl (Cambridge, 1936).

4. For example, Lambert Schenkel, *Gazophylacium artis memoriae* (1595; Strasbourg, 1610), counsels imagining that a great wind has blown through the chambers of your memory places and carried all their images away, or that a servant has swept all the rooms entirely clean. Similar advice occurs in a late-sixteenth-century memory treatise by the Dominican friar Cosmo Rosselli, *Thesaurus artificiosae memoriae*. These and other sixteenth-century examples are discussed by L. Bolzoni, *The Gallery of Memory* (Toronto, 2001), 139–45. It should be noted in all this advice that, although the particular images are cleared away, the basic structure of the memory places remains secure and intact. Erasure of images from the memory places is assumed in the ancient model of the memory places as being like wax tablets and the images like the stylus-incised letters erased from the tablet when they are no longer needed; see *Rhetorica ad Herennium* 3.18.31.

5. Bolzoni, *The Gallery of Memory*, 144.

6. The way in which the monumental map of Late Antique Antioch was "relocated" by the Christians during the struggle between the bones of blessed Babylas and the spring of Apollo in Daphne is a good case in point; see M. J. Carruthers, *The Craft of Thought: Rhetoric, Meditation, and the Making of Images, 400–1200* (Cambridge, 1998), chap. 1, esp. 24–59. The seminal study by M. Halbwachs of "communal memories" based on the holy places in Jerusalem is also relevant: *La topographie légendaire des Evangiles en Terre Sainte* (Paris, 1941; rpt. Paris, 1971).

7. On the trope of recollection as hunting for prey, see M. J. Carruthers, *The Book of Memory: A Study of Memory in Medieval Culture*, 2nd ed. (Cambridge, 2008), 78, 323–24. All further references to *The Book of Memory* are to the second edition.

8. I have argued the case against such a conflation in Carruthers, *The Book of Memory*, xii–xiv, 100–106.

9. Albertus Magnus, *Commentary on Aristotle's De memoria et reminiscentia*; trans. J. Ziolkowski from Albertus Magnus, *Opera omnia*, ed. A. Borgnet (Paris, 1890), 9:97–118, in *The Medieval Craft of Memory: An Anthology of Texts and Pictures*, ed. M. Carruthers and J. Ziolkowski (Philadelphia, 2002), 118–52.

10. Aristotle, *De memoria et reminiscentia* 451b. 20; see also R. Sorabji, *Aristotle on Memory* (Providence, RI, 1972), 42–46.

11. Albertus Magnus, Commentary on Aristotle's *De memoria et reminiscentia*, tractatus 2, capitulum 3 (ed. Borgnet, 112); trans. Ziolkowski, 143: "Et ista est differentia in qua reminisci differt ab eo quod est iterato addiscere, cum reminiscentia possit moveri quodam praedictorum modorum in id principium quod est ante quaesitum jam in memoria, sive ex parte rei, sive ex parte consuetudinis. Iterato autem addiscens talibus non movetur. Cum vero non investigat et movetur per aliquod principium, tunc non recordabitur vel reminiscetur."

12. Hugh of St. Victor, *De tribus maximis circumstantiis historiae* (with tables and a diagram); trans. M. Carruthers in Carruthers and Ziolkowski, *The Medieval Craft of Memory*, 32–40 (reprinted as Appendix A in Carruthers, *The Book of Memory*, 339–44), from the edition of W. M. Green, Speculum, 18 (1943), 484–93.

13. Xenophon, *Memorabilia* 4.2.10; trans. E. C. Marchant, Loeb Classical Library (London, 1923). They are called *akribountas*, "precise in speaking." The comment is made by the young man Euthydemos, in response to a query by Socrates, who asks if he wishes to become a rhapsodist since he possesses a complete copy of Homer. This is one of several specialized professions that Socrates suggests to him as a goal for his education; no, he says. Socrates offers him instead an education that makes good governors and judges as well as persuasive speakers. The distinction being made is between skill and wisdom (or, as we would now say, between a technical and a liberal education). On this ancient debate in the fourth century BCE, see D. S. Hutchinson, "Doctrine of the Mean and the Debate Concerning Skills in Fourth-Century Medicine, Rhetoric and Ethics," *Apeiron*, 21 (1988), 17–52. See also Plato, *Gorgias* 463B; and Aristotle, *Metaphysics* 1.1, on the distinction between "a knack" (*empeiron*) and "an art" (*techne*), or *experimentum* and *ars* in the Latin translation of Aristotle's *Metaphysics* by James of Venice (the earliest medieval translation, ca. mid-twelfth century).

14. Albertus Magnus, *Commentarium in De memoria et reminiscentia*, tractatus 2, capitulum 1 (ed. Borgnet, 107); trans. Ziolkowski, 136: "reminiscentia nihil aliud est nisi investigatio obliti per memoriam." See also Thomas Aquinas, *Sentencia libri . . . de memoria et reminiscentia*, lectio 6, in *Opera omnia* 45.2 of the Leonine edition of Aquinas (Rome, 1985). Aquinas' commentary has been newly translated from this edition by K. White and E. M. Macierowski, *Commentaries on Aristotle's "On Sense and What Is Sensed" and "On Memory and Recollection"* (Washington, DC, 2005). A translation of the Marietti edition of this commentary (ed. R. M. Spiazzi, Turin, 1973) is in Carruthers and Ziolkowski, *The Medieval Craft of Memory*, 153–88 (the differences between the editions are slight).

15. Traditionally thought to have been composed in the fourth century BCE, the dating of the *Dissoi logoi* is now unsettled and may be considerably later than previously thought; see M. Burnyeat, "Dissoi Logoi," in *The Routledge Encyclopedia of Philosophy* (London, 1998), 3:106–7. The treatise has been translated by R. K. Sprague in *Mind*, 77 (1968), 155–67. The exercise of *argumentum in utramque partem* continued through the Middle Ages; see M. C. Woods, "The Teaching of Poetic Composition in the Later Middle Ages," in *A Short History of Writing Instruction*, ed. J. J. Murphy, 2nd ed. (Mahwah, NJ, 2001), 123–43.

16. Aristotle, *Topikōn* 8.14 (as in n. 21 above). See Stump, *Dialectic and Its Place in the Development of Medieval Logic*.

17. Discussed in the general introduction to Carruthers and Ziolkowski, *The Medieval Craft of Memory*, esp. 9–17.

18. Augustine, *Confessiones* 10.14.21: "quasi uenter est animi."

19. See Carruthers, *The Craft of Thought*, 246–54, for a full discussion of the nature of the *pictura* referenced in Adam of Dryburgh's text. *De tripartito tabernaculi* is in Migne, *PL* 198, 609–796; all translations from it are mine.

20. This now-famous passage in the preface to Richard de Foumival's *Bestiaire d'amour* has been often discussed; see esp. V. A. Kolve, *Chaucer and the Imagery of Narrative* (Stanford, 1984); S. Huot, From *Song to Book* (Ithaca, NY, 1987); and E. Sears, "Sensory Perception and Its Metaphors in the Time of Richard of Fournival," in *Medicine and the Five Senses*, ed. W. F. Bynum and R. Porter (Cambridge, 1993), 17–39.

21. *Pictura* can refer equally to both *ekphrasis* and to paintings; so can *descriptio*. The many plans and sketches in Richard of St. Victor's literal exegesis of the Temple compound in Ezekiel are fully copied in all the manuscripts. This work contains several schematics of the sort Adam seems to have in mind. Hugh of St. Victor's "picture" of the ark, a work found in many manuscripts, never contains drawings, nor does Adam of Dryburgh's tabernacle. Both Hugh's and Adam's works are presented as ordering schemes for ethical and theological meditation. See Carruthers, *The Craft of Thought*, esp. 241—54. A different interpretation of Hugh's ark, as instructions for making a fully drawn and colored chart from which Hugh taught, has been put forward by C. Rudolph, *First, I Find the Center Point: Reading the Text of Hugh of Saint Victor's "The Mystic Ark,"* Transactions of the American Philosophical Society, 94 (Philadelphia, 2004). W. Cahn has studied examples of exegetical as well as meditational *picturae*; see "Architecture and Exegesis: Richard of St. Victor's Ezekiel Commentary and Its Illustrations," *AB*, 76 (1994), 26–49; and "The Allegorical Menorah," in *Tributes in Honor of lames M. Marrow*, ed. J. E Hamburger and A. S. Korteweg (Tumhout, 2006), 117—26. The latter is a meditational diagram that focuses on the menorah candlestick, one of the temple furnishings that commonly served as an organizing device for meditation and study, as in Bede's *De templo Solomonis liber* (Migne, PL 91).

MICHAEL E. HOBART AND ZACHARY S. SCHIFFMAN, FROM *INFORMATION AGES: LITERACY, NUMERACY, AND THE COMPUTER REVOLUTION* (1998)

Hobart (b. 1944) is Professor Emeritus of History, Bryant University, and more recently, adjunct professor at Western Washington University and Schiffman is the Bernard J. Brommel Distinguished Research Professor Emeritus in the Department of History at Northeastern Illinois University. The excerpt below is drawn from their book *Information Ages: Literacy, Numeracy, and the Computer Revolution* (1998). The book traces the history of information technology from the ancient Greeks and Sumerians to the mathematical computational inventions of Alan Turing and John von Neumann. Their work treats concepts like information, information age, and information society not simply as products of twentieth century computational and digital innovations, but as long-standing human practices. The historical and cultural developments of orality, literacy, accounting, calculation, numeracy, and computing, they argue, have all shaped how we understand information, its processes, and its technologies today. Such a history approaches information not as a singular information-concept, but as a complex and elusive grappling with the technologies that have for millennia allowed us to organize, manage, transmit, and store the material of culture.

Literacy and List Making in Mesopotamia

Although a late Assyrian collection dating from around 650 B.C., the royal library at Nineveh gives us a glimpse of a Mesopotamian literary tradition preserved religiously by almost two millennia of scribes. Of the seven hundred extant cuneiform tablets in the royal library, the largest group consists of three hundred "omen texts." These lists consist of short, conditional statements correlating various phenomena with predicted outcomes, such as "If a man's chest-hair curls upwards: he will become a slave." The next largest group, two hundred tablets, comprises sign and word lists organized according to a wide variety of principles, largely to aid Akkadian-speaking scribes in mastering Sumerian, a dead language early in the second millennium. A related group of one hundred tablets provide interlinear translations of Sumerian incantations and prayers. Finally, some one hundred tablets contain assorted conjurations, proverbs, and fables, of which only about forty record epics, like the famous story of Gilgamesh. Even taking into account the loss or destruction of tablets, continuous texts—what we call "literature"—constitute only a tiny percentage of the Mesopotamian scribal tradition, which consists chiefly of lists.

To some extent the nonnarrative nature of this literary tradition reflects the requirements of training in a difficult and obscure scribal art, with its emphasis on word lists and copybook phrases, on learning a dead language by rote. But the preponderance of lists also indicates that, as the embodiment of the linguistic propensity to classify, writing tends to encourage further classification. As long as writing remained limited to record keeping, as either pure information or, at most, a technique of information storage with restricted terminology and syntax, the tendency to classify was tightly constrained. But when writing broke free of record keeping and became a technology of communication modeled upon speech, the classifying urge exploded. [. . .]

The word "list" is so commonplace we hardly give it a thought. From the Old English *liste*, "hem" or "border," the term formerly meant a strip of cloth, specifically "the selvage, border, or edge of a cloth, usually of different material from the body of the cloth." It also denoted border in the sense of "boundary," specifically in its plural form as "the palisades or other barriers enclosing a space set aside for jousting," whence the phrase "to enter the lists." The implication of boundaries carries over into our contemporary usage of the word as "a series of names or other items written or printed together in a meaningful grouping or sequence so as to constitute a record." In contrast to the flow of speech, lists create boundaries, which both distinguish the individual entries within the list and separate all its items from those outside. These internal and external boundaries encourage the scrutiny of its entries, individually and as a group, revealing the possibility of new classifications.

The Mesopotamian lists devoted to scribal training give free rein to the impulse to classify. In addition to Sumerian sign lists, and bilingual lists translating Sumerian terms into Akkadian, we find a profusion of topically arranged word lists. According to the noted Assyriologist A. Leo Oppenheim, one such list encompasses topics like "trees, wooden objects, reeds and reed objects, earthenware, leather objects, metals and metal objects, domestic animals, wild animals, parts of the human and animal body, stone and stone objects, plants, fish and birds, wool and garments, localities of all description, and beer, honey, barley, and other foodstuffs." Another list presents various classifications for human beings, under such headings as officials, craftsmen, and cripples. Beginning as a pedagogical device for teaching Akkadian scribes how to write and pronounce Sumerian words, the activity of list making transformed itself into a topical compendium of all received knowledge.

Of course, oral cultures make lists too, as illustrated by tribal genealogies, as well as more complex lists like the "Catalog of Ships" in book 2 of the *Iliad*. This list, which most scholars regard as part of the oral record handed down to Homer, describes the peoples, geography, and rulers of Greece, as well as the numbers of ships and men in the expedition to Troy. Unlike Mesopotamian word lists, the Homeric one is storied, narrating actions: Over the various peoples of Greece, kings are ruling; in the various regions of Greece, sheep are pasturing: and onto the ships from each region, men are embarking. Commemorative patterns of sound and image underlie these concrete situations, subordinating oral list making to community ritual and embedding it in a kind of liturgy. By contrast, writing frees the mind from the mnemonic necessities of oral culture, allowing its energies to flow naturally in the direction of heightened classification. Writing does not so much *create* the urge to classify as *liberate* it, encouraging new forms of intellectual play. [. . .]

The sacral quality of Mesopotamian writing, rooted in its pictographic origins, channels the tendency to classify in a particular and (to our sense) strange direction, epitomized by exhaustive list making. Each list consists of a multitude of systematically elaborated categories. But all this systematizing serves not to classify the things of the world in the kind of hierarchical pyramid we reocentrists would expect, one that analyzes reality by genus and species, reflecting the order of nature. Instead of classifying in this way, the categories exist chiefly to focus the mind and thereby to aid it in a thorough naming of all possible items and phenomena, for if one can name something, one can know it, not as part of the natural hierarchy but purely in itself. The systematic quality of Mesopotamian list making, then, evinces not so much a vertical as a horizontal organization of knowledge, an ever-expansive naming of all the possible phenomena within each category. The Mesopotamians structured knowledge in an additive rather than analytical manner.

The Anatomy of a List

[. . .] A list of lists, the so-called "Sumerian King List" presents an ideal specimen for our purposes, revealing the full extent of the classifying impulse excited by Mesopotamian literacy. It survives in several variants which, taken together, provide an ongoing record of Mesopotamian rulers from the legendary time before the Flood to about 1800 B.C. Philological analysis has revealed that all the variants stem from a common source, composed around 2100 B.C. The King List originated during a period of national revival under the leadership of the Third Dynasty of Ur, when the descendants of the Sumerians regained control of Mesopotamia. Pride awakened by this development gave rise to the notion that all Mesopotamia had always been under a single rule, now finally restored to the proper hands. The King List both sanctions and memorializes this idea.

In contrast to the tales of Homer, the list is clearly of literate origin, being so spare as to provide no story for the memory to grasp. The bulk of the list, running over four hundred lines, reads according to the following simple formula: "B, son of A, reigned X years; C, son of B, reigned Y years." The list of reigns is punctuated every few lines by a conventional transition, generally one stating that "city X was smitten with weapons, and its kingship to city Y was carried," followed by the next enumeration of reigns. In some instances, the list contains anecdotal information concerning the origin and achievements of a ruler, as in the following:

> Etana, a shepherd, the one who to heaven
>   ascended,
> the one who consolidated all lands,
> became king and reigned 1,560 years.

This is one of the most elaborate of these narrative flourishes (if we can call them that), most being limited to a brief mention of the native city or profession of a future king. In short, there is no "story" here, at least none that the oral imagination can lay hold of, with its reliance on heroic action and concrete detail.

Not only is the list a purely literate creation, but it derives from written sources. Philological analysis discloses two kinds of antecedents, corresponding to the two kinds of materials contained in the list. The names and reigns of kings trace to the "date lists" of various cities, enumerations of local rulers and dignitaries extending back to the very remote past. The anecdotal information about kings descends from a host of oral epics and legends preserved in writing. For instance, the above quoted information about Etana derives from the "Etana" epic, probably written down long before the author of the original King List set to work. He thus faced the task of organizing in a single compendium a wealth of information drawn from two very different kinds of documents.

That the date lists would obviously be his primary source, with epic literature restricted to a supplementary role, somewhat eased his conceptual burden. But before using the date lists, he had to find a means of unifying their diverse accounts. Each of these lists commemorates the independent political tradition of a city, generally ruled by a king, that existed in competition with other cities in the region. The ruler was regarded as having been chosen by the god of the city, and struggles between cities were viewed as conflicts within the assembly of gods. Our scribe, however, wanted to commemorate the Sumerian revival, when all Mesopotamia came under the control of a single dynasty in Ur. This phenomenon of a single city's dominance over the entire land required that he devise a new interpretation not only of political power but also of its theological basis, enabling him to merge his sources into a single account.

The scribe's solution to this problem demonstrates his considerable ingenuity, if not genius. He cleverly modified the traditional formula used in the date lists to describe the divine origins of a city and its rulership. The boldness of his departure from tradition, apparent in the opening lines of the King List, is masked by the flat, repetitive, dogmatic style of Mesopotamian writing: "When the kingship was lowered from heaven / the kingship was in Eridu." In place of separate kings, each ordained by the particular god of a city, he has posited a single, divinely ordained "kingship," transferred from one city to the next by an assembly of gods acting in unanimity.

Having found a means of combining the date lists, the scribe could arrange them sequentially, hence charting the course of a kingship that would appear to pass from one city to the next. This posed an added difficulty, though. His other body of sources, epics and legends, revealed that some of the rulers of different cities were contemporaries. The kingship could not reside concurrently in different cities. More so than the preceding problem, this one no doubt taxed our scribe's critical abilities to the utmost.

Logically, he might have resolved the conundrum by determining at what point the kingship was transferred from one city to the next, utilizing only the portion of each date list corresponding to the presence of the kingship in that locality. Although this solution may seem obvious to us, the scribe found it unacceptable because it violated the spirit of Mesopotamian list making, which tends toward completeness, toward the inclusion of all material appropriate to any given heading. Once named, all the rulers of the date lists had attained sufficiently reality as rulers to require their inclusion in the master list, lest it be incomplete. The need to be exhaustive further exacerbated chronological problems, for the scribe could not arrange the unexpurgated date lists successively without creating lengthy chronological separations between contemporaneous rulers.

Given the constraints imposed upon his thinking by the need to be exhaustive, our scribe devised what must have seemed to him a brilliant solution, however imperfect in our eyes. He arranged the material of the date lists sequentially, yet so as to minimize chronological disparities. Dividing each date list into its constituent dynasties, he interspersed the latter to form the King List in such way that contemporaneous rulers became near contemporaries. He thus preserved completeness without egregiously violating chronology.

***

The Sumerian King List demonstrates how writing fostered critical abilities by accentuating the classificatory potential inherent in language. Although the members of an oral culture could conceive the class 'kings'—drawn from their experience, direct or vicarious, of individual rulers—it would exist only as a passing thought. For sustained thinking about kings, they relied on the activity of commemoration, the telling of stories about the heroic actions of specific figures.

Recall that an oral culture retains these stories in its collective memory by means of generalized images to which all members of the community can assent. Although these images are abstracted from the narrative action of the story, they are not themselves abstract; they preserve the generalized image, not of "a king," but of "the king." Generalized and stripped of local detail, the image is nonetheless specific to the story it serves to map.

Writing enables one to do readily what one cannot otherwise so readily do, create a class of "kings" standing apart from the stories told about them. Such is the case with the date lists for individual cities. Their initial, mythological sections, recounting the divine origins of each city, are no doubt abstracted from stories and legends, whether oral or written. The later sections, constituting a quasi-historical enumeration of rulers, are drawn partially from legend, partially from memory, and partially from records.

The author of the Sumerian King List could build upon this initial, classifying effort in two ways. First, he could compare the collected date lists with the collected epic literature, establishing a web of chronological relations between the rulers of different cities. Second, motivated by this new information, he could subdivide the date lists into their constituent dynasties. The latter innovation grows directly out of the activity of list making, which encourages the scrutiny of items, both individually and as a group, and reveals the possibility of new classifications. Writing thus stimulates an expanding range of critical activities whose complexity reaches beyond the confines of an oral culture. [. . .]

The classifying impulse in Mesopotamian writing was thwarted by the urge to be exhaustive, an urge that derived from the pictographic origins of Sumerian script. Despite the growing role of phonetization, the Mesopotamians could never transcend the belief that the nature of things was divinely inscribed in their words. This belief led them to channel their classifying activity not toward higher and higher abstractions but toward an ever more thorough naming that ultimately sought to fix the nature, and thereby the knowledge, of the cosmos.

* * *

The pictographic origins of Sumerian script define the essence of information in ancient Mesopotamia. It originated as writing, the visual expression of language's ability to classify. As further manifestations of this ability were increasingly modeled upon language, writing unleashed the urge to classify the information it had created. And once freed, this urge acquired a momentum of its own, operating upon its own products, which naturally became objects of further scrutiny. The Sumerian King List—a list of lists—exemplifies this tendency. But Mesopotamian list making, though generated by a classifying urge, did not ultimately entail classification.

Of course, the lists were organized by categories, but these existed primarily to facilitate the exhaustive naming of entities and only incidentally to classify them. In fact, the real relations between entities were not classificatory at all; rather, they were inherent in the written names of things, whose constituent signs and their cognates depicted other things, without any obvious connections apparent to the modern mind with its Hellenic predisposition. The very nature of Sumerian script thus encouraged a sequential decoding of names, revealing the myriad pictographic tendrils through which vital sap flowed to animate the things of the world.

We shall now turn to a consideration of the Greek alphabet, which broke the pictorial tie between words and things, removing the barrier to classification. In so doing, it permitted the process of abstraction to operate freely upon its own products, giving rise to different kinds of information at each new level of abstraction. Information thus conceived was not synonymous with the world but rather constituted a body of facts about it. The activity of play accentuated this process of abstraction, yielding a hierarchical vision of the order of things, an order inherent in the things themselves rather than in the words used to express them.

WALTER ONG, FROM *ORALITY AND LITERACY: THE TECHNOLOGIZING OF THE WORD* (1982)

Ong (1912–2003) was a Jesuit priest and Professor of English and Humanities in Psychiatry at St. Louis University. He studied at St. Louis University, where he was briefly a student of Marshall McLuhan. Ong is best known for his work on the cultural and historical shifts from orality and literacy in and their impacts on human consciousness, thought, and Western European society. In his widely influential book *Orality and Literacy: The Technologizing of the Word* (1982), Ong contrasts oral modes of communication with writing—or chirographic models—arguing that underlying different strategies of expression, such as visual, verbal, or aural, change the way we organize, manage, and transmit knowledge. The excerpts below are drawn from two chapters of the book, in which Ong discusses the role of memory, memorization, and the "media model" as a concept predicated on the development of the written word.

From Memory to Written Records

Long after a culture has begun to use writing, it may still not give writing high ratings. A present-day literate usually assumes that written records have more force than spoken words as evidence of a long-past state of affairs, especially in court. Earlier cultures that knew literacy but had not so fully interiorized it, have often assumed quite the opposite. The amount of credence accorded to written records undoubtedly varied from culture to culture, but Clanchy's careful case history of the use of literacy for practical administrative purposes in eleventh- and twelfth-century England (1979) gives an informative sample of how much orality could linger in the presence of writing, even in an administrative milieu.

In the period he studies, Clanchy finds that "documents did not immediately inspire trust."[1] People had to be persuaded that writing improved the old oral methods sufficiently to warrant all the expense and troublesome techniques it involved. Before the use of documents, collective oral testimony was commonly used to establish, for example, the age of feudal heirs. To settle a dispute in 1127 as to whether the customs dues at the port of Sandwich went to St Augustine's Abbey at Canterbury or to Christ Church, a jury was chosen consisting of twelve men from Dover and twelve from Sandwich, "mature, wise seniors of many years, having good testimony." Each juror then swore that, as "I have received from my ancestors, and I have seen and heard from my youth" the tolls belong to Christ Church (232–33). They were publicly remembering what others before them had remembered.

Witnesses were *prima facie* more credible than texts because they could be challenged and made to defend their statements whereas text could not (this, it will be recalled, was exactly one of Plato's objections to writing). Notarial methods of authenticating documents undertake to build authenticating mechanisms into written texts, but notarial methods develop late in literate cultures and much later in England than in Italy (235–6). Written documents themselves were often authenticated not in writing but by symbolic objects (such as a knife, attached to the document by a parchment thong) (24). [. . .]

Early charters conveying land in England were originally not even dated (231, 236–41), probably for a variety of reasons. Clanchy suggests that the most profound reason was probably that "dating required the scribe to express an opinion about his place in time" (238), which demanded that he choose a point of reference. What point? Was he to locate this document by reference to the creation of the world? To the Crucifixion? To the birth of Christ? Popes dated documents this way, from Christ's birth, but was it presumptuous to date a secular document as popes dated theirs? In high technology cultures today, everyone lives each day in a frame of abstract computed time enforced by millions of printed calendars, clocks, and watches. In twelfth-century England there were no clocks or watches or wall or desk calendars. [. . .]

Persons whose world view has been formed by high literacy need to remind themselves that in functionally oral cultures the past is not felt as an itemized terrain, peppered with verifiable and disputed "facts" or bits of information. It is the domain of the ancestors, a resonant source for renewing awareness of present existence, which itself is not an itemized terrain either. Orality knows no lists or charts or figures.

Goody has examined in detail the noetic significance of tables and lists, of which the calendar is one example[2]. Writing makes such apparatus possible. Indeed, writing was in a sense invented largely to make something like lists: by far most of the earliest writing we know, that in the cuneiform script of the Sumerians beginning around 3500 BC, is account-keeping. Primary oral cultures commonly situate their equivalent of lists in narrative, as in the catalogue of the ships and captains in the *Iliad* (ii. 461–879)—not an objective tally but an operational display in a story about a war. In the text of the Torah, which set down in writing thought forms still basically oral, the equivalent of geography (establishing the relationship of one place to another) is put into a formulary action narrative (Numbers 33: 16 ff.): "Setting out from the desert of Sinai, they camped at Kibroth-hattaavah. Setting out from Kibroth-hattaavah, they camped at Hazeroth. Setting out from Hazeroth, they camped at Rithmah . . .," and so on for many more verses. Even genealogies out of such orally framed tradition are in effect commonly narrative. Instead of a recitation of names, we find a sequence of "begats," of statements of what someone did: "Irad begat Mehajael, Mehajael begat Methusael, Methusael begat Lamech" (Genesis 4: 18). This sort of aggregation derives partly from the oral drive to use formulas, partly from the oral mnemonic drive to exploit balance (recurrence of subject-predicate-object produces a swing which aids recall and which a mere sequence of names would lack), partly from the oral drive to redundancy (each person is mentioned twice, as begetter and begotten), and partly from the oral drive to narrate rather than simply to juxtapose (the persons are not immobilized as in a police line-up, but are doing something—namely, begetting).

These biblical passages obviously are written records, but they come from an orally constituted sensibility and tradition. They are not felt as thing-like, but as reconstitutions of events in time. Orally presented sequences are always occurrences in time, impossible to "examine," because they are not presented visually but rather are utterances which are heard. In a primary oral culture or a culture with heavy oral residue, even genealogies are not "lists" of data but rather "memory of songs sung." Texts are thing-like, immobilized in visual space, subject to what Goody calls "backward scanning" (49–50). Goody shows in detail how, when anthropologists display on a written or printed surface lists of various items found in oral myths (clans, regions of the earth, kinds of winds, and so on), they actually deform the mental world in which the myths have their own existence. The satisfaction that myths provide is essentially not "coherent" in a tabular way.

Lists of the sort Goody discusses are of course useful if we are reflectively aware of the distortion they inevitably introduce. Visual presentation of verbalized material in space has its own particular economy, its own laws of motion and structure. Texts in various scripts around the world are read variously from right to left, or left to right, or top to bottom, or all these ways at once as in boustrophedon writing, but never anywhere, so far as is known, from bottom to top. Texts assimilate utterance to the human body. They introduce a feeling for "headings" in accumulations of knowledge: "chapter" derives from the Latin *caput*, meaning head (as of the human body). Pages have not only "heads" but also "feet," for footnotes. References are given to what is "above" and "below" in a text when what is meant is several pages back or farther on. The significance of the vertical and the horizontal in texts deserves serious study. Kerckhove (pp. 10–11 in proofs) suggests that growth in left-hemisphere dominance governed the drift in early Greek writing from right-to-left movement, to boustrophedon movement ("ox-plowing" pattern, one line going right, then a turn around a corner into the next line going left, the letters inverted according to the direction of the line), to *stoichedon* style (vertical lines), and finally to definitive left-to-right movement on a horizontal line.[3] All this is quite a different world of order from anything in the oral sensibility, which has no way of operating with "headings" or verbal linearity. Across the world the alphabet, the ruthlessly efficient reducer of sound to space, is pressed into direct service for setting up the new space-defined sequences: items are marked *a, b, c*, and so on to indicate their sequences, and even poems in the early days of literacy are composed with the first letter of the first word of successive lines following the order of the alphabet. The alphabet as a simple sequence of letters is a major bridge between oral mnemonic and literate mnemonics: generally the sequence of the letters of the alphabet is memorized orally and then used for largely visual retrieval of materials, as in indexes.

Charts, which range elements of thought not simply in one line of rank but simultaneously in horizontal and various criss-cross orders, represent a frame of thought even farther removed than lists are from the oral noetic processes which such charts are supposed to represent. The extensive use of lists and particularly of charts so commonplace in our high-technology cultures is a result not simply of writing, but of the deep interiorization of print (Ong 1958, pp. 307–18, and *passim*), which implements the use of fixed diagrammatic word-charts and other informational uses of neutral space far beyond anything feasible in any writing culture.[4] [. . .]

"Media" Versus Human Communication

In treating the technologizing of the word, for the most part this book has avoided the term media (with its now more and more fugitive singular, medium). The reason is that the term can give a false impression of the nature of verbal communication, and of other human communication as well. Thinking of a "medium" of communication or of "media" of communication suggests that communication is a pipeline transfer of units of material called "information" from one place to another. My mind is a box. I take a unit of "information" out of it, encode the unit (that is, fit it to the size and shape of the pipe it will go through), and put it into one end of the pipe (the medium, something in the middle between two other things). From the one end of the pipe the "information" proceeds to the other end, where someone decodes it (restores its proper size and shape) and puts it in his or her own box-like container called a mind. This model obviously has something to do with human communication, but, on close inspection, very little, and it distorts the act of communication beyond recognition. Hence McLuhan's wry book title: *The Medium is the Massage* (not quite the "message").

Human communication, verbal and other, differs from the "medium" model most basically in that it demands anticipated feedback in order to take place at all. In the medium model, the message is moved from sender-position to receiver-position. In real human communication, the sender has to be not only in the sender position but also in the receiver position before he or she can send anything.

To speak, you have to address another or others. People in their right minds do not stray through the woods just talking at random to nobody. Even to talk to yourself you have to pretend that you are two people. The reason is that what I say depends on what reality or fancy I feel I am talking into, that is, on what possible responses I might anticipate. Hence I avoid sending quite the same message to an adult and to a small child. To speak, I have to be somehow already in communication with the mind I am to address before I start speaking. I can be in touch perhaps through past relationships, by an exchange of glances, by an understanding with a third person who has brought me and my interlocutor together, or in any of countless other ways. (Words are modifications of a more-than-verbal situation.) I have to sense something in the other's mind to which my own utterance can relate. Human communication is never one-way. Always, it not only calls for response but is shaped in its very form and content by anticipated response.

This is not to say that I am sure how the other will respond to what I say. But I have to be able to conjecture a possible range of responses at least in some vague way. I have to be somehow inside the mind of the other in advance in order to enter with my message, and he or she must be inside my mind. To formulate anything I must have another person or other persons already "in mind." This is the paradox of human communication. Communication is inter-subjective. The media model is not. There is no adequate model in the physical universe for this operation of consciousness, which is distinctively human and which signals the capacity of human beings to form true communities wherein person shares with person interiorly, intersubjectively.

Willingness to live with the "media" model of communication shows chirographic conditioning. First, chirographic cultures regard speech as more specifically informational than do oral cultures, where speech is more performance-oriented, more a way of doing something to someone. Second, the written text appears *prima facie* to be a one-way informational street, for no real recipient (reader, hearer) is present when the texts come into being. But in speaking as in writing, some recipient must be present, or there can be no text produced: so, isolated from real persons, the writer conjures up a fictional person or persons. "The writer's audience is always a fiction" (Ong 1977, pp. 54–81).[5] For a writer any real recipient is normally absent (if a recipient is accidentally present, the inscribing of the message itself proceeds as though the person were somehow absent—otherwise, why write?). The fictionalizing of readers is what makes writing so difficult. The process is complex and fraught with uncertainties. I have to know the tradition—the intertextuality, if you wish—in which I am working so that I can create for real readers fictional roles that they are able and willing to play. It is not easy to get inside the minds of absent persons most of whom you will never know. But it is not impossible if you and they are familiar with the literary tradition they work in. I hope that I have somewhat succeeded in laying hold on tradition sufficiently to get inside the minds of readers of this present book.

Notes

1. M. T. Clanchy, *From Memory to Written Record: England, 1066–1307* (Cambridge, MA.: Harvard University Press, 1979), 230. Subsequent page numbers appear parenthetically in the text.
2. Sir J. Goody, *The Domestication of the Savage Mind* (Cambridge: Cambridge University Press, 1977), 52–111.
3. Derrick de Kerckhove, "A Theory of Greek Tragedy," *SubStance* 29 (Summer 1981).
4. Ong, Walter J., *Ramus, Method, and the Decay of Dialogue* (Cambridge, MA: Harvard University Press, 1958).
5. Ong, Walter J., *Interfaces of the Word* (Ithaca and London: Cornell University Press, 1977).

SIGMUND FREUD, FROM "A NOTE UPON THE 'MYSTIC WRITING-PAD'" (1925)

Freud (1856–1939) was an Austrian neurologist, founder of psycho-analysis, and writer. One of the most influential thinkers of the twen-tieth century, Freud was invested in developing a science of the mind to understand human behavior and its psychological manifestations. At the center of psychoanalysis as a method lies the role of the ana-lytic process: to establish, retrieve, collect, and interpret information a patient may share with their doctor during a therapy session (which, before it became known as psychoanalysis, Freud together with Josef Breuer developed as the "talking cure" [*Sprechtherapie*]). Freud was an incredibly productive and avid writer, whose attention to the analysis of human actions, cultural artifacts, and the relationship between symp-toms visible on the surface and their underlying, concealed causes has influenced a wide array of field including Anthropology, Semiotics, and Literary Theory; among his best-known publications are *The Interpre-tation of Dreams* (1899), *Totem and Taboo* (1913), *Beyond the Pleasure Principle* (1920) and *Moses and Monotheism* (1940). The excerpt below is drawn from *"A Note upon the 'Mystic* Writing-Pad,'" an essay pub-lished in 1925. In the essay, Freud imagines the mystic writing pad, a reusable wax tablet covered with a sheet of cellophane used to write notes, as a metaphor for the human mind and the process of recording and storing memories.

If I distrust my memory—neurotics, as we know, do so to a remarkable extent, but normal people have every reason for doing so as well—I am able to supplement and guarantee its working by making a note in writing. In that case the surface upon which this note is preserved, the pocket-book or sheet of paper, is as it were a materialized portion of my mnemic apparatus, the rest of which I carry about with me invisible. I have only to bear in mind the place where this "memory" has been deposited and I can then "reproduce" it at any time I like, with the certainty that it will have remained unaltered and so have escaped the possible distortions to which it might have been subjected in my actual memory.

If I want to make full use of this technique for improving my mnemic function, I find that there are two different procedures open to me. On the one hand, I can choose a writing-surface which will preserve intact any note made upon it for an indefinite length of time—for instance, a sheet of paper which I can write upon in ink. I am then in possession of a "permanent memory-trace." The disadvantage of this procedure is that the receptive capacity of the writing-surface is soon exhausted. The sheet is filled with writing, there is no room on it for any more notes, and I find myself obliged to bring another sheet into use, that has not been written on. Moreover, the advantage of this procedure, the fact that it provides a "permanent trace," may lose its value for me if after a time the note ceases to interest me and I no longer want to "retain it in my memory." The alternative procedure avoids both of these disadvantages. If, for instance, I write with a piece of chalk upon a slate, I have a receptive surface which retains its receptive capacity for an unlimited time and the notes upon which can be destroyed as soon as they cease to interest me, without any need for throwing away the writing-surface itself. Here the disadvantage is that I cannot preserve a permanent trace. If I want to put some fresh notes upon the slate, I must first wipe out the ones which cover it. Thus an unlimited receptive capacity and a retention of permanent traces seem to be mutually exclusive properties in the apparatus which we use as substitutes for our memory: either the receptive surface must be renewed or the note must be destroyed.

All the forms of auxiliary apparatus which we have invented for the improvement or intensification of our sensory functions are built on the same model as the sense organs themselves or portions of them: for instance, spectacles, photographic cameras, ear-trumpets. Measured by this standard, devices to aid our memory seem particularly imperfect, since our mental apparatus accomplishes precisely what they cannot: it has an unlimited receptive capacity for new perceptions and nevertheless lays down permanent—even though not unalterable-memory-traces of them. [...]

Some time ago there came upon the market, under the name of the Mystic Writing-Pad,[1] a small contrivance that promises to perform more than the sheet of paper or the slate. It claims to be nothing more than a writing-tablet from which notes can be erased by an easy movement of the hand. But if it is examined more closely it will be found that its construction shows a remarkable agreement with my hypothetical structure of our perceptual apparatus and that it can in fact provide both an ever-ready receptive surface and permanent traces of the notes that have been made upon it.

The Mystic Pad is a slab of dark brown resin or wax with a paper edging; over the slab is laid a thin transparent sheet, the top end of which is firmly secured to the slab while its bottom end rests upon it without being fixed to it. This transparent sheet is the more interesting part of the little device. It itself consists of two layers, which can be detached from each other except at their two ends. The upper layer is a transparent piece of celluloid; the lower layer is made of thin translucent waxed paper. When the apparatus is not in use, the lower surface of the waxed paper adheres lightly to the upper surface of the wax slab.

To make use of the Mystic Pad, one writes upon the celluloid portion of the covering-sheet which rests upon the wax slab. For this purpose no pencil or chalk is necessary, since the writing does not depend on material being deposited upon the receptive surface. It is a return to the ancient method of writing upon tablets of clay or wax: a pointed stilus scratches the surface, the depressions upon which constitute the "writing."

In the case of the Mystic Pad this scratching is not effected directly, but through the medium of the covering-sheet. At the points which the stilus touches, it presses the lower surface of the waxed paper on to the wax slab, and the grooves are visible as dark writing upon the otherwise smooth whitish-grey surface of the celluloid. If one wishes to destroy what has been written, all that is necessary is to raise the double covering-sheet from the wax slab by a light pull, starting from the free lower end. The close contact between the waxed paper and the wax slab at the places which have been scratched (upon which the visibility of the writing depended) is thus brought to an end and it does not recur when the two surfaces come together once more. The Mystic Pad is now clear of writing and ready to receive fresh notes.

The small imperfections of the contrivance have, of course, no importance for us, since we are only concerned with its approximation to the structure of the perceptive apparatus of the mind.

If, while the Mystic Pad has writing upon it, we cautiously raise the celluloid from the waxed paper, we can see the writing just as clearly on the surface of the latter, and the question may arise why there should be any necessity for the celluloid portion of the cover. Experiment will then show that the thin paper would be very easily crumpled or torn if one were to write directly upon it with the stilus. The layer of celluloid thus acts as a protective sheath for the waxed paper, to keep off injurious effects from without. The celluloid is a "protective shield against stimuli"; the layer which actually receives the stimuli is the paper. I may at this point recall that in *Beyond the Pleasure Principle*.[2] I showed that the perceptive apparatus of our mind consists of two layers, of an external protective shield against stimuli whose task it is to diminish the strength of excitations coming in, and of a surface behind it which receives the stimuli, namely the system Pcpt.-Cs [Perception-Consciousness].

The analogy would not be of much value if it could not be pursued further than this. If we lift the entire covering-sheet—both the celluloid and the waxed paper—off the wax slab, the writing vanishes and, as I have already remarked, does not re-appear again. The surface of the Mystic Pad is clear of writing and once more capable of receiving impressions. But it is easy to discover that the permanent trace of what was written is retained upon the wax slab itself and is legible in suitable lights. Thus the Pad provides not only a receptive surface that can be used over and over again, like a slate, but also permanent traces of what has been written, like an ordinary paper pad: it solves the problem of combining the two functions *by dividing them between two separate but interrelated component parts or systems*. But this is precisely the way in which, according to the hypothesis which I mentioned just now, our mental apparatus performs its perceptual function. The layer which receives the stimuli—the system Pcpt.-Cs.—forms no permanent traces; the foundations of memory come about in other, adjoining, systems.

We need not be disturbed by the fact that in the Mystic Pad no use is made of the permanent traces of the notes that have been received; it is enough that they are present. There must come a point at which the analogy between an auxiliary apparatus of this kind and the organ which is its prototype will cease to apply. It is true, too, that, once the writing has been erased, the Mystic Pad cannot "reproduce" it from within; it would be a mystic pad indeed if, like our memory, it could accomplish that. None the less, I do not think it is too far-fetched to compare the celluloid and waxed paper cover with the system Pcpt.-Cs. and its protective shield, the wax slab with the unconscious behind them, and the appearance and disappearance of the writing with the flickering-up and passing-away of consciousness in the process of perception.

But I must admit that I am inclined to press the comparison still further. On the Mystic Pad the writing vanishes every time the close contact is broken between the paper which receives the stimulus and the wax slab which preserves the impression. This agrees with a notion which I have long had about the method in which the perceptual apparatus of our mind functions, but which I have hitherto kept to myself.[3] My theory was that cathectic innervations are sent out and withdrawn in rapid periodic impulses from within into the completely pervious system Pcpt.-Cs. So long as that system is cathected in this manner, it receives perceptions (which are accompanied by consciousness) and passes the excitation on to the unconscious mnemic systems; but as soon as the cathexis is withdrawn, consciousness is extinguished and the functioning of the system comes to a standstill. It is as though the unconscious stretches out feelers, through the medium of the system Pcpt.-Cs., towards the external world and hastily withdraws them as soon as they have sampled the excitations coming from it. Thus the interruptions, which in the case of the Mystic Pad have an external origin, were attributed by my hypothesis to the discontinuity in the current of innervation; and the actual breaking of contact which occurs in the Mystic Pad was replaced in my theory by the periodic nonexcitability of the perceptual system. I further had a suspicion that this discontinuous method of functioning of the system Pcpt.-Cs. lies at the bottom of the origin of the concept of time.

If we imagine one hand writing upon the surface of the Mystic Writing-Pad while another periodically raises its covering sheet from the wax slab, we shall have a concrete representation of the way in which I tried to picture the functioning of the perceptual apparatus of our mind.

Notes

1. [It is still obtainable as such in England, where, however, it is also known as "Printator."]
2. [Trans., 1922, 22 ff.; new trans., 1950, 30 ff.]
3. [It is hinted at in *Beyond the Pleasure Principle* (English translation, 1922, 32; new translation, 1950, 33).]

VANNEVAR BUSH, FROM
"AS WE MAY THINK" (1945)

Bush (1890–1974) was an American electrical engineer and science administrator. He taught at MIT (where Claude Shannon was one of his students), and in 1932 became vice president of MIT and the dean of the School of Engineering. During the interwar period, Bush was at the forefront of designing and building analog computers, most notably the differential analyzer, a mechanical machine that solved differential equations. He later served as president of the Carnegie Institution of Washington, chairman of the National Advisory Committee for Aeronautics, and, during World War II, as head of the Office of Scientific Research and Development, where he was involved in the Manhattan Project. These appointments across scientific and governmental institutions make clear how Bush's work influenced the institutional landscape of science and policy making in the U.S.: in July 1945, Bush wrote "Science, The Endless Frontier," a landmark report to President Truman urging for greater government support for the sciences. In the same month, he published "As We May Think" in the *Atlantic,* from which the excerpt below is drawn. Here, Bush grapples with the dangers of scientific inventions becoming forces of destructions and lays out ground-breaking visions for technological devices to improve everyday life and human society, amongst them a Vocoder, a machine "which types when talked to," and most famously the memex, a kind of memory machine that could serve as a personal knowledge storehouse for "books, records, and communications." Such a machine, Bush envisioned, would help organize, store, and transmit information in order to create knowledge and make it more accessible.

1

Of what lasting benefit has been man's use of science and of the new instruments which his research brought into existence? First, they have increased his control of his material environment. They have improved his food, his clothing, his shelter; they have increased his security and released him partly from the bondage of bare existence. They have given him increased knowledge of his own biological processes so that he has had a progressive freedom from disease and an increased span of life. They are illuminating the interactions of his physiological and psychological functions, giving the promise of an improved mental health.

Science has provided the swiftest communication between individuals; it has provided a record of ideas and has enabled man to manipulate and to make extracts from that record so that knowledge evolves and endures throughout the life of a race rather than that of an individual. [. . .]

The difficulty seems to be, not so much that we publish unduly in view of the extent and variety of present day interests, but rather that publication has been extended far beyond our present ability to make real use of the record. The summation of human experience is being expanded at a prodigious rate, and the means we use for threading through the consequent maze to the momentarily important item is the same as was used in the days of square-rigged ships.

But there are signs of a change as new and powerful instrumentalities come into use. Photocells capable of seeing things in a physical sense, advanced photography which can record what is seen or even what is not, thermionic tubes capable of controlling potent forces under the guidance of less power than a mosquito uses to vibrate his wings, cathode ray tubes rendering visible an occurrence so brief that by comparison a microsecond is a long time, relay combinations which will carry out involved sequences of movements more reliably than any human operator and thousands of times as fast—there are plenty of mechanical aids with which to effect a transformation in scientific records. [. . .]

3

To make the record, we now push a pencil or tap a typewriter. Then comes the process of digestion and correction, followed by an intricate process of typesetting, printing, and distribution. To consider the first stage of the procedure, will the author of the future cease writing by hand or typewriter and talk directly to the record? He does so indirectly, by talking to a stenographer or a wax cylinder; but the elements are all present if he wishes to have his talk directly produce a typed record. All he needs to do is to take advantage of existing mechanisms and to alter his language.

At a recent World Fair a machine called a Voder was shown. A girl stroked its keys and it emitted recognizable speech. No human vocal chords entered into the procedure at any point; the keys simply combined some electrically produced vibrations and passed these on to a loud-speaker. In the Bell Laboratories there is the converse of this machine, called a Vocoder. The loudspeaker is replaced by a microphone, which picks up sound. Speak to it, and the corresponding keys move. This may be one element of the postulated system.

The other element is found in the stenotype, that somewhat disconcerting device encountered usually at public meetings. A girl strokes its keys languidly and looks about the room and sometimes at the speaker with a disquieting gaze. From it emerges a typed strip which records in a phonetically simplified language a record of what the speaker is supposed to have said. Later this strip is retyped into ordinary language, for in its nascent form it is intelligible only to the initiated. Combine these two elements, let the Vocoder run the stenotype, and the result is a machine which types when talked to.

Our present languages are not especially adapted to this sort of mechanization, it is true. It is strange that the inventors of universal languages have not seized upon the idea of producing one which better fitted the technique for transmitting and recording speech. Mechanization may yet force the issue, especially in the scientific field; whereupon scientific jargon would become still less intelligible to the layman.

One can now picture a future investigator in his laboratory. His hands are free, and he is not anchored. As he moves about and observes, he photographs and comments. Time is automatically recorded to tie the two records together. If he goes into the field, he may be connected by radio to his recorder. As he ponders over his notes in the evening, he again talks his comments into the record. His typed record, as well as his photographs, may both be in miniature, so that he projects them for examination. [. . .]

6

The real heart of the matter of selection, however, goes deeper than a lag in the adoption of mechanisms by libraries, or a lack of development of devices for their use. Our ineptitude in getting at the record is largely caused by the artificiality of systems of indexing. When data of any sort are placed in storage, they are filed alphabetically or numerically, and information is found (when it is) by tracing it down from subclass to subclass. It can be in only one place, unless duplicates are used; one has to have rules as to which path will locate it, and the rules are cumbersome. Having found one item, moreover, one has to emerge from the system and re-enter on a new path.

The human mind does not work that way. It operates by association. With one item in its grasp, it snaps instantly to the next that is suggested by the association of thoughts, in accordance with some intricate web of trails carried by the cells of the brain. It has other characteristics, of course; trails that are not frequently followed are prone to fade, items are not fully permanent, memory is transitory. Yet the speed of action, the intricacy of trails, the detail of mental pictures, is awe-inspiring beyond all else in nature.

Man cannot hope fully to duplicate this mental process artificially, but he certainly ought to be able to learn from it. In minor ways he may even improve, for his records have relative permanency. The first idea, however, to be drawn from the analogy concerns selection. Selection by association, rather than indexing, may yet be mechanized. One cannot hope thus to equal the speed and flexibility with which the mind follows an associative trail, but it should be possible to beat the mind decisively in regard to the permanence and clarity of the items resurrected from storage.

Consider a future device for individual use, which is a sort of mechanized private file and library. It needs a name, and, to coin one at random, "memex" will do. A memex is a device in which an individual stores all his books, records, and communications, and which is mechanized so that it may be consulted with exceeding speed and flexibility. It is an enlarged intimate supplement to his memory.

It consists of a desk, and while it can presumably be operated from a distance, it is primarily the piece of furniture at which he works. On the top are slanting translucent screens, on which material can be projected for convenient reading. There is a keyboard, and sets of buttons and levers. Otherwise it looks like an ordinary desk.

In one end is the stored material. The matter of bulk is well taken care of by improved microfilm. Only a small part of the interior of the memex is devoted to storage, the rest to mechanism. Yet if the user inserted 5000 pages of material a day it would take him hundreds of years to fill the repository, so he can be profligate and enter material freely.

Most of the memex contents are purchased on microfilm ready for insertion. Books of all sorts, pictures, current periodicals, newspapers, are thus obtained and dropped into place. Business correspondence takes the same path. And there is provision for direct entry. On the top of the memex is a transparent platen. On this are placed longhand notes, photographs, memoranda, all sorts of things. When one is in place, the depression of a lever causes it to be photographed onto the next blank space in a section of the memex film, dry photography being employed.

There is, of course, provision for consultation of the record by the usual scheme of indexing. If the user wishes to consult a certain book, he taps its code on the keyboard, and the title page of the book promptly appears before him, projected onto one of his viewing positions. Frequently used codes are mnemonic, so that he seldom consults his code book; but when he does, a single tap of a key projects it for his use. Moreover, he has supplemental levers. On deflecting one of these levers to the right he runs through the book before him, each page in turn being projected at a speed which just allows a recognizing glance at each. If he deflects it further to the right, he steps through the book 10 pages at a time; still further at 100 pages at a time. Deflection to the left gives him the same control backwards.

A special button transfers him immediately to the first page of the index. Any given book of his library can thus be called up and consulted with far greater facility than if it were taken from a shelf. As he has several projection positions, he can leave one item in position while he calls up another. He can add marginal notes and comments, taking advantage of one possible type of dry photography, and it could even be arranged so that he can do this by a stylus scheme, such as is now employed in the telautograph seen in railroad waiting rooms, just as though he had the physical page before him.

7

All this is conventional, except for the projection forward of present-day mechanisms and gadgetry. It affords an immediate step, however, to associative indexing, the basic idea of which is a provision whereby any item may be caused at will to select immediately and automatically another. This is the essential feature of the memex. The process of tying two items together is the important thing.

When the user is building a trail, he names it, inserts the name in his code book, and taps it out on his keyboard. Before him are the two items to be joined, projected onto adjacent viewing positions. At the bottom of each there are a number of blank code spaces, and a pointer is set to indicate one of these on each item. The user taps a single key, and the items are permanently joined. In each code space appears the code word. Out of view, but also in the code space, is inserted a set of dots for photocell viewing; and on each item these dots by their positions designate the index number of the other item.

Thereafter, at any time, when one of these items is in view, the other can be instantly recalled merely by tapping a button below the corresponding code space. Moreover, when numerous items have been thus joined together to form a trail, they can be reviewed in turn, rapidly or slowly, by deflecting a lever like that used for turning the pages of a book. It is exactly as though the physical items had been gathered together from widely separated sources and bound together to form a new book. It is more than this, for any item can be joined into numerous trails.

The owner of the memex, let us say, is interested in the origin and properties of the bow and arrow. Specifically he is studying why the short Turkish bow was apparently superior to the English long bow in the skirmishes of the Crusades. He has dozens of possibly pertinent books and articles in his memex. First he runs through an encyclopedia, finds an interesting but sketchy article, leaves it projected. Next, in a history, he finds another pertinent item, and ties the two together. Thus he goes, building a trail of many items. Occasionally he inserts a comment of his own, either linking it into the main trail or joining it by a side trail to a particular item. When it becomes evident that the elastic properties of available materials had a great deal to do with the bow, he branches off on a side trail which takes him through textbooks on elasticity and tables of physical constants. He inserts a page of longhand analysis of his own. Thus he builds a trail of his interest through the maze of materials available to him.

And his trails do not fade. Several years later, his talk with a friend turns to the queer ways in which a people resist innovations, even of vital interest. He has an example, in the fact that the outraged Europeans still failed to adopt the Turkish bow. In fact he has a trail on it. A touch brings up the code book. Tapping a few keys projects the head of the trail. A lever runs through it at will, stopping at interesting items, going off on side excursions. It is an interesting trail, pertinent to the discussion. So he sets a reproducer in action, photographs the whole trail out, and passes it to his friend for insertion in his own memex, there to be linked into the more general trail.

8

Wholly new forms of encyclopedias will appear, ready made with a mesh of associative trails running through them, ready to be dropped into the memex and there amplified. The lawyer has at his touch the associated opinions and decisions of his whole experience, and of the experience of friends and authorities. The patent attorney has on call the millions of issued patents, with familiar trails to every point of his client's interest. The physician, puzzled by a patient's reactions, strikes the trail established in studying an earlier similar case, and runs rapidly through analogous case histories, with side references to the classics for the pertinent anatomy and histology. The chemist, struggling with the synthesis of an organic compound, has all the chemical literature before him in his laboratory, with trails following the analogies of compounds, and side trails to their physical and chemical behavior.

The historian, with a vast chronological account of a people, parallels it with a skip trail which stops only on the salient items, and can follow at any time contemporary trails which lead him all over civilization at a particular epoch. There is a new profession of trail blazers, those who find delight in the task of establishing useful trails through the enormous mass of the common record. The inheritance from the master becomes, not only his additions to the world's record, but for his disciples the entire scaffolding by which they were erected.

Thus science may implement the ways in which man produces, stores, and consults the record of the race. It might be striking to outline the instrumentalities of the future more spectacularly, rather than to stick closely to methods and elements now known and undergoing rapid development, as has been done here. Technical difficulties of all sorts have been ignored, certainly, but also ignored are means as yet unknown which may come any day to accelerate technical progress as violently as did the advent of the thermionic tube. In order that the picture may not be too commonplace, by reason of sticking to present-day patterns, it may be well to mention one such possibility, not to prophesy but merely to suggest, for prophecy based on extension of the known has substance, while prophecy founded on the unknown is only a doubly involved guess. [. . .]

The applications of science have built man a well-supplied house, and are teaching him to live healthily therein. They have enabled him to throw masses of people against one another with cruel weapons. They may yet allow him truly to encompass the great record and to grow in the wisdom of race experience. He may perish in conflict before he learns to wield that record for his true good. Yet, in the application of science to the needs and desires of man, it would seem to be a singularly unfortunate stage at which to terminate the process, or to lose hope as to the outcome.

MARSHALL MCLUHAN, FROM
UNDERSTANDING MEDIA:
THE EXTENSION OF MAN (1964)

McLuhan (1911–1980) was Professor of English Literature University of Toronto and a media theorist. He is best known for his work on the impacts of media on human society, and in particular for his intellectual and philosophical contribution to media theory as a field. In *The Gutenberg Galaxy* (1962), McLuhan delineates four media epochs of history (oral culture, manuscript culture, Gutenberg galaxy, and electronic age) and argues that with each shift different mass media have changed not only the media landscape and its technologies, but along with it also human perception and consciousness. In *Understanding Media* (1964), McLuhan further develops his argument that media should not simply be treated as tools carrying messages, but instead understood as extensions of human senses and behaviors, fundamentally influencing human society and subjectivity. In the chapter "The Medium is the Message," from which the excerpt below is drawn, McLuhan proposes to shift our attention to the study of media and away from the mere analysis of content.

I n a culture like ours, long accustomed to splitting and dividing all things as a means of control, it is sometimes a bit of a shock to be reminded that, in operational and practical fact, the medium is the message. This is merely to say that the personal and social consequences of any medium—that is, of any extension of ourselves—result from the new scale that is introduced into our affairs by each extension of ourselves, or by any new technology. Thus, with automation, for example, the new patterns of human association tend to eliminate jobs, it is true. That is the negative result. Positively, automation creates roles for people, which is to say depth of involvement in their work and human association that our preceding mechanical technology had destroyed. Many people would be disposed to say that it was not the machine, but what one did with the machine, that was its meaning or message. In terms of the ways in which the machine altered our relations to one another and to ourselves, it mattered not in the least whether it turned out cornflakes or Cadillacs. The restructuring of human work and association was shaped by the technique of fragmentation that is the essence of machine technology. The essence of automation technology is the opposite. It is integral and decentralist in depth, just as the machine was fragmentary, centralist, and superficial in its patterning of human relationships.

The instance of the electric light may prove illuminating in this connection. The electric light is pure information. It is a medium without a message, as it were, unless it is used to spell out some verbal ad or name. This fact, characteristic of all media, means that the "content" of any medium is always another medium. The content of writing is speech, just as the written word is the content of print, and print is the content of the telegraph. If it is asked, "What is the content of speech?", it is necessary to say, "It is an actual process of thought, which is in itself nonverbal." An abstract painting represents direct manifestation of creative thought processes as they might appear in computer designs. What we are considering here, however, are the psychic and social consequences of the designs or patterns as they amplify or accelerate existing processes. For the "message" of any medium or technology is the change of scale or pace or pattern that it introduces into human affairs. The railway did not introduce movement or transportation or wheel or road into human society, but it accelerated and enlarged the scale of previous human functions, creating totally new kinds of cities and new kinds of work and leisure. This happened whether the railway functioned in a tropical or a northern environment, and is quite independent of the freight or content of the railway medium. The airplane, on the other hand, by accelerating the rate of transportation, tends to dissolve the railway form of city, politics, and association, quite independently of what the airplane is used for.

Let us return to the electric light. Whether the light is being used for brain surgery or night baseball is a matter of indifference. It could be argued that these activities are in some way the "content" of the electric light, since they could not exist without the electric light. This fact merely underlines the point that "the medium is the message" because it is the medium that shapes and controls the scale and form of human association and action. The content or uses of such media are as diverse as they are ineffectual in shaping the form of human association. Indeed, it is only too typical that the "content" of any medium blinds us to the character of the medium. It is only today that industries have become aware of the various kinds of business in which they are engaged. When IBM discovered that it was not in the business of making office equipment or business machines, but that it was in the business of processing information, then it began to navigate with clear vision. The General Electric Company makes a considerable portion of its profits from electric light bulbs and lighting systems. It has not yet discovered that, quite as much as AT&T, it is in the business of moving information.

The electric light escapes attention as a communication medium just because it has no "content." And this makes it an invaluable instance of how people fail to study media at all. For it is not till the electric light is used to spell out some brand name that it is noticed as a medium. Then it is not the light but the "content" (or what is really another medium) that is noticed. The message of the electric light is like the message of electric power in industry, totally radical, pervasive, and decentralized. For electric light and power are separate from their uses, yet they eliminate time and space factors in human association exactly as do radio, telegraph, telephone, and TV, creating involvement in depth. [. . .]

Mechanization was never so vividly fragmented or sequential as in the birth of the movies, the moment that translated us beyond mechanism into the world of growth and organic interrelation. The movie, by sheer speeding up the mechanical, carried us from the world of sequence and connections into the world of creative configuration and structure. The message of the movie medium is that of transition from lineal connections to configurations. It is the transition that produced the now quite correct observation: "If it works, it's obsolete." When electric speed further takes over from mechanical movie sequences, then the lines of force in structures and in media become loud and clear. We return to the inclusive form of the icon.

To a highly literate and mechanized culture the movie appeared as a world of triumphant illusions and dreams that money could buy. It was at this moment of the movie that cubism occurred, and it has been described by E. H. Gombrich *(Art and Illusion)* as "the most radical attempt to stamp out ambiguity and to enforce one reading of the picture—that of a man-made construction, a colored canvas." For cubism substitutes all facets of an object simultaneously for the "point of view" or facet of perspective illusion. Instead of the specialized illusion of the third dimension on canvas, cubism sets up an interplay of planes and contradiction or dramatic conflict of patterns, lights, textures that "drives home the message" by involvement. This is held by many to be an exercise in painting, not in illusion.

In other words, cubism, by giving the inside and outside, the top, bottom, back, and front and the rest, in two dimensions, drops the illusion of perspective in favor of instant sensory awareness of the whole. Cubism, by seizing on instant total awareness, suddenly announced that *the medium is the message.* Is it not evident that the moment that sequence yields to the simultaneous, one is in the world of the structure and of configuration? Is that not what has happened in physics as in painting, poetry, and in communication? Specialized segments of attention have shifted to total field, and we can now say, "The medium is the message" quite naturally. Before the electric speed and total field, it was not obvious that the medium is the message. The message, it seemed, was the "content," as people used to ask what a painting was *about.* Yet they never thought to ask what a melody was about, nor what a house or a dress was about. In such matters, people retained some sense of the whole pattern, of form and function as a unity. But in the electric age this integral idea of structure and configuration has become so prevalent that educational theory has taken up the matter. Instead of working with specialized "problems" in arithmetic, the structural approach now follows the lines of force in the field of number and has small children meditating about number theory and "sets." [. . .]

De Tocqueville, in earlier work on the French Revolution, had explained how it was the printed word that, achieving cultural saturation in the eighteenth century, had homogenized the French nation. Frenchmen were the same kind of people from north to south. The typographic principles of uniformity, continuity, and lineality had overlaid the complexities of ancient feudal and oral society. The Revolution was carried out by the new literati and lawyers.

In England, however, such was the power of the ancient oral traditions of common law, backed by the medieval institution of Parliament, that no uniformity or continuity of the new visual print culture could take complete hold. The result was that the most important event in English history has never taken place; namely, the English Revolution on the lines of the French Revolution. The American Revolution had no medieval legal institutions to discard or to root out, apart from monarchy. And many have held that the American Presidency has become very much more personal and monarchical than any European monarch ever could be.

De Tocqueville's contrast between England and America is clearly based on the fact of typography and of print culture creating uniformity and continuity. England, he says, has rejected this principle and clung to the dynamic or oral common-law tradition. Hence the discontinuity and unpredictable quality of English culture. The grammar of print cannot help to construe the message of oral and nonwritten culture and institutions. The English aristocracy was properly classified as barbarian by Matthew Arnold because its power and status had nothing to do with literacy or with the cultural forms of typography.

Said the Duke of Gloucester to Edward Gibbon upon the publication of his *Decline and Fall:* "Another damned fat book, eh, Mr. Gibbon? Scribble, scribble, scribble, eh, Mr. Gibbon?" De Tocqueville was a highly literate aristocrat who was quite able to be detached from the values and assumptions of typography. That is why he alone understood the grammar of typography. And it is only on those terms, standing aside from any structure or medium, that its principles and lines of force can be discerned. For any medium has the power of imposing its own assumption on the unwary. Prediction and control consist in avoiding this subliminal state of Narcissus trance. But the greatest aid to this end is simply in knowing that the spell can occur immediately upon contact, as in the first bars of a melody. [. . .]

* * *

It is, however, no time to suggest strategies when the threat has not even been acknowledged to exist. I am in the position of Louis Pasteur telling doctors that their greatest enemy was quite invisible, and quite unrecognized by them. Our conventional response to all media, namely that it is how they are used that counts, is the numb stance of the technological idiot. For the "content" of a medium is like the juicy piece of meat carried by the burglar to distract the watchdog of the mind. The effect of the medium is made strong and intense just because it is given another medium as "content." The content of a movie is a novel or a play or an opera. The effect of the movie form is not related to its program content. The "content" of writing or print is speech, but the reader is almost entirely unaware either of print or of speech. [. . .]

Today when we want to get our bearings in our own culture, and have need to stand aside from the bias and pressure exerted by any technical form of human expression, we have only to visit a society where that particular form has not been felt, or a historical period in which it was unknown. Professor Wilbur Schramm made such a tactical move in studying *Television in the Lives of Our Children.* He found areas where TV had not penetrated at all and ran some tests. Since he had made no study of the peculiar nature of the TV image, his tests were of "content" preferences, viewing time, and vocabulary counts. In a word, his approach to the problem was a literary one, albeit unconsciously so. Consequently, he had nothing to report. Had his methods been employed in 1500 A.D. to discover the effects of the printed book in the lives of children or adults, he could have found out nothing of the changes in human and social psychology resulting from typography. Print created individualism and nationalism in the sixteenth century. Program and "content" analysis offer no clues to the magic of these media or to their subliminal charge. [. . .]

FRIEDRICH KITTLER, FROM "THERE IS NO SOFTWARE" (1993)

Kittler (1943–2011) was a German literary scholar, philosopher, and media theorist. His work on technical media, materiality, and culture changed the German landscape of intellectual history in profound ways—not only because of his interest in French poststructuralism (in particular Foucault and Lacan) as a counterpoint to the Frankfurt School and hermeneutics, but also because of his radical and often controversial focus on media technologies as a priori to human experience. This kind of techno-determinism and ontological approach to media distinguishes Kittler from McLuhan, whose understanding of media as "extensions of men" Kittler rejected for its illusion that humans are capable of controlling their media. Rather, he writes in *Gramophone, Film, Typewriter (1999)*, "media determine our situation"; human subjectivity can neither fully free itself from nor establish control over the media that shape our interactions and experiences. In his earlier book *Discourse Networks 1800/1900* (1984), Kittler focuses on the technological and institutional conditions for "selecting, storing, and processing data" by pairing Foucauldian discourse analysis with Claude Shannon's information theory. Kittler found in Shannon a highly functional and useful information concept, which, unconcerned with human subjectivity and meaning, allowed him to decentralize questions of meaning in favor of analyzing the systems, networks, sources, channels, and receivers that have shaped our relationship to media ecologies. For this volume, we chose a lesser-known essay, "There Is No Software," which touches upon many of Kittler's interests: mathematical rigor, materiality, writing, memory, and the logic of the machine.

The present explosion of the signifying scene, which, as we know from Barry McGuire and A. F. N. Dahran, coincides with the so-called Western world, is instead an implosion. The bulk of written texts—including the paper I am actually reading to you—no longer exist in perceivable time and space, but in a computer memory's transistor cells. And since these cells, in the last three decades of Silicon Valley exploits, have shrunk to spatial extensions of less than one micrometer, our writing scene may well be defined by a self-similarity of letters over some six orders of decimal magnitude. This state of affairs does not only make a difference to history, in which, at its alphabetical beginning, a camel and its hebraic letter gamel were just two and a half orders of decimal magnitude apart. It also seems to hide the very act of writing.

As one knows without saying, we do not write anymore. The crazy kind of software engineering that was writing suffered from an incurable *confusion between use and mention*. Up to Hölderlin's time, a mere mention of lightning seems to have been sufficient evidence of its possible poetic use. Nowadays, after this lightning's metamorphosis into electricity, manmade writing passes instead through microscopically written inscriptions, which, in contrast to all historical writing tools, are able to read and write by themselves. The last historical act of writing may well have been the moment when, in the early seventies, the Intel engineers laid out some dozen square meters of blueprint paper (64 square meters in the case of the later 8086) in order to design the hardware architecture of their first integrated microprocessor. This manual layout of two thousand transistors and their interconnections was then miniaturized to the size of an actual chip and, by electro-optical machines, written into silicon layers. Finally, this 4004-microprocessor found its place in the new desk calculators of Intel's Japanese customer,[1] and our postmodern writing scene could begin. Actually, the hardware complexity of microprocessors simply discards such manual design techniques. In order to lay out the next computer generation, the engineers, instead of filling countless meters of blueprint paper, have recourse to Computer Aided Design, that is, to the geometrical or autorouting powers of the actual generation.

In constructing the first integrated microprocessor, however, Intel's Marcian E. Hoff had given an almost perfect demonstration of a Turing machine. After 1937, computing, whether done by men or by machines, can be formalized as a countable set of instructions operating on an infinitely long paper band and the discrete signs thereon. Turing's concept of such a paper machine,[2] whose operations consist only of writing and reading, proceeding and receding, has proven to be the mathematical equivalent of any computable function. Universal Turing machines, when fed the instructions of any other machine, can imitate it effectively. Thus, precisely because eventual differences between hardware implementations do not count anymore, the so-called Church-Turing hypothesis in its strongest or physical form is tantamount to declaring nature itself a universal Turing machine.

This claim in itself has had the effect of duplicating the implosion of hardware by an explosion of software. Programming languages have eroded the monopoly of ordinary language and grown into a new hierarchy of their own. This postmodern Tower of Babel reaches from simple operation codes whose linguistic extension is still a hardware configuration, passing through an assembler whose extension is this very opcode, up to high-level programming languages whose extension is that very assembler. In consequence, far-reaching chains of self-similarities in the sense defined by fractal theory organize the software as well as the hardware of every writing. What remains a problem is only recognizing these layers which, like modern media technologies in general, have been explicitly contrived to evade perception. We simply do not know what our writing does. [. . .]

When meanings come down to sentences, sentences to words, and words to letters, there is no software at all. Rather, there would be no software if computer systems were not surrounded by an environment of everyday languages. This environment, however, ever since a famous and twofold Greek invention, has consisted of letters and coins, of books and bucks.[3] For these good economical reasons, nobody seems to have inherited the humility of Alan Turing, who, in the stone age of computing, preferred to read his machine's outprint in hexadecimal numbers rather than in decimal numbers.[4] On the contrary, the so-called philosophy of the so-called computer community tends systematically to obscure hardware with software, electronic signifiers with interfaces between formal and everyday languages. In all philanthropic sincerity, high-level programming manuals caution against the psychopathological risks of writing assembler code.[5] In all friendliness, "BIOS services" are currently defined as designed to "hide the details of controlling the underlying hardware from your program."[6] Consequently, in a perfect gradualism, DOS services would hide the BIOS, WordPerfect the operating system, and so on and so on until, very recently, two fundamental changes in computer design (or DoD politics) have brought this system of secrecy to closure. First, on an intentionally superficial level, perfect graphic user interfaces, since they dispense with writing itself, hide a whole machine from its users. Second, on the microscopic level of hardware, so-called protection software has been implemented in order to prevent "untrusted programs" or "untrusted users" from any access to the operating system's kernel and input/output channels.[7]

This ongoing triumph of software is a strange reversal of Turing's proof that there can be no mathematically computable problem a simple machine could not solve. Instead, the physical Church-Turing hypothesis, by identifying physical hardware with the algorithms forged for its computation, has finally gotten rid of hardware itself. As a result, software has successfully occupied the empty place and profited from its obscurity. The ever-growing hierarchy of high-level programming languages works exactly the same way as one-way functions in recent mathematical cryptography. Such functions, when used in their straightforward form, can be computed in reasonable time, for instance, in a time growing only in polynomial expressions with the function's complexity. The time needed for its inverse form, however (that is, for reconstructing from the function's output its presupposed input), would grow at exponential and therefore unviable rates. One-way functions, in other words, hide an algorithm from its result. For software, this cryptographic effect offers a convenient way to bypass the fact that by virtue of Turing's proof the concept of mental property as applied to algorithms has become meaningless. Precisely because software does not exist as a machine-independent faculty, software as a commercial or American medium insists on its status as property all the more. Every license, every dongle, every trademark registered for WP, as well as for WordPerfect, proves the functionality of one-way functions. In this country, notwithstanding all mathematical tradition, even a copyright claim for algorithms has recently succeeded. And, finally, IBM has done research on a mathematical formula for measuring the distance in complexity between an algorithm and its output. Whereas in the good old days of Shannon's mathematical theory of information, the maximum in information coincided strangely with maximal unpredictability, or noise,[8] the new IBM measure, called logical depth, has been defined as follows: "The value of a message . . . appears to reside not in its information (its absolutely unpredictable parts), nor in its obvious redundancy (verbatim repetitions, unequal digit frequencies), but rather in what may be called its buried redundancy-parts predictable only with difficulty, things the receiver could in principle have figured out without being told, but only at considerable cost in money, time, or computation. In other words, the value of a message is the amount of mathematical or other work plausibly done by its originator, which the receiver is saved from having to repeat."[9] Thus, logical depth in its mathematical rigor could advantageously replace all the old, everyday language definitions of originality, authorship, and copyright in their necessary inexactness, were it not for the fact that precisely this algorithm intended to compute the cost of algorithms in general is Turing-uncomputable itself.[10]

Under these tragic conditions, criminal law, at least in Germany, has recently abandoned the very concept of software as mental property; instead, it defines software as necessarily a material thing. The high court's reasoning, according to which no computer program could ever run without the corresponding electrical charges in silicon circuitry,[11] can illustrate the fact that the virtual undecidability between software and hardware by no means follows, as systems theorists would probably like to believe, from a simple variation of observation on points. On the contrary, there are good grounds to assume the indispensability and, consequently, the priority of hardware in general. [. . .]

[M]aximal connectivity, on the other, physical side, defines nonprogrammable systems, be they waves or beings. That is why these systems show polynomial growth rates in complexity and, consequently, why only computations done on nonprogrammable machines could keep up with them. In all evidence, this hypothetical, but all too necessary, type of machine would constitute sheer hard-ware, a physical device working amidst physical devices and subject to the same bounded resources. Software in the usual sense of an ever-feasible abstraction would not exist any longer. [. . .]

In what I have tried to describe as badly needed machines that are probably not too far in the future (and drawing quite heavily on recent computer science), certain Dubrovnik observers' eyes might be tempted to recognize, under evolutionary disguises or not, the familiar face of man. Maybe. At the same time, however, our equally familiar silicon hardware obeys many of the requisites for such highly connected, nonprogrammable systems. Between its million transistor cells, some million to the power of two interactions always already take place. There is electron diffusion; there is quantum-mechanical tunneling all over the chip.[12] Technically, however, these interactions are still treated in terms of system limitations, physical side effects, and so on. To minimize all the noise that it would be impossible to eliminate is the price we pay for structurally programmable machines. The inverse strategy of maximizing noise would not only find the way back from IBM to Shannon, it may well be the only way to enter that body of real numbers originally known as chaos.

Notes

1. See Klaus Schrödl, "Quantensprung," *DOS* 12/1990: 102f.
2. See Alan M. Turing, *On Computable Numbers, with an Application to the Entscheidungs Problems*, Proceedings of the London Mathematical Society, 2nd ser. 42 (1937), 249.
3. See Johannes Lohmann, "Die Geburt der Tragödie aus dem Geiste der Musik," *Archiv für Musikwissenschaft* (1980), 174.
4. See Andrew Hodges, *Alan Turing: The Enigma* (New York: Simon and Schuster, 1983), 399.
5. See *TOOL Praxis: Assembler-Programmierung auf dem PC*, 1st ed. (Würzburg: Vogel, 1989), 9.
6. Nabajyoti Barkalati, *The Waite Group's Macroassembler Bible* (Carmel, Indiana: Howard H. Sams, 1989), 528.
7. See Friedrich Kittler, "Protected Mode."
8. See Friedrich Kittler, "Signal-Rausch-Abstand," in Hans Ulrich Gumbrecht and Karl Ludwig Pfeiffer, eds., *Materialität der Kommunikation* (Frankfurt a. M.: Suhrkamp 1988), 343–45.
9. Charles H. Bennet, "Logical Depth and Physical Complexity," in Herken, ed., 230.
10. With thanks to Oswald Wiener/Yukon.

11. *The German says* Vgl. M. Michael König, 1991, Sachlich sehen. Probleme bei der Über-
    lassung von Software. C't, Heft 3, 5.73. (Bundesgerichtshofentscheidung vom 2.5, 1985,
    Az. IZB 8/84, NIW-RR 1986, 2019). Programs are defined as "Verkörperungen der geis-
    tigen Leistung damit aber Sachen" ("embodiments of intellectual achievement, but in
    material things").

12. See Conrad, 303f.

VILÉM FLUSSER, FROM FORM AND
MATERIAL (1993) AND RECODING (1987)

Flusser (1920–1991) was a Czech philosopher and writer. Forced to leave
Czechoslovakia in 1939 when the Nazis occupied Prague, he emigrated
first to England and then to Brazil, where he taught philosophy of science at the University of São Paolo and later became Professor of Philosophy of Communication at Escola Superior de Cinema. Flusser wrote
and published in English and French, though the majority of his work
was in Portuguese and German. He left Brazil in the 1970s, and accepted
Friedrich Kittler's invitation to a Visiting Professorship at Ruhr University Bochum in 1991, shortly before he died. His work only became more
widely known and translated into English in the past two decades, and
has since then received significant attention. Flusser's interdisciplinary
interest in media philosophy, communication studies, and cultural theory mirrors his dialogic style of thinking and writing, which is as idiosyncratic as it is enjoyable: in brief, poignant, sometimes speculative,
and often provocative essays, he analyzes the objects, words, images,
and concepts around us—from *telephone* and *atlas* to *history, myth,* and
religion. What both these concrete objects and abstract human concepts
have in common is, Flusser thought, their involvement as processes of
human communication. His own neologism—communicology—aimed
to establish a new intellectual field of study, which would pay attention
to the organization, storage, transmission, and—most importantly—
new production of information that make up these communicative
processes. The two excerpts below showcase two very different kinds

of Flusser's approaches to thinking: one, through etymological conceptual work, reaching back into the past and the other speculating about the future, expanding in this way the history of information beyond the Shannon knot.

from "Form and Material" (1993)

A lot of nonsense has been talked about the word *immaterial*. But when people start to speak of "immaterial culture," such nonsense can no longer be tolerated. This essay aspires to clear away the distorted concept of the "immaterial."

The word *materia* is the result of the Romans' attempt to translate the Greek term *hyle* into Latin. *Hyle* originally meant "wood," and the fact that the word *materia* must have meant something similar is still suggested by the Spanish word *madera*. When, however, the Greek philosophers took up the word *hyle*, they were thinking not of wood in general but of the particular wood stored in carpenters' workshops. In fact, what they were concerned with was finding a word that could express the opposite of the term *form* (Greek *morphe*). Thus *hyle* means something amorphous. The basic idea here is this: The world of phenomena that we perceive with our senses is an amorphous stew behind which are concealed eternal, unchanging forms which we can perceive by means of the supersensory perspective of theory. The amorphous stew of phenomena (the "material world") is an illusion, and reality, which can be discovered by means of theory, consists of the forms concealed behind this illusion (the "formal world"). Discovered, indeed, in such a way that one recognizes how the amorphous phenomena flow into forms, occupy them in order to flow out into the amorphous once more.

We get closer to this opposition *hyle/ morphe* or "matter"/ "form" if we translate the word *matter* as "stuff." The word *stuff* is both a noun and a verb ("to stuff"). The material world is that which is stuffed into forms; it gives them a filling. This is much more plausible than the image of wood being cut into forms. For it demonstrates that the world of stuff only comes about when it is stuffed into something. The French word for filling is *farce*; this makes it possible to claim that, from a theoretical perspective, everything material in the world, everything made up of stuff, is a farce. This theoretical perspective, in the course of the development of science, entered into a dialectical relationship with the sensory perspective ("observation—theory—experiment"), and this can be seen as a stumbling-block to theory. It could even lead to the sort of materialism for which matter (stuff) is reality. Nowadays, however, under pressure from information technology, we are returning to the original concept of "matter" as a temporary filling of eternal forms.

For reasons that would go way beyond the scope of this essay, there grew up, independently of the philosophical concept of matter, the opposition "matter-spirit." The original conception here was that solid bodies could be turned into liquid and liquid bodies into gas, in so doing escaping the field of vision. Thus, for example, breath (Greek *pneuma*, Latin *spiritus*) can be seen as a turning of the solid human body into gas. The transformation from solid to gas (from body to spirit) can be observed in one's breath in cold weather.

In modern science, the concept of changing states of aggregation (solid > liquid > gas and back again) has given rise to a different world-view, according to which, roughly speaking, this change takes place between two horizons. On the one horizon (the point of absolute zero), everything whatsoever is solid (material), and on the other horizon (at the speed of light), everything whatsoever is more than gaseous (high energy). (One is reminded that "gas" and "chaos" are the same word.) The "matter-energy" opposition that arises here makes one think of spiritualism: One can transform matter into energy (fission) and energy into matter (fusion) (this is expressed in Einstein's formula). According to the world-view of modern science, everything is energy—i.e. the possibility of chance, improbable agglomeration, of the formation of matter. In such a world-view, "matter" equals temporary islands consisting of agglomerations (warps) in high-energy fields of possibility which intersect with one another. Hence all the fashionable nonsense talked nowadays about "immaterial culture." What is meant by this is a culture in which information is entered into the electromagnetic field and transmitted there. What is nonsense is not just the misuse of the term immaterial (instead of *high-energy*) but also the uninformed use of the term *inform*.

To return to the original opposition "matter-form"—i.e. "content-container." The basic idea is this: When I see something, a table for example, I see wood in the form of a table. It is true that the table is being hard as I am seeing it (I bump into it), but I know that this state is transitory (it will be burnt and decompose into amorphous ash). But the table-form is eternal, since I can imagine it anywhere and at any time (see it in my mind's theoretical eye). Hence the form of the table is real, and the content of the table (the wood) is only apparent. This illustrates what carpenters do: They take the form of a table (the "idea" of a table) and impose it upon an amorphous piece of wood. The tragedy here is that in so doing they not only in-form the wood (impose the table form on it) but also deform the idea of the table (distort it in the wood). The tragedy is therefore that it is impossible to make an ideal table.

This all sounds very archaic, but it is in fact so up-to-date that it deserves to be called a "burning issue." Take a simple, and hopefully plausible, example: Heavy bodies appear to roll around without following any rules, but in *reality* they behave according to the formula of free fall. The movement perceived by the senses (that which is material about the bodies) is apparent, and the theoretically intelligible formula (that which is formal about the bodies) is real. And this formula, this form, is without time and space, unalterably eternal. The formula of free fall is a mathematical equation, and equations are without time and space. There is no point in trying to ask whether "$1 + 1 = 2$" is also true at 4:00 P.M. in Vladivostok. There is just as little point, however, in saying of the formula that it is "immaterial." It is the *How* of the material, and the material is the *What* of the form. To put it another way: The information "free fall" has a content (body) and a form (a mathematical formula). [. . .]

In short: Forms are neither discoveries nor inventions, neither Platonic Ideas nor fictions, but containers cobbled together for phenomena ("models"). And theoretical science is neither "true" nor "fictitious" but "formal" (model-designing).

If "form" is the opposite of "matter," then no design exists that could be called "material": It is always in-forming. And if form is the "How" of matter, and "matter" the "What" of form, then design is one of the methods of giving form to matter and making it appear as it does and not like something else. Design, like all cultural expressions, illustrates that matter does not appear (is not apparent) except insofar as one in-forms it, and that, once in-formed, it starts to appear (become a phenomenon). Thus matter in design, as everywhere in culture, is the way in which forms appear. [. . .]

The "burning issue" is therefore the fact that in the past (since the time of Plato and even earlier), it was a matter of forming the material to hand to make it appear, but now what we have is a flood of forms pouring out of our theoretical perspective and our technical equipment, and this flood we fill with material so as to "materialize" the forms. In the past, it was a matter of giving formal order to the apparent world of material, but now it is a question of making a world appear that is largely encoded in figures, a world of forms that are multiplying uncontrollably. In the past, it was a matter of formalizing a world taken for granted, but now it is a matter of realizing the forms designed to produce alternative worlds. That means an "immaterial culture," though it should actually be called a "materializing culture."

What is at issue is the concept of in-formation. In other words, imposing forms on materials. This has been apparent since the Industrial Revolution. A steel tool in a press is a form, and it in-forms the flood of glass or plastic flowing past it into bottles or ashtrays. In the past, it was a question of distinguishing between true and false information. True information was when the forms were discoveries, and false information was when the forms were fictions. This distinction is becoming pointless since we have started to see forms neither as discoveries (*aletheiai*) nor as fictions, but as models. In the past, there was a point in distinguishing between science and art, and now this has become pointless. The criteria for criticizing information is now more like the following questions: To what extent are the forms being imposed here capable of being filled with material? To what extent are they capable of being realized? To what extent is the information practical or productive?

It is therefore not a question of whether images are the surfaces of materials or the contents of electromagnetic fields. But a question of the extent to which they arise from material, as opposed to formal, thinking and seeing. Whatever "material" may mean, it cannot mean the opposite of "immaterial." For the "immaterial" or, to be more precise, the form is that which makes material appear in the first place. The appearance of the material is form. And this is of course a post-material claim.

from "Recoding" (1987)

W e will have to relearn many things. That is difficult because what we have to learn is hard to acquire but, above all, because that which has once been learned is hard to forget. One advantage of artificial intelligences is that they have no difficulty forgetting. From them, we are learning the importance of forgetting. It is a tremendous thing to relearn, for it demands that we rethink the function of memory. In our tradition, memory is the seat of immortality: in Judaism, for example, one of life's goals is to remain in memory as a blessing. We must learn that it is just as important to be extinguished from memory. Death and immortality must be relearned, fame and anonymity must be revalued.

First among those things we must relearn in the context of the new as it emerges is process-oriented, progressive linear thought, the way of thinking that is articulated in linear writing. We will have to erase the alphabet from memory to be able to store the new codes there.

But might it be possible to learn the new codes without erasing what was stored in memory already? Isn't the brain a memory that is hardly used, that has a great deal of space available for new things, and is this not even more the case for those giant artificial memories we have begun to build? Doesn't the dialectic say that what has become obsolete is not lost but lifted up? Might it be that in the future, the new codes will be grounded in the alphabet, which they will assimilate into themselves and beyond, to new heights, so that rather than becoming illiterate, we become superliterate?

That is unthinkable. We will not be able to store the new codes over the alphabet in memory because these codes cannot tolerate the alphabet. They are impatiently imperialistic toward the alphabet. They cannot let a thought process geared toward criticizing images remain active behind their backs. The relationship between digital and alphabetic codes is no dialectic contradiction between image-producing and image-criticizing codes, capable of lifting each other to some sort of synthesis as it runs its course. It is rather about the formation of a new experience of space and time and so of a new concept of space and time into which the old experiences and concepts cannot go. This can no longer be grasped dialectically. Kuhn's concept of a "paradigm" works better: a sudden, previously unthinkable leap from one level to another rather than a synthesis from opposites. With digital codes, a new experience of time and space is emerging. Like a paradigm, it must obliterate everything that came before: all experiences that cannot yet be aligned under the old concepts of "omnipresence" and "simultaneity." Such experience cannot absorb but rather must destroy the alphabet. [. . .]

We will have to learn to write digitally, should *writing* still be a suitable designation for such a means of notation, and should anyone still be able to see it as a recoding from old into new codes. One who regards digital codes as written codes and sees a continuity between them and prealphabetic image making and alphabetic text making could claim to need to learn to recode everything: not only everything written but also everything still to write. We will have to recode the whole of literature, the whole factual and imaginary library of our culture into digital codes to be able to feed them to artificial memories and call them down from there. We will have to recode everything still to be written all those unfinished thought processes set out in texts, into digital codes. One who sees digital code as the articulation of a radically new way of thinking that can't be called writing, on the other hand, could say that we will be forced to erase the whole factual and imaginary library from memory, with all its achievements and all its unfinished beginnings, to clear a space for the new. But basically, these two formulations amount to the same thing: we will have to learn to rethink our entire history, backward and forward—a dizzying assignment after all.

How dizzying it all is becomes clear when we put ourselves in the position of a future reader. Let's assume that the world's literature has already been digitally recoded, stored in artificial memories, and its original alphabetic form erased. The future reader sits in front of the screen to call up the stored information. This is no longer a passive taking in (pecking) of information fragments along a prewritten line. This is more like an active accessing of the cross-connections among the available elements of information. It is the reader himself who actually produces the intended information from the stored information elements. To produce the information, the reader has various methods of access available, which are suggested to him by the artificial intelligence (methods currently called "menus"), but he can also apply his own criteria. And certainly we should expect a whole future science concerned with criteria for and links to bits of information (so-called documentation sciences are starting to do this). What happens in such reading can be seen more clearly in an example.

Let's assume that the reader is interested in the history of science, that is, in pieces of information that follow one another in a chronological order from the standpoint of the reader's present. According to our current ways of reading and thinking, "Aristotle" would, for example, come before "Newton": To the future reader, "Aristotle" and "Newton" are simultaneously accessible, both coded digitally. So he can access both systems at the same time, and in such a way that they overlap and disturb one another. In the Newton system, for example, "inertia" will run up against "motive" in the Aristotle system, and the principle of "justice" in Aristotle's system will bump into the chains of causality in Newton's system. The reader will be able to manipulate the two overlapping systems so that an intermediate stage emerges in which Aristotle's system could arise from Newton's as well as Newton's from Aristotle's. From the available data, the reader will find out that the Newtonian system is, in fact, more recent than the Aristotelian, but he can just as easily reverse the history.

The example was chosen to show that the future reader will be free to access linear, historical cross-links between elements of information among others. He will be able to read the history of science, among other things, from his data. But the history that comes from such a reading is precisely not what we mean by "history." Historical consciousness—this awareness of being immersed in a dramatic and irreversible flow of time—has vanished from the future reader. He is above it, able to access his own flow of time. He doesn't read along a line but rather spins his own nets.

Recoding literature into the new codes is a dizzying assignment. It demands that we translate our thought world into a foreign one: from the world of spoken languages into that of ideographic images, from the world of logical rules into that of mathematical ones, and above all, from the world of lines into that of particulate nets.

We probably will not be able to begin before we have developed a theory and philosophy of translation. We are very far from this. Still we can see recoding under way everywhere (although not yet, except in fantasy, the destruction of recoded texts). [. . .]

In the matter of recoding, we face two opposing tendencies. On one hand we have people who don't want to learn to recode for they don't believe it is necessary to learn afresh. On the other hand, we have people who approach everything written and yet to be written with the intention of recoding it, either because they sense an adventure or simply because they have begun to be repulsed by all the scribbling. Between these two extremes are some who are simultaneously aware of both the necessity and the difficulty of recoding that is, relearning. These are the people from whom a theory and philosophy of translation is to be expected. If it is achieved, the transition from the alphabetic into the new culture will become a conscious step beyond current conditions of thought and life. If it is not achieved, a descent into illiterate barbarism is to be feared.

[. . .] To those of us who spell things out, the current transition from the alphabet to the new looks like a dangerous step on a ridge between abysses. It may seem like a pleasant stroll to our grandchildren, but we are not our grandchildren, who will learn the new with ease in kindergarten. Do we have to go back to kindergarten?

LISA GITELMAN, FROM *PAPER KNOWLEDGE: TOWARD A MEDIA HISTORY OF DOCUMENTS* (2004)

Gitelman (b. 1962) is Professor of English and media historian at New York University. Her research focuses on the history and economies of media technologies, from sound recording, writing machines, and print culture to digital networks. Gitelman's work more generally belongs to new media studies, a field that emerged to address the social, cultural, and technological consequences of computer technologies, communication theory, and digital media. But the distinction between old and new media is not merely a historical one: in *Always Already New: Media, History, and the Data of Culture* (2006), Gitelman reminds us that newness is part of the logic of media, which she defines as "socially realized structures of communication." As such, media, she argues, are both historical subjects and the instruments through which we understand history and historicity. This is true for both media forms and their content. In the introduction to *"Raw Data" Is an Oxymoron* (2013), Gitelman writes that "data are abstract"; they are not objective figments of reality, but they require our participation. The following excerpt comes from the introduction to her book *Paper Knowledge: Toward a Media History of Documents* (2014), in which she traces the "scriptural economy" of mundane media formats and documents from the last 150 years.

[. . .] The word "document" descends from the Latin root *docer*, to teach or show, which suggests that the document exists in order to document. Sidestepping this circularity of terms, one might say instead that documents help define and are mutually defined by the know-show function, since documenting is an epistemic practice: the kind of knowing that is all wrapped up with showing, and showing wrapped with knowing. Documents are epistemic objects; they are the recognizable sites and subjects of interpretation across the disciplines and beyond, evidential structures in the long human history of clues.[1] Closely related to the know-show function of documents is the work of no show, since sometimes documents are documents merely by dint or their potential to show: they are flagged and filed away for the future, just in case. Both know show and no show depend on an implied self-evidence that is intrinsically rhetorical. As John Guillory notes, "persuasion is implicit in *docer*."[2] If all documents share a certain "horizon of expectation," then, the name of that horizon is accountability.[3] [. . .]

But what *is* a document? Bibliographers and other information specialists have persisted in puzzling over this question for at least the last hundred years. Most famously the French librarian and "documentalist" Suzanne Briet proposed in 1951 that an antelope running wild would not be a document but an antelope taken into a zoo would be one, presumably because it would then be framed—or reframed—as an example, specimen, or instance.[4] She was pushing a limit case as Michael Buckland explains, drawing attention to the properties of documents: they are material objects intended as evidence and processed or framed—if not always caged—as such.[5] Although I think it is probably best to remain agnostic on the question of antelopes, Briet and Buckland help underscore the context-dependent character of the know-show function. Any object can be a thing but once it is framed as or entered into evidence—once it is mobilized—it becomes a document, an instance proper to that genre. What is notably obscured by the exoticism of Briet's instance is just how intricately entangled the genre and the thing can be and have become over the last several centuries.[6] [. . .]

Documents are important not because they are ubiquitous, I should be clear, but rather because they are so evidently integral to the ways people think and live. The epistemic power of the know-show function is indisputable, and the properties of documents matter in all kinds of far-reaching ways. As Geoffrey Nunberg describes it, information is understood today to come in discrete "morsels" or bits partly because of the way the concept of information reifies the properties of paper documents; they are separate and separable, bounded and distinct. Likewise, information has an objective, autonomous character partly because of the way it reflects the authoritative institutions and practices to which documents belong.[7] What this reflection of authority suggests is that documents—unlike information, interesting enough—are importantly situated; they are tied to specific settings. Again, the know-show function is context-dependent in space and time: consider the poor antelope, trapped within the zoological garden. Or consider the 1839 *American Slavery as It Is*, a key document in the history of the abolitionist movement in the United States. Compiled in part from Southern newspapers, it altered the contexts of advertisements describing runaway slaves by recognizing their value for republication in the North.[8] Republication turned the ads into a powerful indictment of slavery because they so frequently described runaways in terms of bodily mutilations. Embedded in local newsprint these advertisements had been documents, to be sure, but collecting them and reproducing them in another context for another audience made them know-show with much greater force. What had been published first as instruments calling the slave system into complicity, to aid in slaves' recapture, were now republished as instruments of moral suasion whereby the slave system became paradoxically enrolled in the antislavery cause: slavery "as it is" condemns itself. Because it implies accountability, knowing and showing together constitute an epistemic practice to which ethics and politics become available, even necessary. [. . .]

The history of communication typically defines print by distinguishing it from manuscript, yet there is considerable poverty in that gesture. Far from being a simple precursor, manuscript stands as a back formation of printing. (That is, before the spread of printing there wasn't any need to describe manuscript as such.[9]) Meanwhile print itself has come to encompass many diverse technologies for the reproduction of text, despite its primary, historical association with letterpress printing à la Johannes Gutenberg. Until the nineteenth century every "printed" text was printed by letterpress, using a process of composition, imposition, and presswork very like the one that Gutenberg and his associates and competitors developed in the mid-fifteenth century, although saying so admittedly overlooks xylography (woodblock printing) and intaglio processes like printing from copperplate engravings. Since 1800, however, multiple planographic, photochemical, and electrostatic means of printing have been developed and variously deployed, to the point that in the twenty-first century virtually nothing "printed" is printed by letterpress. With the tables turned, the term "print" has floated free of any specific technology, if indeed it was ever securely moored in the first place. Instead "print" has become defined—as if in reflexive recourse to its own back formation-by dint of "a negative relation to the [writer's] hand."[10] Any textual artifact that is not handwritten or otherwise handmade letter by letter (typed, for example) counts as "printed," and lately even the printer's hand has gone missing, since today "printers" are usually not human: now the term more familiarly designates machines proper to the realm of consumer electronics. (Curiously— and unlike human hands—office printers have been almost without exception beige in color, although that norm appears to be changing.) The fact that

Gutenberg's bible and the assortment of drafts and documents rolling out of my laser printer all count as "printed" only goes to show how difficult it can be to speak or write about media with any great precision. This is partly due to the poverty of terminology, but it is also partly due to the persistent if idiosyncratic power of the media concept. [. . .]

With some exceptions, the documents produced by job printers in the later nineteenth century were instruments of corporate speech proper to the conduct of businesses of every sort, as well as to the operation of institutions such as schools, churches, voluntary associations, and municipalities. These were contexts in which the know-show function might hinge triply on what documents said, on their format (the size, weight, and folds of the paper on which they were printed), and on their formatting (their layout and typographical design) created by the compositors who set them in type.[11] The meaning of documents thus inheres symbolically, materially, and graphically, according to the contexts in which documents make sense as visible signs and/as material objects.[12] A multitude of forms—some of them literally fill-in-the-blank forms—helped to shape and enable, to define and delimit, the transactions in which they were deployed. In their sheer diversity and multiplicity, documents originating with job printers point toward a period of intense social differentiation, as Americans became subject to a panoply (or, rather, a pan-opoly) of institutions large and small, inspiring a prolific babble of corporate speech. Beyond the simple logic of spheres—public and domestic—job printing indicates an intersecting tangle of transaction, as individuals used printed and written documents variously to negotiate—with greater and lesser success, one must imagine—their everyday relationships to and amid many institutions, and institutionalized realms all at once. [. . .]

More clearly than either job printing or scholarly mimeographs and microforms, photocopied documents form the site and substance of modern bureaucracy, part of its strategic repertoire. Ellsberg in particular works as something like a latter-day addition to the colorful cast of historical actors described in Ben Kafka's The Demon of Writing: Powers and Failures of Paperwork. Like Charles Hippolyte Labussière, for instance—who is said to have saved hundreds of people from the guillotine by surreptitiously destroying the relevant paperwork during the Reign of Terror—Ellsberg risked much in acting against the Vietnam War. He worked from a position inside the machinery of state—or at least inside the scriptural economy of the military-industrial complex—while he did so in ways that gestured as much toward the contradictory "psychic reality" of bureaucracy, in Kafka's terms, as toward its specific material features.[13] Whereas tactics à la Labussière involved the misdirection and destruction of documents, Ellsberg's tactics involved their proliferation through photocopying. [. . .]

So many of the popular stories we continue to tell ourselves about what we refer to as print are big-boned affairs that rely on gross analogies. McLuhan probably locked this pattern in, with his 1962 account of a "Typographic Man" who is woefully "unready" for the electronic media of his day. Readers today may be shocked at having to slog through so much about classical antiquity and medieval Europe in *The Gutenberg Galaxy*, because McLuhan proceeds with such certainty that letterpress printing in the Renaissance "was an event nearly related to the earlier technology of the phonetic alphabet."[14] The connection starts to seem typological. It has similarly become a commonplace of late to compare the ascendance of digital networks and the World Wide Web with the rapid dissemination of letterpress printing in Renaissance Europe and the supposed emergence of print culture. Clay Shirky, for instance, has suggested that the "mass amateurization of publishing" on the Internet could be likened to the mass amateurization of "literacy after the invention of moveable type."[15] Three analogical revolutions by these lights, one vast historical arc: if one accepts this premise, then the history of the West may be figured as a self-celebrating page, written first in phonetic characters, printed next by movable type, and finally and triumphantly generated and published online. [. . .] Following documents reveals both the abundant diversity of the scriptural economy and its ever widening scope, as knowing-showing has again and again been worked by new and different means as well as by additional and increasingly diverse actors. Following documents hints further at intricate and proliferating techniques of control, as subjects know and show within and against the demands of an increasingly dense overlay of institutions and institutionalized realms.

Notes

1. See Annelise Riles, "Introduction: In Response," in *Documents: Artifacts of Modern Knowledge*, ed. Annelise Riles (Ann Arbor: University of Michigan Press, 2006), 6–7. See also Carlo Ginzburg, *Clues, Myths, and the Historical Method*, trans. John Tedeschi and Anne C. Tedeschi (Baltimore, MD: Johns Hopkins University Press, 1989), 96–155; Anthony Grafton, *The Footnote: A Curious History* (Cambridge, MA: Harvard University Press, 1997).
2. John Guillory, "The Memo and Modernity," *Critical Inquiry* 31, no. 1 (2004): 120.
3. Lauren Berlant, *The Female Complaint: The Unfinished Business of Sentimentality in American Culture* (Durham, NC: Duke University Press, 2008), 314.
4. Briet was a proponent of the European bibliographical movement called Documentation. See Suzanne Briet, *What Is Documentation? English Translation of the Classic French Text*, trans. Ronald E. Day, Laurent Martinet, and Hermina G. B. Anghelescu (Lanham, MD: Scarecrow, 2006). See also Bernd Frohmann, "The Documentality of Mme. Briet's Antelope," in *Communication Matters: Materialist Approaches to Media, Mobility, and Networks*, ed. Jeremy Packer and Stephen B. Crofts Wiley (New York: Routledge, 2012), 173–82.
5. Michael Buckland, "What Is a Digital Document?," 1998, http://people.ischool.berkeley.edu/~buckland/digdoc.html, accessed 25 June 2013.

6. "Mobilized" is a Bruno Latourism (see below). For the recent interest in "things," see Bill Brown, "Thing Theory," *Critical Inquiry* 28 (Autumn 2001): 1–22. See also, Lorraine Daston, ed., *Things That Talk: Object Lessons from Art and Science* (New York: Zone, 2004); Lorraine Daston, ed., *Biographies of Scientific Objects* (Chicago: University of Chicago Press, 2000); Hans-Jörg Rheinberger, *Toward a History of Epistemic Things: Synthesizing Proteins in the Test Tube* (Stanford, CA: Stanford University Press, 1997).

7. Geoffrey Nunberg, "Farewell to the Information Age," in *The Future of the Book*, ed. Geoffrey Nunberg (Berkeley: University of California Press, 1996), 120.

8. See Ellen Gruber Garvey, " '*facts* and FACTS': Abolitionists' Database Innovations," in *"Raw Data" Is an Oxymoron*, ed. Lisa Gitelman (Cambridge, MA: MIT Press, 2013), 89–102; Trish Loughran, *The Republic in Print: Print Culture in the Age of U.S. Nation Building, 1770–1870* (New York: Columbia University Press, 2007).

9. Indeed, manuscript is a back formation that likely took a good deal of time to evolve; see Peter Stallybrass, "Printing and the Manuscript Revolution," in *Explorations in Communication and History*, ed. Barbie Zelizer (New York: Routledge, 2008), 115. For at least two centuries after Johannes Gutenberg, libraries in Europe made no distinction between their manuscript codices and their printed ones; see David McKitterick, *Print, Manuscript and the Search for Order, 1450–1830* (Cambridge: Cambridge University Press, 2003), 13.

10. Michael Warner, *The Letters of the Republic: Publication and the Public Sphere in Eighteenth-Century America* (Cambridge, MA: Harvard University Press, 1990), 7.

11. On formatting as part of what memos say, see Guillory, "The Memo and Modernity," 126–27.

12. Apologies for the ugly "and/as"; see Lisa Gitelman, *Always Already New: Media, History, and the Data of Culture* (Cambridge, MA: MIT Press, 2006), 91. On materiality, see especially Johanna Drucker, "Entity to Event: From Literal, Mechanistic Materiality to Probabilistic Materiality," *Paralax* 15, no. 4 (2009): 7–17.

13. B. Kafka, *The Demon of Writing*, chapter 2.

14. Marshall McLuhan, *The Gutenberg Galaxy: The Making of Typographic Man* (Toronto: University of Toronto Press, 1962), 30, 152.

15. Clay Shirky, *Here Comes Everybody: The Power of Organizing without Organizations* (New York: Penguin, 2008), 79.

INFORMED SOCIETY

This section considers the social dimensions of information regimes, past and present. Since its coinage in Japan in the 1960s, the topic of "information society" within the social sciences has grown into an analytical field, well covered in economics, political science, and communication and media studies, not to mention sociology. It denotes a broad spectrum of societal transformations linked to the advent of post-industrialism, the rise of digital networks like the World Wide Web, and the subsequent virtualization of everyday life. By now, after half a century of discussion—often breathless with excitement—in scholarly writing and popular media, it is nearly a cliché to call the term a cliché. Nonetheless, its heuristic use-value is far from exhausted, particularly on account of its lingering role as a substrate to discussions of the so-called Information Age and the information revolution. In order to make sense of the present, we keep returning to the work of sorting out basic issues: Which societies qualify as information societies, and why? Within them, how is information distributed? Who is included, and who is left out? How does information impact the ways in which people relate, work, and play with one another?

The urgency of the latter question, in particular, has inspired a significant number of works featured here. In making our selections, we have emphasized scholarship that expands the scope of the discussion by virtue of its focus on periods or cultures that fall outside of the conventional boundaries of what is considered to be "the" information society. We have accordingly shed the definitive article in favor of a looser title, Informed Society, with the aim of exploring how information can be purposive for innovative work on social history within the humanities—a task that is equally crucial to information studies given the fact that human relations constitute the underlying context that gives meaning to information in the first place. To be clear: our intent is not to police boundaries between disciplines. Readers interested primarily in delving into a more mainstream tradition of information society studies are advised to refer to one of the many anthologies on the topic.[1]

While the term informed society nominally sidesteps potential issues of definition and ahistoricity that come with an overdetermined category like information society, a reader may very well wonder whether it now swings too far the other way, toward a fuzzy universalism capable only of eliciting bland truisms. After all, informing others and being informed by them are essential forms of social exchange. Communities communicate. Without information exchange, cooperation, resource allocation, and consensus building are impossible. If any society can be described in these terms, what kind of conceptual leverage do we gain with an alternative approach to informed society? The answer lies in the adjective *informed*, which calls attention to processes and their social effects rather than to a stable category, per se. Studying the process of informing requires an accounting of interactions between social epistemology, language, technoscientific development, material forms of communication, and relations of power. So far, the history of human society has proven to trend toward ever more complex ways of informing and being informed, as divisions of labor become more refined and symbolic forms such as writing and codes proliferate. As the selections here illustrate, studying changes in the informedness of a particular sociohistorical context deepens our understanding of the ways in which this course has been negotiated, potentially challenging assumptions about the uniqueness of our present epoch.

Our first excerpt is from a work that exemplifies the pivot toward such an expanded consideration: *The Control Revolution*, by the sociologist James Beniger. Published in 1986, the book responds to a compiled list of seventy scholarly works dealing with some facet of "the" information society in postwar Euro-America. While agreeing that a major social transformation has in fact taken place, Beniger disputes its origin point, arguing that the logic of control through information management was already manifest in the late nineteenth century, in response to a crisis of control created by the Industrial Revolution. According to Beniger, this crisis of control arose when the capacity for processing material and energy outpaced the capacity to process information, precipitating the innovation of control for coordinating movement and labor across distances and at scales previously unimaginable. At stake, for Beniger, is more than the periodization of the information society and its relationship to Shannon and digital computing. Rather, he is interested in pursuing broader questions of how and why information has become so central to a modern, integrated economy and advanced industrial societies. Furthermore, the book demonstrates how a distinctly interdisciplinary approach that incorporates concepts and metaphors from biology, economics, engineering, and systems analysis, can pinpoint trends that are gradual and architectonic, but, as Beniger stresses, critical in the long run. Such an informatic approach to history produced fascinating results—and helped launch a discussion within the humanities a generation ago.

Two other pieces help round out a consideration of postwar information society by situating its development in the late twentieth century and envisioning its possible futures. One of the earliest to combine information and society into a compound noun (in Japanese: *jōhōka shakai*), Yoneji Masuda proposes that telecommunications and computing be harnessed for new forms of knowledge work and democratic governance. In contrast to Masuda's optimism over the liberating potential of information, Paul Virilio sounds the alarm on the effects of an "information bomb" on Euro-American society, surveying an increasingly dystopic landscape where the operationalization of cybernetics across state and corporate institutions has resulted in increased surveillance and management of social interactions, leaving us helplessly distracted and enthralled. These futurological relics exemplify how the Shannon knot binds the stakes of the histories of political liberalism, the nation state, and the global expansion of capitalism.

The remaining selections variously showcase the historiographic possibilities of informed society for pre-Shannon contexts, highlighting cases in which practices or understanding of information passed a threshold within a society or group, transforming dominant modes of labor and consumption or precipitating new modes of self-understanding. Readers will notice how many of these selections contribute to decentering—geographically, temporally, and culturally—historiography on informed societies. Mary E. Berry describes urban readers' experience in Japan's Tokugawa period (1603–1868), which witnessed a massive uptick in printed and ephemeral facts. The result: a "public library of information," reflective of early modern society's new appetite for knowing itself. Ann Blair provides a counterpart from early modern Europe, detailing important changes in scholars' attitudes toward information management. Such scholars' feelings of information overload helped precipitate new textual forms and writing practices, including encyclopedism, an impulse that echoes developments in the fourteenth-century Arabic world, where, as Elias Muhanna shows, new institutions of learning similarly put unprecedented emphasis on the collection and organization of textual information.

Several of the pieces adopt transcultural and comparative approaches. In her book, Blair compares the reference tools of early modern Europe with similar genres in contemporary Byzantium, the Islamic world, and imperial China. By contrast, Steven G. Marks places his informatic history of capitalism within a global framework, contrasting medieval and Renaissance Europe with contemporary polities such as Ming China. Examining nineteenth-century India and the Rebellion of 1857, C.A. Bayly introduces the notion of an "information order" to navigate the complex series of gaps and intersections that obtained between the knowledge systems of indigenous groups and English administrators.

By foregrounding encounters between different epistemes, Bayly's postcolonial approach raises questions about language and the way in which information and informing—or something like them—have been perceived and talked about in different sociohistorical settings. Words like *khabr* and *suchna*, as we learn from Bayly, are (or were) possible counterparts to information, epistemic tokens whose exchange value and truth value were in broad use; at the same time, he defines them schematically vis-à-vis other terms for knowledge. But how universal are such terms and schemas? Do information or informed-ness appear in similar guises in Tokugawa-era Edo, Renaissance Italy, and the Mamluk Sultanate? From the standpoint of scholarly study, the possibility of translation and definition does not need to be over-limiting. After all, people do not always have the terms to describe their experiences or conditions. Here, the authors of several works bring their own definition of information to bear upon the subject, or simply circumvent discourse to instead focus on practices and material conditions. Whether acknowledged or not, the role of language and translatability, in the form of linguistic difference or absence, helps further expose historical contingency and the slipperiness of a seemingly commonsensical term like information—and, by extension, the information society itself. As John Durham Peters emphasizes in his essay in this volume—which originally grew out of Peters's extended critical review of the *Control Revolution*—"*information* is a term that does not like history . . . [but it] is, after all, a word with a history." By extension, to acknowledge the many histories and experiences of informed societies is to expose the promise of digital information to unify all human experience and culture today.

Anatoly Detwyler

Note

1. See, for example, the four-volume collection *The Information Society* (New York: Routledge, 2009).

JAMES BENIGER, FROM *THE CONTROL REVOLUTION: TECHNOLOGICAL AND ECONOMIC ORIGINS OF THE INFORMATION SOCIETY* (1986)

Trained as a sociologist, James R. Beniger (1946–2010) began working on information in the form of data visualization and statistical graphics during the 1970s. A decade later came *The Control Revolution*, whose publication proved to be a landmark in the historiography of technology, communications, and information. In it, Beniger argues that the rise of the post-WWII "information society" did not begin with Shannon's formula or the advent of digital computing. Instead, it was manifested in the spatial and temporal compression of Industrial Revolution–era innovations: telegraph, train timetable, Taylorism, and bureaucracy—powerful ways of managing an increasingly integrated system of production, circulation, and consumption. In the following excerpt from the book's introduction, Beniger evaluates such nineteenth-century technologies and institutions using cybernetic notions of feedback and control. Together with John Durham Peters's critical review charging the book with ignoring the human and cultural dimensions of information, *The Control Revolution* helped inaugurate a vital discussion regarding the historical origins of the information society.

Crisis of Control

The later Industrial Revolution constituted, in effect, a consolidation of earlier technological revolutions and the resulting transformations of society. Especially during the late nineteenth and early twentieth centuries industrialization extended to progressively earlier technological revolutions: manufacturing, energy production, transportation, agriculture—the last a transformation of what had once been seen as the extreme opposite of industrial production. In each area industrialization meant heavy infusions of capital for the exploitation of fossil fuels, wage labor, and machine technology and resulted in larger and more complex systems—systems characterized by increasing differentiation and interdependence at all levels.

One of the earliest and most astute observers of this phenomenon was Emile Durkheim (1858-1917), the great French sociologist who examined many of its social ramifications in his *Division of Labor in Society* (1893). As Durkheim noted, industrialization tends to break down the barriers to transportation and communication that isolate local markets (what he called the "segmental" type), thereby extending distribution of goods and services to national and even global markets (the "organized" type). This, in turn, disrupts the market equilibrium under which production is regulated by means of direct communication between producer and consumer:

> Insofar as the segmental type is strongly marked, there are nearly as many economic markets as there are different segments. Consequently, each of them is very limited. Producers, being near consumers, can easily reckon the extent of the needs to be satisfied. Equilibrium is established without any trouble and production regulates itself. On the contrary, as the organized type develops, the fusion of different segments draws the markets together into one which embraces almost all society . . . The result is that each industry produces for consumers spread over the whole surface of the country or even of the entire world. Contact is then no longer sufficient. The producer can no longer embrace the market in a glance, nor even in thought. He can no longer see limits, since it is, so to speak, limitless. Accordingly, production becomes unbridled and unregulated. It can only trust to chance . . . From this come the crises which periodically disturb economic functions. (1893, pp. 369-370)

What Durkheim describes here is nothing less than a crisis of control at the most aggregate level of a national system—a level that had had little practical relevance before the mass production and distribution of factory goods. Resolution of the crisis demanded new means of communication, as Durkheim perceived, to control an economy shifting from local segmented markets to higher levels of organization—what might be seen as the growing "systemness" of society. This capacity to communicate and process information is one component of what structural-functionalists following Durkheim have called the problem of integration, the growing need for coordination of functions that accompanies differentiation and specialization in any system.

Increasingly confounding the need for integration of the structural division of labor were corresponding increases in commodity flows through the system—flows driven by steam-powered factory production and mass distribution via national rail networks. Never before had the processing of material flows threatened to exceed, in both volume and speed, the capacity of technology to contain them. For centuries most goods had moved with the speed of draft animals down roadway and canal, weather permitting. This infrastructure, controlled by small organizations of only a few hierarchical levels, supported even national economies. Suddenly—owing to the harnessing of steam power— goods could be moved at the full speed of industrial production, night and day and under virtually any conditions, not only from town to town but across entire continents and around the world.

To do this, however, required an increasingly complex system of manufacturers and distributors, central and branch offices, transportation lines and terminals, containers and cars. Even the logistics of nineteenth-century armies, then the most difficult problem in processing and control, came to be dwarfed in complexity by the material economy just emerging as Durkheim worked on his famous study.

What Durkheim described as a crisis of control on the societal level he also managed to relate to the level of individual psychology. Here he found a more personal but directly related problem, what he called anomie, the breakdown of norms governing individual and group behavior. Anomie is an "abnormal" and even "pathological" result, according to Durkheim (1893, p. 353), an exception to his more general finding that increasing division of labor directly increases normative integration and, with it, social solidarity. As Durkheim argued, anomie results not from the structural division of labor into what he called distinct societal "organs" but rather from the breakdown in communication among these increasingly isolated sectors, so that individuals employed in them lose sight of the larger purpose of their separate efforts:

> The state of anomie is impossible wherever solidary organs are sufficiently in contact or sufficiently prolonged. In effect, being continuous, they are quickly warned, in each circumstance, of the need which they have of one another, and, consequently, they have a lively and continuous sentiment of their mutual dependence . . . But, on the contrary, if some opaque environment is interposed, then only stimuli of a certain intensity can be communicated from one organ to another. Relations, being rare, are not repeated enough to be determined; each time there ensues new groping. The lines of passage taken by the streams of

movement cannot deepen because the streams themselves are too intermittent. If some rules do come to constitute them, they are, however, general and vague. (1893, pp. 368–369)

Like the problem of economic integration, anomie also resulted—in Durkheim's view—from inadequate means of communication. Both problems were thus manifestations, at opposite extremes of aggregation, of the nineteenth-century control crisis . . . [Just] as the problem of control threatened to reach crisis proportions late in the century, a series of new technological and social solutions began to contain the problem. This was the opening stage of the Control Revolution.

Rationalization and Bureaucracy

Foremost among all the technological solutions to the crisis of control—in that it served to control most other technologies—was the rapid growth of formal bureaucracy first analyzed by Max Weber at the turn of the century. Bureaucratic organization was not new to Weber's time, as we have noted; bureaucracies had arisen in the first nation-states with centralized administrations, most significantly in Mesopotamia and ancient Egypt, and had reached a high level of sophistication in the preindustrial empires of Rome, China, and Byzantium. Indeed, bureaucratic organization tends to appear wherever a collective activity needs to be coordinated by several people toward explicit and impersonal goals, that is, to be *controlled*. Bureaucracy has served as the generalized means to control any large social system in most institutional areas and in most cultures since the emergence of such systems by about 3000 B.C.

Because of the venerable history and pervasiveness of bureaucracy, historians have tended to overlook its role in the late nineteenth century as a major new control technology. Nevertheless, bureaucratic administration did not begin to achieve anything approximating its modern form until the late Industrial Revolution. As late as the 1830s, for example, the Bank of the United States, then the nation's largest and most complex institution with twenty-two branch offices and profits fifty times those of the largest mercantile house, was managed by just three people: Nicholas Biddle and two assistants (Redlich 1951, pp. 113–124). In 1831, President Andrew Jackson and 665 other civilians ran all three branches of the federal government in Washington, an increase of sixty-three employees over the previous ten years. The Post Office Department, for example, had been administered for thirty years as the personal domain of two brothers, Albert and Phineas Bradley (Pred 1973, chap. 3). Fifty years later, in the aftermath of rapid industrialization, Washington's bureaucracy included some thirteen thousand civilian employees, more than double the total—already swelled by the American Civil War—only ten years earlier (U.S. Bureau of the Census 1975, p. 1103).

Further evidence that bureaucracy developed in response to the Industrial Revolution is the timing of concern about bureaucratization as a pressing social problem. The word *bureaucracy* did not even appear in English until the early nineteenth century, yet within a generation it became a major topic of political and philosophical discussion. As early as 1837, for example, John Stuart Mill wrote of a "vast network of administrative tyranny . . . that system of *bureaucracy*, which leaves no free agent in all France, except the man at Paris who pulls the wires" (Burchfield 1972, p. 391); a decade later Mill warned more generally of the "inexpediency of concentrating in a dominant bureaucracy . . . all power of organized action . . . in the community" (1848, p. 529). Thomas Carlyle, in his *Latter-Day Pamphlets* published two years later, complained of "the Continental nuisance called 'Bureaucracy' " (1850, p. 121). The word *bureaucratic* had also appeared by the 1830s, followed by *bureaucrat* in the 1840s and *bureaucratize* by the 1890s.

That bureaucracy is in essence a control technology was first established by Weber, most notably in his *Economy and Society* (1922). Weber included among the defining characteristics of bureaucracy several important aspects of any control system: impersonal orientation of structure to the information that it processes, usually identified as "cases," with a predetermined formal set of rules governing all decisions and responses. Any tendency to humanize this bureaucratic machinery, Weber argued, would be minimized through clear-cut division of labor and definition of responsibilities, hierarchical authority, and specialized decision and communication functions. The stability and permanence of bureaucracy, he noted, are assured through regular promotion of career employees based on objective criteria like seniority.

Weber identified another related control technology, what he called *rationalization*. Although the term has a variety of meanings, both in Weber's writings and in the elaborations of his work by others, most definitions are subsumed by one essential idea: control can be increased not only by increasing the capability to process information but also by decreasing the amount of information to be processed. The former approach to control was realized in Weber's day through bureaucratization and today increasingly through computerization; the latter approach was then realized through rationalization, what computer scientists now call preprocessing. Rationalization must therefore be seen, following Weber, as a complement to bureaucratization, one that served control in his day much as the preprocessing of information prior to its processing by computer serves control today.

Perhaps most pervasive of all rationalization is the increasing tendency of modern society to regulate interpersonal relationships in terms of a formal set of impersonal and objective criteria. The early technocrat Claude Henri Comte de Saint-Simon (1760–1825), who lived through only the first stages of industrialization, saw such rationalization as a move "from the government of men to the administration of things" (Taylor 1975, pt. 3). The reason why people can be governed more readily *qua* things is that the amount of information about them that needs to be processed is thereby greatly reduced and hence the degree of control—for any constant capacity to process information—is greatly enhanced. By means of rationalization, therefore, it is possible to maintain large-scale, complex social systems that would be overwhelmed by a rising tide of information they could not process were it necessary to govern by the particularistic considerations of family and kin that characterize preindustrial societies.

In short, rationalization might be defined as the destruction or ignoring of information in order to facilitate its processing. This, too, has a direct analog in living systems . . . One example from within bureaucracy is the development of standardized paper forms. This might at first seem a contradiction, in that the proliferation of paperwork is usually associated with a growth in information to be processed, not with its reduction. Imagine how much more processing would be required, however, if each new case were recorded in an unstructured way, including every nuance and in full detail, rather than by checking boxes, filling blanks, or in some other way reducing the burdens of the bureaucratic system to only the limited range of formal, objective, and impersonal information required by standardized forms.

Equally important to the rationalization of industrial society, at the most macro level, were the division of North America into five standardized time zones in 1883 and the establishment the following year of the Greenwich meridian and International Date Line, which organized world time into twenty-four zones. What was formerly a problem of information overload and hence control for railroads and other organizations that sustained the social system at its most macro level was solved by simply ignoring much of the information, namely that solar time is different at each node of a transportation or communication system. A more convincing demonstration of the power of rationalization or preprocessing as a control technology would be difficult to imagine.

So commonplace has such preprocessing become that today we dismiss the alternative—that each node in a system might keep a slightly different time—as hopelessly cumbersome and primitive. With the continued proliferation of distributed computing, ironically enough, it might soon become feasible to return to a system based on local solar time, thereby shifting control from preprocessing back to processing—where it resided for centuries of human history until steam power pushed transportation beyond the pace of the sun across the sky.

New Control Technology

The rapid development of rationalization and bureaucracy in the middle and late nineteenth century led to a succession of dramatic new information-processing and communication technologies. These innovations served to contain the control crisis of industrial society in what can be treated as three distinct areas of economic activity: production, distribution, and consumption of goods and services.

Control of production was facilitated by the continuing organization and preprocessing of industrial operations. Machinery itself came increasingly to be controlled by two new information-processing technologies: closed-loop feedback devices like James Watt's steam governor (1788) and preprogrammed open-loop controllers like those of the Jacquard loom (1801). By 1890, Herman Hollerith had extended Jacquard's punch cards to tabulation of U.S. census data. This information-processing technology survives to this day—if just barely—owing largely to the corporation to which Hollerith's innovation gave life, International Business Machines (IBM). Further rationalization and control of production advanced through an accumulation of other industrial innovations: interchangeable parts (after 1800), integration of production within factories (1820s and 1830s), the development of modern accounting techniques (1850s and 1860s), professional managers (1860s and 1870s), continuous-process production (late 1870s and early 1880s), the "scientific management" of Frederick Winslow Taylor (1911), Henry Ford's modern assembly line (after 1913), and statistical quality control (1920s), among many others.

The resulting flood of mass-produced goods demanded comparable innovation in control of a second area of the economy: distribution. Growing infrastructures of transportation, including rail networks, steamship lines, and urban traction systems, depended for control on a corresponding infrastructure of information processing and telecommunications. Within fifteen years after the opening of the pioneering Baltimore and Ohio Railroad in 1830, for example, Samuel F. B. Morse—with a congressional appropriation of $30,000—had linked Baltimore to Washington, D.C., by means of a telegraph. Eight years later, in 1852, thirteen thousand miles of railroad and twenty-three thousand miles of telegraph line were in operation (Thompson 1947; U.S. Bureau of the Census 1975, p. 731), and the two infrastructures continued to coevolve in a web of distribution and control that progressively bound the entire continent. In the words of business historian Alfred Chandler, "the railroad permitted a rapid increase in the speed and decrease in the cost of long-distance, written communication, while the invention of the telegraph created an even greater transformation by making possible almost instantaneous communication at great distances. The railroad and the telegraph marched across the continent in unison . . . The telegraph companies used the railroad for their rights-of-way, and the railroad used the services of the telegraph to coordinate the flow of trains and traffic" (1977, p. 195).

This coevolution of the railroad and telegraph systems fostered the development of another communication infrastructure for control of mass distribution and consumption: the postal system. Aided by the introduction in 1847 of the first federal postage stamp, itself an important innovation in control of the national system of distribution, the total distance mail moved more than doubled in the dozen years between Morse's first telegraph and 1857, when it reached 75 million miles—almost a third covered by rail (Chandler 1977, p. 195). Commercialization of the telephone in the 1880s, and especially the development of long-distance lines in the 1890s, added a third component to the national infrastructure of telecommunications.

Controlled by means of this infrastructure, an organizational system rapidly emerged for the distribution of mass production to national and world markets. Important innovations in the rationalization and control of this system included the commodity dealer and standardized grading of commodities (1850s), the department store, chain store, and wholesale jobber (1860s), monitoring of movements of inventory or "stock turn" (by 1870), the mail-order house (1870s), machine packaging (1890s), franchising (by 1911 the standard means of distributing automobiles), and the supermarket and mail-order chain (1920s). After World War I the instability in national and world markets that Durkheim had noted a quarter-century earlier came to be gradually controlled, largely because of the new telecommunications infrastructure and the reorganization of distribution on a societal scale.

Mass production and distribution cannot be completely controlled, however, without control of a third area of the economy: demand and consumption. Such control requires a means to communicate information about goods and services to national audiences in order to stimulate or reinforce demand for these products; at the same time, it requires a means to gather information on the preferences and behavior of this audience—reciprocal feedback to the controller from the controlled (although the consumer might justifiably see these relationships as reversed).

The mechanism for communicating information to a national audience of consumers developed with the first truly mass medium: power-driven, multiple-rotary printing and mass mailing by rail. At the outset of the Industrial Revolution, most printing was still done on wooden handpresses—using flat plates tightened by means of screws—that differed little from the one Gutenberg had used three centuries earlier. Steam power was first successfully applied to printing in Germany in 1810; by 1827 it was possible to print up to 2,500 pages in an hour. In 1893 the New York World printed 96,000 eight-page copies every hour—a 300-fold increase in speed in just seventy years.

The postal system, in addition to effecting and controlling distribution, also served, through bulk mailings of mass-produced publications, as a new medium of mass communication. By 1887 Montgomery Ward mailed throughout the continent a 540-page catalog listing more than 24,000 items. Circulation of the Sears and Roebuck catalog in-creased from 318,000 in 1897 (the first year for which figures are available) to more than 1 million in 1904, 2 million in 1905, 3 million in 1907, and 7 million by the late 1920s. In 1927 alone, Sears mailed 10 million circular letters, 15 million general catalogs (spring and fall editions), 23 million sales catalogs, plus other special catalogs—a total mailing of 75 million (Boorstin 1973, p. 128) or approximately one piece for every adult in the United States.

Throughout the late nineteenth and early twentieth centuries uncounted entrepreneurs and inventors struggled to extend the technologies of communication to mass audiences. Alexander Graham Bell, who patented the telephone in 1876, originally thought that his invention might be used as a broadcast medium to pipe public speeches, music, and news into private homes. Such systems were indeed begun in several countries—the one in Budapest had six thousand subscribers by the turn of the century and continued to operate through World War I (Briggs 1977). More extensive application of telephony to mass communication was undoubtedly stifled by the rapid development of broadcast media beginning with Guglielmo Marconi's demonstration of long-wave telegraphy in 1895. Transatlantic wireless communication followed in 1901, public radio broadcasting in 1906, and commercial radio by 1920; even television broadcasting, a medium not popular until after World War II, had begun by 1923.

Many other communication technologies that we do not today associate with advertising were tried out early in the Control Revolution as means to influence the consumption of mass audiences. Popular books like the novels of Charles Dickens contained special advertising sections. Mass telephone systems in Britain and Hungary carried advertisements interspersed among music and news. The phonograph, patented by Thomas Edison in 1877 and greatly improved by the 1890s in Hans Berliner's "gramophone," became another means by which a sponsor's message could be distributed to households: "Nobody would refuse," the United States Gramaphone Company claimed, "to listen to a fine song or concert piece or an oration—even if it is interrupted by a modest remark, Tartar's Baking Powder is Best' " (Abbot and Rider 1957, p. 387). With the development by Edison of the "motion picture" after 1891, advertising had a new medium, first in the kinetoscope (1898) and cinematograph (1895), which sponsors located in busy public places, and then in the 1900s in films projected in "movie houses." Although advertisers were initially wary of broadcasting because audiences could not be easily identified, by 1930 sponsors were spending $60 million annually on radio in the United States alone (Boorstin 1973, p. 392).

These mass media were not sufficient to effect true control, however, without a means of feedback from potential consumers to advertisers, thereby restoring to the emerging national and world markets what Durkheim had seen as an essential relationship of the earlier segmental markets: communication from consumer to producer to assure that the latter "can easily reckon the extent of the needs to be satisfied" (1898, p. 369). Simultaneously with the development of mass communication by the turn of the century came what might be called mass feedback technologies: market research (the idea first appeared as "commercial research" in 1911), including questionnaire surveys of magazine readership, the Audit Bureau of Circulation (1914), house-to-house interviewing (1916), attitudinal and opinion surveys (a U.S. bibliography lists nearly three thousand by 1928), a Census of Distribution (1929), large-scale statistical sampling theory (1930), indices of retail sales (1933), A. C. Nielsen's audimeter monitoring of broadcast audiences (1935), and statistical-sample surveys like the Gallup Poll (1936), to mention just a few of the many new technologies for monitoring consumer behavior.

Although most of the new information technologies originated in the private sector, where they were used to control production, distribution, and consumption of goods and services, their potential for controlling systems at the national and world level was not overlooked by government. Since at least the Roman Empire, where an extensive road system proved equally suited for moving either commerce or troops, communications infrastructures have served to control both economy and polity. As corporate bureaucracy came to control increasingly wider markets by the turn of this century, its power was increasingly checked by a parallel growth in state bureaucracy. Both bureaucracies found useful what Bell has called "intellectual technology":

> The major intellectual and sociological problems of the post-industrial society are . . . those of "organized complexity"—the management of large-scale systems, with large numbers of interacting variables, which have to be coordinated to achieve specific goals . . . An *intellectual technology* is the substitution of algorithms (problem-solving rules) for intuitive judgments. These algorithms may be embodied in an automatic machine or a computer program or a set of instructions based on some statistical or mathematical formula; the statistical and logical techniques that are used in dealing with "organized complexity" are efforts to formalize a set of decision rules. (1973, pp. 29–30)

Seen in this way, intellectual technology is another manifestation of bureaucratic rationality, an extension of what Saint-Simon described as a shift from the government of men to the administration of things, that is, a further move to administration based not on intuitive judgments but on logical and statistical rules and algorithms. Although Bell sees intellectual technology as arising after 1940, state bureaucracies had begun earlier in this century to appropriate many key elements: central economic planning (Soviet Union after 1920), the state fiscal policies of Lord Keynes (late 1920s), national income accounting (after 1933), econometrics (mid-1930s), input-output analysis (after 1936), linear programming and statistical decision theory (late 1930s), and operations research and systems analysis (early in World War II).

In the modern state the latest technologies of mass communication, persuasion, and market research are also used to stimulate and control demand for governmental services. The U.S. government, for example, currently spends about $150 million a year on advertising, which places it among the top thirty advertisers in the country; were the approximately 70 percent of its ads that are presented free as a public service also included, it would rank second—just behind Procter and Gamble (Porat 1977, p. 137). Increasing business and governmental use of control technologies and their recent proliferation in forms like data services and home computers for use by consumers have become dominant features of the Control Revolution.

YONEJI MASUDA, FROM
THE INFORMATION SOCIETY AS POST-INDUSTRIAL SOCIETY (1981)

Masuda (1905–1995), a sociologist and futurist from Japan, belongs within the group of popular writers seeking to characterize and predict information's role in the social and economic transformations of capitalist countries following WWII. Alongside Fritz Machlup's knowledge industry and the postindustrial society of Daniel Bell, Masuda adds information society or informatized society (*jōhōka shakai*), a term he and others first used in Japan in the 1960s to describe a new chapter in the history of civilization's advance. From the following excerpt's schematic comparison of industrial society and the new information society emerges a utopian vision, where human-computer synergy will lead to a non-coercive state, one whose beneficence is represented by the institution of information utilities through which society will democratically govern itself.

Image of the Future Information Society

What is the image of the information society? The composition of the concept will be built on the following two premises:

1. The information society will be a new type of human society, completely different from the present industrial society. Unlike the vague term 'post-industrial society', the term 'information society' as used here will describe in concrete terms the characteristics and the structure of this future society.

The basis for this assertion is that *the production of information values and not material values will be the driving force* behind the formation and development of society. Past systems of innovational technology have always been concerned with material productive power, but the future information society must be built within a completely new framework, with a thorough analysis of the system of computer-communications technology that determines the fundamental nature of the information society.

2. The developmental pattern of industrial society is the societal model from which we can predict the overall composition of the information society. Here is another bold 'historical hypothesis': *the past developmental pattern of human society can be used as a historical analogical model for future society.*

Putting the components of the information society together piece by piece by using this historical analogy is an extremely effective way for building the fundamental framework of the information society.

The Overall Composition of the Information Society

Table 1 presents the overall framework of the information society based upon these two premises. This table presents the overall composition of the information society based on a historical analogy from industrial society. Let me explain each of the major items. Of course the entire picture of the future information society can not be given at this stage, but at least this table will help the reader understand the composition and overall relations between chapters that unfold later in the book.[1]

1. The prime innovative technology at the core of development in industrial society was the steam engine, and its major function was to substitute for and amplify the physical labor of man. In the information society, 'computer technology' will be the innovational technology that will constitute the developmental core, and its fundamental function will be to *substitute for and amplify the mental labor of man.*

2. In industrial society, the motive power revolution resulting from the invention of the steam engine rapidly increased material productive power, and made possible the mass production of goods and services and the rapid transportation of goods. In the information society, 'an information revolution' resulting from development of the computer will rapidly expand information productive power, and make possible *the mass production of cognitive, systematized information, technology, and knowledge.*

3. In industrial society, the modern factory, consisting of machines and equipment, became the societal symbol and was the production center for goods.

TABLE 36.1 Pattern Comparison of Industrial Society and the Information Society

		Industrial Society	Information Society
Innovational Technology	Core	Steam engine (power)	Computer (memory, computation, control)
	Basic function	Replacement, amplification of physical labor	Replacement, amplification of mental labor
	Productive power	Material productive power (increase in per capita production)	Information productive power (increase in optimal action-selection capabilities)
Socioeconomic structure	Products	Useful goods and services	Information, technology, knowledge
	Production center	Modern factory (machinery, equipment)	Information utility (information networks, data banks)
	Market	New world, colonies, consumer purchasing power	Increase in knowledge frontiers, information space
	Leading industries	Manufacturing industries (machinery industry, chemical industry)	Intellectual industries (information industry, knowledge industry)
	Industrial structure	Primary, secondary, tertiary industriies	Matrix industrial structure (primary, secondary, tertiary, quaternary/ systems industries)
	Economic structure	Commodity economy (division of labor, separation of production and consumption)	Synergetic economy (joint production and shared utilization)
	Socioeconomic principle	Law of price (equilibrium of supply and demand)	Law of goals (principle of synergetic feedforward)
	Socioeconomic subject	Enterprise (private enterprise, public enterprise, third sector)	Voluntary communities (local and informational communities)
	Socioeconomic system	Private ownership of capital, free competition, profit maximization	Infrastructure, principle of synergy, precedence of social benefit
	Form of society	Class society (centralized power, classes, control)	Functional society (multicenter, function, autonomy)
	National goal	GNW (gross national welfare)	GNS (gross national satisfaction)
	Form of government	Parliamentary democracy	Participatory democracy
	Force of social change	Labor movements, strikes	Citizens' movements, litigation
	Social problems	Unemployment, war, fascism	Future shock, terror, invasion of privacy
	Most advanced stage	High mass consumption	High mass knowledge creation
Values	Value standards	Material values (satisfaction of physiological needs)	Time-value (satisfaction of goal achievement needs)
	Ethical standards	Fundamental human rights, humanity	Self-discipline, social contribution
	Spirit of the times	Renaissance (human liberation)	Globalism (symbiosis of man and nature)

In the information society *the information utility* (a computer-based public infrastructure) consisting of information networks and data banks will replace the factory as *the societal symbol*, and become the production and distribution center for information goods.

4. Markets in industrial society expanded as a result of the discovery of new continents and the acquisition of colonies. The increase in consumption purchasing power was the main factor in expansion of the market. In the information society, 'the knowledge frontier' *will become the potential market*, and the increase in the possibilities of problem solving and the development of opportunities in a society that is constantly and dynamically developing will be the primary factor behind the expansion of the information market.

5. In industrial society, the leading industries in economic development are machinery and chemicals, and the total structure comprises primary, secondary, and tertiary industries. In the information society the leading industries will be *the intellectual industries*, the core of which will be the knowledge industries. *Information-related industries* will be newly added as *the quaternary group* to the industrial structure of primary, secondary, and tertiary. This structure will consist of a matrix of information-related industries on the vertical axis, and health, housing and similar industries on the horizontal axis.

6. The economic structure of industrial society is characterized by (1) a sales-oriented commodity economy, (2) specialization of production utilizing divisions of labor, (3) complete division of production and consumption between enterprise and household. In the information society (1) information, the axis of socio-economic development, will be produced by the information utility, (2) self-production of information by users will increase; information will accumulate, (3) this accumulated information will expand through synergetic production and shared utilization and (4) the economy will change structurally from an exchange economy to *a synergetic economy*.

7. In industrial society the law of price, the universal socio-economic principle, is the invisible hand that maintains the equilibrium of supply and demand, and the economy and society as a whole develop within this economic order. In the information society *the goal principle* (a goal and means principle) will be the fundamental principle of society, and the synergetic feedforward, which apportions functions in order to achieve a common goal, will work to maintain the order of society.

8. In industrial society, the most important subject of social activity is the enterprise, the economic group. There are three areas: private enterprise, public enterprise, and a third sector of government ownership and private management. In the information society the most important subject of social activity will be *the voluntary community*, a socio-economic group that can be broadly divided into local communities and informational communities.

9. In industrial society the socio-economic system is a system of private enterprise characterized by private ownership of capital, free competition, and the maximization of profits. In the information society, the socio-economic system will be a voluntary civil society characterized by the superiority of its infrastructure, as a type of both public capital and knowledge-oriented human capital, and by a fundamental framework that embodies *the principle of synergy and social benefit*.

10. Industrial society is a society of centralized power and hierarchical classes. The information society, however, will be a multi-centered and complementary voluntary society. It will be horizontally functional, maintaining social order by *autonomous and complementary functions of a voluntary civil society*.

11. The goal of industrial society is to establish a Gross National Welfare Society, aiming to become a cradle-to-grave high welfare society. The information society will aim for *the realization of time value* (value that designs and actualizes future time), for each human being. The goal of society will be for everyone to enjoy a worthwhile life in the pursuit of greater future possibilities.

12. The political system of industrial society is a parliamentary system and majority rule. In the information society the political system will become a *participatory democracy*. It will be the politics of participation by citizens; the politics of autonomous management by citizens, based on agreement, participation and synergy that take in the opinions of minorities.

13. In industrial society, labor unions exist as a force for social change, and labor movements expand by the use of labor disputes as their weapon. In the information society, *citizen movements* will be the force behind social change; their weapons will be litigation and participatory movements.

14. In industrial society there are three main types of social problems: recession-induced unemployment, wars resulting from international conflict, and the dictatorships of fascism. The problems of the information society will be future shocks caused by the inability of people to respond smoothly to rapid societal transformation, acts of individual and group terrorists such as hijackings, *invasions of individual privacy* and the crisis of *a controlled society*.

15. The most advanced stage of industrial society is a high mass consumption stage, centering on durable goods, as evidenced by motorization (the diffusion of the automobile). The most advanced stage of the information society will be *the high mass knowledge creation society*, in which computerization will make it possible for each person to create knowledge and to go on to self-fulfillment.

16. In industrial society, the materialistic values of satisfying physiological and physical needs are the universal standards of social values; but in the information society, seeking *the satisfaction of achieved goals* will become the universal standard of values.

17. Finally, the spirit of industrial society has been the renaissance spirit of human liberation, which ethically means respect for fundamental human rights and emphasis on the dignity of the individual, and a spirit of brotherly love to rectify inequalities.

The spirit of the information society will be *the spirit of globalism, a symbiosis in which man and nature* can live together in harmony, consisting ethically of *strict self-discipline and social contribution.*

8
The Information Utility: Societal Symbol of the Information Society

While industrial society is a society formed and developed around the production of material values, the information society will be formed and developed around the production of information values. In industrial society the modern factory is a large machinery production facility which has the central function in the production of goods. This modern factory, the present societal symbol, supplanted the farm, which had been the main base of production in agricultural society. In the information society of the future the *information utility* will become the base of production of information values, and thus could appropriately be called the societal symbol of the information society.[2]

What Is an Information Utility?

An 'information utility' is *an information infrastructure* consisting of public information processing and service facilities that combine computer and communication networks. From these facilities *anyone, anywhere, at any time will be able easily, quickly, and inexpensively to get any information which one wants to get.*

The following four requirements will be essential to an information utility.

1. Central facilities equipped with large scale computers capable of simultaneous parallel processing, connected with large capacity memory devices, a large number of program packages and extensive data bases. Such facilities will be able to do information processing and provide services for a large number of users at the same time.
2. Such information process and service facilities will be provided for the use of the general public, for which purpose the computers of the central facilities will be connected by means of a communications circuit directly to terminals in businesses, schools, and homes.

3. Any user will be able to call the local center of the information utility to have data processed, or one will even be able to process the necessary data for oneself.
4. The cost of using the services of the center must be low to enable the general public to use the center for day-to-day needs.

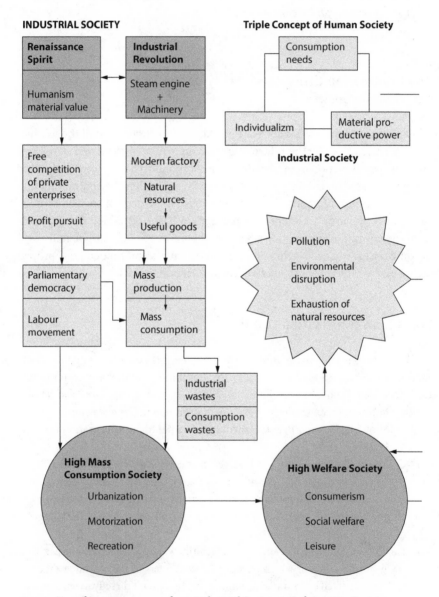

36.1A–B Transformation process from Industrial Society to Information Society

There is a system already in existence which partly meets these conditions. It can be seen in the commercial time-sharing service and the utilization of computer networks operating between universities. But these systems are restricted to certain social strata (large enterprises and universities), and the costs are high. It was once thought that it would be several decades before information utilities could become available to meet all these conditions fully,

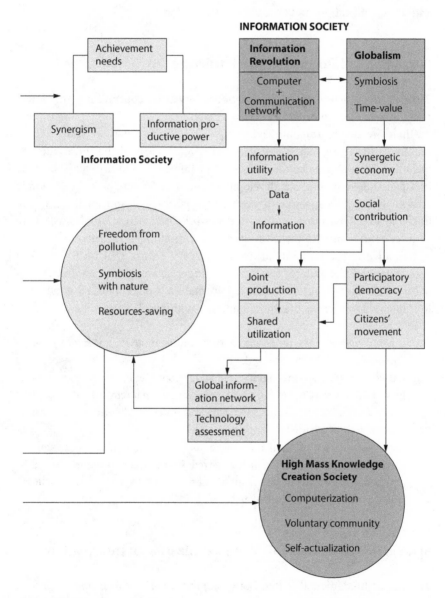

36.1A-B *Continued*

but the development of ICs (integrated circuits) in the early 1970s ushered in the era of full-fledged information utilities.

. . .

Can we now project the picture of a future information utility as the societal symbol of the information society?

A desirable and feasible future information utility will represent the integration of three concepts—(1) information and infrastructure, (2) joint production and shared utilization, and (3) citizen participation.

Formation of Information Infrastructure

The first fundamental of the information utility as we conceive it is that *it will take the form of an information infrastructure.*

There are two reasons for saying this. *First*, the information utility will be required to have all that is essential to the other parts of the infrastructure, including electricity, water, railroads, etc. The information utility will (1) become indispensable to the support, development and maintenance of socio-economic activity, (2) require massive investments in equipment and facilities, (3) be linked in a regional and/or nationwide network. Information utilities will share all three conditions with the existing components of the infrastructure.

Second, the information utility by its very nature will be for the use and benefit of the public, its service being of a unique character, that is *self-multiplication*. In the first place, information, unlike material goods, has four inherent properties that have made self-multiplication possible.

1. It is *not consumable*—goods are consumed in being used, but information remains however much it is used.
2. It is *non-transferable*—in the transfer of goods from A to B, they are physically moved from A to B, but in the transfer of information it remains with A.
3. *Indivisible*—materials such as electricity and water are divided for use, but information can be used only as 'a set'.
4. *Accumulative*—the accumulation of goods is by their non-use, but information cannot be consumed or transferred, so it is accumulated to be used repeatedly. The quality of information is raised by adding new information to what has already been accumulated.

Synergetic Production and Shared Utilization of Information

The second fundamental is that both *the production and utilization will be a combined operation.* This means that the production structure of information is *self-multiplying*.

'Self-multiplication' does not mean the successive production of new information, but *the utility's continuous expansion in the production of information,
both in quantity accumulation and qualitative improvement.* All information
produced by the information utility is cumulative, with new information constantly being added. In simpler terms, *the accumulation of information leads to
further accumulation of information which in turn means still further accumulation of information over time and space.* One can say that information utilities
are systems that demonstrate to the maximum the self-multiplication function
of information by man-machine methods . . .

***

The third fundamental is *citizen participation.* Three possible types of management can be envisaged for the information utility: the business, government
managed and the citizen managed types.

In the long run, the citizen oriented mixed type will probably become pre-
dominant because citizen participation will be essential to the management of
information utilities. This becomes clear if one looks at the shape that these
three types of management can assume, and then notes, from a macro point of
view, the socio-economic merits and demerits of each . . .

TABLE 36.2 Three Types of Information Utilities

	Business Type	Government Managed Type	Citizen Managed Type
Management Goal	Profit	Welfare	Information accumulation
Type of Capital	Private capital	Government capital	Civil capital
Type of Management	Private	Government	Autonomous
Form of Production	Time sharing services	Data banks	Synergetic production
Area of Service	Daily convenience, leisure	Medical care, education	Problem solving, opportunity developments
Operations Base	Sales revenue	Usage rates, taxes	Voluntary contributions, usage rates
Price System	Free price system	Public utility rate system	Income standard system
Merits	Efficient, good service	Operated in the public interest, inexpensive	Autonomous, creative
Demerits	Commercialism, mental degeneration	Danger of control, inefficiency	Weak, unstructured operations base

Citizen Participation Is Essential

Whatever the combination, citizen participation is an essential condition, the most desirable form of which would be mixed and citizen-oriented. The main reason is that (1) only by citizen participation in the management of information utilities will the self-multiplicative production effect of information be expanded, (2) autonomous group decision making by ordinary citizens will be promoted, and (3) the dangerous tendency toward a centralized administrative society will be prevented.

The Macro-Cumulative Effect of Information. *The first* reason why information utilities will tend toward citizen management is that this type of information utility, more than any other, will facilitate the macro-cumulative effect of information. I have already mentioned that self-multiplication of information production gives the information utility the nature of an information infrastructure. When viewed from the perspective of the national economy, the self-multiplication can be called *the macro cumulative effect* of information; the effect being in sharp contrast to *the mass production effect* of goods produced in the modern factories of industrial society.

In the production of goods, the expansion in manufacturing that follows a big increase in production equipment has a great mass production effect. That is to say, the greater the investment in capital equipment, the more productive power increases and production costs decrease. This decrease in costs expands the market and encourages further profits and further accumulation of capital. This mass production effect of goods is, from the enterprise's point of view, the multiplying effect of capital, in the sense that any accumulation of capital results in further accumulation of capital.

The self-multiplication of private capital has been a fundamental cause of the formation and expansion of modern manufacturing industries as a whole.

In the case of information also, expansion in the scale of production cannot be ignored, but here the cumulative effect is more important.

The most important point in the production of information from a macro standpoint is *the self-multiplication of information value* itself—how to accumulate information and how to continue the further accumulation of information by adding new information to what has already been accumulated.

The information utility is not used simply by a limited group of users; it is widely used in the public interest by people in general. Moreover, it is the general public themselves that operate the information utility freely. Having the information utility take the form of synergetic production and shared use will raise the macro-cumulative effect of information utilities to the highest level. The citizen management type that is oriented toward voluntary synergistic production and shared use of information by citizens themselves is the

form of management of the information utility that will have the greatest macro-cumulative effect, rather than the business type that aims to increase profits
through the self-multiplication of capital, or the government managed type
that prevents citizens from using the information utility freely.

Autonomous Group Decision Making. *The second* ground for confidence is
that *this type makes autonomous group decision making possible*, with the aim of
solving complex socio-economic problems through autonomous decisions by
the citizens themselves.

The inadequacy of governmental compulsion and monetary compensation
in solving the problems of human existence will stimulate these possibilities
even further. The future information society will be a society in which autonomous decision making will be the most basic human right. The causes of
problems that will arise in the future will be very complex and interrelated,
and in complex opposition to these will be the individual group interests of
the citizens. In solving such problems, *mutual understanding* and *voluntary
cooperation* of each citizen in selecting the action that corresponds to one's own
situation will be essential.

Avoiding a Controlled Society. *The third* reason is that only through this type
can *the information society avoid the dangers of a controlled society*. For the
information society to become an ideal society of voluntary decision making,
and to avoid the ultimate fearful Orwellian automated state, will depend on the
form of management adopted for the information utility.

If information utilities were to be completely dominated by a despotic
state organization, the information society would be the ultimate controlled
society, in which the abuses would by far exceed the alienation of man in the
present industrial society or the abuse of human rights under dictatorships.
This could occur because, in information utilities, both public and personal
information concerning each individual is filed and accumulated, and, in
addition, information about one's major activities in society would be added
constantly to this file.

But if the information utilities are completely entrusted to the voluntary
management of the citizenry, and if the personal information of individuals
is completely protected and used to improve the private life of each individual
and the quality of one's social activities, then the information utility will be
of immeasurable benefit to all citizens. For example, the information utility
will not simply provide the individual with information that is useful in solving everyday problems (illness, work, learning, housing, etc.) of the citizens,
but will also contribute greatly to maintaining the individual's life in a healthy
active state, by combining this sort of social information with personal data
about each individual.

Looked at in this way, the information utility is a socio-economic institution which concentrates the ultimate in scientific technology. In this sense also *the autonomous management by citizens* of the information utility is an essential prerequisite for the ideal information society.

Notes

1. Yoneji Masuda, "Social Impact of Computerization. An Application of the Pattern Model for Industrial Society." *Challenges from the Future*. Tokyo: Kodansha, 1970.
2. Yoneji Masuda, "Future Perspectives for Information Utility," *Proceedings of the 4th International Conference on Computer Communication*. Kyoto, Japan, September 1978.

PAUL VIRILIO, FROM
THE INFORMATION BOMB (1999)

Paul Virilio (1932–2018) was an architect and urban planner-cum-cultural theorist whose work explores interconnected themes of militarization, media history, and "dromology," Virilio's name for the logic of speed that dominates modern society. Written in the author's typically aphoristic style, *The Information Bomb* figures the postwar information revolution as an explosive device, one whose field of catastrophic destruction extends across all modern society and humanity more generally. In sharp contrast to Masuda's emphasis on the liberating potential of technology, Virilio takes a pessimistic stance, arguing that the virtualization of social life leads to subjugation by the state and private institutions who surveil our every move. The essay's call for a form of "social deterrence" to resist the consequences of the information bomb has become all the more poignant since the subsequent rise of online social media platforms such as Facebook and Twitter.

Chapter 12

Every political revolution is a drama, but the coming technical revolution is without doubt more than just a drama. It is a *tragedy of knowledge*, the Babelish confusion of individual and collective bodies of learning.

As Aesop said of language, the Internet is both the best and the worst of things. It is the advance of a limitless—or almost limitless—communication; and at some point it is also the disaster—the meeting with the iceberg—for this *Titanic* of virtual navigation.

The cybernetics of the network of networks, the product of a "techno-sophic" illusion contemporaneous with the end of the Cold War as "end of history," is a techno-system of strategic communication which brings with it the *systemic risk* of a chain reaction of damage that will occur as soon as globalization has become effective.

There is no point today speculating on the regional character—or otherwise—of the recent Asian stock market crash. If the cybernetics of the financial market had actually been globalized, the crash of autumn 1997 would have been instantaneously planetary and the economic catastrophe would have been total.

Thus, after the *atom* bomb and the deployment for over forty years of generalized nuclear deterrence, the *information bomb* which has just exploded will very soon require the establishment of a new type of *deterrence*—in this case, a *societal* one, with "automatic circuit-breakers" put in place capable of avoiding the over-heating, if not indeed the fission, of the social cores of nations.

With the real-time globalization of telecommunications—the unofficial model for which is provided by the Internet—the information revolution shows itself to be also a *systematic snooping operation*, which triggers a panic phenomenon of rumour and suspicion, and which is set to ruin the foundations of "truth" in a professional ethics and hence the freedom of the press. Everyone can see this from the role of the Internet, for example, in the Clinton-Lewinsky scandal, with the doubts cast on the veracity of the facts asserted/denied, the uncontrollable development of a manipulation of sources and hence of public opinion itself—all of which are so many warning signs that prove the revolution of *real information* is also a revolution in *virtual disinformation* and hence in history as currently being written.

Radioactivity of the elements of matter, interactivity of the constituents of information—the harm done by irradiation is discreet and multifarious, at times amounting to general contamination.

The actors and tele-actors of the cybernetic telecommunications revolution, acting and interacting in real time, set a technical pace or tempo which now lords it over the properly historical importance of the *local time* of societies and countries. This works to the exclusive advantage of a *world time* which no longer belongs so much to the history of nations as to the abstraction of a **universal chrono-politics** for which no political representative is truly responsible, except for certain military general staffs in the case of *cyberwar being declared.*

What are we to say, for example, of researchers' silence on the role of the National Security Agency in the history of the development of the Internet?

How are we to analyse today the resolve of the American State Department to make military strikes against a country which offends against the new world order—as it happens, Iraq—*automatic*?

Behind the libertarian propaganda for a *direct (live) democracy*, capable of renovating party-based *representative democracy*, the ideology of an *automatic democracy* is being put in place, in which the absence of deliberation would be compensated by a "social automatism" similar to that found in opinion polls or the measurement of TV audience ratings.

A reflex democracy, without collective reflexion, in which conditioning would have greater importance than "electoral campaigning" and in which the "demonstrative" character of the party programmes would give way to the strictly "demonstrative" and spectacular character of a drilling of individual behaviour, the parameters of which were long ago tested out by advertising.

Moreover, has not the network of networks, established on the basis of the Arpanet system, which was designed to resist the electromagnetic effects of an atomic war, presented an occasion—since the Gulf War—for launching the very *first universal advertising campaign* for a systemic product which interests *no one in particular* and *everyone in general*?

The promotion of the Web and its on-line services, an unprecedented phenomenon of ideological contamination, no longer bears any resemblance to the marketing of a practical technology, such as the sale of a vehicle or even of some kind of broadcasting equipment (radio, television), since what is involved in this case is the *most immense enterprise of opinion transformation* ever attempted in "peacetime," an undertaking which has scant regard for the collective intelligence or the culture of nations.

Hence, among other things, the general excessiveness—of the provisions of the Multilateral Agreement on Investment (MAI), for example, or of the NTM, the "transatlantic free-trade project."

These are globalitarian campaigns and they have about them the intensity of American propaganda for "info-war," that *revolution in military affairs* initiated by the Pentagon at the end of the Cold War.

Yet one would understand nothing of the Internet and the future information superhighways if one forgot the interactive dimension of the arrangement and the birth of a real **comparative advertising** which is no longer content merely to vaunt the excellence of a particular product, but is concerned, first and foremost, to *impugn the commercial competitor*, to disarm the resistance of consumers, by denigrating their position, or merely their reticence.

Not content to satisfy the legitimate curiosity of the purchasers of their goods, the advertising agencies are now intent on calling for the *symbolic murder* of their competitors. Hence the decision of the European Parliament to adopt effective legislation against these "campaigns of systematic denigration."[1]

We should also point out that the Web can no longer be separated from the technical development which aims to replace the totality of *analogue* information by a digitalization of the knowledge media over the next ten years.

With the *digital* on the verge of winning out in all spheres of audiovisual production, the European Community is currently examining a *Green Paper on convergence.*

According to the authors of this report, the fact that a single technology—the digital—is used for different purposes (telephone, television or computers) should lead to a re-examination of the special treatment accorded to the Community's audiovisual sector and to that sector being brought solely under market control, as is the case with telecommunications.

The second strand in this *tentacular* convergence clearly concerns the Internet, with the idea that, on this network of American origin, since anything goes, future jurisdiction over the system should be solely a matter for the United States.

We are thus moving imperceptibly towards a sort of **image crash**.

An eye for an eye—the competition between icons is currently on the agenda and that competition, in assuming worldwide proportions, is, like everything else in the era of the great planetary market-place, destabilizing for the regime of temporality of the whole of iconic information.

Screen against screen—the home computer *terminal* and the television *monitor* are squaring up to each other in a fight to dominate *the global perception market*, control of which will, in the near future, open up a new era both in aesthetics and in ethics.

* * *

"With 500,000 screens throughout the world tracking a totally computerized stock market, the Asian crash was watched everywhere as it happened," declared a French trader in autumn 1997.

But when there are 5 million *live-cams* spread all over the world and several hundred million Internet users capable of observing them simultaneously at their consoles, we shall see the first **visual crash**, and so-called *television* will then give way to the generalized tele-surveillance of a world in which the famous *virtual bubble* of the financial markets will be supplanted by the *visual bubble* of the collective imaginary, with the attendant risk of the explosion of the information bomb announced back in the 1950s by Albert Einstein himself.

If, today, the *irrational* is amplified in the various sectors of financial globalization, it will flourish even more tomorrow in the field of the *globalization of the collective imaginary*, since the multiplier effect of the old television (responsible, among other things, for the Rodney King affair, the O.J. Simpson trial and the *post mortem* coronation of Princess Diana) will be infinitely reinforced by the **over-reactive** character of world tele-surveillance.

"The generalization of individual positions, when they are all moving in the same direction, generates unstable global conjunctures," observed a CNRS analyst writing of the Asian crash. *The rationality of individual behaviours makes for an overall irrationality.*[2]

As **world** time ("live") takes over from the ancient, immemorial supremacy of the **local** time of regions, both the next step in *interactive* advertising and the even more fearsome conditions for *comparative* advertising between brands and investors are set to appear. This is a veritable cold civil war, a guerrilla war involving the symbolic execution of competitors, for which the European Council is set to give the go-ahead.

In this globalitarian conjuncture, the "advertising space" is no longer to be found in the breaks between films or the TV slots between programmes: *it is now the real space-time of all communication.* Virtual inflation no longer relates solely to the economy of manufactured products, the financial bubble, but to the very understanding of our relation to the world.

As a result, the great *"danger to the system"* is no longer that of the bankruptcy of companies or banks in a chain reaction, such as we have recently seen in Asia, but the formidable threat of a blinding, of a collective blindness on the part of humanity—the unprecedented possibility of a *defeat of facts* and hence a disorientation of our relation to reality.

The bankruptcy of phenomena, the catastrophic slump of the visible, from which economic and political *disinformation* alone could derive advantage: with the *analogue* yielding its prerogatives to the *digital*, and with the recently achieved "data compression" making it possible henceforth to speed up—that is to say, to concertina—our relation to reality . . . but to do so on condition that we accept the increasing impoverishment of sensory appearances.

In this way, with the progressive **digitalization** of audiovisual, tactile and olfactory information going hand in glove with the decline of immediate sensations, the *analogue resemblance* between what is close at hand and comparable would yield primacy to the *numerical probability* alone of things distant—of all things distant. And would in this way pollute our sensory ecology once and for all.

Notes

1. In May 1998 Fashion-TV, a women's fashion chain founded by Adam Lisowski, took the Walt Disney Company (Europe SA) to court for spreading defamatory rumours, and for a "campaign to blacken its name among the clients and partners of Fashion-TV," which might be explained by the imminent launch of a rival fashion chain by Disney. See *Le Nouvel Observateur*, 30 May 1998, TV supplement.
2. André Orlan, *Le Mende*, 5 November 1997.

C. A. BAYLY, FROM
EMPIRE AND INFORMATION :
INTELLIGENCE GATHERING AND
SOCIAL COMMUNICATION IN INDIA,
1780-1870 (1996)

Bayly (1945–2015) was an influential historian of colonial India and the British empire. His earlier work on urban history, especially on bazaars and markets, helped engender his interest in the topic of social communication. Offering a counterpart to Thomas Richards's emphasis on literary and metropolitan perspectives of colonial information management, Bayly makes the case for a more empirical study of a region's "information order," placing the dispensation of knowledge at the forefront of social history. Applied to nineteenth-century northern India, this emphasis reveals an intricate picture of intersecting but separate knowledge systems: amongst the Indians, an emerging public sphere or "ecumene" independent from that of the colonial administrators. Meanwhile, for the British: a growing reliance on statistics and literary stereotypes at the cost of gathering local intelligence—resulting in their surprise over the large-scale rebellion in 1857.

Introduction

A central purpose of this book is to examine British political intelligence in north India between the 1780s and the 1860s. It describes the networks of Indian running-spies, newswriters and knowledgeable secretaries whom officials of the East India Company recruited and deployed in their efforts to secure

military, political and social information. It considers how the colonial authorities interpreted and misinterpreted the material derived from these sources.
It draws attention to the gaps, distortions and "panics" about malign "native"
plots which afflicted the system of imperial surveillance within north India
and, for comparison's sake, outside its borders, in Nepal, Burma and beyond the
north-western frontier. Finally, the book examines the extent to which intelligence failures and successes contributed to the course of the Rebellion of
1857–9, the collapse of the East India Company's government and the form of
the following pacification.

The quality of military and political intelligence available to European colonial powers was evidently a critical determinant of their success in conquest
and profitable governance. Equally, this information provided the raw material
on which Europeans drew when they tried to understand the politics, economic activities and culture of their indigenous subjects. The book, therefore,
addresses some of the most traditional as well as some of the most recent and
controversial issues in imperial and south Asian historiography.

The study also concerns communication and the movement of knowledge
within Indian society, examining the role of communities of writers in the
bazaars and the culture of political debate. It is a study of social communication in the sense used in Karl Deutsch's pioneering work.[1] It considers those
specialists who helped to articulate indigenous systems of knowledge and keep
information, ideas and gossip flowing: the astrologers, physicians, experts in
the philosopher's stone, midwives, marriage-makers, and other knowledgeable
people who brought news from one community and region to another. It was
the density and flexibility of indigenous routines of social communication
which explains why north Indians were able to make such striking use of
the printing press, the newspaper and the public meeting once those innovations finally began to spread rapidly amongst them in the 1830s and 1840s.
While modern Indian history should certainly not be depicted as a single
grand narrative culminating in the emergence of nationalism, the density of
social communication demonstrated by this book does, in fact, help to explain
why political leaders in a poor country with a relatively low rate of general literacy should have been able to create a widely diffused and popular nationalist
movement so early.

These two systems—the colonial state's surveillance agencies and the autonomous networks of social communicators—overlapped and interpenetrated. But
the overlap was incomplete. The meeting between British and Indian agencies
was riven by suspicion, distortion and violence. For here, at the point of intersection between political intelligence and indigenous knowledge, colonial rule
was at its most vulnerable. Here, new communities of knowledgeable Indians
which used the colonial state's communications and ideologies independently
of it, or against it, began to emerge even in the early nineteenth century.

As the expatriate newspaper, *The Friend of India*, remarked in 1836 echoing the administrator, Sir John Malcolm, "our Indian Empire is one of opinion" and "the progress of knowledge" would probably "entail the separation of India from England."[2] A contemporary British officer seeing a pile of newly printed vernacular books in the office of Mountstuart Elphinstone, Governor of Bombay, exclaimed in similar terms: "it is our highroad back to Europe."[3]

Neither Indian historians nor historians of other European dependencies have paid very much attention to the intelligence or propaganda systems of colonial powers,[4] though intelligence studies have become a major industry for European and American historians who have come to regard political surveillance and social communication as a critical feature of the modern state and society.[5] Recent works on India have considered the related area of "colonial knowledge" or "discourse," focusing on the learned theories of orientalism, rather than on day-to-day information and its sources.[6] Several scholars, too, have begun to consider the "native informant" and the impact of the press and print capitalism.[7] Nevertheless, state surveillance and social communication remains a poorly studied area. By contrast, some of the more important works of fiction to emerge from the Indo-British encounter are located precisely on that cusp between British intelligence and indigenous knowledge. Rudyard Kipling's *Kim*,[8] to take the most celebrated example, introduces a cast of characters which find pale reflections in this study. In Kipling's novel the reader meets Kim himself, the Eurasian spy in the Great Game of espionage in central Asia, and Hurree Babu, the learned native informant. Alongside them Kipling memorably pictures the eddies of news and gossip flowing down the Grand Trunk Road from Lahore to Banaras, carried onward by Afghan horse-dealers, Hindu bankers and pilgrims destined for the holy places of Hinduism and Buddhism.

The information order

The book seeks to establish a broad framework for the study of these two elements—state's intelligence and social communication—by using the concept of the "information order." This term has been adapted from the work of the economic geographer Manuel Castells who has written of the "informational city."[9] Castells treats the new information technology of the late twentieth century as a type of social formation rather than as a simple adjunct to existing economic forces or a neutral technological process. He shows how in North America after 1960, information technology changed the pattern of urban living, speeded processes of deindustrialization and income differentiation, and "de-skilled" large parts of the work force, especially those already disadvantaged such as poorly educated minority groups and women. What is important about his approach is that he sees the generators of knowledge, the institutions of information collection and diffusion and the discourses to which they give rise as autonomous forces for economic and social change. They are not reduced to the status of contingencies of late-industrial capitalism or the modern state. Knowledge itself is a social formation; knowledgeable people form distinct and active social segments with their own interests. For Castells, intellectual property, including education, was as much the foundation of social class and economies as financial or landed property was for earlier generations of social theorists. Rather than being residual categories relegated to the end of the history book in chapters entitled "intellectual developments" or "communications," these considerations should be central to studies of social change. Such an approach ought to bring benefits to Indian history, a subject whose proponents have until recently been preoccupied with the sociology of institutions to the detriment of the sociology of knowledge. Equally, Indian intellectual history has been more radically divorced from its social context than in many other areas of historical study. It needs to be restored to that context.

What we have called the information order should not be seen as a "thing," any more than a state or an economy is a thing; it is a heuristic device, or a field of investigation, which can be used to probe the organisation, values and limitations of past societies. It is not separate from the world of power or economic exploitation, but stands both prior to it and dependent on it. It can be considered to have a degree of autonomy from politics or economic structure. Thus some powers, or powerful groups, with finite economic resources and little brute force—the Republic of Venice in the eighteenth century[10] or the House of Rothschild in the nineteenth, for instance—have had exceptionally well-organised and flexible information systems which allowed them to make their limited caches of power and resources work harder. Likewise, societies at similar levels of economic development, when judged by per capita income, had different styles of information order which shaped their capacity to change internally or resist external pressures.

In early modern societies, the information order was decentralised, consisting of many overlapping groups of knowledge-rich communities. It was not mediated as in contemporary industrial societies by a dominant state or commercial communications sector. Schooling and literacy were specialist resources open only to particular elites who used their learning as badges of status. Knowledge was only slowly becoming a public good, a citizen's right, or an adjunct of state power. As yet, it was deeply embodied in the status of the particular informant or knowledge community. Kings and their officials collected and deployed knowledge in unstandardised forms because what should be known was not yet determined by any dominant notion of a critical bureaucracy or public. All the same, the school, the royal writers' chancellery, the public scribe, the spy, the runner, the body of physicians and astrologers, and other specialists tended to make up a loosely-knit constellation of powers in society. In Indian soothsaying as in its European equivalent, all these actors were conjoined under the sign of Mercury, messenger of the Gods, or Budh-Graha, affording us an indigenous licence for the category.[11]

Viewed from the perspective of information, however, pre-modern societies differed greatly from one another in the status and uses of literacy and also in the quality and effectiveness of the systems of information collection and distribution deployed by the state and other agencies. Later Tokugawa Japan, for example, supporting more than 40 per cent male education, mass lithography and a system of commercial horseback messengers,[12] stands in sharp contrast to contemporary societies, such as the Ottoman Middle East[13] and South Asia, which possessed broadly similar levels of per capita wealth. In the latter two societies, lithography was slow to develop and a clerical elite monopolised literacy which was the preserve of little more than 10 per cent of the male population. The level of state surveillance common in Tokugawa Japan was also rarely aspired to in India, though comprehensive records of land measurement and assessment had evolved early in the subcontinent. In contrast again, the early modern states of southeast Asia were more concerned with counting people than with counting revenue, partly because they were constrained by shortages of labour rather than of cash. Burmese and Thai rulers, therefore, organised general population censuses earlier than their counterparts in India and parts of west Asia.

These differences were partly determined by economics. Monetised economies required different forms of knowledge collection and archive-making from those where customary labour dues or shares of produce were taken by the elites. At the same time, differences in ideology and religious practice also moulded contrasting information orders. The reformed Buddhist hierarchies of early modern Thailand and Burma, for example, attempted to impart standard rules of life to the wider population[14] in a way which was impossible for the loose networks of Indian Brahmin priests. Monks and kings consequently encouraged a more widespread system of popular education than existed in most parts of north India.

Colonial knowledge

European colonial states faced obvious problems in engaging with the information order of a conquered society, an essential task if they were to build an intelligence system capable of securing their grip on the territory's resources. The conquerors needed to reach into and manipulate the indigenous systems of communication in new colonies. But because these indigenous systems differed from each other in important respects, colonial regimes in turn came to preside over widely differing information orders. Simple difficulties of language made the Europeans initially dependent on the skills of "linguists," "translators" and "men of two tongues" or, as the Hindustani has it, *dubashs*. These informants were inevitably drawn from the very communities which the Western powers sought to dominate. Even if they served their alien masters loyally, they moved in realms of life and thought which they wished to keep hidden from the rulers. The basic fear of the colonial official or settler was, consequently, his lack of indigenous knowledge and ignorance of the "wiles of the natives." He feared their secret letters, their drumming and "bush telegraphy" and the nightly passage of seditious agents masquerading as priests and holy men.

Some contemporary social theorists have gone further and concluded that Europeans never knew anything significant about indigenous societies, and indeed can never know anything about them because of European conceptual biases. What passed, or passes, for European knowledge of the Other is, in fact, a mere web of rhetorical devices designed to give legitimacy to conquest.[15] This position is too extreme. European rule over Asians and Africans could not have been sustained without a degree of understanding of the conquered societies. In India, colonial knowledge was derived to a considerable extent from indigenous knowledge, albeit out of context and distorted by fear and prejudice. People from different races and cultures, possessing different degrees of power, could and did achieve a broad agreement over claims to truth about the phenomena they observed. This study, therefore, broadly accepts Stuart Schwartz's view that "despite the haze of linguistic and cultural assumptions that limit observation . . . other cultures existed outside the mind of the observer" and they could be observed and understood "in an admittedly imperfect approximation of a reality."[16]

In our view, the problems the British faced in understanding and controlling events in south Asia derived as much from the shape of India's information order and the superficiality of colonial rule as from any particular cultural bias or prejudice resulting from the assimilation of knowledge to power. The British never controlled the bulk of capital, the means of production or the means of persuasion and communication[17] in the subcontinent. Because they were not, in general, concerned to spread their faith or mingle their genes with the Indian population, the British could not count on an inflow of "affective knowledge," that is knowledge which derived from the creation of moral communities within the colonial society by means of conversion, acculturation or interbreeding. Indian Christians and Armenians were, of course, important informants; Eurasians played a big role, especially in the generation of military knowledge for the British conquerors in the later eighteenth century. But the situation was quite different from that obtaining, for example, in early southern Africa where large mixed-race communities and acculturated or converted Africans ("Hottentots"; Khoikhoi) provided guides, mediators and informants.[18] Again, the British in India could not rely on that "patrimonial knowledge" on which independent states and some colonial governments could draw. This was the knowledge of the expatriate or mixed-race landowner or commercial man who acted, albeit in his own interest, as the eyes and ears of the colonial government. In India, as opposed to French Algeria or British southern Africa, white or mixed-raced farmers, or sub-imperialist commercial men, such as the Indians in East Africa, were not widely available to create and transmit information to the rulers.

In India, then, the British were forced to master and manipulate the information systems of their Hindu and Mughal predecessors; this was especially true before 1830. Later, there was indeed change in these systems, though this was limited in its geographical range and impact. Indigenous agencies were modified, given new tasks and set to collecting different types of information from their predecessors. Public instruction created a new type of native informant. The statistical movement, which gathered pace after 1830, had a powerful impact. It raised the status of the expatriate expert, the "old India hand" in the Indian Medical Service or the Posts and Intelligence Department of the Army and gave the colonial authorities a superficial knowledge of conditions in the major stations and among subordinate Indian servants. Away from the purview of the district offices, however, the British were still ignorant of much that was transpiring, as the events of 1857 brutally revealed. Their chain of surveillance was at its most vulnerable where the body of elite, literate officers stretching down from the district town linked up with the hereditary servants and information collectors of the village. This link snapped in 1857, was partly welded together in the later nineteenth century but was rapidly corroded again during the twentieth century. In short, the surveillance agencies of both pre-colonial and colonial government in India were flexible and at times penetrating, but they also seem labile and thinly spread when compared, for instance, to the density of state institutions at village level in Japan. In parallel with political power through long periods of Indian history, information and knowledge was decentralised. From the heyday of Mughal rule to the present this has confronted the emerging state with serious obstacles in its dealings with regional and village elites.

When we move on to consider the broader impact of British rule on the information order of north India, similar patterns will emerge. On the face of it, the simultaneous introduction of public instruction, the printing press, public debate in newspapers, the English language, libraries and dense archives transformed Indian society in the nineteenth century more thoroughly than colonial capitalism transformed its economy. This study does not, however, go as far as postulating a revolution in mentalities consequent on the rise of "print capitalism" as Benedict Anderson does for Indonesia and other colonial territories.[19] It argues that north India's response to these modern forms of information diffusion and retrieval was determined to a considerable extent by existing communities of knowledge, styles of reasoned debate and patterns of social communication. Even in realms of scientific knowledge such as the disciplines of astronomy, geography and medicine, where western theories and techniques were to achieve dominance in the long term, the imprint of earlier indigenous sciences and the virtue of indigenous practitioners remained significant for most Indians. The information order of colonial India retained distinctly Indian features, even while it was absorbing and responding to the profound influences set in motion by the European rulers. The first chapter examines this indigenous inheritance.

Notes

1. Karl Deutsch, *Nationalism and Social Communication. An Enquiry Into the Foundations of Nationality* (Cambridge, Mass., 1960); Paul R. Brass, *Language, Religion and Politics in North India* (Cambridge, 1974).

2. 'Report of the General Committee for Public instruction', *Friend of India* 27 Oct, 1836 cf. J. Malcolm, *Political History of India* (London, 1826), I, 82. He defined 'opinion' in terms of Gramscian ideological hegemony as 'that respect and awe with which the comparative superiority of knowledge, justice and system of rule, have inspired the inhabitants of our own territories . . .' I am grateful to Mr. Nigel Chancellor for pointing out the original reference.

3. Cited in K. Ballhatchet, *Social Policy and Social Change in Western India 1817–1830* (London, 1957), p. 249.

4. But see Milton Israel, *Communications and Power. Propaganda and the Press in the Indian Nationalist Struggle, 1920–47* (Cambridge, 1994).

5. For the early modern period, Ian K. Steele, *The English Atlantic 1675–1740. An exploration of communications and community* (New York, 1986); P. Fritz, 'The Anti-Jacobite intelligence system of the English ministers, 1715–45', *Historical Journal*, 16, 1973, 265–89; H.A. Innis, *Empire and Communications* (Oxford, 1990); for the modern period the journal *Intelligence and National Security*, R.J. Poplewell, *Intelligence and Imperial Defence* (London, 1995).

6. The most celebrated example is Ronald Inden, *Imagining India* (Oxford, 1990).

7. e.g. Nicholas Dirks, 'Castes of Mind', *Representations*, 37, winter 1992, 56–77; Eugene F. Irschick, *Dialogue and History. Constructing South India, 1795–1895* (California, 1994); Francis Robinson, 'Technology and religious change. Islam and the impact of print', *Modern Asian Studies*, 27, 1, 1993, 229–51.

8. cf. Thomas Richards, *The Imperial Archive: knowledge and the fantasy of empire* (London, 1993), pp. 22–30, who notes that in *Kim*, social knowledge has become coextensive with military intelligence; in the Indian system they had always been closely allied.

9. Manuel Castells, *The Informational City. Information technology, economic restructuring and the urban-regional process* (Oxford, 1989). No 'information' can, of course, be perceived and ordered unless the observer has conceptual paradigms within which to apprehend it. Our use of the word 'information', however, implies observations perceived at a relatively low level of conceptual definition, on the validity of whose claims to truth people from different regions, cultures and linguistic groups might broadly agree. 'Knowledge' implies socially organised and taxonomised information, about

which such agreement would be less sure. In north Indian languages 'information' would be rendered by words such as *khabr* and *suchna*; knowledge by *ilm* or *vidya*, though under some circumstances vidya might mean something more akin to 'occult' knowledge, while spiritual knowledge would be represented by *gyana* or *jnan*.

10. Venice maintained a complex system of internal and external espionage, besides controlling the movement of the commercial secrets of glassmaking, etc.

11. The *Bhuvana-Dipaka* cited in M. Ramakrishna Bhat, *Essentials of Horary Astrology or Prasnapadavi* (Delhi, 1992), p. 40.

12. K Moriya, 'Urban networks and information networks', in C. Nakane and S. Oishi (eds.), C. Totman (tr.), *Tokugawa Japan* (Tokyo, 1990), pp. 97–124; as early as 1692, 7,300 book titles had been published in Japan. Kyoto alone had 494 publishing houses in the eighteenth century. No book was published in India, by Indians, until *c.* 1800.

13. See, e.g., Cornell H. Fleischer, *Bureaucrat and Intellectual in the Ottoman Empire: the historian Mustafa Ali. 1541–1600* (Princeton, 1986).

14. Nicholas Tarling, *Cambridge History of South East Asia*, I, (Cambridge, 1992), 537–42.

15. This position has sometimes been associated with Edward Said, *Orientalism* (1978), but it is much more typical of his radical disciples, see John M. MacKenzie, *Orientalism. History, theory and the arts* (Manchester, 1995).

16. Stuart B. Schwartz, 'Introduction' in Schwartz (ed.) *Implicit Understandings. Observing, reporting and reflecting on the encounters between Europeans and other peoples in the early modern era* (New York, 1994), p. 19.

17. This term is taken from Anthony Giddens, *The Constitution of Society. Outline of a theory of structuration* (Cambridge, 1984), and conveys part of what I mean by information order.

18. Leonard Thompson and Monica Wilson, *The Oxford History of South Africa*, I (Oxford, 1969), 69–70; Robert Ross, *Adam Kok's Griquas. A study in the development of stratification in South Africa* (Cambridge, 1976).

19. Benedict Anderson, *Imagined Communities* (revised ed., London, 1994).

MARY ELIZABETH BERRY, FROM *JAPAN IN PRINT: INFORMATION AND NATION IN THE EARLY MODERN PERIOD* (2006)

Mary Elizabeth Berry (b. 1947) is a historian and specialist of Japan's transition from the late medieval period (16th c.) to the early modern era (17th–18th c). Exploring the latter period, *Japan in Print* shows how the Tokugawa state's relative political stability, urbanization, and flourishing print culture formed the conditions for an information revolution, characterized by a massive uptick in the publication of details regarding contemporary people, places, things, and words, endlessly collected and republished to meet the demands of a growing readership. Such a proliferation of ephemeral, empirical facts resulted in what Berry terms a "public library of information," whose taxonomic structures and standardized units of analysis helped make "society visible to itself" as an integrated nation—preceding by several centuries the modern newspapers and telegraph that are so central to Benedict Anderson's account of national imagination. In the opening chapter, Berry introduces this information commons, imaginatively surveying its myriad of travel guides, street maps, personnel lists, and other resources.

A Traveling Clerk Goes to the Bookstores

Suppose you lived in Kyoto about three hundred years ago and were facing your first trip to Edo, the Tokugawa shogun's capital, some five hundred kilometers away. To flesh out this fantasy, let's make you a senior clerk in a firm that retails silk cloth. You are being sent on a temporary assignment from the main shop in Kyoto to a branch in Edo.

You might prepare for your journey, as novices have always prepared in the past, by canvassing seasoned travelers and then trusting to advice along the way. If fortunate and well connected, you might also scan travel diaries in manuscript. But because you live around 1700, you have a further choice—one barely available to your grandparents. You can prepare for your journey by seriously hitting printed books. Since 1640 or so, remarkable numbers of commercially published texts have been converting private knowledge into public information. The mysteries of the road, and many others besides, have been unlocked for both solitary readers and the radiating circles of relations around them. You are one of the readers and, for our purposes, quite a methodical and practiced one. To give you a good budget for buying and borrowing material, which can be costly, we'll make you the heir to that silk shop.

Being something of a bibliophile, you begin your research by consulting recent booksellers' catalogues, rough equivalents of *Books in Print*, which have been appearing in major cities since at least 1659. *Kōeki shojaku mokuroku* (A Catalogue of Publications for Public Utility), published by a consortium of

39.1 "Bookseller," from *Jinrin kinmōzui*

(An Illustrated Encyclopedia of Humanity, 1690). National Diet Library, Tokyo.

Kyoto firms in 1692, contains entries on over 7,000 current titles divided into 46 main categories (and numerous subcategories).[1] You winnow leads from some obvious sections ("Geography," "Travel," "Famous Places") and from a few less obvious ones as well ("Erotica," "Military Affairs"), hoping to come across additional items—ephemera, privately printed matter, texts published outside Kyoto that may not have made it into the catalogue—as you browse the shops. There are over 100 of them. Some are small printing houses stocking their own titles. Others retail texts on specialized subjects such as Chinese learning or poetry or medicine or Zen Buddhism. Yet others, and the ones you frequent, distribute disparate material from disparate firms in both Kyoto and more distant publishing centers, principally Edo and Osaka. There you will gather a generous selection of texts, borrowing many of them for fixed but renewable terms at a fraction of the list prices.[2]

To orient yourself geographically, you start with maps. Although your choice is substantial, in both sheet and atlas form, you will probably settle on a current edition of Ishikawa Ryūsen's *Nihon kaisan chōrikuzu* (Map of the Seas,

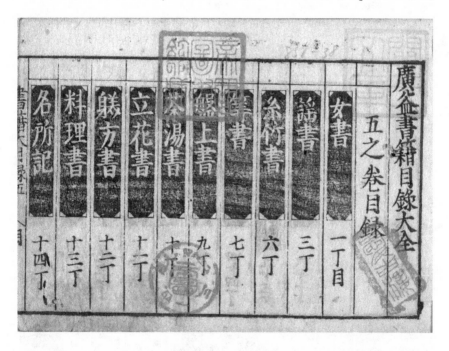

39.2 *Kōeki shojaku mokuroku taizen* (A Catalogue of Publications for Public Utility, 1692), partial table of contents for fascicle 5, listing the following subject categories (and their beginning page numbers): women, noh chanting, musical instruments, calculation, board games, tea ceremony, flower arrangement, etiquette, cooking, and accounts of famous places.

Courtesy of the East Asian Library, University of California, Berkeley.

Mountains, and Lands of Japan)—a map so legible and packed with information that it has been revised and reissued annually since its first publication in 1689.[3]

It charts the nation's provinces and castle towns, land and water routes, famous sites and scenic places. It labels every ferry crossing and every post station along the major highways, listing the distances between stops in an index. Thick with social and political geography, it also identifies all regional lords, or daimyo, with notes on the gross productivity of their domains. The map is a large one (81 × 171 cm), made by pasting together numerous individual sheets and folding them for convenience. In a print market tailored to most imaginable needs, you could certainly find smaller, handier maps—single-sheet or accordion-pleated editions, for example, tuckable into a kimono sleeve. But the big maps attract you, and most consumers, because they offer space for exploding detail and many indexes. They also offer space itself, mimicking in their size the expanse of real terrain. You will spread out Ryūsen's map on the floor and crawl over and around it to capture the relationship between carto-graphic representation and the physical landscape. I suspect you may change

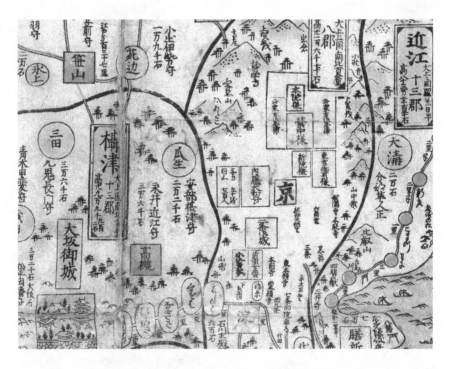

39.3 Ishikawa Ryūsen, *Nihon kaisan chōrikuzu* (Map of the Seas, Mountains, and Lands of Japan, 1694), detail centered on Kyoto and showing the provinces of Ōmi, Yamashiro, and Settsu. Woodblock, 81 × 171 cm.

Courtesy of the East Asian Library, University of California, Berkeley.

your socks and walk across the map as well, perhaps pacing the main highways from Kyoto to Edo.[4] Reading it presents no particular problems. Your school primers (including *Nihon ōrai* [Japan Basics], published in 1688) have taught you the basic nomenclature, cultural landmarks and economic features of the national scene.[5] And to help with obscure names, you keep to hand both family encyclopedias and dictionaries.

Your geographical knowledge refreshed, but your route undecided, you turn next to *Shokoku annai tabi suzume* (The Traveling Sparrow's Guide to the Provinces, first published in seven fascicles in 1687).[6] A compendium of itineraries issued individually in previous years, the Sparrow takes you along the country's principal highways, noting not only post stations and distances but travel times, road conditions, fees for porters and pack horses, licensed accommodations, seasonal pleasures, and notable touring sites. It also moves outside the highway system to cover the secondary roads and paths that connect scores of popular destinations. Thus you will find itineraries not only from Kyoto to Edo (two principal routes with hints on detours and byways), but from Kyoto to Mount Kōya, the Arima hot springs, Yoshino, and other fabled locales. Finally, the Sparrow moves beyond roadways to describe sea routes. If you hanker for a sail, the Sparrow will guide you by land to the Inland Sea and then by water to Edo Bay.

Suppose, though, that comparison of the Sparrow's data persuades you to choose the fastest and best-maintained land course from Kyoto to Edo, the Tōkaidō, or Eastern Sea Highway. At this point, you may want a convincing visual image of the impending journey. So spend some time with *Tōkaidō bunken ezu* (The Pictorial Survey of the Tōkaidō, published in five fascicles in 1690).[7] Instead of individual pages, each fascicle consists of a long scroll of paper, formed of separate sheets pasted end to end, that folds every 12 centimeters to make an accordion-style book. Together the fascicles picture the mighty sweep of the Tōkaidō on a scale of 1:12,000, reproducing the 486 kilometers between Edo and Kyoto in just over 40 meters of drawing.

The Pictorial Survey, drafted by the cartographer Ochikochi Dōin and illustrated by the painter Hishikawa Moronobu, resembles a photographic record. It portrays the wide road (mostly about 5.5 meters across) packed with sand or stone, the abutting gutters and streams, the fifty-three post stations and their buildings, the transport and lodging facilities available along the way, the bridges and fords and ferries, the shade trees and Buddhist statues standing like sentries, the sanctuaries and villages located in the distance. Accurately depicting bends in the highway, the Survey also enters every distance marker (at intervals of one *ri*, or about four kilometers), every stone guidepost at the intersections, and every barrier where officials monitor travelers and check their papers. The cartographer adds compass points from span to span, indicating the gently changing orientations of a road that curves where a scroll cannot.

Juxtaposed on this businesslike log of the highway are myriad vignettes that invite all viewers "from the loftiest nobles to the lowliest women and children to see themselves as if in a brilliant mirror" (as the preface puts it). Hishikawa Moronobu's illustrations provide an ethnography in motion, depicting long military processions, travelers of all ages and stations, farmers and fishers at work, vendors and peddlers of tea and tobacco and souvenirs, sightseers exploring famous sites and viewing Mount Fuji from the optimal vantage points. Travel is thus transformed in the Survey from tough and unpredictable work into a seeming occasion for pleasure and discovery, casual companionship and shopping for novelties.

Now that you know the way and what to expect, you are ready for background on the places you will pass. Again, you have some basic proficiency in historical and social geography, not only from school primers but the family encyclopedias (such as *Banmin chōhōki* [Everybody's Treasury], published in two fascicles in 1692) that assemble knowledge about past and present rulers, calendars and chronologies, the distribution of local lords, and the like.[8] But for denser accounts, you turn to a national gazetteer. You choose a recent one, *Kokka man'yōki* (The Ten-Thousand Leaf Record of the Provincial Flowers, published in 1697 in 21 fascicles and over 2,000 pages), which decants each of the provinces into conventional categories.[9] You concentrate on the fifteen provinces along the Tōkaidō, reencountering some material familiar from the Sparrow (the numbers of districts, geographical features, annual productivity totals, chief crops and manufactures, the names of castle holders, principal sanctuaries and famous places). Yet you also find capsule histories of each of the provinces, their ruling families, and their many monuments—not only temples and shrines but castle ruins, old battlegrounds, graves, and stone stellae. Entries include poems inspired by various sites, typically from classical and medieval anthologies, to improve your literary education. The Ten-Thousand Leaf Record contains a fair amount of administrative detail as well. Beyond providing the names and genealogical tables of daimyo, this gazetteer identifies an unusual number of local office-holders: domainal elders, regional intendants, municipal magistrates, and heads of the military guard.

If you plan to linger on the way for pleasure, spending perhaps twenty days on a trip normally requiring about twelve (unless the Ōi and Abe Rivers flood, stranding you indefinitely), you might use the Ten-Thousand Leaf Record for sightseeing information. But a better bet is a specialized guide to a single site or the sequential attractions on your route. *Tōkaidō meishoki* (An Account of Famous Places of the Tōkaidō, published in 1661 in six fascicles), a travelogue covering the Eastern Sea Highway, pairs a worldly priest with an insouciant commoner, whose adventures and dialogues construct a narrative of the road.[10] Between the theaters and brothels of Edo (where they start out) and the fashionable streets of Kyoto (where they end up), the companions barrel

39.4 Ochikochi Dōin and Hishikawa Moronobu, *Tōkaidō bunken ezu* (Pictorial Survey of the Tōkaidō, 1690), opening page of fascicle 3, "From Fuchū to Yoshida," showing the post station and castle town of Fuchū and listing castle officials, transporters, and portage fees. National Diet Library, Tokyo.

through dozens of noteworthy sites—all apparently open to the curious—while exchanging remarks on the lore and landmarks of temples, the histories of martial families and legendary men, the properties of the better hot springs. All such material is offered as ready information for the traveler rather than privileged insider learning.

Finally ready to concentrate on Edo itself, you might stagger under the weight of available intelligence were you not familiar with the even more voluminous, and prototypical, texts concerning Kyoto. Again, you start with maps. And, again, you have an enormous choice, since over 200 different maps of the military capital have been printed since the early part of the century, including the Great Map of Edo, a set of five sectional maps based on an exhaustive survey by the Tokugawa shogunate (first published section by section between 1670 and 1673). But you prefer a version by Ishikawa Ryūsen, which is less exact but more legible and vivid in detail.[11] It measures 100 by 160 centimeters. Like most of its counterparts, this map centers on the Tokugawa castle, fastidiously depicts the moats, canals, and rivers that thread the city, and extends to the bay on the east and the agrarian outreaches at the other cardinal points. It identifies all bridges and embankments and most fields for martial sport. It tracks every street (and most alleys), labeling every ward. It also locates dozens of temples and shrines, scores of warehouses, and hundreds of military mansions (with prodigious details about their occupants). To clarify social topography, Ryūsen's map uses family crests and regalia to mark daimyo residences, color-coding to distinguish the commoner and religious zones. The pleasure quarters are labeled too, if inconspicuously.

You can find a verbal equivalent of the map in another Sparrow—the Edo Sparrow, this time (*Edo suzume*, published in twelve fascicles in 1677).[12] Principally a heroic street index, it moves through the city section by section, noting the sites that front each step of the way. If you fail to keep count yourself, the author concludes with assurances that he has covered "over 520 mansions of great lords, 2,870 lesser military mansions, 850 temples, 120 shrines, 900 neighborhoods, and 2,880 *chō* of distance [roughly 300 kilometers]."

Classification is a contagion, you discover, as you turn to an urban directory, *Edo kanoko* (The Dappled Fabric of Edo, published in six fascicles in 1687 and regularly revised thereafter).[13] This encyclopedic source offers you many versions of many Edos as it organizes and reorganizes the city in a kaleidoscope of patterns. You will probably buy rather than borrow the Dappled Fabric, since its punishing catalogues defy any summary consultation, and you will probably select the celebrated edition of 1690. This directory includes a list in 26 categories of over 300 physical features (natural and manmade); the annual ritual calendars of both the commoners and the military houses; a list in 22 categories of almost 400 famous tea objects, with the names of owners; a list in 10 categories of major Buddhist and Shinto icons; a list of over 60 shrines

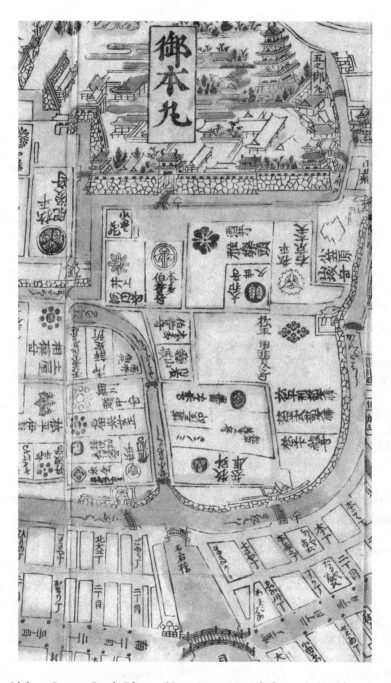

39.5 Ishikawa Ryūsen, *Bundo Edo ōezu* (Great Survey Map of Edo, 1710), detail featuring Edo castle and the Bridge of Japan. Daimyo residences are marked by family names, titles, and crests. Commoner neighborhoods appear as white space. Woodblock, 100 × 160 cm.

Courtesy of the East Asian Library, University of California, Berkeley.

with notes on history, administration, and income; a list of over 100 temples, organized by sect, with notes on history, administration, and income; a street-by-street survey of Edo with selective inventories of shops; a guide to the principal entertainment quarters; a list of famous vistas; a list in 43 categories of roughly 300 pro prominent artists, teachers, and providers of services (doctors of various specialties, poets of different schools, removers of ear wax), most with addresses; a list in 193 categories of almost 700 prominent craftspeople and merchants (the gold and silver guildsmen, textile dealers, incense blenders, handlers of Buddhist goods), most with addresses; and a list of 21 licensed wholesale firms.

Awesome in its lists but sparing in exposition, the Dappled Fabric leaves you ready for fuller accounts of the Edo scene. Narrative tour guides help close the breach. You have something of a choice, since the earliest dates from 1621 and the most recent from 1694. The habit of recycling a substantial amount of old material under new titles may reduce the appeal of the later work, but it is still best to stick with a current text, since sheer coverage improves. Edo's "places of fame," roughly a dozen according to a guide of 1621, numbered 46 by 1643, 80 by 1662, and 100 by 1687. (By the nineteenth century they would total 1,043.)[14] The inflation results not so much from new building as from greater inclusion: once-parochial sites have been converted into public places in response to both competition between metropolitan centers for fame-studded landscapes and changing attitudes toward the landscape itself. A wide common gaze is invading, and appropriating, the space of a putatively common history. Famous places do include scenes of beauty and pleasure. But you will find most of them defined by notable pasts that seemingly bind countrymen together. The sort of friendly raconteurs who led you along the Tōkaidō reappear in the Edo guides to exchange more lore about miracles and battles, priests and generals, elite customs and great events. And they deliver their stories with the same sort of casual knowingness that presumes popular access to a shared historyscape.[15]

Game for more? Specialized books of all kinds beckon, if only you can figure out what you want to know. Perhaps your interest in administrative detail has been whetted rather than sated by ubiquitous references to daimyo and their castles. You are headed, after all, for a political capital where official arcana are a daily diet. So refer to a Mirror of the Military Houses, or full personnel roster of the Tokugawa shogunate (first published in 1643 and continually revised thereafter by competitive firms).[16] These rosters start with current lists of all daimyo lords, roughly 250 of them, each identified by his family crest and regalia and described in up to 44 categories (family and personal name, courtly rank and title, age, location and gross productivity of the local domain, addresses of all residences in Edo, names of heirs and other family members and major retainers . . .). The rosters also continue, if you buy an amplified edition, with lists of the principal office holders in the Tokugawa shogunate—almost two thousand of them, serving in Edo as well as the provincial centers of shogunal authority, all lined up under as many as 231 job titles. These entries, too, are long. They typically include (among other items) each official's name, address, stipend, crest, deputies, tenure in office, and previous appointments.

The Military Mirrors will probably seem familiar to you, perhaps because you have seen equivalent treatments of the courtly aristocracy in various family encyclopedias, gazetteers, and guides to Kyoto. The emperor and his household, the 200-some noble families, the princely abbots and abbesses—all appear in rosters that, like the Military Mirrors, specify name, rank, title, crest, income, residence, and major deputies.[17] But you are just as likely to recognize the style of the Mirrors because you have seen equivalent treatments of the demimonde.

Circulating since the 1650s, and now numbering in the hundreds, rosters of prostitutes and actors have long treated the universe of play as the Mirrors treat the universe of power. Texts like *Yoshiwara hito tabane* (A Bundle of Personages from the Yoshiwara, published in 1680) list courtesans with their names, ranks, crests, professional houses, and residences.[18] Most include maps and illustrations as well, and some go so far as to state fees (which appear to parallel military stipends). Similarly, rosters of actors, like the *Yarōmushi* (Rogue Bugs, 1660),[19] note their names, troupes, managers, principal roles, and crests. But while mimicking the schemes of honor and identity characteristic of the Military Mirrors, the rosters of the demimonde depart from the model by offering critiques of performance. Love and entertainment are for sale. Best to buy prudently. So you are given appraisals of physical attributes and artistic skills, warned away from women who surrender too soon or actors who rely on bombast. If you are worried about your own performance in the quarters, you can find guides to etiquette that will take you from bath to table to bed. And, indeed, so popular is the coverage of the sex trade that storytellers are appropriating the style of the rosters for comic purposes. The current rage is Ejima Kiseki's *Keisei iro jamisen* (Sex Music), which covers over 1,750 women, in seven principal ranks, who work the great cities.[20]

* * *

Now you are tired, eager to quit a literature of lists and categories. Your brain swollen with numbers, you're ready for the comfort of fiction, where story will replace inventory. So you turn to the master, Ihara Saikaku. The book you select, *Kōshoku gonin onna* (Five Women Who Chose Love), worries you a bit with its arithmetical title. Still, you are soon distracted by the tale of Oman, a merchant's daughter who is as ravishing as she is rich. She loves Gengobei, who is nearly as ravishing (if somewhat worn) but no longer rich (since he has spent the family fortune on eight years of single-minded sex). Resolute before the obstacles that love requires, Oman manages to lure Gengobei from both the boys he prefers and the clerical vows he professes. Eventually, after some low-life misadventure, Oman brings the rake home. With a marriage in view, her oddly overjoyed parents welcome the prospective groom. And you welcome the end to a good story free of inventory. But too soon. Closing his tale, Saikaku tells us that Oman's parents hand over to Gengobei.

> The various keys of the house—three hundred and eighty-three in all. Then, an auspicious day having been determined, they set about a Storehouse Opening. First they inspected six hundred and fifty chests, each marked "Two Hundred Great Gold Pieces," and eight hundred others, each containing one thousand small gold pieces. The hundred-weight boxes of silver, which they next examined, were mildewed from disuse and a fearful groaning came from those underneath. . . . [C]opper coins lay scattered about like grains of sand. . . .
>
> Proceeding now to the outside storehouse, they found treasures galore: fabrics brought over from China in the olden days were piled to the rafters; next to them precious incense lay stacked like so much firewood; of flawless coral gems, from ninety grains to over one pound in weight, there were one thousand two hundred and thirty-five; there was an endless profusion of granulated shark skin and of the finest willow-green porcelain; all this, together with the Asukawa tea canister and such other precious ware, had been left there pell-mell. . . . Other wonders too were in that storehouse: a mermaid picked in salt, a pail wrought of pure agate. . . .[21]

As vigorously as any author of a gazetteer or urban directory, Saikaku, too, counts and calculates, lists and labels. He delights in things of wonder, and in things made wonderful by their names and variety and plenitude. If he does not unlock every single storehouse, Saikaku pushes toward the exhaustive tour. And if he classifies the goods more casually than not, he works down a rough catalogue of metal currency, bulk storage, and masterpieces. There is no escape for you. You live in a world of numeration and classification. You swoon. You sleep.

Notes

1. A good sample of booksellers' catalogues appears in Shidō Bunko, ed., *(Edo jidai) Shorin shuppan shoseki mokuroku shūsei* (Tokyo: Inoue Shobō, 1962–64). For the 1692 catalogue mentioned here, see ibid., 1: 223–317, *Kōeki shojaku mokuroku* (also called *Kōeki shojaku mokuroku taizen*, both standard titles for numerous works). There are four copies of the woodblock edition of this text in the East Asian Library of the University of California, Berkeley. For publishing and cataloguing information concerning

this and subsequently cited books in the EAL collection, see Oka Masahiko, Kodama Fumiko, Tozawa Ikuko, and Ishimatsu Hisayuki, comps., *Edo Printed Books at Berkeley, Formerly of the Mitsui Library in the Collection of the University of California at Berkeley* (Tokyo: Yumani Shobō, 1990).

2. For two major studies of printing history and bookselling, see Peter Kornicki, *The Book in Japan: A Cultural History from the Beginnings to the Nineteenth Century* (Boston: Brill, 1998), esp. pp. 169–205, and Henry D. Smith II, "The History of the Book in Edo and Paris," in James L. McClain, John M. Merriman, and Ugawa Kaoru, eds., *Edo and Paris: Urban Life and the State in the Early Modern Era* (Ithaca, N.Y.: Cornell University Press, 1994), pp. 332–52. Also see David Chibbett, *The History of Japanese Printing and Book Illustration* (Tokyo: Kodansha International, 1977), and Peter Kornicki, "Obiya Ihei: A Japanese Provincial Publisher," *British Library Journal* 11 (1985): 131–42. The names and addresses of booksellers appear in such urban directories as the *(Zōho) Edo sōkanoko meisho taizen*, in Edo Sōsho Kankōkai, ed., *Edo sōsho* (Tokyo: Edo Sōsho Kankōkai, 1916–17), 3: 1–88, and 4: 1–131; see 4: 94–95.

3. The East Asian Library at the University of California, Berkeley, holds copies of this map from the 1689, 1691, and 1694 editions. (No printed catalogue of the Japanese maps in the EAL exists as yet.) The library also holds several copies of a very similar map, Ryūsen's *Dai Nihon ōezu*. For a reproduction of a 1691 edition of *Nihon kaisan chōrikuzu*, see Unno Kazutaka, Oda Takao, and Muroga Nobuo, eds., *Nihon kochizu taisei* (Tokyo: Kōdansha, 1972–75), vol. 1, pl. 31. I have used Marcia Yonemoto's translation of the title. See, for a discussion focused on Ryūsen's *Honchō zukan kōmoku*, her *Mapping Early Modern Japan: Space, Place, and Culture in the Tokugawa Period (1603–1868)* (Berkeley: University of California Press, 2003), pp. 26–35.

4. I am guessing here, although colleagues in Japan agree that the size of most early modern maps invites viewers to walk on them. Because neither the woodblock technology nor the density of entries required maps as large as those produced, bigness itself appears to have been a desideratum. And because sheet maps were not displayed (but folded and put away), I suspect their size suited a taste for physical as well as visual exploration of the surface.

5. *Nihon ōrai*, discussed in Ishikawa Matsutarō, *Ōraimono kaidai jiten* (Tokyo: Ōzorasha, 2001), 1: 648, and reproduced in Kaigo Tokuomi, ed., *Nihon kyōkasho takei: Kindai-hen* (Tokyo: Kōdansha, 1961–67), *Ōrai-hen*, vol. 9. Also see the dis cussion of geographical primers in Ishikawa Matsutarō, *Ōraimono no seiritsu to tenkai* (Tokyo: Yūshōdō Shuppan, 1988), pp. 99–129 and, for an almost exhaustive collection of texts, Ishikawa Matsutarō, ed., *Ōraimono taikei* (Tokyo: Ōzorasha, 1992–94).

6. *Shokoku annai tabi suzume*, facsimile in Asakura Haruhiko, ed., *Kohan chishi sōsho* (Tokyo: Sumiya Shobō, 1969–71), vol. 9. A 1720 variant of this text, the *Shokoku tabi suzume*, is held by the East Asian Library at the University of California, Berkeley. For a survey of geographical texts published early in the Edo period, see Wada Mankichi and Asakura Haruhiko, *(Shintei zōho) Kohan chishi kaidai* (Tokyo: Kokusho Kankōkai, 1974).

7. For a facsimile, see Ochikochi Dōin and Hishikawa Moronobu, *Tōkaidō bunken ezu*, ed. Kohan Edozu Shūsei Kankōkai (Tokyo: Kohan Edozu Shūsei Kankōkai, 1970). Also see Asakura Haruhiko, ed., *Kohan chishi sōsho*, vol. 12. For discussion, see Koji Hasegawa, "Road Atlases in Early Modern Japan and Britain," in John Sargent and Richard Wiltshire, eds., *Geographical Studies and Japan* (Sandgate, Folkestone, Kent: Japan Library, 1993), pp. 15–24.

8. *Banmin chōhōki*, facsimile in Kinsei Bungaku Shoshi Kenkyūkai, ed., *Kinsei bungaku shiryō ruijū: Sankō bunken-hen* (Tokyo: Benseisha, 1975–81), 10: 129–261.

9. Kikumoto Gahō, comp., *Kokka man'yōki*, facsimile in Asakura Haruhiko, ed., *Kohan chishi sōsho*, vols. 1–4. Two woodblock editions of this text, dated 1697 and 1835, are held by the East Asian Library at the University of California, Berkeley.

10. Asai Ryōi, *Tōkaidō meishoki*, ed. Asakura Haruhiko (Tokyo: Heibonsha, 1979). For a facsimile, Kinsei Bungaku Shoshi Kenkyūkai, ed., *Kinsei bungaku shiryō ruijū: Kohan chishi-hen* (Tokyo: Benseisha, 1975–81), vol. 8. For discussion of this text and several of the Edo sources mentioned in the following paragraphs, see Jurgis Elisonas, "Notorious Places: A Brief Excursion in the Narrative Topography of Early Edo," in James McClain et al., eds., *Edo and Paris*, pp. 253–91.

11. For a detailed history of Edo mapmaking, see Iida Ryūichi and Tawara Motoaki, *Edozu no rekishi* (Tokyo: Tsukiji Shokan, 1988).

12. *Edo suzume* in Kokusho Kankōkai, ed., *Kinsei bungei sōsho* (Tokyo: Kokusho Kankōkai, 1910), 1: 1–177.

13. *Edo kanoko* in Asakura Haruhiko, ed., *Kohan chishi sōsho*, vol. 8. The following description of the city appears in a revised and expanded edition of this text from 1690, the *(Zōho) Edo sōkanoko meisho taizen*. See citation in n. 2 above. A 1751 edition of the text, the *(Saitei) Edo sōkanoko shinzō taizen*, is held by the East Asian Library at the University of California, Berkeley.

14. For these tallies and discussion of successive Edo guides, see Suzuki Norio, "Meishoki ni miru Edo shūhen jisha e no kanshin to sankei," in Chihōshi Kenkyū Kyōgikai, ed., *Toshi shūhen no chihōshi* (Tokyo: Yūzankaku Shuppan, 1990), pp. 108–26.

15. See, e.g., Asai Ryōi, *Edo meishoki*, in Edo Sōsho Kankōkai, ed., *Edo sōsho*, 2: 1–160; facsimile in Kinsei Bungaku Soshi Kenkyūkai, ed., *Kinsei bungaku shiryō ruijū: Kohan chishi-hen*, vol. 8.

16. For a large selection of texts, see Hashimoto Hiroshi, ed., *(Kaitei zōho) Daibukan* (Tokyo: Meichō Kankōkai, 1966). For discussion, see Fujizane Kumiko, "Bukan no shoshigakuteki kenkyū," *Nihon rekishi* 525 (February 1992): 47–62.

17. Courtly rosters circulated most widely in popular reference works such as the *Banmin chōhōki* (see pp. 141–45) and the Kyoto city directories. See, e.g., the *Kyō habutae*, ed. Shinshū Kyōto Sōsho Kankōkai, *(Shinshū) Kyōto sōsho* (Kyoto: Rinsen Shoten, 1969, second printing 1976), 2: 155–77. Woodblock editions of the *Kyō habutae* (1811) and the *Kyō habutae taizen* (1768) are held by the East Asian Library of the University of California, Berkeley.

18. For the *Yoshiwara hito tabane*, see Ono Susumu, ed., *Kinsei shoki yūjo hyōbankishū* (Tokyo: Koten Bunko, 1965), 1: 465–570. For additional texts, see both that series and Kinsei Bungaku Shoshi Kenkyūkai, ed., *Kinsei bungaku shiryō ruijū: Kanazōshi-hen* (Tokyo: Benseisha, 1972–79), vols. 34–36.

19. *Yarōmushi*, in Kabuki Hyōbanki Kenkyūkai, ed., *Kabuki hyōbanki shūsei* (Tokyo: Iwanami Shoten, 1972–79), 1: 15–42. For similar texts, see both this volume and the full series.

20. Ejima Kiseki, *Keisei iro jamisen*, annot. Hasegawa Tsuyoshi, in Satake Akihiro et al., eds., *Shin Nihon koten bungaku taikei* (Tokyo: Iwanami Shoten, 1989), 78: 3–248.

21. Ihara Saikaku, "The Tale of Gengobei, the Mountain of Love," in id., *Five Women Who Chose Love*, in *The Life of an Amorous Woman and Other Writings*, ed. and trans. Ivan Morris (New York: New Directions, 1963), pp. 100–118; quotation, pp. 117–18.

ANN BLAIR, FROM
TOO MUCH TO KNOW: MANAGING
SCHOLARLY INFORMATION BEFORE
THE MODERN AGE (2010)

Blair (b. 1961) is a cultural and intellectual historian of early modern Europe. In *Too Much to Know*, she elegantly demonstrates that the recent feeling of "information overload" is by no means historically unique, arguing that already between 1500 and 1700 a burgeoning book culture— made up of both printed texts and manuscripts—produced a body of available scholarship too large for even the most dedicated reader to master. As a coping mechanism, scholars adapted and innovated a variety of practices and textual forms, from notetaking to the genre of the reference book. Here we excerpt the book's introduction, where Blair spells out the importance for studying early modern book history and provides a typology of textual information management to do so.

Introduction

We describe ourselves as living in an information age as if this were something completely new. In fact, many of our current ways of thinking about and handling information descend from patterns of thought and practices that extend back for centuries. This book explores the history of one of the longest-running traditions of information management—the collection and arrangement of textual excerpts designed for consultation in what I call, as a convenient shorthand, "reference books."[1] Large collections of textual material, consisting typically of quotations, examples, or bibliographical references, were used in many times and places as a way of facilitating access to a mass of texts considered authoritative. Reference books have sometimes been mined for evidence about commonly held views on specific topics or the meanings of words, and some (encyclopedias especially) have been studied for the genre they formed.[2] My purpose in studying reference tools in early modern Europe, and how they were conceived, produced, and used by contemporaries, is to gain insight into the ideals and practices of what one can anachronistically call "information management" in a period prior to our own. To that end I have combined a wide contextual net, spanning multiple periods, places, and reference genres, with a specific focus on several exemplary general reference books in Latin that were in print between 1500 and 1700.

The term "information" has a long history, attested in English from the fourteenth century in the sense of "instruction" and from the fifteenth century in the sense of "knowledge concerning some particular fact."[3] We use it today in many contexts, from biology, which studies the transmission of information at many levels, from DNA to neural processes, to computer science, which analyzes information mathematically without attention to its semantic content.[4] More colloquially, the notion of an "information age" (a term coined in 1962) is premised on the idea that computers radically changed the availability and methods of producing and using higher-order information (e.g. as recorded in language or numbers).[5] I use the term "information" in a nontechnical way, as distinct from data (which requires further processing before it can be meaningful) and from knowledge (which implies an individual knower). We speak of storing, retrieving, selecting, and organizing information, with the implication that it can be stored and shared for use and reuse in different ways by many people—a kind of public property distinct from personal knowledge. Furthermore, information typically takes the form of discrete and small-sized items that have been removed from their original contexts and made available as "morsels" ready to be rearticulated.[6]

I follow other scholars in applying the term to premodern contexts, cautiously due to the risk of anachronism, because it is effective in describing how authors and readers of early reference books handled their material, even though they themselves articulated their goals in terms not of information but of knowledge and edification. To use actors' categories, that is, the terms most commonly used at the time, early reference books were designed to store and make accessible words and things (*verba et res*).[7] These ranged from definitions and descriptions from the natural world (e.g., this plant has that property or that phenomenon has this cause) to human actions and sayings (X wrote this book, Y said that in these circumstances, this happened to Z). The authors of reference books presented themselves as compilers responsible for the accurate reporting of what others had written elsewhere but not for the veracity of those statements themselves. Compilers were therefore conveyors of information rather than of their own opinions or positions (as I discuss in chapter 4). As such they would also boast of the many and diverse sources from which they had gathered material; they might name and list their sources, but they did not discuss them or offer a contextual interpretation of the material they selected. Instead readers were exhorted to use their own judgment and to pick and choose from among these treasuries something to suit their needs, a nugget to integrate into their own knowledge production, whether oral or written—typically a composition of some kind (e.g., oration, letter, or treatise). For these reasons I argue that the authors and users of premodern reference tools were indeed engaged in "information management" before either term had been coined.

* * *

These days we are particularly aware of the challenges of information management given the unprecedented explosion of information associated with computers and computer networking. One study has estimated that 5 exabytes of new information (an exabyte is 10^{18} bytes) was produced in 2002, 92 percent of it stored on magnetic media, and that "new stored information grew about 30 percent per year between 1999 and 2002."[8] We complain about overload in almost every field, from hardware-store stocking to library holdings to Internet searches.[9] A Google search for "information overload" itself generates more than 1.5 million hits, with the promise of solutions from office supply stores, management consultants, and stress relief services, among many others. But the perception of and complaints about overload are not unique to our period. Ancient, medieval, and early modern authors and authors working in non-Western contexts articulated similar concerns, notably about the overabundance of books and the frailty of human resources for mastering them (such as memory and time).

The perception of overload is best explained, therefore, not simply as the result of an objective state, but rather as the result of a coincidence of causal factors, including existing tools, cultural or personal expectations, and changes in the quantity or quality of information to be absorbed and managed. It is also a plausible and interesting suggestion (but not one that I have the expertise or the method to assess) that what we take to be innate human capacities, say, of memory and recollection, change over time under the impact both of cultural expectations and of the technologies with which we operate.[10] But the feeling of overload is often lived by those who experience it as if it were an utterly new phenomenon, as is perhaps characteristic of feelings more generally or of self-perceptions in the modern or postmodern periods especially. Certainly the perception of experiencing overload as unprecedented is dominant today.[11] No doubt we have access to and must cope with a much greater quantity of information than earlier generations on almost every issue, and we use technologies that are subject to frequent change and hence often new. Nonetheless, the basic methods we deploy are largely similar to those devised centuries ago in early reference books. Early compilations involved various combinations of four crucial operations: storing, sorting selecting, and summarizing, which I think of as the four S's of text management. We too store, sort, select, and summarize information, but now we rely not only on human memory, manuscript, and print, as in earlier centuries, but also on computer chips, search functions, data mining, and Wikipedia, along with other electronic techniques.

Of course reference books constitute only one form of information management, trained on textual information—words or sentences or bibliographical details, which were selected, collected and made accessible in some kind of order. Information of many other kinds was also stored, transmitted and managed in pre- and early modern cultures—in collections of objects, natural and artificial (in cabinets of curiosities, museums, botanical and zoological gardens) in the records of commercial or administrative transactions (archives), or in the oral or experiential transmission of skills and speech in all kinds of settings (home, marketplace, or workshop). Recent scholarship has in many cases begun to examine these forms of accumulation as sites of information management, each of which posed distinctive practical, intellectual, and political challenges. In due course, by drawing on many specific studies, we can hope to identify parallels and lines of exchange in methods of working and organization, over time and across different areas, for example, between the treatment of words and of things and among scholarly, mercantile, and administrative practices.[12] In this book I focus on two areas of especially active accumulation in the Renaissance: manuscript notes and printed reference books inspired by the humanist study of ancient language and culture. I find that the two are closely connected: reference books were initially formed from the reading notes taken by their compilers, and in turn they offered buyers a stockpile of notes ready for use without the difficulties of taking them directly.

Developed from medieval and ancient models, early modern reference tools spanned a wide range of genres that can be difficult to distinguish from one another by hard and fast criteria. Setting aside the specialized reference books in theology, law, and medicine, I focus on the genres that offered access to information that was considered essential for the educated in any occupation. These comprised principally (using current category terms): dictionaries of words (mono- and polyglot) and of things (e.g., biographical and geographical dictionaries), collections of quotations or of historical anecdotes, and miscellaneously arranged commentaries designed for consultation through an index. In addition I consider various kinds of "books about books" such as bibliographies and library and booksellers' catalogs, which guided readers toward other books. Depending on their arrangement (alphabetic, systematic, or miscellaneous), reference works typically deployed one or more finding aids including tables of contents, alphabetical indexes, outlines, dichotomous diagrams, cross-references, and a hierarchy of sections and subsections made visible on the page through the use of layout, symbols, and different scripts or fonts. Of course many other kinds of early modern books were meant to be consulted, including how-to books or books of recipes and secrets, for example, and relied on the same range of finding devices, but I have focused on the major humanist reference genres because their exceptional size and broad scope offer especially good opportunities to study the methods by which they were composed, arranged, and used.[13]

The four S's approach to managing an ever-increasing accumulation of material was not the only response to the information explosion in the early modern period. Instead of methods that coped with ambitious accumulation of information, René Descartes (1596–1650), for example (among other seventeenth-century thinkers calling for an overhaul of received philosophy), recommended ignoring the accumulated stock of texts and starting afresh to ground philosophy from first principles: "Even if all knowledge could be found in books, where it is mixed in with so many useless things and confusingly heaped in such large volumes, it would take longer to read those books than we have to live in this life and more effort to select the useful things than to find them oneself."[14] The accumulation of past authorities had become so great and so discordant that it seemed to Descartes simpler to do without them. Although others shared Descartes' scorn for ancient authority (including Francis Bacon in some passages), a mastery of ancient culture and literature remained central to European education and the principal criterion of distinction between the educated and the uneducated. But the rejection and drastic culling of accumulated information always held intermittent appeal: mystics, for example, generally emphasized divine inspiration rather than the management of accumulated human knowledge; after Descartes, who reported that his new philosophy came to him in a dream, the rejection of received opinion became a stance common even among authors who were otherwise consumers and producers of information. In the eighteenth century a number of writers articulated fantasies of destroying useless books to stem the never-ending accumulation: for Gibbon the books to destroy included "the ponderous mass of Arian and Monophysite controversy"; for d'Alembert, "useless historical works."[15] One critic has identified the articulation of the sublime as another kind of response to overabundance; Kant and Wordsworth are among the authors who described an experience of temporary mental blockage due to "sheer cognitive exhaustion," whether triggered by sensory or mental overload.[16] In these cases as the moment passed (whether it was sublime or destructive), the philosopher would generally return to more traditional methods of work—including those that enabled him to access and use accumulated information. Reference books certainly do not represent the full range of responses to the challenges of managing overabundant information, but they offer some of the best sources we have from which to consider how textual information was managed in the early modern and premodern periods.

* * *

My purpose in this book is not just to offer some historical perspective on our current concerns but to shed new light on the intellectual culture of early modern Europe. Neither the perception of overabundance nor the basic methods of text management (the four S's) were new or unique to the Renaissance. Furthermore, many of the features of the printed reference book, such as alphabetical ordering and indexing and consultation-friendly layouts were adapted to print from medieval manuscript practices. What was distinctive to the Renaissance was the large scale of accumulation of textual excerpts both in personal collections of manuscript notes and in printed compilations. Certainly printing facilitated the explosion in the number and size of printed reference works. Printing made it less expensive to produce books, including large ones, and aided large-scale compilation indirectly, for example, by increasing the number of books available for excerpting and by stimulating the production of paper, which was also the optimal medium for stockpiling manuscript notes. But printing and the availability of paper do not of themselves explain why the learned were willing to invest so much effort and money in amassing large collections of textual information in their manuscript notes and in printed reference books. Renaissance discoveries of ancient texts and distant places offered new material to sort and store, in addition to more traditional sources, but underlying the learned reaction to all this input was the most important causal factor of all: a newly invigorated info-lust that sought to gather and manage as much information as possible. The abundant note-takers and compilers who are the focus of my book articulated a new enthusiasm for attending to every book and every discipline in the search for potentially useful information. They hoped to safeguard the material they collected against a repetition of the traumatic loss of ancient learning of which they were keenly aware. The compilers also saw their work as a contribution to the public good that benefited from their catering to as many different themes and interests as possible.

My account focuses on large-scale compilations in manuscript and print and is not exhaustive. Some Renaissance authors advocated a restrictive canon of texts and excerpts rather than the expansive vision of those who amassed the biggest collections of excerpts.[17] But the largest reference books offer unique perspectives on both ordinary and extraordinary methods of working with texts, on the impact of printing, on the nature and spread of reference reading among the Latin-educated, and on the anxieties that this diffusion elicited. The large Latin reference works I study were designed to aid in reading and composing Latin texts, oral and written, and were used by students, teachers, and preachers and also by scholars, authors, and "men of action." Most early modern reference genres drew heavily in form and content from medieval models that originated in the thirteenth century. But by the early sixteenth century a number of new books were larger and more diverse than the medieval models on which they drew. The most successful of them went through dozens of editions, with frequent modifications and additions, down to the last decades of the seventeenth century, when most Latin reference works were printed for the last time.

These large folio books represent a tremendous collective investment of human and material resources on the part of authors and printers who produced them (ranging from the 430,000 words of Domenico Nam Mirabelli's *Polyanthea* of 1503 to the 10 million words of the eight-volume *Magnum theatrum humane vitae* of 1631 by Laurentius Beyerlinck). The institutions and individuals who purchased them also invested significantly. Of course, as one book historian wisely pointed out, most printed books have never been read, given that printers have always speculated on the numbers of copies they would sell.[18] But these large reference works sold well, especially considering their large size and cost, and I document how they were actually used despite the fact that few authors acknowledged using them. I argue that buyers sought in them the kinds of reading notes they wished they had taken themselves if they had had the resources (time, energy, money) to read the originals of the texts excerpted there. In wondering how these reference books were physically produced, from manuscript notes to final printed volume, I have uncovered some unusual methods devised by compilers to lessen their arduous task, including the manipulation of notes on slips of paper and the cutting and pasting from manuscripts and printed works to save the labor of copying.

The working methods studied here are those characteristic of humanist and late humanist ambitions, designed to produce and display mastery of ancient literature and culture. Attention to working methods has grown in recent years in other areas of intellectual history as well. For a long time the main group of scholars attending to manuscript notes and drafts in addition to finished works were literary scholars practicing "genetic criticism" and focused on those major authors of the nineteenth and twentieth centuries for whom abundant papers were available. Some medievalists have also investigated working methods and the terms for them, notably those distinctive to scholasticism.[19] But new interest in working methods has stemmed from recent work in the history of science, specifically in the early modern period, which emphasizes the interdependence of ideas with the social and material contexts of their formation. Some studies have focused on places peculiar to scientific work, such as the laboratory, the anatomy theater, the botanical garden, or the observatory. Other studies originating in the history of science have explored contexts relevant to intellectual work more generally, including the domestic setting in which intellectuals often worked and the economy of manuscript and print in which ideas were formed and diffused. Careful attention to the work performed in various contexts has also pointed to the presence of many helpers, from wives and children to laboratory assistants and amanuenses, who were often treated as "invisible" and are difficult to identify precisely.[20] Reference books shed light on how compilers worked, in collaborations both across time and at one time, as well as how those who used them worked.

To understand the work of those who operated in the humanist mode broadly conceived—who strove to produce knowledge principally from the study of ancient texts—it is particularly helpful to learn more about the kinds of books and of reading with which they engaged. We have studies of the furniture and rooms where humanists worked and of how the best-known humanists read and annotated ancient texts.[21] But humanists and those less learned among the Latin literate had increasing opportunities between 1500 and 1700 to engage in consultation reading, accessing a text in parts thanks to finding devices, with or without pen in hand.[22] Although any book with an index or for which one had a precise reference could be read by consultation, we can learn about methods of consultation especially well by examining those genres that were designed to be consulted rather than read through. The large Latin reference works I examine here accumulated myriad small units of information (quotations, definitions, or examples) from which readers were invited to select items of interest by consulting the text itself and the accompanying finding devices. Given the compilers' promises of the accuracy of their material, reference books offered a repository of textual facts akin to the facts increasingly invoked in many areas of early modern culture, especially in England.[23] Reference books could substitute for reading or rereading, or they complemented other kinds of reading depending on the circumstances. We have a more complete picture of the reading methods used by the learned and the broader public of the Latin literate by including the kinds of books that were taken for granted—omitted from citations or direct discussion but printed and owned in ever greater numbers between 1500 and 1700.

* * *

Reference books also offer a new angle from which to consider the impact of printing in early modern Europe. Since its beginnings as a subfield in the 1980s, the history of the book has generated much new work on the impact of printing and the notion of "print culture." Elizabeth Eisenstein has made the most extensive claims for the impact of printing, emphasizing the cumulative improvement across successive editions and the rapid and broad diffusion of books. Recent controversy surrounding her work has questioned whether handpress printing, with its artisanal variability and unscrupulous commercial practices, fostered the kind of standardization and reliability we associate with printing in the industrial age.[24] Another response to Eisenstein's claims has questioned the abruptness of the changes she associates with printing and suggested that late medieval manuscripts presented many of the features characteristic of the modern book, including, for example, indexes, page layout designed to facilitate consultation, and production on speculation rather than on commission in commercial scriptoria.[25] From my survey of reference works in a number of premodern settings, including ancient and medieval Europe and the worlds of Islam and China, I conclude that the central features of reference tools, including large-scale compilation, finding devices, and layouts to facilitate consultation reading, all developed independently of printing. But I also argue that in early modern Europe printing shaped in important ways the form, contents, and impact of these works.

The diffusion of printed reference books elicited a steady flow of complaints throughout the early modern period. The complaints became especially strident in the late seventeenth century, when Latin learning itself seemed threatened by the dominance of vernaculars (especially in England and France) and by the increasing sense that ancient authors and ideas should be abandoned in favor of more recent ones. I interpret these anxieties as additional evidence for the spread of consultation reading to ever-broader swaths of the educated. By the time the Latin reference books ceased being printed ca. 1700, they had spread familiarity with the methods of consultation reading, originally the purview of a narrow intellectual elite in the Middle Ages, to the much broader audience of the Latin-educated. The eighteenth century became known as the "age of dictionaries" because compilers and readers alike took for granted the justifications, tools, and methods of reference reading developed in the large Latin reference books of the sixteenth and seventeenth centuries, even though these works are little known today and had only an indirect impact on the "modern" and vernacular genres of the eighteenth century.

* * *

This book proceeds through increasingly focused layers of contextual analysis in chapters 1 to 3 before considering a few specific works in chapters 4 and 5. In chapter 1, I survey the reference genres produced in a variety of premodern contexts to highlight the remarkable similarities in the basic methods and problems of text management across many cultures and also the peculiarities of early modern Europe. In chapter 2, I argue that methods of note-taking in early modern Europe served as a more immediate context for the development of reference books in two ways: printed compilations typically originated in the collections of personal notes of one or more compilers, and they offered ready-made in print the kinds of notes readers wished to have available even if they had not taken them themselves. The accumulation of manuscript notes posed problems of management, collaboration, and sharing that also characterize printed compilations. In chapter 3, I survey the nonspecialist Latin reference genres in print between 1500 and 1700 and their finding devices, with careful attention to the terms contemporaries used to describe them and to those historians have deployed, including the notion of "encyclopedia." In chapter 4, I focus on the career and composition of several major reference works (especially the *Polyanthea* and the *Theatrum*), drawing on the texts, on their printing histories, and on some extant working papers of Conrad Gesner of Zurich and Theodor Zwinger of Basel. In chapter 5, I document the reception of these reference works through surviving copies and their annotations, explicit citations and tacit use, and complaints about them. Though they were no longer in print after 1710 and were rarely acknowledged as models, the Latin reference works laid the groundwork for the explosion of vernacular reference works and encyclopedias in the eighteenth century. For some two centuries printed humanist reference genres spread the use of increasingly sophisticated methods and tools of information management among compilers, printers, and readers. These techniques were easily adapted to the modern languages and contents characteristic of Enlightenment reference works, and they are familiar enough today to remind us that many habits that we take for granted are indebted to the transmission of practices developed centuries ago in medieval and early modern Europe.

Notes

1. In chapter 3 I discuss this and similar terms (e.g., "repertory") in use before the modern period. By "reference book" I mean a large collection of textual information designed to be consulted rather than read through.
2. See Moss (1996) on commonplace books; on encyclopedias, see below, ch. 3.
3. *OED*, "information," esp. I.1a and I.3a.
4. On information in the life sciences, see Wright (2007), ch. 1; in information science, Shannon (1948).
5. Machlup (1962) is credited with coining the term; see Beniger (1986), 21.
6. My discussion of information is indebted to Nunberg (1996) and Brown and Duguid (2000), 118–20.
7. For other applications of the term to the past, see Hobart and Schiffman (1998). On res et verba in the Renaissance, see Kessler and Maclean (2002).
8. Lyman and Varian (2003), executive summary.
9. The 300,000 items in the McGuckins hardware store, for example, exceed the number of entries in many dictionaries; Norman (1993), 168.
10. Sutton (2002).
11. For the point that each generation perceives overload afresh, see Rosenberg (2003), 2.

12. Recent work in this vein includes: Park and Daston (2006), part 2 on sites of knowledge; Te Heesen and Spary (2002) on collecting; Soll (2009), Friedrich (2008), Blair and Milligan (2007), Blair and Stallybrass (2010) on administrative practices. Soll (2009) offers a rich example of cross-fertilization between different fields.
13. See Long (2001) and Eamon (1994) on how-to manuals and books of secrets.
14. Descartes (1996), 10:497–98.
15. On Gibbon, see Yeo (2001), 90–91; d'Alembert, *Mélanges de littérature, d'histoire et de philosophie*, 2 vols. (Berlin, 1753), 2:3–4, as cited in Désormeaux (2001), 61.
16. Hertz (1985), 40–60.
17. See the advice of the Jesuit Antonio Possevino in *Bibliotheca selecta* (1606); the contrast is discussed in Zedelmaier (1992).
18. Amory (1996), 51.
19. See, among their many works, Weijers (1996) and Rouse and Rouse (1991a).
20. See the seminal article of Shapin (1989); for recent studies of scientific notebooks, see Holmes et al. (2003); on the domestic context of scientific work in particular, see Cooper (2006), Algazi (2003), and Harkness (1997).
21. See, e.g., Thornton (1997) and Grafton (1997).
22. On the many kinds of discontinuous reading, see Stallybrass (2002).
23. For the historiography on facts, see Shapiro (2000), Daston (2001), Poovey (1998).
24. See Eisenstein (1979), Johns (1998) and Eisenstein and Johns (2002).
25. See Grafton (1980) and Needham (1980).

ELIAS MUHANNA, FROM "WHY WAS THE FOURTEENTH CENTURY A CENTURY OF ARABIC ENCYCLOPAEDISM?" (2013)

Muhanna (b. 1978) is a scholar of classical Arabic literature and Islamic intellectual history. He is translator of an abridged edition of the monumental fourteenth-century compendium of knowledge, *The Ultimate Ambition in the Arts of Erudition,* by Shihab al-Din al-Nuwayri, one of the major encyclopedists under discussion here. Seeking to answer his title's question, Muhanna here argues that the vast, encyclopedia-like projects that emerged in the Arabic world in the wake of Mongol conquest were less a response to a traumatic loss of texts, and rather the product of the new institutions of learning that emerged from the relative sociopolitical stability of the Mamluk era. Paralleling other historical contexts described by Berry and Blair in our volume, educated readers in fourteenth-century Egypt and Syria responded to a glut of information by developing new forms of textual collection and organization.

Centers of Knowledge and Power

In Islamic history, the year 1258 looms large. In February, the armies of the Mongol Ilkhanids sacked the Abbasid capital at Baghdad, bringing an end to a dynasty that had reigned—through periods of glory and ignominy—for half a millennium. The ferocity of the attack is the stuff of legend: hundreds of thousands were said to have been slaughtered, buildings were razed to the ground, and the historic libraries of the city were gutted and destroyed, making the waters of the Tigris run black with the ink of discarded books. Following its victory at Baghdad, the Mongol army marched west where, two years later, it would be defeated decisively by the Mamluks at the Battle of 'Ayn Jālūt.

The traditional narrative has held that after the fall of Baghdad, Cairo inherited its mantle as the political and cultural epicentre of the Muslim world.[1] Scholars and poets fled from Iraq, finding a welcome home in the colleges of the Mamluk realms even as they spread the news of smoking libraries to their counterparts in Egypt and Syria. The sense of terror that this catastrophe provoked, so the theory goes, was one of the principal factors leading to the rise of the Mamluk encyclopaedic movement, which aimed to forestall the loss of an entire civilisation's intellectual heritage.[2]

One can understand the attraction of this hypothesis given the existence of a similar discourse in the context of Renaissance encyclopaedism, but there is very little primary evidence from the sources themselves that bears out this view.[3] Furthermore, recent scholarship on the Mongol conquests has complicated the picture of a glorious cultural capital ravaged by alien marauders. Literary reports about Baghdad suggest that the city seemed to have been a cultural backwater long before the Mongols sacked it,[4] and we now know that the post-conquest flow of emigrants was not unidirectional: some escaped from the oncoming tide of the Mongol advance only to duck back behind it once the armies reached as far as Syria.[5]

These qualifications notwithstanding, there can be little doubt that in the two and a half centuries following the sack of Baghdad, the cosmopolitan centers of the Mamluk realms became magnets for scholars and students from all over the Muslim world. The stability and security provided by a rapidly consolidating imperial state represented a fundamental break with several centuries of fractiousness and political turmoil in the central Islamic lands. Among the consequences of this new order was the emergence of an increasingly universal vision in much of the historical and geographical literature of the period, which began to regard its object of study as the Islamic world writ large, rather than a more narrowly defined region or time span.[6] This is borne out in remarkable fashion by Ibn Faḍl Allāh al-'Umarī, the author of the encyclopaedic *Masālik: al-abṣār*, who states in the preface of his work that he would not have been able to produce such a text had it not been for his position as a high-ranking secretary in the bureaucracy of a powerful empire, which enabled him to meet travellers from all over the Islamic and Mediterranean worlds. As Zayde Antrim has argued, it was only through "the lens of empire [that he was] able to see and describe the diverse and distant lands, from India and Iran, to Mali and Ethiopia, to Morocco and Spain, that together constituted for al-'Umarī the 'realms of Islam.' "[7]

The case of al-'Umarī was not unique; all three members of the Mamluk encyclopaedic triumvirate served as career bureaucrats within the imperial government, as did many other scholars and compilers. Meanwhile, those who did not work as direct servants of the state were similarly implicated within the aggregative ethos of the time by virtue of their participation in an increasingly institutionalised scholarly system. As is well known, the Mamluk period witnessed a dramatic rise in the number of educational institutions—particularly *madrasas*, colleges of Islamic law—in its urban centers, in which a variety of subjects were taught.[8] Prior to this period, however, and for much of Islamic history, education did not take place in *madrasas*, but was rather conducted through informal associations between independent scholars who often traveled great distances in pursuit of knowledge, and typically had to find alternate means to sustain themselves while carrying out their scholarly endeavours.[9] In the Mamluk empire, this activity took on an increasingly institutional character through the creation of salaried positions in a wide range of educational loci—a development which presaged, as Joan Gilbert has argued, the emergence of a "professionalized and bureaucratized" scholarly class.[10]

A distinctive token of the self-consciously corporate nature of this class was the explosion of biographical literature during this period, primarily in the form of multi-volume, alphabetically-arranged onomastica. Many of these texts were devoted to the notable jurists of different legal schools, but others mapped the intellectual boundaries of other scholarly communities as well, from grammarians to Qur'anic exegetes to hadith transmitters. As Wadad al-Qadi has suggested, the production of these texts marked an important development in the self-consciousness of the learned elite. Not merely lists of names, these works rather presented an "alternative history" of the Muslim community, written by scholars for scholars, as opposed to the historical chronicle, which was primarily written by scholars for rulers.[11]

Al-Nuwayrī, the author of the encyclopaedic *Nihāyat al-arab fī funūn al-adab*, is a prime example of an individual whose professional and intellectual trajectory was defined by his experience within this world of institutions. Born in Upper Egypt, he went to Cairo when he was 19 to work in the office of the sultan's private funds, studying and residing at a local college. Showing talent in his administrative duties, he was given greater responsibility, overseeing various institutions in the course of his career, from the imperial fisc itself to the Bīmāristān al-Manṣūrī, a famous hospital containing "wards for various diseases, a lecture room, laboratories, a dispensary, baths, kitchens and storerooms" and a school mosque with a library of medical, theological, and legal texts.[12] In 1310, al-Nuwayrī was put in charge of the Nāṣiriyya, the college where he had resided as a young man. He was an astute observer of its workings, even supplying the text of its endowment deed in his encyclopaedia. When he eventually retired to devote the rest of his life to composing his encyclopaedia, he availed himself of the Nāṣiriyya's library, drawing upon its considerable holdings in multiple fields to compile his enormous work.

Al-Nuwayrī's encyclopaedia was, like its author, something of an institutional product: a work that came to fruition in the context of colleges, imperial chanceries, and libraries. This environment did not only facilitate the work of a compiler, but also engendered it, insofar as the growing numbers of books and learned people circulating within the network of scholarly institutions could not but convey a sense of the expanding boundaries of knowledge. On the other hand, however, these conditions also made it possible to envision a solution to the problem of too much information, which took the form of the capacious compilatory texts that began to appear in such profusion. The historian Ibn Khaldūn (d. 1406) observed in the late fourteenth century that "among the things that are harmful to the human quest for knowledge and to the attainment of a thorough scholarship are the great number of works available . . . and the numerous (different) methods (used in those works)."[13] The solution to this dilemma (which Ibn Khaldūn regarded as quite unsatisfactory) seemed to be the production of even more books—abridgements, epitomes, commentaries, and compendia—to help the novice wend his way through the great forest of specialised treatises. The production of such works was not aimed at preventing the loss of knowledge (as has been previously supposed), but was more likely a response to the feeling of an overcrowding of authoritative sources, a feeling made especially palpable in the scholarly centers of the Mamluk empire.[14]

To reiterate, the boom of encyclopaedic and otherwise compilatory literature during the fourteenth century took place against a cultural backdrop characterised by the consolidation of political power and centralisation of intellectual exchange. In this regard, there are certain congruities in the relationship of encyclopaedism to empire, which may repay investigation, between the Mamluk period and other imperial settings. As Jason König and Tim Whitmarsh have argued, the essential functions of the archive ("itemisation, analysis, ordering, hierarchisation, synthesis, synopsis") belong to a discursive form that is "characteristically imperial."[15] Such processes undergird the work of the encyclopaedist no less than that of the chancery official. As we will discuss in the next section, it is little wonder that, during the Mamluk period, these two figures were often one and the same.

The Cleric and the Clerk

The earliest manifestations of Arabic encyclopaedism have typically been traced to a period predating the rise of the Mamluk empire by several centuries: that of the Abbasid caliphate and its glorious literary and intellectual apogee during the ninth and tenth centuries. This was a period that witnessed a florescence of *adab*, a term that has come to refer generically to "literature" in modern Arabic, but which encompassed a broader set of acceptations in the medieval period, including, correct, polite behaviour (i.e., what one scholar has referred to as the Arabic equivalent of the Latin *urbanitas*); a genre of quotable aphorisms and *bons mots* to be cited in polite society; and a collection of philological disciplines which included grammar, knowledge of poetry, and other subjects.[16]

The main practitioners and originators of *adab* were the *kuttāb* (singular *kātib*), the class of secretaries who served in the Abbasid administration, whose urbane outlook was modeled upon that of their predecessors, the *dibhērān*, Persian scribes in the employ of the Sassanid empire. For this class of officials, a well-rounded education was essential. In addition to being an accomplished litterateur, a secretary was steeped in "theology and law . . . philosophy, music, medicine and the natural and mathematical sciences like astronomy, alchemy, arithmetic, geometry and mensuration, mechanics and hydraulics."[17] Testifying to the importance of this encyclopaedic ideal is a wide range of multi-topic compendia from the period in question—works by such figures as al-Jāhiẓ (d. 868/9), Ibn Qutayba (d. 889), and al-Masʿūdī (d. 956)—that comprise what might be called a "first wave" of medieval Arabic encyclopaedism.[18]

While several parallels between the worlds of Abbasid and Mamluk officialdom might be noted, it is the differences that are most salient to an understanding of what characterised the encyclopaedism of the fourteenth century. In the Mamluk empire, the principal nexus of intellectual and literary exchanges shifted away from the court, where it had been centred in previous centuries, and came to occupy other milieus such as the educational and administrative institutions.[19] Furthermore, the increased involvement by religious scholars (the ʿulamāʾ) in the production of poetry and belles-lettres (*adab*) betokens a blending of the religious and secular ethics, or what Thomas Bauer has called "the adabization of the ʿulamāʾ."[20] In contrast to earlier periods, when litterateurs (particularly within the highly specialised professional class of clerks) stood apart from the religious establishment, it is difficult to draw a clear division between secretaries and scholars during the Mamluk period.[21] Many scholars worked in administration during their careers, and one could rarely rise very high as a bureaucrat without some kind of traditional training in Islamic law. Administration, therefore—and particularly the chancery—served as a key meeting point for individuals with a wide range of specialties, interests, and abilities.[22]

The copious administrative literature of the period provides a window onto the encyclopaedic culture of the Mamluk secretarial-scholarly classes. In one of the longest chapters of his work—occupying approximately 850 pages— al-Nuwayrī lays out a kind of professional manual, a *vade mecum* comprising a multitude of subjects relevant to the day-to-day dealings of a clerk: samples of praiseworthy epistles, styles of greeting and salutation, guidelines for the practices of good bookkeeping and proper penmanship, and boiler-plate language for every manner of legal transaction, from royal letters of investiture to common divorces.[23]

In addition to the mass of administrative minutiae, however, al-Nuwayrī also speaks more generally about the education of the secretary and his cultivation of eloquence, a process which required the study of various materials—a kind of scribal curriculum.[24] At the head of this curriculum, naturally, is the Qur'an, which the secretary must memorise and make a part of his consciousness, such that the appropriate quotation will leap to his mind spontaneously in the course of penning an epistle. Following the Qur'an the secretary should develop a mastery of hadith, Arabic grammar, rhetoric, classical Arabic poetry, belletristic prose, proverbs, constitutional and administrative law, and political history.[25] Just when one thinks the curriculum is complete, al-Nuwayrī casually reminds his reader that, in addition to these basics, the scribe must also be familiar with different kinds of animals, birds, plants, trees, geographic locales, etc., as he will be called upon to test this multifaceted knowledge in the service of his craft:

> As for letters that include descriptions of weapons and implements of war, horses, birds of prey, types of sport, and things of that nature, the scribe is given free rein to do what he can with his own eloquence . . . With regard to horses and birds of prey, and everything related to them from cheetahs and [other] hunting animals, the knowledge of their qualities and the tokens of their skill is essential to the scribe . . . And as for letters meant to exercise the mind and test one's talents—such as boasting jousts between fruits and blossoms, and descriptions of aromatic plants, rivers, streams, canals, creeks, seas, ships, and things of that nature . . . we will present some of them [in a later volume][26]

The chapter on the scribal arts, therefore, serves two functions. On the one hand, it presents a wealth of technical and administrative information pertaining specifically to chancery affairs. On the other hand, the chapter also gestures towards the rest of the encyclopaedia—the parts containing cosmological, political, literary, zoological, botanical, and historical information—and insists that these materials are not just relevant, but essential to the formation of the model clerk. This treatment of clerkly erudition prompts several questions. Firstly, we would be justified in wondering just how idealised a picture it was. In other words, was it actually crucial for a scribe to know who the Caliph al-Ma'mūn's favourite singing slave-girl was? Did he truly need to be well-versed in the nesting habits of flamingoes, or the rituals of moon-worshipping cults? Was he really expected to know which aromatic blossoms were capable of being distilled (roses, white willows, and water lilies), and which ones were not (violets, jasmine, myrtle, saffron, and mint)? Did one, in other words, have to be a walking encyclopaedia, just to wield the *kātib*'s pen?

As tempting as it is to accept al-Nuwayrī's description at face value, one must assume a certain amount of exaggeration, for, as Maaike van Berkel has shown, the testimony of the administrative literature regarding the profile of the ideal clerk can be unreliable. Just because famous scribes such as 'Abd al-Ḥamīd ibn Yaḥyā (d. 750), Ibn al-Athīr (d. 1239) and al-Qalqashandī were "well-versed *adībs* (men of letters) and set great store to erudition," this does not mean that all scribes conformed to this model.[27] On the other hand, even if al-Nuwayrī and his contemporaries exaggerated somewhat about their job descriptions, the profile does not seem to stray that far afield from what we know of the wide-ranging interests of many Mamluk intellectuals. The blending of the cultures of 'ilm (knowledge) and adab meant, for one thing, that circulating in learned society required fluency in multiple domains, and it is here that one begins to perceive how a text like al-Nuwayrī's fits into the processes of cultivating, deploying, and constantly renewing and expanding one's eloquence and erudition.

The Mamluk encyclopaedias were textual products of this ethos. A resurgence of the cosmopolitan, "humanistic" culture of Abbasid literary circles was in evidence, but it had a far broader reach, including religious scholars in its midst, which also changed its character substantially. At the same time, increasing literacy among the "middle strata" of Mamluk society (merchants, craftsmen, etc.) resulted in a vibrant book market, which provided alternatives to patronage for those who wanted to make a living from their scholarly and literary activities.[28] By all accounts, this was a good time to be in the book business, good enough for al-Nuwayrī to leave a rewarding job in the imperial administration to work as a copyist of popular manuscripts while he labored away on his encyclopaedia.

Notes

1. See Chapoutot-Remadi (1991); Blachère (1970).
2. 'The [invasion] certainly provoked serious disquiet which was translated into the composition of enormous encyclopaedias intended to some extent to preserve the acquisitions of preceding generations at the moment when the Arabo-Islamic world could be seen as despairing of achieving new progress and felt itself threatened by the worst calamities. In the following centuries, the Black Death (749/1348) was further to aggravate this feeling of insecurity': see Pellat (1991) 906.
3. See Ann Blair's contribution in chapter 18 [of the original volume], which documents the efforts of Renaissance compilers to prevent 'a repetition of the traumatic loss of ancient learning of which they were keenly aware' (p. 382).
4. As Michael Cooperson has shown, the Andalusian traveler Ibn Jubayr (d. 1217) visited Baghdad as early as 1184 and described it as something of an intellectual wasteland: 'This ancient city, though it still serves as the Abbasid capital, has lost much of its distinctive character and retains only its famous name. Compared to what it once was—before it fell victim to recurrent misfortunes and repeated calamities—the city resembles a vanished encampment or a passing phantom': see Cooperson (1996) 99.

5. The Baghdad-based philosopher Ibn Kammūna (d. 1284-5) was one such example. He moved to Aleppo following the sack of Baghdad, but then returned to the east when the Mongols sacked Aleppo in 1260: see Langermann (2007) 14. In other instances, the Mongols singled out scholars as booty but then patronised them, as was the case of the astronomer al-Ṭūsī (d. 1274), who built his famed observatory under the auspices of Hülegü at Maragha, where a library was also built with the books carried off from the conquests of Iraq and Syria: see DeWeese (2006); Gilli-Elewy (2000).

6. As Zayde Antrim has shown in her study of place and belonging in medieval Syria, Mamluk geographers exhibited a 'broader vision of place' than their antecedents, whose own writings reflected a preoccupation with more circumscribed territorial referents. Particularly in the fourteenth century, which represented 'the height of prosperity and stability in medieval Syria', Antrim argues that the region's inhabitants conceived of themselves 'as belonging to and in an empire billed as Dār al-Islām [the Abode of Islam]': see Antrim (2004) 280-1.

7. Antrim (2004) 333.

8. The historical development of the *madrasa* was studied in magisterial fashion by the late George Makdisi, who argued that the first institutional locus of instruction in the Islamic sciences was the *masjid* (mosque). Over time, mosques became centres for jurisprudential activity, as Muslims sought to connect their study of scripture and tradition with the legal and social questions facing society. The turning point for the mosque as an educational space, says Makdisi, occurred in the mid-ninth century when the demand for such legal instruction grew, prompting the building of larger mosques with attached *khan* (inns), for out-of-town students and teachers. The final step in the development of the madrasa took place in the eleventh century, and was marked by the combination of the duties of the masjid and those of the khan in a single institution under a single endowment (*waqf*). See Makdisi (1981); Pedersen (1986).

9. Michael Chamberlain, in his study of knowledge and social practice in medieval Damascus, emphasises the political-financial aspect of *madrasas* and the degree to which they represented lucrative positions (*manāṣib*) for scholars, who jockeyed endlessly with each other for the patronage of powerful *amīrs*: see Chamberlain (1994). Jonathan Berkey, while recognising the important role that institutions played, argues that we should not overstate the institutional character of the transmission of knowledge in Islam, suggesting that most learning took place outside the *madrasa* even during its heyday, and that education remained a largely personal and flexible affair; see Berkey (1992).

10. Gilbert (1980) 134

11. al-Qadi (2006).

12. Rabie (1978).

13. Ibn Khaldūn (1958) vol. 3, 288-91. The anxiety about an overabundance of books is common to many intellectual traditions and historical epochs, and, as recent research has shown, was often mitigated in similar ways. For an excellent discussion of this trope as it appears throughout classical Arabic literature and historiography, see Rosenthal (1995). For approaches to dealing with textual overabundance in the European context, see Blair (2003).

14. Cf. chapter 2 in this volume for a similar discussion of literary 'overcrowding' in the Roman Empire.

15. König and Whitmarsh (2007b) 38.

16. See Bonebakker (1960); Bonebakker (1984); Heinrichs (1995).

17. Bosworth (1963) 98-9.

18. Pellat (1966); Pellat (1991); Chapoutot-Remadi (1991).
19. See al-Musawi (2006).
20. See Bauer (2007b).
21. See Carter (1971) 46–7.
22. This is apparent from a study of the vocational patterns of Mamluk clerks. As Joseph Escovitz has shown, unlike their Abbasid forebears, most officials in the Mamluk administration had a religious education, and over one third held posts as vocational *ulamā* (e.g., *madrasa* instructors, judges, etc.) or *hadith* transmitters. In other words, the secretaries were not 'a homogeneous caste of "men of the pen" drawn from a small number of scribal families, and devoted only to the smooth running of the Mamluk administration, but rather a heterogeneous group from diverse backgrounds, with strong and active ties to the religious institution': see Escovitz (1976) 55.
23. See al-Nuwayrī (1923–97) 7, 8, 9: 1–223.
24. This discussion takes the form of an extended quotation from a treatise by another Mamluk scribe: see Ibn Fahd al-Ḥalabī (1897).
25. al-Nuwayrī (1923–97) 7: 27–35.
26. al-Nuwayrī (1923–97) 8: 212–13.
27. Van Berkel (2001) 89. Al-Qalqashandī himself evinces a prejudice towards the financial clerks who served in the imperial fisc, claiming that they were intellectually inferior to the clerks of the chancery. One wonders if he knew that al-Nuwayrī—whose text contains far more literature than al-Qalqashandī's—had once been the head clerk in charge of the imperial fisc: the height of philistinism, indeed!
28. See Bauer (2007a 54–5). On the growth of the Mamluk book market, see also Larkin (2006) 220.

STEVEN MARKS, FROM *THE INFORMATION NEXUS: GLOBAL CAPITALISM FROM THE RENAISSANCE TO THE PRESENT* (2016)

Marks (b. 1958) is a specialist of Russian and world economic history. Emphasizing the relationship between mercantile knowledge and information management, *The Information Nexus* ascribes the origins of modern business and capitalism to the establishment of information systems such as double-entry bookkeeping and postal networks at the end of the middle ages. By juxtaposing such communications infrastructures and practices with those of Ming China (1368–1644) and Tokugawa Japan (1603–1868), Marks tells a story of historical divergence, using the difference in each region's capacity to circulate information to explain why capitalism first developed in western Europe. We have selected the opening gambit to Marks's comparison in order to give a sense of his argument.

Early Modern Europe's Expanding Field of Vision

The Origins of Capitalism

In 1870, workmen in a house in Prato, Italy, near Florence, knocked down a wall and came upon an old boarded-up stairwell filled with sacks of documents. It turned out they belonged to Francesco di Marco Datini, the head of a late-fourteenth-century import-export firm, and included more than 150,000 letters, 500 account books, 400 insurance policies, 300 deeds of partnership, and tens of thousands of commercial bills and instruments.[1] This was the discovery of a medieval "database" compiled by a businessman who spent so much time sending and receiving letters that one can imagine him adjusting very quickly to email had it been introduced in the 1300s.[2]

It is important to understand that Datini was not all that unusual for his time and place. Nor would he be out of place in today's world—although he might store his documents in a file cabinet or online rather than in sacks. If his obsession with collecting and communicating information seems familiar from the behavior of corporations in the twenty-first century, that is because Renaissance Italy's merchants had the same need to find out news that might affect their business and the same need to achieve coordination and control of their operations.[3]

Why the similarity? Because business, whether ancient, medieval, or modern, needs information to function. The most basic feature of a market economy is a price, which is a "mechanism for communicating information" about any product being bought or sold.[4] Besides supply and demand, what economists call "transaction costs" influence prices. The cost of doing business is obviously less, for instance, if property rights are protected, contracts are enforced, and transportation is more advanced, as these make it easier to buy, sell, and produce. Conversely, the costs are higher if these conditions do not exist. The lower such transaction costs, the more efficient the market.[5]

Acquiring information about something one might buy, sell, or invest in is another transaction cost with an impact on market efficiency. Following the lead of economists dating back to the eighteenth century, Friedrich A. Hayek emphasized that relationship in his writings of the 1930s and 1940s: "The economic problem of society," he wrote, "is a problem of the utilization of knowledge not given to anyone in its totality."[6] Several decades later, George Stigler won a Nobel Prize for coming to grips with the implications of Hayek's statement. Stigler argued that information costs had to be considered in economics, especially since businessmen or consumers make most decisions on the basis of incomplete information about almost everything: the future cost of raw materials, the exact price shoppers are willing to pay, or the quality of a product.[7] Similarly, in a study of used-car sales called "The Market for Lemons," George A. Akerlof laid bare the problem of "hidden information" in all economic transactions.[8] They and other economists who studied the impact of information—or the lack thereof—ended up qualifying standard neo-classical assumptions about the functioning of the free market: without fully accessible information, economic decision-making can be flawed, which implies that the market economy is not perfectly constructed.[9]

But businessmen have always intuited this. It is precisely because the information available is imperfect that they strive to gather as much as they can: the more of it they have and the faster they get it, the better able they are to make decisions that help them earn a profit and best their competitors. For a company, information acquisition entails a reduction of transaction costs, uncertainties, and risks, and with that an enhancement of opportunities.[10]

That takes us to the heart of my argument: in parts of early modern Western Europe, businessmen overcame informational deficiencies to an unprecedented degree. They made the collection and transfer of information, to borrow the terminology of another economist, less "sticky" than they had ever been before.[11] For reasons we will explore, the societies they lived in and the political regimes they lived under made it easier for them to open information channels and reduce informational blockages, thereby diminishing transaction costs. The sheer volume of information seeking, accumulating, analyzing, and dispensing was unprecedented in human history.

To elaborate, by information I mean more than the narrow consideration of price or an enterprise's profitability; I include in this institutions that expand useful knowledge in the widest sense.[12] Therefore, transportation, communications, literacy, book production, and the press all play a large role in this chapter. Information encompasses everything from inventing new accounting methods to sniffing out shifts in the political winds that would affect market conditions. As we will see, all of these manifold efforts reflect societies that were driven to learn about the world in all its dimensions and developed the tools to do so.[13] Europe's expanding field of vision helps to account for the economic successes of Western business and the relative deficiencies of the leading Asian economies. With that assessment, this chapter challenges the "California" school of economic history, which argues that the "great divergence" between East and West occurred only late in the day, around 1800, and resulted from Western Europe's access to "coal and colonies," the twin juggernauts of imperialism and industrialization.[14] In doing so, the chapter also disputes the implication in the works of anthropologist Jack Goody that all notions of Western uniqueness are Eurocentric myths, which he labels "the theft of history."[15] What I am arguing is that the initial divergence took place much earlier, and was a byproduct of the information deficit within Asia and the superior information-gathering abilities of the West. This is what opened the door of economic development for the one and shut it (at least for a while) for the other.

The dense information nexus that was first built in Italy, Holland, and England is the essence of capitalism. Yes, the profit motive is an essential driving force of the system, which is lubricated by credit and cash. But as argued in Chapter 3, these also existed in many other places and time periods, so we cannot say capital or the "cash nexus" are defining aspects of capitalism, despite the name. As we saw in Chapter 3, most people still view capital, wage labor, the division of labor, and private property rights as the fundamental features of the capitalist system. Yet however crucial these features may be, they have existed in so many places that they cannot be taken to constitute the building blocks of capitalism as a unique economic system. The only characteristic that is *exclusive* to capitalism is the enhanced ability to marshal information.

The information nexus has its roots in the Middle Ages and first came to fruition in certain nations of early modern Western Europe. This is why bestselling authors Alvin Toffler and Peter Drucker, among others, are mistaken when they announce that in our own digital age, knowledge and information have "gone from being an adjunct of money power" to being "the most important ingredient of force and wealth."[16] In reality, we entered the "Information Age" centuries ago. Let us return to Datini's day and see how it came about.

The Middle Ages: Communications and Commercial Revolutions

Stepped-up information gathering and processing in Renaissance Italy of the kind we see evidenced in Datini's sacks of documents were both the cause and effect of a revolution in commerce and communications that took place in medieval Europe.

After the long hiatus following the collapse of the Roman empire, aristocrats and peasants alike were drawn into a money economy. From the twelfth century onward, trade boomed, both locally and across national boundaries. In the long run, even deadly outbreaks of warfare and plague could not keep it in check. Regularly scheduled fairs tied all the commercial activity together and improved information exchange about commodities, credit, and the reputations of fellow traders. The largest fairs were French, and served as meeting grounds for Northern and Southern European merchants: the Champagne fairs of Provins, Troyes, Lagny, and Bar-sur-Aube; to the south and east in Chalon, Geneva, and Lyons; and to the west at Saint-Denis near Paris. Soon they also appeared in the Low Countries, southwest Germany, Italy, and Castile. In England, over the course of the thirteenth and fourteenth centuries people congregated at well over a thousand local fairs and markets, plugging small towns into regional and international trade grids that were pulsating with commercial life.[17]

Commerce grew as conditions for transportation eased on upgraded land, river, and sea routes across Western Europe in the Middle Ages. Local and regional authorities constructed thousands of small bridges, expanded ports, opened mountain passes, canalized riverways, and repaired Roman highways that had fallen into disuse centuries earlier. This was an interlinked, "integrated transport network for carrying goods," a "road revolution" that affected the entire continent. Medieval thoroughfares were now clogged with mercantile travelers taking advantage of wagons, whose newly invented front axles and iron-rimmed wheels offered a higher carrying capacity for freight. A dense network of inns cropped up, where innkeepers often provided money-changing and other banking services.[18]

People in the northern Italian city-states were the first to capitalize on these developments. Some of their businesses became large multi-branched firms financed in part through transferable shares. Investors who congregated in the financial quarters formed bourses—the earliest being the open-air *Loggia dei Mercanti* located on the Piazza di Rialto in Venice from 1322. Wealthy individuals ploughed their money into these shares or government bonds. Companies like the Datini, Acciaiuli, Peruzzi, and Bardi groups started as family firms, then grew into separate and multiple partnerships whose international operations spanned banking, mining, textile manufacturing, and the bulk trade in grain. They had more employees than contemporary government bureaucracies and opened satellite offices to capture new business. In 1335, the Peruzzi Company had five agents in England, four in France, four in Avignon, four in Flanders, six in Sicily, six in Naples, and five at the grain exporting port of Barletta. In the next century, the Medici Bank had branches in eleven cities.[19]

The Italian companies were able to establish a permanent presence away from their home bases because of numerous innovations in communications and control that allowed for a flow of regular information from me field to headquarters. Among them were seemingly simple but new devices that helped track commercial activity like invoices, bills of lading, and shipping manifests.[20] Perhaps most momentous was the development of a regular mail service. Starting in the 1260s, courier services called *scarselle* (after the leather letter bags) began operating between Italy and the French fairs. By the 1340s, seventeen firms in Florence agreed to support a joint mail cooperative called the *Scarsella dei Mercanti Fiorentini* to avoid duplicating costs. The *scarselle genovesi* regularly ran correspondence between businesses in Genoa and their agents in Barcelona, Paris, Cologne, and Bruges. Routes crisscrossed Italy and reached as far as England, but companies could always hire their own private couriers if they needed to send something faster than the average 50 kilometers a day (which meant around a month and a half for a letter to go between Naples and London). Private entrepreneurs ran most of these services, which profited from the massive number of letters being mailed: the Datini company alone was responsible for at least 10,000 a year for three decades. But in the 1300s, the Venetian government founded its own postal system, the *Compagnia dei Corrieri*. Beginning in 1516, the Habsburg crown farmed out postal operations between Austria and their dominions in the Low Countries, Burgundy, Italy, and Spain to the Taxis family (Tassis in Italy and France), whose Italian forbears had been postmen in Lombardy. This was the "first public communications system in Europe," available for use by everyone.[21]

What was in these letters?[22] Information on market conditions, for one. In the 1380s, for example, darker furs came into style for men of substance, which shifted demand from Russian squirrel to black sable; those merchants with the fastest communications link to the Russian suppliers of the fur profited (judging from a later traveler's account, it could have taken up to ten months to go from Hamburg to Moscow via Riga on the Baltic coast, and thence over land and river routes).[23] Letters often included political news relevant to investment conditions and sales opportunities—whatever could be gleaned from friends, contacts, diplomats, spies, and gossip-mongers about the financial needs of monarchs or their inclination toward war and peace.

But above all, it was commodities prices and exchange rates that were the sought-after information in these missives, prices being the basic indicator of supply and demand in every market, a signal of where to conduct business and what to buy and sell. A 1588/1589 price list from Venice included the values of currencies from other Italian states, Germany, France, and England; the prices of gold, silver, various kinds of cloth, metals, grain; and a panoply of spices and herbs: pepper, ginger, gum arabic, asafoetida, sugar, mastic, camphor, and on and on. A similar document from Florence in 1631 includes these items plus almonds, apples, amber, cinnamon, nutmeg, saffron, and verdigris.[24] These lists were usually appended to letters and transcribed in standardized form. What the Italians called *listini dei prezzi* covered every commodity from every potential market of Europe and the Levant. At first, such firms as the Datini or, in the German lands, the giant financial and commercial concern of the Fugger family wrote them up internally. Soon price lists were more widely distributed for sale in manuscript form and by the late sixteenth century in print—due to the invention of the Gutenberg printing press. These so-called "commodity price currents" were the earliest precursors of our business press.[25]

Add political information and you have the birth of newspapers. These were essential tools for merchants, who were the main suppliers and consumers of news in Europe in the late medieval and early modern periods. In Venice, known by European contemporaries as the "metropolis of news," *reportiste* (reporters) wrote *avvisi* (notices) by hand; after Gutenberg the *gazette*, or printed newsletter, appeared—a word derived from the Venetian halfpenny, which was the price of each copy.[26] With the publishing of commodity price currents, a greater number of people engaged in commerce could now exploit this kind of intelligence, which was formerly restricted to a tiny, well-connected merchant elite. That number was still relatively small, but it was an important step in making commercial expansion possible.

If the birth of newspapers was directly related to the European adoption of the world-changing invention of printing with moveable type, so was the expansion of book production. That too helped encourage the profit-seeking activities of businessmen by giving them ready access to new techniques and broadening their horizons with information about the world at large. Surpassing all others as a book-publishing center was Venice, which in the first fifty years after Gutenberg issued 4,500 titles, amounting to 2.5 million copies of books. In Europe as a whole by 1600, around 150,000 titles had come out, with estimates of the number of books in circulation before that date ranging from 150,000,000 to 230,000,000.[27]

Aside from religious and secular literature in every European and Middle Eastern language, publishers issued numerous aids to businessmen with the sale of almanacs, atlases, descriptions of tradable goods, multilingual dictionaries, travel itineraries, etiquette guides for behavior in foreign emporia, tips on maneuvering around customs in every port, and an array of manuals designed to shortcut calculations and currency conversions. Books for the merchant were as popular as do-it-yourself, self-help, and inspirational books aimed at the businessman are today.[28]

Among the books that had the greatest impact were those on accounting and financial analysis—both of which aided the continuing growth of business in the West. The bible of medieval finance was *Liber Abaci* (The Book of the Abacus), published in 1202, a practical guide on the mathematics of money, trade, arbitrage, and the calculation of profits written by Fibonacci, a.k.a. Leonardo of Pisa.

Fibonacci's father had been a customs official in the Pisan colony of Bugia (now Bejaia) in Algeria. There the son learned the Arabic language and Arabic numerals—he was in fact the first person to demonstrate to Europeans their convenience for business purposes. To quote Fibonacci, he traveled widely throughout the Mediterranean region and studied "with whoever was learned in [mathematics], from . . . Egypt, Syria, Greece, Sicily."[29] What he did was to bring together the advanced mathematical traditions of the East—the Arab world and India—and bestow them upon subsequent generations in the West. As *Liber Abaci* begins, "these are the nine figures of the Indians: 9 8 7 6 5 4 3 2 1. With these nine figures and with this sign 0 which in Arabic is called zephirum, any number can be written, as will be demonstrated."[30]

But he also surpassed his Asian predecessors—and allowed European commerce to surpass them—insofar as he was the first anywhere to analyze relative value and present value mathematically. How does one decide, for instance, which is worth more when dealing with Arab merchants: their saffron or their pepper? How does one decide whether to speculate in grain or invest in the government annuities offered by the Italian city-states in return for the purchase of their bonds? How does one divide profits among partners with different amounts of capital invested in a company? These problems, all presented in *Liber Abaci*, had never been addressed before, although they drew on Asian mathematical principles. The book was translated almost immediately from Latin into the vernacular Italian and imparted in the business schools that were appearing in the late thirteenth and early fourteenth centuries in every Italian commercial city. The hundreds of Renaissance-era business math textbooks that were first handwritten then printed in Italy, France, and beyond all drew directly or indirectly on Fibonacci.

Robust commercial exchange and international trade created a ready-made audience for Fibonacci, and it also gave rise to "Italian bookkeeping," as it was long known. Double-entry bookkeeping was invented in the thirteenth century in northern Italy, where the complexity of business operations made accounting necessary to monitor the large amounts of money changing hands between clients, suppliers, investors, and customers. Like Fibonacci's work, it was taught in the proliferating business schools of Renaissance Italy. It spread farther and wider with the publication of *Summa di Arithmetica* (Venice, 1494). The author was Luca Bartolomeo de Pacioli, a neo-Platonist philosopher and friend of Leonardo da Vinci, whose fame throughout Europe came with his aphoristic nuggets of practical wisdom: "If you cannot be a good accountant, you will grope your way forward like a blind man and may meet great losses."[31] Not only was double-entry bookkeeping, once invented, recommended for making sure one's business was not "a confusion of Babel," in the words of another fifteenth-century writer, it was also how the owners of the Italian super-companies mentioned above could keep control of their long-distance operations: that is, through regular accounting audits of their highly paid branch managers.[32]

What Pacioli was saying seems obvious: the more information you have and the more effectively it is analyzed the stronger your business; conversely, those who fail to adopt new methods of information-processing limit the scope and scale of their operations and risk being outrun by their competitors. But self-evident though Pacioli's words are to us, in his day they had the force of novelty. European businessmen also had access to new techniques and new ideas that made it possible for them to follow his advice. Why that was so has to do with a unique concatenation of circumstances to be explained more fully below. For now, suffice it to say that the seeds were planted in parts of Western Europe during the Middle Ages, to sprout in the early modem era and come to fruition in later centuries. In other parts of the world, by contrast, it was much harder to acquire the kinds of information Western European merchants increasingly had available to them thanks to steadily improving means of communications, above all the business and financial press.

To support those claims we need to examine the status of information in medieval and early modern China, Japan, India, and the Middle East, then follow with the early modern Dutch Republic, England, and France.

Notes

1. Iris Origo, *The Merchant of Prato: Francesco di Marco Datini* (NY: Knopf, 1957), vi.
2. John Micklethwait and Adrian Wooldridge, *The Company: A Short History of a Revolutionary Idea* (NY: Modern Library, 2003), 10.

3. Jonathan Barton Baskin and Paul J. Miranti, Jr., *A History of Corporate Finance* (Cambridge: Cambridge University Press, 1997), 29–30.

4. Friedrich A. Hayek, "The Use of Knowledge in Society," *American Economic Review* (Sept. 1945), 526.

5. Douglass C. North, "Markets," in *Oxford Encyclopedia of Economic History*, ed. Joel Mokyr, vol. III (Oxford: Oxford University Press, 2003), 432–433; Douglass C. North, "Institutions, Transaction Costs, and the Rise of Merchant Empires," in *The Political Economy of Merchant Empires*, ed. James D. Tracy (Cambridge: Cambridge University Press, 1991), 22–40; Douglass C. North and Robert Paul Thomas, *The Rise of the Western World* (Cambridge: Cambridge University Press, 1973). Although North considers the acquisition of information as a transaction cost, his main emphasis is on law.

6. Hayek, "Use of Knowledge," 519–520. Hayek was prompted to consider the issue in reaction to post-World War I socialist ambitions for economic planning, which presupposed the omniscience of government. But economists for over a hundred years before him were conscious of the problem of inadequate information. See Fritz Machlup, *Knowledge: Its Creation, Distribution, and Economic Significance*, vol. III: *The Economics of Information and Human Capital* (Princeton: Princeton University Press, 1984), 15–17 and passim; Philip Mirowski, *Machine Dreams: Economics Becomes a Cyborg Science* (Cambridge: Cambridge University Press, 2002), 370; Yuval P. Yonay, *The Struggle over the Soul of Economics* (Princeton: Princeton University Press, 1998), 131; Frank H. Knight, *Risk, Uncertainty, and Profit* (Boston: Houghton Mifflin, 1921), 197 and chaps. 7–8 passim; Robert E. Wright, *The Wealth of Nations Rediscovered: Integration and Expansion in American Financial Markets, 1780–1850* (Cambridge: Cambridge University Press, 2002), 214.

7. George J. Stigler, *The Organization of Industry* (Chicago: University of Chicago Press, 1968), chap. 16.

8. George A. Akerlof, "The Market for Lemons: Quality Uncertainty and the Market Mechanism," *Quarterly Journal of Economics* (Aug. 1970), 488–500. I borrow the term "hidden information" from John Cassidy, *How Markets Fail* (NY: Farrar, Straus and Giroux, 2009), chap. 12.

9. Naomi R. Lamoreaux, Daniel M. G. Raff, and Peter Temin, "Introduction," in *Learning by Doing in Markets, Firms, and Countries*, ed. Naomi R. Lamoreaux, Daniel M. G. Raff, and Peter Temin (Chicago: University of Chicago Press, 1999), 5–6; Cassidy, *How Markets Fail*, chap. 12; Kenneth J. Arrow, "Limited Knowledge and Economic Analysis," *American Economic Review* (March 1974), 1–10.

10. John J. McCusker, "Information and Transaction Costs in Early Modern Europe," in *Weltwirtschaft und Wirtschaftsordnung*, ed. Rainer Gömmel and Markus A. Denzel (Stuttgart: Franz Steiner Verlag, 2002), 69.

11. Eric von Hippel, "'Sticky Information' and the Locus of Problem Solving," in *The Dynamic Firm*, ed. Alfred D. Chandler, Jr. et al. (Oxford: Oxford University Press, 1998), 60–77. Von Hippel identifies the nature of the problem in today's world, but does not delve into the history of information transfer.

12. A distinction is often made between "information," which some economists define as unprocessed data, and "knowledge," which they define as applied or "socially useful" information: see Joel Mokyr, *The Gifts of Athena: Historical Origins of the Knowledge Economy* (Princeton: Princeton University Press, 2002), chap. 1, and David Warsh, *Knowledge and the Wealth of Nations* (NY: Norton, 2006), 295–297. Since my emphasis is on the *potential* for acquiring information and knowledge, the distinctions between them are less important and I will use the two terms interchangeably.

13. Similar arguments for the early industrial era can be found in Joel Mokyr, "The Market for Ideas and the Origins of Economic Growth in Eighteenth Century Europe," online at http://faculty.wcas.northwestern.edul-jmokyr/Marketforideas.PDF; Robert C. Allen, *The British Industrial Revolution in Global Perspective* (Cambridge: Cambridge University Press, 2009), chap. 10; and Margaret C. Jacob, *The First Knowledge Economy: Human Capital and the European Economy, 1750–1850* (Cambridge: Cambridge University Press, 2014).

14. Kenneth Pomeranz, *The Great Divergence: China, Europe, and the Making of the Modern World Economy* (Princeton: Princeton University Press, 2000). Peer Vries, in both a review essay, "Are Coal and Colonies Really Crucial? Kenneth Pomeranz and the Great Divergence," *Journal of World History* (Fall 2001), 407–446, and a book. *Escaping Poverty: The Origins of Modern Economic Growth* (Goettingen: V&R Unipress, 2013), offers a sustained rebuttal of Pomeranz et al., but does not consider information as a factor in the debate as I do here.

15. Jack Goody, *The Theft of History* (Cambridge: Cambridge University Press, 2006).

16. Quote from Alvin Toffler, *Powershift* (NY: Bantam Books, 1990), xix, 18. For similar statements, see Peter F. Drucker, *Post-Capitalist Society* (NY: HarperBusiness, 1993), 5–6; Manuel Castells, *The Rise of the Network Society*, vol. I (Oxford: Blackwell, 1996), 469–478; and Thomas Stewart, *Intellectual Capital: The New Wealth of Organizations* (NY: Currency Doubleday, 1997), xx.

17. Peter Spufford, *Power and Profit: The Merchant in Medieval Europe* (London: Thames and Hudson, 2002), 48–50, 144–150; John Hatcher and Mark Bailey, *Modelling the Middle Ages: The History and Theory of England's Economic Development* (Oxford: Oxford University Press, 2001), 142–144; S. R. Epstein, *Freedom and Growth: The Rise of States and Markets in Europe, 1300–1750* (London: Routledge, 2000),74–88. For a glimpse at the thriving regional and international trade of Iberia in the high Middle Ages, see Bernard F. Reilly, *The Medieval Spains* (Cambridge: Cambridge University Press, 1993), 140–144.

18. Spufford, *Power and Profit*, 12ff, 48ff, chaps. 3–4, with quotes on 164 and 181; Christopher Dyer, *An Age of Transition? Economy and Society in England in the Later Middle Ages* (Oxford: Oxford University Press, 2005), 170–172; Hatcher and Bailey, *Modelling the Middle Ages*, 146–149, 154–156. This picture based on recent scholarship is a rebuttal of Fernand Braudel, who insisted on the sluggishness of late medieval communications, perhaps because he was comparing them to the modern era: see his *The Mediterranean and the Mediterranean World in the Age of Philip II*, trans. Siân Reynolds, vol. I (NY: Harper and Row, 1972), 283–284, 355–375 passim, and *Civilization and Capitalism*, vol. I: *The Structures of Everyday Life*, trans. Siân Reynolds (NY: Harper and Row, 1981), 424. Citing new documentary and archeological evidence, Michael McCormick, *Origins of the European Economy: Communications and Commerce, AD 300–900* (Cambridge: Cambridge University Press, 2001), finds extensive international maritime and overland travel by Europeans in an even earlier period. But it was nothing compared to what occurred later.

19. Edwin S. Hunt and James M. Murray, *A History of Business in Medieval Europe, 1200–1550* (Cambridge: Cambridge University Press, 1999), chap. 5; Spufford, Power and Profit, 19–25, 43, 50–52; Baskin and Miranti, *History of Corporate Finance*, 40–41; David Abulafia, "The Impact of Banking in the Late Middle Ages and the Renaissance, 1300–1500," in *Banking, Trade, and Industry: Europe, America, and Asia from the Thirteenth to the Twentieth Century*, ed. Alice Teichova et at. (Cambridge: Cambridge University Press, 1997), 24; Micklethwait and Wooldridge, *The Company*, 7–10.

20. Baskin and Miranti, *History of Corporate Finance*, 33

21. Wolfgang Behringer, "Communications Revolutions: A Historiographical Concept," *German History* (Aug. 2006), 340–346, with quote on 342. Spufford, *Power and Profit*, 25–29; Peter Burke, "Early Modem Venice as a Center of Information and Communication," in *Venice Reconsidered*, ed. John Martin and Dennis Romano (Baltimore: Johns Hopkins University Press, 2000), 391; Andrew Pettegree, *The Invention of News* (New Haven: Yale University Press, 2014), 43–46, 51–57, 168–181.

22. For a sample of mainly Italian international commercial correspondence, see Robert S. Lopez and Irving W. Raymond, eds, *Medieval Trade in the Mediterranean World* (NY: Columbia University Press, 1990), chap. 23.

23. Jean Favier, *Gold and Spices: The Rise of Commerce in the Middle Ages*, trans. Caroline Higgitt (NY: Holmes and Meier, 1998), 65–67. On the Russian side of the business, see Janet Martin, *Treasure of the Land of Darkness: The Fur Trade and Its Significance for Medieval Russia* (Cambridge: Cambridge University Press, 1986), chaps. 3–4. For the slow and difficult travel conditions even centuries later, see Samuel H. Baron, trans. and ed., *The Travels of Olearius in Seventeenth-Century Russia* (Stanford: Stanford University Press, 1967), chap. 1.

24. John J. McCusker and Cora Gravesteijn, *The Beginnings of Commercial and Financial Journalism: The Commodity Price Currents, Exchange Rate Currents, and Money Currents of Early Modern Europe* (Amsterdam: Nederlands Economisch-Historisch Archief, 1991), 192 on Florence, 397 on Venice.

25. John J. McCusker, "The Demise of Distance: The Business Press and the Origins of the Information Revolution in the Early Modem Atlantic World," *American Historical Review* (April 2005), 299; John J. McCusker, "Information and Transaction Costs in Early Modem Europe," in *Weltwirtschaft und Wirtschaftsordnung*, ed. Gömmel and Denzel, 74–76; McCusker and Gravesteijn, *Beginnings of Commercial and Financial Journalism*, 22–23, 38n20; Spufford, *Power and Profit*, 28–29.

26. Burke, "Early Modem Venice as a Center of Information," 397; Pettegree, *Invention of News*, 5–6; Paul Arblaster, "Posts, Newsletters, Newspapers," *Media History*, XI, nos. 1–2 (2005), 22–23, 34n9.

27. Burke, "Early Modem Venice as a Center of Information," 392, 398, 400–402; Erdmann Weyrauch, "Das Buch als Träger der frühneuzeitlichen Kommunikationsrevolution," in *Kommunikationsrevolutionen: Die neuen Medien des 16. und 19. Jahrhunderts*, ed. Michael North, 2nd ed. (Cologne: Böhlau Verlag, 2001), 2–3; Eltjo Buringh and Jan Luiten van Zanden, "Charting the 'Rise of the West': Manuscripts and Printed Books in Europe, A Long-Term Perspective from the Sixth through Eighteenth Centuries," *Journal of Economic History* (June 2009), 417.

28. Spufford, *Power and Profit*, 52–56; Lopez and Raymond, *Medieval Trade in the Mediterranean World*, 342–343 and chap. XXI passim; Armando Sapori, *The Italian Merchant in the Middle Ages*, trans. Patricia Ann Kennen (NY: Norton, 1970), 36.

29. William M. Goetzmann, "Fibonacci and the Financial Revolution," in *The Origins of Value: The Financial Innovations that Created Modern Capital Markets*, ed. William M. Goetzmann and K. Geert Rouwenhorst (Oxford: Oxford University Press, 2005), 123–143, with quote on 127.

30. Jane Gleeson-White, *Double Entry: How the Merchants of Venice Created Modem Finance* (NY: Norton, 2011), 19.

31. Alfred W. Crosby, *The Measure of Reality: Quantification and Western Society, 1250–1600* (Cambridge: Cambridge University Press, 1997), 212–216, with quote on 216; Gleeson-White, *Double Entry*, chaps. 2–4; Spufford, *Power and Profit*, 29–31; and Lopez and

Raymond, *Medieval Trade in the Mediterranean World*, chap. XXII. On the first English translation of Pacioli in 1543, see Geoffrey Poitras, *The Early History of Financial Economics, 1478–1776* (Cheltenham: Edward Elgar, 2000), 117.

32. Baskin and Miranti, *History of Corporate Finance*, 42, 44. The quote is from Benedetto Cotrugli, *Della mercatura et del mercante perfetto* (Naples, 1458), excerpted in Lopez and Raymond, *Medieval Trade in the Mediterranean World*, 377.

ACKNOWLEDGMENTS

We have made every effort to contact the original copyright holders of the texts printed in this reader. If any have been overlooked, the publisher will be pleased to make the necessary arrangements at the first opportunity.

Gregory Bateson, *Steps to an Ecology of Mind*, 315–320, 408–410. Copyright © 1972, 1999 University of Chicago Press (print), Brockman, Inc. (e-book). Print edition reprint rights granted by University of Chicago Press; permission conveyed through Copyright Clearance Center, Inc.

C.A. Bayly, *Empire and Information: Intelligence Gathering and Social Communication in India*, 1–9. Copyright © 1996 Cambridge University Press. Reprinted by permission of Cambridge University Press.

James Beniger, *The Control Revolution: Technological and Economic Origins of the Information Society*, 6–21, 25–26. Copyright © 1986 the President and Fellows of Harvard College. Reprinted by permission of Harvard University Press, Cambridge, Mass.

Walter Benjamin, "The Storyteller: Reflections on the Works of Nikolai Leskov," in *Illuminations*, trans. Harry Zohn, 83–85, 87–90, 91–93. Copyright © 1955 by Suhrkamp Verlag, Frankfurt A.M. English translation copyright © 1968 and renewed 1996 by Houghton Mifflin Harcourt Publishing Company. Reprinted by permission of Mariner Books, an imprint of HarperCollins Publishers. All rights reserved.

Mary Elizabeth Berry, *Japan in Print: Information and Nation in the Early Modern Period*, 1–12, 253–256. Copyright © 2006 The Regents of the University of California. Reprinted by permission of the publisher, the University of California Press.

Ann Blair, *Too Much to Know*, 1–10. Copyright © 2010 Yale University Press. Reprinted by permission of Yale University Press.

Vannevar Bush, "As We May Think," *The Atlantic Monthly* 176.1 (July 1945): 101–108. Copyright © 1945 Vannevar Bush. Reprinted with the permission of the Bush family.

Haroldo de Campos, "The Informational Temperature of the Text," trans. Jon Tolman, *Poetics Today* 3.3 (1982): 177–187. Copyright © 1982 the Porter Institute for Poetics and Semiotics, Tel Aviv University. All rights reserved. Republished by permission of the copyright holder, and the present publisher, Duke University Press.

Mary J. Carruthers, "*Ars oblivionalis, ars inveniendi*: The Cherub Figure and the Arts of Memory," *Gesta* 48.2 (2009): 99–103, 114–117. Copyright © 2009 University of Chicago Press. Reprinted by permission of University of Chicago Press, Journals Division; permission conveyed through Copyright Clearance Center, Inc.

Umberto Eco, *The Open Work*, trans. Anna Cancogni, 57–60, 66–69. Copyright © 1989 the President and Fellows of Harvard College. Reprinted by permission of Harvard University Press, Cambridge, Mass.

Vilém Flusser, "Form and Material," in *The Shape of Things*, 22–26, 28–29. Copyright © 1999 Reaktion Books Limited. Reproduced with permission of Reaktion Books Limited through PLSclear.

Vilém Flusser, "Recoding," in *Does Writing Have a Future?* trans. Nancy Ann Roth, 149–150, 152–155. Originally published in German in *Die Schrift. Hat Schreiben Zukunft?* Copyright © 1987 European Photography, Andreas Müller-Pohle, P.O. Box 08 02 27, D-10002, Berlin, Germany, www.equivalence.com. Edition Flusser, Volume V (20025). English translation copyright © 2011 the Regents of the University of Minnesota. Reprinted by permission of the publisher, the University of Minnesota Press.

Michel Foucault, *The Order of Things: An Archaeology of the Human Sciences*, trans. Alan Sheridan-Smith, xv-xxi, 50–58. Translation copyright © 1970 by Penguin Random House LLC. Used by permission of Pantheon Books, an imprint of the Knopf Doubleday Publishing Group, a division of Penguin Random House LLC. All rights reserved.

Sigmund Freud, "A Note upon the Mystic Writing-Pad," trans. James Strachey, *International Journal of Psychoanalysis* 21 (1940): 469–474. Copyright © 1925, 1940 Institute of Psychoanalysis. Reprinted by permission of Taylor & Francis Ltd., on behalf of the Institute of Psychoanalysis http://www.theijp.org/.

Harold Garfinkel, *Toward a Sociological Theory of Information*, 110–112, 158–159. Copyright © 1952 Paradigm Publishers. Reprinted by permission of Taylor & Francis Group LLC Books.

Lisa Gitelman, *Paper Knowledge*, 1–20. Copyright © 2014 Duke University Press. All rights reserved. Reprinted by permission of the copyright holder. www .dukeupress.edu.

Ian Hacking, *The Taming of Chance*, 16–26, 218–219. Copyright © 1990 Cambridge University Press. Reproduced with permission of Cambridge University Press through PLSclear.

Friedrich Hayek, "The Use of Knowledge in Society," *The American Economic Review* 35.4 (September 1945): 520–528. Copyright © 1945 American Economic Association. Reproduced with permission of the *American Economic Review* and the Hayek family.

N. Katherine Hayles, *How We Became Posthuman: Virtual Bodies in Cybernetics, Literature, and Informatics*, 50–52, 53–56, 74–75. Copyright © 1999 University of Chicago Press. Reprinted by permission of University of Chicago Press; permission conveyed through Copyright Clearance Center, Inc.

Martin Heidegger, "The Origin of the Work of Art," in *Poetry, Language, Thought*, 26–29, 70–72, 77–79. Originally published in *Holzwege*. Copyright © 1950 Vittorio Klostermann GmbH. English translation by Albert Hofstadter. Copyright © 1971 HarperCollins Publishers. Reproduced by permission of HarperCollins Publishers.

Michael E. Hobart and Zachary S. Schiffman, *Information Ages: Literacy, Numeracy, and the Computer Revolution*, 45–47, 50–56. Copyright © 1998 Johns Hopkins University Press. Reprinted with permission of Johns Hopkins University Press.

Peter Janich, *What is Information?* eds. and trans. Eric Hayot and Lea Pao, 70–76. Originally published as *Was ist Information? Kritik einer Legende*. Copyright © 2006 Suhrkamp Verlag Frankfurt am Main. English translation copyright © 2018 The Regents of the University of Minnesota. Used by permission of the publisher, the University of Minnesota Press.

Lily Kay, *Who Wrote the Book of Life? A History of the Genetic Code*, 115–127, 354–356. Copyright © 2000 Stanford University Press.

Friedrich Kittler, "There Is No Software," in Kittler, *Literature, Media, Information Systems: Essays*, ed. John Johnston, 147–148, 150–152, 154–155. English translation copyright © 1989 Stanford Humanities Review.

Claude Lévi-Strauss, "The Mathematics of Man," *International Social Science Bulletin* 6.4 (1954): 581–590. Copyright © 1954 UNESCO. Reprinted by permission of UNESCO.

Jurij M. Lotman, "The Future for Structural Poetics," *Poetics* 8 (1979): 501–507. Copyright © 1979 North-Holland Publishing Company. Reprinted by permission of Elsevier.

Donald MacKay, "The Place of 'Meaning' in the Theory of Information," in *Information Theory*, ed. E.C. Cherry, Butterworths, 1956, 215–225. Copyright © 1956 Donald MacKay. Reprinted with the permission of Elsevier and the MacKay family.

Steven Marks, *The Information Nexus: Global Capitalism from the Renaissance to the Present*, 75–86. Copyright © 2016 Steven G. Marks. Reprinted by permission of the publisher, Cambridge University Press.

Yoneji Masuda, *The Information Society as Post-Industrial Society*, 29–35, 75–83. Copyright © 1980 Institute for the Information Society, Tokyo, Japan. First US printing in 1981 by World Future Society.

Marshall McLuhan, "The Medium Is the Message," in *Understanding Media: The Extenstions of Men*, critical ed., ed. W. Terrence Gordon, 19–21, 24–26, 27–28, 30–31, 32–33. Copyright © 1964, 1994, 2003 Corinne McLuhan. Reprinted by permission of the publisher, Gingko Press.

Abraham Moles, *Information Theory and Esthetic Perception*, 191–193, 197–201, 207–209. Originally published as *Théorie de l'information et perception esthétique*. Copyright © 1958 Flammarion. English translation copyright © 1973 University of Illinois Press.

Elias Muhanna, "Why was the fourteenth century a century of Arabic encyclopaedism?" in *Encyclopaedism from Antiquity to the Renaissance*, eds. Jason König and Greg Woolf, 347–355. Copyright © 2013 Cambridge University Press. Reprinted by permission of Cambridge University Press.

Walter J. Ong, *Orality and Literacy: The Technologizing of the Word*, 30th anniversary edition, ed. John Hartley, 96, 99–101, 175–177. Copyright © 1982, 2002 Walter J. Ong; selected content © 2012 John Hartley. Reprinted by permission of the publisher Routledge, an imprint of Taylor & Francis Ltd.

William R. Paulson, *The Noise of Culture: Literary Texts in a World of Information*, 83–89. Copyright © 1988 Cornell University. Used by permission of the publisher, Cornell University Press.

John Durham Peters, "Information: Notes Toward a Critical History," *Journal of Communication Inquiry* 12.2 (July 1988): 9–23. Copyright © 1988 SAGE Publishing. Reprinted by permission of SAGE Publishing.

Mary Poovey, *A History of the Modern Fact: Problems of Knowledge in the Sciences of Wealth and Society*, 33–65, 337–341. Copyright © 1998 University of Chicago Press. Reprinted by permission of University of Chicago Press; permission conveyed through Copyright Clearance Center, Inc.

Thomas Richards, *The Imperial Archive: Knowledge and the Fantasy of Empire*, 1, 3–9. Copyright © 1994 Verso. Reprinted by permission of Verso.

Claude Shannon, "A Mathematical Theory of Communication," *Bell Labs Technical Journal* 27.3 (July 1948): selected excerpts. Copyright © 1948 Nokia Bell Labs. Reused with permission of Nokia Corporation and AT&T Archives.

Claude Shannon, "The Bandwagon," *IRE Transactions on Information Theory*, March 1956: 3. Copyright © 1956 Institute of Electrical and Electronics Engineers (IEEE). Reprinted by permission of IEEE.

Mathieu Triclot, *Le moment cybernétique*, trans. Eric Hayot and Julien Jeusette, 405–411. Copyright © Éditions Champ Vallon. English translation copyright

© 2021 Eric Hayot and Julien Jeusette. Reprinted by permission of Éditions Champ Vallon.

Paul Virilio, *The Information Bomb*, trans. Chris Turner, 107–114. Originally published as *La Bombe informatique*. Copyright © 1998 Éditions Galilée. English translation copyright © 2000 Chris Turner. Reprinted by permission of the English translation publisher, Verso; permission conveyed through PLSclear.

Norbert Wiener, *Cybernetics; or, Control and Communication in the Animal and the Machine*, 2nd ed., 5–6, 10–11, 27–28, 157–158, 161–164. Copyright © 1961 Massachusetts Institute of Technology. Reprinted by permission of the MIT Press.

Frances Yates, *The Art of Memory*, in *Selected Works of Frances Yates*, vol. 3, 84–88, 103–106, 123–125, 128. Copyright © 1966 Frances A. Yates. Reprinted by permission of the publisher Routledge, an imprint of Taylor & Francis Ltd.

INDEX